THE COMPLETE POETICAL WORKS
OF THOMAS HARDY

With Hardy's original illustrations to *Wessex Poems*

That which I have seen I will declare. *Job**

THE COMPLETE
POETICAL WORKS
OF
THOMAS HARDY

EDITED BY
SAMUEL HYNES

VOLUME I
Wessex Poems
Poems of the Past and the Present
Time's Laughingstocks

OXFORD
AT THE CLARENDON PRESS
1982

Oxford University Press, Walton Street, Oxford OX2 6DP

London Glasgow New York Toronto
Delhi Bombay Calcutta Madras Karachi
Kuala Lumpur Singapore Hong Kong Tokyo
Nairobi Dar es Salaam Cape Town
Melbourne Auckland

and associates in
Beirut Berlin Ibadan Mexico City Nicosia

Published in the United States by
Oxford University Press, New York

OXFORD is a trade mark of Oxford University Press

The preparation of this edition was made possible (in part) by a grant from the Program for Editions of the National Endowment for the Humanities, an independent federal agency of the United States government.

British Library Cataloguing in Publication Data
Hardy, Thomas, 1840–1928
The complete poetical works of Thomas Hardy.
Vol. I: Wessex poems; Poems of the past and the
present; Time's laughingstocks.—(Oxford English Texts)
I. Title   II. Hynes, Samuel
821'.8   PR4741
ISBN 0-19-812708-1

Library of Congress Cataloging in Publication Data
Hardy, Thomas, 1840–1928.
The complete poetical works of Thomas Hardy.
(Oxford English Texts)
Includes index.
Contents: v. 1. Wessex poems. Poems of the past
and the present. Time's laughingstocks.
I. Hynes, Samuel Lynn.
PR4741.H9   821'.8 17   81-22456
ISBN 0-19-812708-1 (v. 1.) AACR2

Printed in Great Britain
at the University Press, Oxford
by Eric Buckley
Printer to the University

ACKNOWLEDGEMENTS

THE editor of an edition such as this incurs many debts over many years, and I am glad to have an opportunity to acknowledge mine here. The Program for Editions of the National Endowment for the Humanities provided generous financial support, as did Princeton University. The staff of the Princeton University Library assisted me in many ways: I particularly wish to thank Richard Ludwig, Susanne McNatt, and Deborah Raikes. Roger Peers, Curator of the Dorset County Museum, was endlessly patient and helpful, as he has been to so many Hardy scholars. Frederick B. Adams, David Holmes, Richard Purdy, and Robert H. Taylor allowed me access to their collections of Hardy manuscripts and other materials. James Gibson shared with me his knowledge of Hardy's texts.

I have benefited from the advice and help of many other scholars and friends: the late J. O. Bailey, Alan Bell, Hilde D. Cohn, Richard Ellmann, Barbara Hardy, Caroline Hobhouse, John Howard, Joanna Hynes, Patricia Ingham, Michael Meredith, Michael Millgate, Frank Pinion, Anthony Preston, Miranda Preston, Lola Szladits, James Thorpe, Audrey Wintour, Charles Wintour, and Beth Witherell. And I have been aided by a series of able graduate assistants: Annette Cafarelli, Bruce Gardiner, Candace Killam, Thomas McCavera, Marion Meilaender, and Roberta Tovey.

For permission to quote from manuscript materials I wish to thank the following: the Trustees of the Hardy estate; the University Court, Aberdeen University; Frederick B. Adams; Birmingham City Museums and Art Gallery; the Bodleian Library, Oxford; the British Library; the Poetry/Rare Books Collection of the University Libraries, the State University of New York at Buffalo; the Bancroft Library of the University of California at Berkeley; the Research Library of the University of California at Los Angeles; the Library of the University of California at Riverside; the Miller Library, Colby College, Waterville, Maine; the Trustees of the Thomas Hardy Memorial Collection in the Dorset County Museum, Dorchester; the William R. Perkins Library, Duke University; Eton College Library; the Syndics of the Fitzwilliam Museum, Cambridge; the Houghton Library, Harvard University;

David Holmes; the Huntington Library, San Marino, California; the E. M. Forster Papers, King's College Library, Cambridge; the Library of Congress; the Master and Fellows of Magdalene College, Cambridge; the Pierpont Morgan Library; the National Trust, Stourhead, Wiltshire; the Henry W. and Albert A. Berg Collection, New York Public Library Astor, Lenox and Tilden Foundations; the Fales Collection, New York University Library; the Library, The Queen's College, Oxford; Richard Little Purdy; the Trustees of the Street Library, Somerset; the Robert H. Taylor Collection, Princeton University Library; the Humanities Research Center, University of Texas at Austin; the London Borough of Wandsworth, Libraries and Arts Division; the Beinecke Rare Book and Manuscript Library, Yale University.

Many individuals and institutions provided me with information; I would especially like to thank A. R. Augier, Administrator of Stourhead House, Wilts.; the Librarian of Cheltenham College; the Book Department of Christie, Manson & Wood Ltd.; The Dudley Library, Dudley, West Midlands; the English Folk Dance & Song Society; the late Lew David Feldman; the librarians of Birkbeck College, Queen Mary College, University College, and Westfield College of the University of London; the Reverend P. S. Macpherson, Vicar of St. George's Church, Fordington, Dorchester; the staff of the National Library of Scotland; Bernard Quaritch Ltd.; Maurice G. Rathbone, County Archivist, the Wiltshire County Record Office; Bertram Rota Ltd.; Sotheby Parke Bernet & Co.; George Stevens Cox; the University of Sussex Library; the Alderman Library, University of Virginia; the Superintendent, Windsor Castle.

Over the many years during which this edition has been in preparation, the officers of the Oxford University Press have been unfailingly helpful and patient, and I am happy to have this opportunity to express my gratitude to them.

CONTENTS

ABBREVIATIONS USED IN THIS VOLUME

CP	*Collected Poems* (all reported editions)
CP19	*Collected Poems* (London: 1919)
CP20	*Collected Poems*, 2nd impression (London: 1920)
CP23	*Collected Poems*, 2nd edition (London: 1923)
ME	Mellstock Edition (London: 1919–20): Volume XXXIV, *Wessex Poems/Poems of the Past and the Present* (1920); Volume XXXV, *Time's Laughingstocks* (1920)
PE	Pocket Edition (London: 1906–30): *Wessex Poems/Poems of the Past and the Present* (1907)
PP	*Poems of the Past and the Present* (all reported impressions)
PP01	*Poems of the Past and the Present* (London and New York: 1902 [1901])
PP02	*Poems of the Past and the Present*, 2nd impression (New York and London: 1902)
PP03	*Poems of the Past and the Present*, 2nd edition (London: 1903)
SP	*Selected Poems* (London: 1916)
TL	*Time's Laughingstocks* (all reported impressions)
TL09	*Time's Laughingstocks* (London: 1909)
TL10	*Time's Laughingstocks*, 2nd impression (London: 1910)
WE	Wessex Edition (London: 1912–31), including 1st and 2nd impressions
WE12	Wessex Edition, Verse Volume I: *Wessex Poems/Poems of the Past and the Present* (1912)
WE13	Wessex Edition, Verse Volume III: *Time's Laughingstocks* (with *The Dynasts*, Part Third) (1913)
WE20	2nd impression of Wessex Edition, Verse Volumes I–III (1920)
WP	*Wessex Poems* (all reported editions)
WP98	*Wessex Poems* (London and New York: 1898)
WP03	*Wessex Poems*, 2nd edition (London: 1903)
Adams	the collection of Frederick B. Adams
Bailey	J. O. Bailey, *The Poetry of Thomas Hardy* (Chapel Hill: 1970)
Bancroft	the Bancroft Library, University of California, Berkeley
Berg	the Henry W. and Albert A. Berg Collection, New York Public Library
BL	the British Library
Clark	correspondence and corrected proofs in papers of R. & R. Clark Ltd., in the National Library of Scotland
Colby	the Hardy collection at Colby College, Waterville, Maine
Collins	Vere H. Collins, *Talks with Thomas Hardy at Max Gate 1920–1922* (London: 1928)

DCM   the Hardy collection in the Dorset County Museum; particular documents in this collection are identified as follows:

     DCM1   revisions in Hardy's copies of Verse Volumes I and III of the Wessex Edition

     DCM2   revisions in Hardy's copy of *Selected Poems* (1916)

     DCM3   revisions in Hardy's copy of *Collected Poems* (1923)

     DCM4   revisions in Hardy's copy of *Selected Poems* (1917)

EL   Florence Emily Hardy, *The Early Life of Thomas Hardy* (London: 1928)

Eton   the Hardy collection at Eton College

FEH   pamphlets of Hardy's poems privately printed for Florence Emily Hardy

Holmes   the collection of David Holmes

HRC   the Humanities Research Center, University of Texas

H/L   Hardy's notes to Hermann Lea (see Appendix A)

Lea   Hermann Lea, *Thomas Hardy's Wessex* (London: 1913)

Letters I   Richard Little Purdy and Michael Millgate, eds., *The Collected Letters of Thomas Hardy*, Volume I (Oxford: 1978)

Letters II *Collected Letters*, Volume II (Oxford: 1980)

LY   Florence Emily Hardy, *The Later Years of Thomas Hardy* (London: 1930)

Orel   Harold Orel, ed., *Thomas Hardy's Personal Writings* (London: 1967)

ORFW   Evelyn Hardy and F. B. Pinion, eds., *One Rare Fair Woman: Thomas Hardy's Letters to Florence Henniker* (London: 1972)

Pinion   F. B. Pinion, *A Commentary on the Poems of Thomas Hardy* (London: 1976)

Purdy   Richard Little Purdy, *Thomas Hardy: A Bibliographical Study* (Oxford: 1954, reissued 1978)

RLP   the Hardy collection of Richard Little Purdy

Yale   the Beinecke Library, Yale University

cap.   capitalized

del.   deleted

Hol.   the bound holograph printer's copies of the individual volumes of Hardy's verse. Locations are given in explanatory notes at the end of this volume.

ital.   italic type, or underlined (in manuscript texts)

l.c.   lower-case

MS1, etc.   other single manuscripts, as identified in textual notes.

om.   omitted

P1, etc.   proofs and revises, as identified in textual notes.

rom.   roman type

INTRODUCTION

A General History of the Texts

THE materials with which the editor of Hardy's poetry must work are copious: at least one manuscript exists for every poem. Some 200 of the more than 900 poems were published separately before (and occasionally after) book publication. Of the eight individual volumes of verse, all went into a second impression, or a second edition, or both. The *Collected Poems* was published in two editions during Hardy's lifetime and a third immediately after his death. Verse was also included in the four collected editions of Hardy's works published during his lifetime: the Uniform Edition, the Pocket Edition, the Wessex Edition, and the Mellstock Edition.

There are also many other relevant documents. Copies of Hardy's books of verse—most of them from his own library—containing corrections in his own hand are in public and private collections. There is a complete set of corrected page proofs of *Human Shows* in the Dorset County Museum, and corrected proofs of a number of the poems from their periodical publication in various collections. Diaries, notebooks, and letters commenting on poems also exist. And, finally, an unusually extensive correspondence between Hardy and his principal publisher, Macmillan, and between Macmillan and R. & R. Clark, the firm's printer, has been preserved.

Among the many texts the variants are very numerous, and occur throughout Hardy's works, from his first published poem, 'The Bride-Night Fire', which appeared in 1875, to the *Chosen Poems*, which he revised just before his death—a span of more than fifty years. Certainly his second wife was right when she wrote after his death of his 'artistic inability to rest content with anything that he wrote until he had brought the expression as near to his thought as language would allow'. He would, she wrote, 'often go on revising his poems for his own satisfaction after their publication in book form';[1] and she might have added that, having done so, he might

---

[1] Florence Emily Hardy, *The Later Years of Thomas Hardy* (New York: 1930), p. 272n.

make these revisions in the next publication of the poem—or he might not.

Manuscripts

Holographs of all Hardy's eight volumes of verse exist. These are fair copies, showing many corrections; they were prepared as printer's copy, and in all but one case were used as such and then returned to Hardy. They were later bound—each volume separately—and presented to various libraries and museums (locations are given in the explanatory notes to the individual volumes). The holograph of the posthumous *Winter Words* was prepared by Hardy like the others, but it was evidently not used as printer's copy (it bears none of the usual printer's marks); pencil notes and erasures on its pages suggest that at the time of his death Hardy had not settled on the final texts of some of the poems.

Of the many separate manuscripts of individual poems, some are fair copies made for a friend or to be sold for charity; others are copies sent to newspaper and magazine editors; a few are early drafts. The largest group of the latter, marked '24 Draft Lyric Poems' in Hardy's hand, is in the Dorset County Museum. Also in that collection are five books from Hardy's own library, marked with revisions: the first and third volumes of verse in the Wessex Edition; *Selected Poems* 1916; *Selected Poems* 1917 (prepared by Hardy as the copy text for the revised and expanded *Chosen Poems*); and *Collected Poems* 1923. In addition, there are four lists of corrections, made up by Hardy for the Mellstock Edition and for the 1920 reprint of the Wessex Edition, and sent by him to Macmillan at various dates in 1919 and 1920. (These items are described in Appendix D of Volume Three.)

Hardy's handwriting is unusually clear, and the manuscripts present few problems of legibility; though he sometimes cancelled heavily, even the cancelled words can almost always be made out.

Periodical Publication

Only two poems by Hardy—'The Bride-Night Fire' and 'Lines'— were printed separately before *Wessex Poems*, his first book of verse, appeared in 1898. But beginning in 1899, with his poems on the Boer War, Hardy began to place poems in periodicals before collecting them into a volume; thirteen of the poems in his second collection, *Poems of the Past and the Present* (1902 [1901]), were first published separately, and every subsequent volume included some poems that had had periodical publication. Occasionally poems were published in periodicals after book publication, sometimes in revised versions. For example, the editor of the *Dorset Yearbook* wrote in an obituary notice of Hardy, 'From his published and unpublished collection he gave me poems from time to time with the necessary permission to reproduce them, and if they had already appeared in print he never spared himself the trouble of revising them if he thought it necessary and desirable'; and he quotes a stanza from 'News for her Mother', published in *Time's Laughingstocks* in 1909, and in the *Dorset Yearbook* in a slightly different version in 1922.[2]

Proofs of some of these periodical publications exist, and in a few cases both proofs and revises. There are also letters to a number of editors.

Book Publication

The history of Hardy's poems in book publication includes five principal stages: first, the eight individual collections, with their later impressions and editions, from *Wessex Poems* (1898) to the posthumous *Winter Words* (1928); second, the Pocket Edition (1906–30); third, the Wessex Edition (1912–31); fourth, the *Collected Poems*, first published in 1919, with subsequent editions incorporating later books of verse in 1923, 1928, and 1930; and fifth, the Mellstock Edition, a limited, de luxe edition of the works, published in 1919–20, but not extended to include the later books. In addition to these five, three others may be mentioned: the Uniform Edition (of which more below), the *Selected Poems* (1916), and the enlarged version of that selection, *Chosen Poems* (1929). Each of these separate publications of the poems differs in some textual details from the others: all but the Pocket Edition and the Uniform Edition are separate settings of the text.

Hardy's first two books of verse, *Wessex Poems* and *Poems of the Past and the Present*, were published by Harper & Brothers (London and New York). When Hardy moved to Macmillan in 1902, his new publisher acquired the plates of these books. The first Macmillan printing of *Wessex Poems* (1903), described on the verso of the title-page as a 'new edition', was printed from the Harper plates, somewhat corrected; so was *Poems of the Past and the Present*,

[2] Stanley I. Galpin, 'He was very kind to me', *Dorset Yearbook* (1928), p. 4.

which appeared in the same year as a 'second edition'. The half-titles of the two books identify them respectively as volumes XVIII and XIX of *Thomas Hardy's Works*. This is the so-called Uniform (or sometimes Popular) Edition, begun by Osgood, McIlvaine in 1895, passed on to Harper, and ultimately to Macmillan. It is an important edition of Hardy's fiction, but it has no separate textual identity as an edition of the poetry. The corrected plates remained in use through later reprints: of *Wessex Poems* in 1911, 1916, and 1923, of *Poems of the Past and the Present* in 1911 and 1919.

The Pocket Edition, first issued in eighteen volumes in 1906-7, is essentially a reprint of the Uniform Edition, using smaller pages and thin paper. The first volume of verse in this 'edition', containing *Wessex Poems* and *Poems of the Past and the Present* (1907), incorporates a few corrections that Hardy had sent to Macmillan since the printing of the Uniform Edition, and is therefore of some textual interest; subsequent volumes were simply reprinted from the latest corrected plates.

The Wessex Edition was the first complete resetting of the poems to be published: the first volume of verse—*Wessex Poems* and *Poems of the Past and the Present*—appeared in 1912. Hardy prepared printer's copy for the edition by making corrections in volumes of the Uniform Edition sent to him by Macmillan;[3] he spent much of 1911 at this task, and read proofs in the early months of 1912. This edition represents a very considerable revision of the poetic texts. In *Wessex Poems*, for example, all but five of the fifty-one poems differ in some detail from the text of the 1903 impression, and in some cases the changes are extensive—an entire stanza added to 'San Sebastian', several consecutive lines rewritten in 'Her Death and After'.

The next edition in order of publication is the *Collected Poems* of 1919. The position of this text in the chronology of Hardy's revisions is not, however, quite so easily established as is that of the other editions. The history of the *Collected Poems* begins in January 1909, when Macmillan proposed to Hardy a one-volume complete poetical works, to include *The Dynasts* and the two books of verse then published. Hardy agreed, and by mid-February he was

---

[3] Hardy to Macmillan, 3 May 1913 (BL Add. MS 54924): 'In respect of the volumes generally I should, of course, much like the corrections in the Wessex edition to be incorporated into the other editions, as you suggest. I have not destroyed the corrected volumes of the 3/6 edition that were used as copy for the Wessex edition . . .'.

'getting on with the corrections to the copy for the complete volume of poems, the Wessex Poems, and Poems of the Past and the Present, being finished', and he offered to send this copy 'whenever you would like to begin printing'.[4]

By April, however, he had begun to draw back: would there not be a difficulty about announcing a 'complete poetical works' while he was publishing poems in periodicals which would not be included in the book? And besides, he had enough new poems for another separate volume: 'I have wondered', he wrote to Macmillan, 'whether, when I have finished these proofs that are at hand, it would be advisable to keep back the book awhile till the others can be brought out, trotted round, and afterwards added to the volume we are now doing; though this would keep back the latter some months.' Macmillan agreed; no announcement of the complete edition would be made for some time.[5]

Hardy was soon distracted from this enterprise by the preparation of his new book of poems, *Time's Laughingstocks*, which he formally offered to Macmillan in May 1909, and prepared over the summer: it was published in December 1909. In September of the following year he returned to the question of a collected edition: would it be advisable, he asked Macmillan, to add the new book to the one-volume edition of the poetry and bring it out now? Macmillan replied that so long as *Time's Laughingstocks* was selling well it would be a mistake to issue it in a collection, and the project was once more postponed.[6]

Hardy then offered an alternative proposal: 'As the 3 parts of *The Dynasts* are in type for the collected edition,' he wrote to Macmillan on 22 September 1910, 'could the interim between now and its publication be filled by issuing The Dynasts by itself in one vol—say at 7/6? There would be nothing to do to the type except change the paging.'[7] (The change in pagination would be necessary because the original plan had been that the *Collected Poems* should be arranged in order of publication—1, *Wessex Poems*; 2, *Poems of the Past and the Present*; 3, *The Dynasts*—and these had all been set.) Macmillan agreed, and the one-volume edition of *The Dynasts* was published two months later, in November 1910.

[4] Hardy to Macmillan, 14 Feb. 1909 (BL Add. MS 54923).
[5] Hardy to Macmillan, 14 and 20 Apr. 1909 (BL Add. MS 54923).
[6] Hardy to Macmillan, 20 and 22 Sept. 1910 (BL Add. MS 54923).
[7] BL Add. MS 54923.

The next two years were given over to the preparation of the
Wessex Edition, and the period from late 1913 to early 1914 to
gathering together the poems for *Satires of Circumstance* (and, one
might add, to mourning his first wife, who had died in November
1912, and to marrying his second wife in February 1914). Then the
war came, and put a stop to ambitious publishing ventures for a
time. An indication of the restraining force that the war exercised
on publishing activities is that even Hardy's little *Selected Poems*,
when first discussed in 1915, was thought of as a post-war
publication. In a letter dated 2 July 1915, Hardy referred to 'the
little volume of selections we discussed publishing after the war—
whenever that may be',[8] and asked Macmillan to send him the three
volumes of verse in the Wessex Edition in sheets, along with *Satires
of Circumstance* (which had appeared in 1914).

The sheets arrived four days later, but Hardy was not ready to
send copy until the end of the following February. Notes in the
Dorset County Museum show that he had had some difficulty in
making his selections—perhaps because of the principle on which
he had elected to work: 'You will see', he wrote to his friend Gosse,
'that all poems likely to lead to controversy, and those of the franker
kind, have been necessarily omitted—though they are some of the
strongest.' But another reason for the delay was that he was once
more revising his poems; he told Gosse that 'one poem by the way
—the "Lyonnesse" one—is improved in the Selection',[9] but a
number of others had also been changed, and a few re-titled (some
of these revisions occur only in *Selected Poems*).

During the war years Hardy was also busy revising his recently
published volumes. He sent Macmillan a list of corrections for
Satires of Circumstance in February 1915, and a month after the
publication of *Moments of Vision* in November 1917 he sent in the
first of three sets of corrections to that volume.

When the war had ended, Hardy again raised the question of a
collected edition of his verse. In the course of a letter to Macmillan
he first proposed a new volume in the Wessex Edition, to include
Satires of Circumstance and *Moments of Vision*, and then went on:

I also get inquiries for a compact edition of all the poetry only. And I have
thought that we might some day carry this out by making a companion

---

[8] BL Add. MS 54924.
[9] Hardy to Gosse, 28 Jan. and 23 Feb. 1918 (collection of Frederick B. Adams).

volume to the one-volume *Dynasts* of all the rest of my verse—so that there may be an edition of the complete poetical works in two volumes. You may remember that some of the miscellaneous poems were put in type corresponding with the one-volume *Dynasts*, with the idea that the one volume would hold the whole. But I think two volumes would be better, the present one-volume *Dynasts* being one of the volumes.[10]

Macmillan agreed, and the *Collected Poems* was published in October 1919, as volume I of *The Poetical Works of Thomas Hardy*.

It did not, however, appear alone; it was only one of *ten* volumes of Hardy's poetry issued that month, as Macmillan hastened to replenish depleted stock. In addition to the *Collected Poems*, and the new volume in the Wessex Edition, there were reprints of four volumes in the Uniform Edition and one in the Pocket Edition, and three new volumes in the Pocket Edition.

Of these volumes, Hardy gave personal attention only to the first two. In May 1919 he wrote to Macmillan for sheets of *Satires of Circumstance* and *Moments of Vision*, so that he might 'combine the title pages, contents, etc. into the one volume' of the Wessex Edition.[11] He changed the order of the poems, and revised some of them, preparing the copy carefully: 'I am very anxious', he told Macmillan, 'that no errors in this edition should be made by the printers.'[12] In June and July he read proofs of the *Collected Poems*, completing the task on 15 July.[13] It is not clear how thorough this reading was, but six weeks after the book was published Hardy sent Macmillan a list of fourteen errata 'that I and other people have noted in the Collected Poems'.[14] In fact only one of these was clearly an erratum, in the customary sense of a printer's error; most of them were simple revisions, of the sort that Hardy usually made in proofs or earlier.

On 12 June 1919 Hardy wrote to Macmillan agreeing to a de luxe edition. This was a project that he had had in mind for almost two

[10] Hardy to Macmillan, 22 Mar. 1919 (BL Add. MS 54924).

[11] Hardy to Macmillan, 12 May 1919 (BL Add. MS 54924).

[12] Hardy to Macmillan, 15 May 1919 (BL Add. MS 54924).

[13] 'I have just finished reading the proofs of the "collected" Edition of my verse.' Letter to Sydney Cockerell, 15 July 1919 (in Viola Meynell, ed., *Friends of a Lifetime* (London: 1940), p. 286).

[14] Hardy to Macmillan, 22 Nov. 1919 (BL Add. MS 54924). Macmillan ordered the errata slip printed on 26 Nov.; at the same time these corrections were made in the plates, and all appear in the 1920 reprint of *Collected Poems*. A copy of the errata slip is tipped into Cockerell's copy of the 1920 impression (now in the Bodleian Library), with a note in Hardy's hand that 'these corrections are made in the 1923 edition and after'.

decades: he clearly saw such an edition as a kind of honour, evidence that he was held in high esteem, like his Order of Merit. In 1902, in the course of arranging his move to Macmillan, he had remarked in a letter: 'I have had some offers for the publication of a large limited edn.; but this too has been left in abeyance.' Frederick Macmillan responded that 'A so-called "Edition deluxe" very handsomely printed and limited in number is well worth consideration. We have had great success with Tennyson, Kipling, Charles Lamb, and Pater in that form.'[15] Five years later, when Macmillan proposed a new cheap edition of a novel, Hardy replied: 'I should, however, be more interested in an *edition de luxe*. But that, too, can wait.'[16] And wait it did. Two years later, in a letter agreeing to the one-volume *Collected Poems*, Hardy remarked sadly: 'I suppose I shall never reach the dignity of an edition-de-luxe!'[17]

Macmillan was slow in responding to Hardy's hopes, but in October 1910 the firm did propose a limited edition, to be published jointly with Harper & Brothers in New York. In agreeing to the edition Hardy made it clear that he regarded it as the definitive one: 'I conclude', he wrote, 'that the type of all the volumes will be re-set, and that I shall correct the proofs, there being many errors in the New York editions.'[18] He began revising the Uniform Edition texts in June 1911, and sent in copy for the first volume, *Tess*, with a newly written 'General Preface', in October. But by then the arrangement with Harper was collapsing, and by January 1912 the plans for a de luxe, limited edition had been abandoned. Macmillan offered instead a 'definitive edition' published by themselves alone, and Hardy agreed. The work that he had already done became the basis for the Wessex Edition.

The idea of a de luxe edition continued to be discussed, however, and in July 1914 Macmillan made a new proposal to Hardy, which he accepted on the 15th. In his letter of acceptance Hardy suggested 'The Mellstock Edition' as a possible title, and argued strongly for including his poetry, pointing out that the presence of both prose and verse in Macmillan's Bombay Edition of Kipling had contributed to the success of that edition.[19] But in less than three

[15] Hardy to Macmillan, 18 Mar. 1902 (BL Add. MS 54923); Macmillan to Hardy, 19 Mar. 1902 (DCM).
[16] Hardy to Macmillan, 25 Jan. 1907 (BL Add. MS 54923).
[17] 18 Jan. 1909 (BL Add. MS 54923).
[18] Hardy to Macmillan, 12 Oct. 1910 (BL Add. MS 54923).
[19] BL Add. MS 54924.

weeks the declaration of war had caused the project to be set aside once more.

After the war, the de luxe edition finally appeared. Author and publisher agreed on details in June 1919, and Hardy sent in two lists of corrections to the texts, which were to follow the Wessex Edition but would be completely reset. 'I do not want to read the proofs of the edition', Hardy decided, '—having had enough of reading them, as you will imagine';[20] but as the verse volumes came to be set he changed his mind: 'In respect of the 7 volumes of verse . . . what do you think about my reading them over? The Clarks are quite excellent printers, but as no human printer, or even one sent from Heaven direct, can be trusted with verse, I don't mind reading them . . .'.[21] Two days later he repeated his concern: 'As to the proofs of the verse-volumes, it is certainly safer that I should read them, and whenever the printers begin to send them . . . I shall be ready for them.'[22] Mrs Hardy's correspondence confirms that indeed he did carefully read the proofs of the Mellstock volumes.[23] The Mellstock Edition differs from the Wessex Edition only in minor ways, but it has this importance, that it was the last collected edition of the poems that Hardy is known to have proof-read. And though he was reading the Mellstock proofs only a week after he had finished proof-reading the *Collected Poems*, the revisions he made were *different*—he was really revising all over again.

Hardy never again worked so hard on a text—which is not surprising when one considers that he was eighty when the Mellstock Edition was completed in 1920—but he continued to send in corrections to new printings of his verse, and to revise in his own copies. In April and May 1920 he sent two lists of corrections to the Wessex Edition, which was being reprinted; in October 1922 he cut up and sent in a copy of the *Collected Poems*, 'marked with the corrections that have been made from time to time',[24] to be used in preparing the second edition, and he asked to see proofs of the part that had been added—the poems of *Late Lyrics and Earlier*, which

---

[20] Hardy to Macmillan, 18 June 1919 (BL Add. MS 54924).

[21] Hardy to Macmillan, 29 Jan. 1920 (BL Add. MS 54924).

[22] 31 Jan. 1920 (BL Add. MS 54924).

[23] Florence Hardy to Louise Yearsley, 23 July 1919 (collection of Eton College): 'My husband is correcting proofs for a new expensive edition—to be called "The Mellstock Edition". Between ourselves I shall be so glad when it is over for the job seems to be trying him very much.'

[24] Hardy to Macmillan, 28 Oct. 1922 (BL Add. MS 54925).

had just been published; and at the same time he sent a list of corrections for a reprint of *Late Lyrics*. He published *The Queen of Cornwall* in 1923, and then corrected it twice in the next two years. In 1925 he sent Macmillan lists of revisions for *Human Shows*, and for the Wessex Edition of *Late Lyrics*. And in the autumn of 1927, well past his eighty-seventh birthday, he prepared the copy-text of *Chosen Poems*, and insisted on reading the proofs, which he did in November, less than two months before his death.

Conclusions

One point should be clear from this account of Hardy's poetic career: he was a lifelong reviser of his poems. But though they might be said to have been in a constant process of revision, individual changes in the texts were rarely extensive. Hardy did not 'remake himself', as Yeats and Auden did; it would be nearer the mark to say that he tried to make himself *more* himself, by correcting and improving what he had written, rewriting a line, altering a word, improving a rhyme.

A second and equally important point to make is that these revisions were not systematically cumulative: there is no *final* text. Clearly Hardy intended that there should be one; in 1913, when the first printing of the Wessex Edition had been completed, he wrote to Macmillan: 'I should, of course, much like the corrections in the Wessex edition to be incorporated into the other editions, as you suggest',[25] but this was not done—at least not in the volumes of verse. In later years he was always careful to specify the best corrected text to be used in quoting from his works, but the fact that he chose now one edition and now another suggests that one correct text was not evolving in a direct line of descent. On the last page of his last notebook, almost certainly within a few months of his death, Hardy wrote this note to himself: '*Things to be done.* See how corrections stand in respect of each edition: get a set properly corrected: & destroy useless proofs in cupboard.'[26] This entry is not cancelled, as some others under this heading are; it was a thing still to be done.

One reason for the complex relationships among Hardy's later editions is that they exist in two genetic lines. To understand how this came about, we must go back to the crucial years 1909-12: for

---

[25] See p. xiv n. 3 above.   [26] The notebook is in DCM.

in those years Hardy prepared two editions of his collected poetry, containing the same poems but substantially different in textual details. From the evidence of the publishing history and of Hardy's correspondence with Macmillan, this is what happened. Hardy prepared copy for the first part of the *Collected Poems*—that is, for the texts of *Wessex Poems* and *Poems of the Past and the Present*— early in 1909; the copy was set in type, and Hardy read proofs in April (see the letter quoted above, p. xv). It seems probable that the plates from this setting were still on hand at R. & R. Clark, Macmillan's Edinburgh printer, in 1919, and that they were used to print the first edition of *Collected Poems*.[27]

In 1911 Hardy began work on the Wessex Edition. He used as his working text the volumes of poetry in the latest reprints of the Uniform Edition—the 1911 reprints of *Wessex Poems* and *Poems of the Past and the Present*, and the 1910 reprint of *Time's Laughing-stocks*—rather than proofs of the *Collected Poems* plates for the first two, as might have seemed reasonable. In other words, he began again. Some of the revisions that he had made for the *Collected Poems* were incorporated into the Wessex Edition, but others were not; and revisions made in the Wessex Edition were not included in the *Collected Poems* when it was printed eight years later, in spite of Hardy's explicit wish that this should be done.

Each of these separate versions of the poetry became the trunk of its own family tree of editions. *Collected Poems* went into new editions as new volumes were added—the second edition in 1923, the third in 1928, the fourth in 1930; this edition remained in print for more than forty years, being reprinted from its original plates

[27] See the letter quoted above, p. xvii. Letters from Macmillan to Clark (BL Add. MS 55339) confirm that the entire one-volume edition of 1909 (that is, *Wessex Poems, Poems of the Past and the Present*, and *The Dynasts*) was set in that year, and that proofs were sent to Hardy. By 1919 Macmillan was not sure how much of the volume was set up, but assumed that some was. A note of 27 Mar. from Macmillan to Clark (BL Add. MS 55345) reads: '*Hardy's Complete Poetical Works.*

'In the year 1909 we started this volume, part of which was set up, when we took from it "The Dynasts" which we published separately.

'We now want the Poems completed to consist of
  Wessex Poems
  Poems Past and Present
  Time's Laughingstocks
  Satires of Circumstance
  Moments of Vision

'We don't know how much you have already set up, but you can complete the volume and let us have the proofs.'

and, when those wore out, from lithographic plates made from the most recent impression. The Wessex Edition was also expanded as new books of poems appeared: new volumes were added in 1919, 1926, and 1931, and the earlier volumes were reprinted in 1920. Hardy used this edition as the text for his *Selected Poems* (1916, and many reprints thereafter), and for the Mellstock Edition.

One might add, as a further complication, that the individual books of poems continued to be reprinted, usually with some corrections. For these new impressions Hardy customarily sent Macmillan lists of corrections—three sets for *Moments of Vision*, for example, and three for *Late Lyrics*—but he did not read proofs again, and he did not attempt to collate the texts with other revised versions. Consequently some later impressions of early books contain texts that preserve some first-edition readings that had been revised in both the Wessex Edition and the *Collected Poems*, while incorporating some of the revisions that Hardy had made in other editions. (The 1923 *Wessex Poems* is a good example of such a text.)

Perhaps if Hardy had begun his full-time poetic career earlier, he might have had the energy and the patience to co-ordinate all the different versions of his poems, and so produce an ideal text. But he was fifty-eight when his first book of verse was published, over seventy when he prepared the Wessex Edition, and nearly eighty when the first *Collected Poems* appeared. There is no evidence that his mental faculties diminished in any way—indeed the post-humous *Winter Words* argues strongly to the contrary—but his physical strength did decline in his later years, he was intermittently ill, and he suffered periods of physical weakness and enforced inactivity. One can scarcely complain if he put such energy as he had into new poems, in a burst of late creativity that has few parallels in English poetry, rather than into the tedious business of collation.

Hardy did make some efforts to integrate his scattered revisions, and to bring the texts of his poems to final corrected form. These efforts are embodied in seven books from Hardy's library: five verse volumes of the Wessex Edition; a copy of the thin-paper edition of *Collected Poems* (1923); and a set of proofs of *Human Shows*, sewn together to make a book. Each of these contains several sets of corrections, entered at different times and in different coloured pencils or inks. A few of the corrections are tentative—marked with a query, or one of several alternatives—but most are firmly entered, and the words or marks of punctuation that they replace are firmly cancelled. Some of these revisions are new; others simply record a change already made in another edition (for example, entering a Wessex Edition change in the *Collected Poems* text). They are not major revisions: a cadence is smoothed, a faulty punctuation corrected, a word or a phrase replaced by a clearer or more idiomatic one. It was the sort of tidying up that a neat old man who cared for his work might do, at the end of a long literary career.

On the flyleaves of the bound volumes, Hardy wrote notes to himself, recording which corrections had been sent to Macmillan and which had not. The notes are not always exactly correct— obviously it was a confusing business keeping track of so many sets of changes—but they show what the function of these corrected volumes was: they were the gathering-places for Hardy's revisions, from which he could compile lists of textual changes to be transmitted to Macmillan, for inclusion in later printings. Hardy did indeed use the Wessex Edition volumes in that way in 1919 and 1920, when he sent lists of corrections for the second impression of the Wessex Edition, and for the Mellstock Edition. No doubt he intended to do the same with the *Collected Poems* volume and with the *Human Shows* proof, though he apparently never got round to preparing the lists. Consequently, though many of the marked changes did appear in one printed text or another, no text contains all of them, and some never appeared at all.

Since Hardy did not accomplish a text incorporating all his final revisions, that task remains for Hardy's editor. He must take authorial revisions from many sources, and at the same time must correct the errors that have crept into existing versions of the poems. His goal will be to establish that ideal text that Hardy might have prepared, and wished to prepare, but did not. And I have added to that task another, and related one: to provide, through textual notes, an account of the process, as recorded both in manuscripts and in printed books, by which Hardy worked towards that final text.

A Note on the Present Edition

THE copy-texts for this edition are the first editions of Hardy's first seven volumes of poems, and the holograph of *Winter Words*. These copy-texts have been emended according to the following principles:

Substantives. I have considered substantive revisions that reached print to be expressions of Hardy's fixed intention, and have incorporated these revisions into the established text. Where there is more than one revised version of a line or a word, I have taken the latest one where chronology can be determined with certainty (as is usually the case); in those instances where the chronology is uncertain, I have relied on my critical judgement and my sense of what is characteristic of Hardy's mature style. In considering revisions, I have not accepted the third edition of *Collected Poems* (1928), or the printed texts of *Winter Words* (1928) and *Chosen Poems* (1929) as authoritative; these were all printed after Hardy's death, and the evidence of the printer's copy of *Chosen Poems* makes it clear that Mrs Hardy and an unknown editor (no doubt at Macmillan) made textual decisions that were contrary to Hardy's own.

All substantive variants occurring in manuscripts and in printed texts are reported in textual notes, with the following exceptions:

(1) the revisions that Hardy made in his own copies of his books that are clearly tentative—those marked with a query, or including more than one alternative reading;

(2) the pencilled revisions that Hardy made in manuscripts and in his own books, but then erased.

It seemed desirable that these tentative changes should be clearly distinguished from Hardy's firm decisions; I have therefore omitted them from the textual notes, and have reported them separately in the explanatory notes at the back of each volume.

Accidentals. Hardy was not careful about punctuation in the holographs that he prepared as printer's copies: clearly he was one of those writers who expected his copy to be corrected by the printer, and who would alter in proofs any corrections that displeased him. That he was a meticulous proof-reader the existing proofs make very clear; he not only made many substantive corrections, but he also caught faulty characters—even a lower-case i with the dot missing!—and numerous errors of punctuation. I have therefore taken the first editions of all the volumes except *Winter Words* as the best authority in punctuation, unless there is reason to think that later changes were authorial. In some cases this can be proved from Hardy's corrections in his own books, or from the lists that he prepared for Macmillan, or from corrected proofs and notes sent to the printer, but in other cases I have had to trust my sense of Hardy's style and practice. For example, he had a nineteenth-century taste for capitalized personifications, and frequently used them; but his practice was not consistent, and sometimes personifications appear in lower case in early texts, and are later capitalized. I have concluded that this is more likely to have been Hardy's decision than a printer's, and have adopted the capital in such instances. Similarly in the case of the strings of full points—conventionally the mark of an elision—that Hardy customarily used to indicate the passage of time in a narrative poem: where this symbol first appears in a late text of a poem I have taken it to be an authorial change. I have been more cautious about adopting late insertions of question marks and marks of exclamation, but have done so when the text justifies them, on the grounds that these, too, are more likely to be authorial than an editor's or printer's changes. In a few cases I have adopted manuscript readings of accidentals where that reading is supported by a second manuscript, or where the sense clearly requires it. These adoptions are indicated in textual notes.

In the case of *Winter Words*, which Hardy did not live to see through the press, I have followed the punctuation of the holograph text except in cases where it is manifestly incorrect. But Hardy's punctuation was as wayward in this, his last book of poems, as it was in his first, and if he had lived he would surely have passed editorial changes in proofs; I have therefore not hesitated to adopt the punctuation of the printed text of *Winter Words* where it clearly corrects a holograph mis-punctuation. The instances where I have done so are reported in the textual notes.

I have reported all variant accidentals in manuscripts, with the following exceptions: obvious slips of the pen (e.g. the omission of closing quotation marks), minor spelling variants (*vigilling* for *vigiling*, *abyssmal* for *abysmal*), and variants in hyphenation. In the case of printed texts I have reported variant accidentals only when (*a*) a corroborating correction in Hardy's hand exists, in a manuscript or a revised proof, or in one of Hardy's own books; or (*b*) a change of sense is involved—though I have interpreted this rule broadly, to include all changes in capitalization, and in question marks and exclamation marks. In manuscript quotations, ampersands have been replaced by 'and'. In the placement of quotation marks relative to punctuation, and in the typographical form of sub-titles, I have uniformly adopted the house style of the Oxford University Press.

Where the established text of a poem carries a date and/or place of composition, the form of this notation has been made uniform. For example, Hardy recorded his 1865-7 address variously as W. P. V., 16 W. P. V., etc.; I have written these out in the fullest of the forms he used: 16 Westbourne Park Villas—even in cases where no version of the particular text actually contains the full form.

An asterisk following the title of a poem indicates an explanatory note at the back of the volume. Hardy's own explanatory notes are placed with the others, but are marked with an (H). His glossarial notes have been incorporated into the Glossary (Appendix F of Volume Three), and are also marked (H).

I have taken as texts for four of Hardy's prefaces—those for *Wessex Poems*, *Poems of the Past and the Present*, *Time's Laughing-stocks*, and *Late Lyrics and Earlier*—the 'supplemented' versions printed in the Wessex Edition, which Hardy preferred;[1] in one case a minor emendation from the Mellstock Edition has been adopted. The *Winter Words* preface is that of the first edition, which differs from the holograph in a single mark of punctuation.

Textual Notes. Textual notes are keyed to the text by a line number and, when necessary for clarity of reference, by a keyword. When the variant is a single word, the word as it appears in the established text is quoted, followed by a closing square bracket; to the right of this bracket all variants are listed in chronological order of transcription and/or publication, with their sources. For example:

36 —Unanswered,] —Unenlightened, *PP*; So, baffled, *CP19*

When the variation is in punctuation only, the word or words that

---

[1] In a letter dated 7 May 1915 (DCM), Hardy advised Harold Child to use the Wessex Edition in his research, 'the prefaces having all been supplemented in it'.

precede the variant mark of punctuation are indicated by a tilde, thus:

8 fire!] ~. *Hol.*

When an entire line has been revised, the variant line is simply quoted, with its source, thus:

32 Even ghosts tend thereto! *SC14*

The source or sources of the established text are cited in the notes, to the left of the square bracket, wherever this information cannot readily be inferred from the variants: for example, where the number of variants might cause confusion, or where Hardy vacillated between readings from text to text, or where the source is an unusual one—a manuscript, or one of the lists of corrections that Hardy sent to his publisher, or an annotation in one of his own books, or a combination of sources, as in the following instance:

24 *WE, DCM3*] There rest we. *LL, CP23*

Where no source is given, it is to be assumed that the established reading occurs in all significant texts except those cited as variants. Where variants occur in a periodical publication, the periodical source is cited at the beginning of the textual note, and is thereafter abbreviated: e.g. *A* for *Academy*, *ER* for *English Review*.

In reporting manuscript variants I have indicated words that Hardy cancelled by enclosing them in angle brackets. In the few instances where a cancelled word is illegible I have recorded a question mark between angle brackets. Where letters were added to or subtracted from a word, I have treated the entire original word as cancelled. (Cancellations of a letter or two, from which no word can be inferred, have been omitted.) I have also treated changes in word-order and inserted words as cancellations; for example, in the first line of the holograph of 'Rome: At the Pyramid of Cestius' Hardy first wrote 'Who was Cestius?' and then inserted between the first two words the word *then*. I have recorded this change as

1 Who, then, was] ⟨Who was⟩ *Hol.*

I have not reported cancellations where the same word was simply restored; however, it does seem of interest that in some cases Hardy cancelled a word, tried an alternative, and then returned to the first, and I have reported these changes, as in 'At the Royal Academy':

11 verdures] ⟨verdures⟩ ⟨carpets⟩ *Hol.*

In a number of instances a poem in Hardy's holograph printer's copy contains an entire line from an earlier text (usually from a periodical version), which Hardy has struck through and replaced, or heavily revised. In the textual notes I have indicated this process by quoting the first version, with its source, followed by the notation: *variant line del. Hol.*

I have tried to restrict the numbers of sources cited to the minimum necessary for a clear understanding of the relations between texts. Manuscript versions and/or proofs of poems are cited only if they differ from the printed version that they precede, or where the manuscript confirms a variant accidental as Hardy's; and Hardy's revisions and corrections in his own books, and in the lists that he prepared for his publisher, are cited only when the reading is unique, or supports a unique printed text. The Mellstock Edition is not reported except where it differs from the 1919-20 impression of the Wessex Edition (which was its copy-text). The Pocket Edition, *Selected Poems*, *Collected Poems* 1920, and later reprints of individual volumes are only cited when they contain the first instance of a variant.

WESSEX POEMS
AND OTHER VERSES

"---- At mothy curfew-tide,
They've a way of whispering to me."
FRIENDS BEYOND.

CONTENTS

PREFACE*

OF the miscellaneous collection of verse that follows, only four pieces have been published, though many were written long ago, and others partly written. In some few cases the verses were turned into prose and printed as such in a novel, it not having been anticipated at that time that they might see the light in their original 5 shape.

Here and there, when an ancient and legitimate word still current in the district, for which there was no close equivalent in received English, suggested itself, it has been made use of, on what seemed good grounds. 10

The pieces are in a large degree dramatic or personative in conception; and the dates attached to some of the poems do not apply to the rough sketches given in illustration, which have been recently made, and, as may be surmised, are inserted for personal and local reasons rather than for their intrinsic qualities. 15

September 1898.

PREFACE. 3 some few cases] ⟨some cases⟩ *Hol.*   4 as such in a novel,] as such, *WP, CP*
5 anticipated] ⟨foreseen⟩ *Hol.*; it having been unanticipated *WP, CP*   5–6 see . . . shape.]
⟨be printed.⟩ *Hol.*; see the light. *WP, CP*   7 Here and there, when] Whenever *WP,*
CP   7–8 word . . . for] local word, for *Hol.*; word of the district, for *WP, CP*
8 close equivalent] equivalent *WP, CP*   9 itself,] itself as the most natural, nearest,
and often only expression of a thought, *WP, CP*   9–10 of, . . . grounds.] of. *Hol.*
12 conception; and the dates] conception; and this even where they are not obviously so. The
dates *WP, CP*   13 given in illustration,] ⟨that illustrate them,⟩ given in illustration,
⟨but⟩ *Hol.*   14 *all after* made *om. Hol.*
    Signed with initials T. H. *WP, CP*

THE TEMPORARY THE ALL

(Sapphics)

Change and chancefulness in my flowering youthtime
Set me sun by sun near to one unchosen;
Wrought us fellowlike, and despite divergence,
    Fused us in friendship.

'Cherish him can I while the true one forthcome—   5
Come the rich fulfiller of my prevision;
Life is roomy yet, and the odds unbounded.'
    So self-communed I.

'Thwart my wistful way did a damsel saunter,
Fair, albeit unformed to be all-eclipsing;   10
'Maiden meet,' held I, 'till arise my forefelt
    Wonder of women.'

Long a visioned hermitage deep desiring,
Tenements uncouth I was fain to house in;
'Let such lodging be for a breath-while,' thought I,   15
    'Soon a more seemly.

THE TEMPORARY THE ALL. *Headnote SP, CP20, WE20*
  1 flowering] bloothing *Hol.*   3 fellowlike,] fellowly, *WP*   divergence,]
misfitness *Hol.*   4 Friends ⟨interwove⟩ interknit us. *Hol.*; Friends interblent us.
WP; Friends interlinked us. *PE*   5 while] ⟨till⟩ *Hol.*   9 'Thwart *DCM4*]
Thwart *WP–CP*   10 Fair not fairest, good not best of her feather; *WP98*   albeit] the
while *WP03*   14 Tenement uncouth did I fain abide in; *Hol.*   15 lodging]
lodgment *Hol.*

'Then high handiwork will I make my life-deed,
Truth and Light outshow; but the ripe time pending,
Intermissive aim at the thing sufficeth.'
        Thus I . . . But lo, me!   20

Mistress, friend, place, aims to be bettered straightway,
Bettered not has Fate or my hand's achievement;
Sole the showance those of my onward earth-track—
        Never transcended!

AMABEL

I marked her ruined hues,
Her custom-straitened views,
And asked, 'Can there indwell
        My Amabel?'

I looked upon her gown,   5
Once rose, now earthen brown;
The change was like the knell
        Of Amabel.

Her step's mechanic ways
Had lost the life of May's;   10
Her laugh, once sweet in swell,
        Spoilt Amabel.

I mused: 'Who sings the strain
I sang ere warmth did wane ?
Who thinks its numbers spell   15
        His Amabel ?'—

17 Then *DCM4*] ∼ , *WP–CP*   high handiwork] achievement large *Hol.*
18 pending,] ∼ *Hol.*   19 Intermissive] ⟨Curt and casual⟩ *Hol.*   20 ⟨So⟩
Thus I . . . But woe me, *Hol.*   21 place,] ⟨house,⟩ ⟨bower⟩ home, *Hol.*   aims]
⟨deed⟩ *Hol.*   straightway,] forthwith, *Hol.*   22 Bettered not have I by the full in
each kind, *Hol.*   achievement] achieving *WP*   23 They as tokens sole of my sorry
earth-way *Hol.*   showance *WP, DCM1 and 4, WE20, CP23*] showings *WE12, SP, CP19*
24 Stand in their ⟨poorness⟩ scantness! *Hol.*

AMABEL. 2 ⟨Her outworn orbs of blue,⟩ Her faded iris-blues, *Hol.*   11 once . . .
swell,] ⟨which coldly fell⟩ *Hol.*

Knowing that, though Love cease,
Love's race shows no decrease;
All find in dorp or dell
        An Amabel.   20

—I felt that I could creep
To some housetop, and weep
That Time the tyrant fell
        Ruled Amabel !

I said (the while I sighed   25
That love like ours had died),
'Fond things I'll no more tell
        To Amabel,

'But leave her to her fate,
And fling across the gate,   30
"Till the Last Trump, farewell,
        O Amabel !"'

                                1865.

18 no decrease;] undecrease; *WP*   23 tyrant] *cap. Hol.*   26 died),] ~)
Hol.   27 'Fond] "Sweet *Hol.*   30 fling] ⟨say⟩ cry *Hol.*   31 fare-
well,] ~ *Hol.*
  Date 1866 *Hol., SP*   *Place* 16 Westbourne Park Villas *WE, SP; del. DCM4*

HAP

If but some vengeful god would call to me
From up the sky, and laugh: 'Thou suffering thing,
Know that thy sorrow is my ecstasy,
That thy love's loss is my hate's profiting!'

Then would I bear it, clench myself, and die,   5
Steeled by the sense of ire unmerited;
Half-eased in that a Powerfuller than I
Had willed and meted me the tears I shed.

But not so. How arrives it joy lies slain,
And why unblooms the best hope ever sown?   10
—Crass Casualty obstructs the sun and rain,
And dicing Time for gladness casts a moan. . . .
These purblind Doomsters had as readily strown
Blisses about my pilgrimage as pain.

1866.
16 Westbourne Park Villas.

'IN VISION I ROAMED'

To——

In vision I roamed the flashing Firmament,
So fierce in blazon that the Night waxed wan,
As though with awe at orbs of such ostént;
And as I thought my spirit ranged on and on

In footless traverse through ghast heights of sky,   5
To the last chambers of the monstrous Dome,
Where stars the brightest here are lost to the eye:
Then, any spot on our own Earth seemed Home!

HAP. *Title* Chance *Hol.*
    5 bear it,] bear, and *WP*   6 unmerited;] ~, *Hol.*   7 Half-eased in]
Half-eased, too, *WP98*   12 gladness] laughter *Hol.*   14 pain.] ~! *Hol.*
    Place W. P. V. *WE, ME*; *om. all other texts*

'IN VISION I ROAMED'. 2 wan,] ~ *Hol.*   3 awe at orbs] an awed sense *WP*
5 sky,] ~ *Hol.*   6 Dome,] *l.c., Hol.*   7 are lost to the eye:] to darkness die:
WP   8 Home!] ⟨*l.c.*⟩ *Hol.*

And the sick grief that you were far away
Grew pleasant thankfulness that you were near,   10
Who might have been, set on some foreign Sphere,
Less than a Want to me, as day by day
I lived unware, uncaring all that lay
Locked in that Universe trackless, distant, drear.

1866.

AT A BRIDAL

Nature's Indifference

When you paced forth, to await maternity,
A dream of other offspring held my mind,
Compounded of us twain as Love designed;
Rare forms, that corporate now will never be!

Should I, too, wed as slave to Mode's decree,   5
And each thus found apart, of false desire,
A stolid line, whom no high aims will fire
As had fired ours could ever have mingled we;

And, grieved that lives so matched should miscompose,
Each mourn the double waste; and question dare   10
To the Great Dame whence incarnation flows,
Why those high-purposed children never were:
What will she answer? That she does not care
If the race all such sovereign types unknows.

1866.
8 Adelphi Terrace.

11 foreign Sphere,] outstep sphere, *WP*   12 Less] ⟨Lest⟩ *Hol.*   me,] ∼
Hol.   as day] ⟨?⟩ *Hol.*   by day] ∼ ⟨,⟩ *Hol.*   13 lived unware,] ⟨should have
lived⟩ *Hol.*   14 Locked] ⟨Hid⟩ *Hol.*   trackless, distant, drear.] taciturn and
drear. *WP, CP*

AT A BRIDAL. *Subtitle om. Hol.*; To —— *WP*
1 await] wait *WP*   8 we;] ∼ ⟨;⟩, *Hol.*   11 flows,] ∼ *Hol.*
14 If all such aimed ideals have such a close. *Hol.*
Place DCM1, WE20

POSTPONEMENT*

Snow-bound in woodland, a mournful word,
Dropt now and then from the bill of a bird,
Reached me on wind-wafts; and thus I heard,
    Wearily waiting:—

'I planned her a nest in a leafless tree,   5
But the passers eyed and twitted me,
And said: "How reckless a bird is he,
    Cheerily mating!"

'Fear-filled, I stayed me till summer-tide,
In lewth of leaves to throne her bride;   10
But alas! her love for me waned and died,
    Wearily waiting.

'Ah, had I been like some I see,
Born to an evergreen nesting-tree,
None had eyed and twitted me,   15
    Cheerily mating!'

                                        1866.

A CONFESSION TO A FRIEND IN TROUBLE*

Your troubles shrink not, though I feel them less
Here, far away, than when I tarried near;
I even smile old smiles—with listlessness—
Yet smiles they are, not ghastly mockeries mere.

A thought too strange to house within my brain   5
Haunting its outer precincts I discern:
—*That I will not show zeal again to learn*
Your griefs, and, sharing them, renew my pain. . . .

POSTPONEMENT. 3 on wind-wafts;] from windward; *Hol.*   thus] this *Hol.*   8 Cheerily]
Dreaming of *Hol.*   9 ⟨"I stayed me, and hoped at the summer-tide,⟩ "Stricken, I
stayed till the summer-tide, *Hol.*   10 lewth of] ⟨shielding⟩ *Hol.*   throne]
⟨throne⟩ house *Hol.*   16 Cheerily] Dreaming of *Hol.*

A CONFESSION TO A FRIEND. *Title* ⟨A Confession of Selfishness⟩ *Hol.*
  2 tarried] ⟨halted⟩ lingered *Hol.*   6 precincts] chambers *Hol.*

It goes, like murky bird or buccaneer
That shapes its lawless figure on the main,   10
And staunchness tends to banish utterly
The unseemly instinct that had lodgment here;
Yet, comrade old, can bitterer knowledge be
Than that, though banned, such instinct was in me!

1866.
16 Westbourne Park Villas.

NEUTRAL TONES

We stood by a pond that winter day,
And the sun was white, as though chidden of God,
And a few leaves lay on the starving sod;
— They had fallen from an ash, and were gray.

Your eyes on me were as eyes that rove   5
Over tedious riddles of years ago;
And some words played between us to and fro
On which lost the more by our love.

The smile on your mouth was the deadest thing
Alive enough to have strength to die;   10
And a grin of bitterness swept thereby
Like an ominous bird a-wing. . . .

Since then, keen lessons that love deceives,
And wrings with wrong, have shaped to me
Your face, and the God-curst sun, and a tree,   15
And a pond edged with grayish leaves.

1867.

---

11 And each new impulse tends to make outflee *WP, CP19*   12 here;] ~ : *Hol.*
13 Yet,] ~ *Hol.*
   Place W. P. V. *WE, ME; om. all other texts*

NEUTRAL TONES. 1 day,] ~ *Hol.*   2 of] ⟨by⟩ *Hol.*   3 starving] withered
Hol.   sod; *Hol., CP, DCM4*] ~ , *WP, WE*   6 of *CP23, DCM4*] solved *WP,
WE, CP19*   7 some words *WP, CP, DCM4*] ⟨a query⟩ *Hol.*; words *WE, SP*   fro
CP, DCM4] fro— *WP, WE, SP*   8 ⟨Which was most wrecked by our love?⟩ On
which the more lost ⟨of⟩ by our love. *Hol.*   16 pond] ~ , *Hol.*
   Place W. P. V. *WE*; Westbourne Park Villas. *SP*; *del. DCM4*

SHE AT HIS FUNERAL*

They bear him to his resting-place—
In slow procession sweeping by;
I follow at a stranger's space;
His kindred they, his sweetheart I.
Unchanged my gown of garish dye,   5
Though sable-sad is their attire;
But they stand round with griefless eye,
Whilst my regret consumes like fire!

187-.

SHE AT HIS FUNERAL. *Title DCM3*] She *WP-CP*; At his Funeral *SP*   *Subtitle* At his
Funeral *WP-CP*
  8 fire!] ~ . *Hol.*

HER INITIALS

Upon a poet's page I wrote
Of old two letters of her name;
Part seemed she of the effulgent thought
Whence that high singer's rapture came.
—When now I turn the leaf the same   5
Immortal light illumes the lay,
But from the letters of her name
The radiance has waned away!

1869.

HER INITIALS. 2 two letters] the initials *Hol.*   name;] ~ , *Hol.*   3 For she seemed
woven of the thought *Hol.*   6 Immortal] ⟨Perennial⟩ *Hol.*   7 letters of her]
margin-written *Hol.*   8 waned] died *WP*   away!] ~ . *Hol.*
  Divided into two four-line stanzas WE, SP

HER DILEMMA

(In —— church)

The two were silent in a sunless church,
Whose mildewed walls, uneven paving-stones,
And wasted carvings passed antique research;
And nothing broke the clock's dull monotones.

Leaning against a wormy poppy-head,   5
So wan and worn that he could scarcely stand,
—For he was soon to die,—he softly said,
'Tell me you love me!'—holding long her hand.

She would have given a world to breathe 'yes' truly,
So much his life seemed hanging on her mind,   10
And hence she lied, her heart persuaded throughly
'Twas worth her soul to be a moment kind.

HER DILEMMA. 1 The] ⟨We⟩ *Hol.*   3 carvings] ∼, *Hol.*   7 die,—] die—
Hol.   8 long] hard *WP*   her] ⟨my⟩ *Hol.*   9 She] ⟨I⟩ *Hol.*   'yes']
cap. Hol.   10 her] ⟨my⟩ *Hol.*   11 she] ⟨I⟩ *Hol.*   her] ⟨my⟩ *Hol.*
12 her] ⟨my⟩ *Hol.*

But the sad need thereof, his nearing death,
So mocked humanity that she shamed to prize
A world conditioned thus, or care for breath   15
Where Nature such dilemmas could devise.

1866.

REVULSION

Though I waste watches framing words to fetter
Some unknown spirit to mine in clasp and kiss,
Out of the night there looms a sense 'twere better
To fail obtaining whom one fails to miss.

For winning love we win the risk of losing,   5
And losing love is as one's life were riven;
It cuts like contumely and keen ill-using
To cede what was superfluous when given.

Let me then never feel the fateful thrilling
That devastates the love-worn wooer's frame,   10
The hot ado of fevered hopes, the chilling
That agonizes disappointed aim!
So may I live no junctive law fulfilling,
And my heart's table bear no woman's name.

186–.
16 Westbourne Park Villas.

14 she] ⟨I⟩ *Hol.*   16 Nature] *l.c. Hol.*

REVULSION. 2 Some ... mine] Some spirit to mine own *WP*   3 night] *cap. Hol.*
8 superfluous when] superfluously *WP, CP*   9 never feel] feel no more *WP*
13 fulfilling,] ∼ *Hol.*
 Date 1866 *WP, CP*   Place *WE, ME; om. all other texts*

SHE, TO HIM*

I

When you shall see me in the toils of Time,
My lauded beauties carried off from me,
My eyes no longer stars as in their prime,
My name forgot of Maiden Fair and Free;

When in your being heart concedes to mind,   5
And judgment, though you scarce its process know,
Recalls the excellencies I once enshrined,
And you are irked that they have withered so:

Remembering mine the loss is, not the blame,
That Sportsman Time but rears his brood to kill,   10
Knowing me in my soul the very same—
One who would die to spare you touch of ill!—
Will you not grant to old affection's claim
The hand of friendship down Life's sunless hill?

                                        1866.

SHE, TO HIM I. 1 in the toils] lined by tool *WP98*   5 When alienation comes of heart
and mind, *Hol.*   7 I once] ⟨it us⟩ *Hol.*   9 Remembering that with me lies
not the blame, *WP*   11 soul] heart *Hol.*   12 ill!—] ∼; *Hol.*
13 grant] ⟨cede⟩ ⟨yield⟩ *Hol.*

SHE, TO HIM*

II

Perhaps, long hence, when I have passed away,
Some other's feature, accent, thought like mine,
Will carry you back to what I used to say,
And bring some memory of your love's decline.

Then you may pause awhile and think, 'Poor jade!' 5
And yield a sigh to me—as ample due,
Not as the tittle of a debt unpaid
To one who could resign her all to you—

And thus reflecting, you will never see
That your thin thought, in two small words conveyed, 10
Was no such fleeting phantom-thought to me,
But the Whole Life wherein my part was played;
And you amid its fitful masquerade
A Thought—as I in your life seem to be!

1866.

SHE, TO HIM

III

I will be faithful to thee; aye, I will!
And Death shall choose me with a wondering eye
That he did not discern and domicile
One his by right ever since that last Good-bye!

SHE, TO HIM II. *Title* To Him *SP, where the poem stands alone*
1 Perhaps,] ~ *Hol.*   5 awhile] ~ , *Hol.*   jade!'] Maid!" *Hol.*
6 ample due,] gift benign, *WP98*   7 as] ⟨at⟩ *Hol.*   8 resign her all to
you—] to you her all resign— *WP98*   14 your life seem to be!] yours but seem to be.
WP, WE
    Place Westbourne Park Villas. *SP*; *del. DCM4*

SHE, TO HIM III. 1 will!] ~ , *Hol.*   4 ever since] e'ersince *Hol.*

I have no care for friends, or kin, or prime   5
Of manhood who deal gently with me here;
Amid the happy people of my time
Who work their love's fulfilment, I appear

Numb as a vane that cankers on its point,
True to the wind that kissed ere canker came;   10
Despised by souls of Now, who would disjoint
The mind from memory, making Life all aim,

My old dexterities in witchery gone,
And nothing left for Love to look upon.

1866.

SHE, TO HIM

IV

This love puts all humanity from me;
I can but maledict her, pray her dead,
For giving love and getting love of thee—
Feeding a heart that else mine own had fed!

How much I love I know not, life not known,   5
Save as one unit I would add love by;
But this I know, my being is but thine own—
Fused from its separateness by ecstasy.

And thus I grasp thy amplitudes, of her
Ungrasped, though helped by nigh-regarding eyes;   10

---

12 making] and make *WP*   13 in witchery] of hue quite *WP*   gone,] ~ *Hol.*

SHE, TO HIM IV. 2 dead,] ~ *Hol.*   3 giving love] ~, *Hol.*   6 one] some *WP, WE*

Canst thou then hate me as an envier
Who see unrecked what I so dearly prize?
Believe me, Lost One, Love is lovelier
The more it shapes its moan in selfish-wise.

1866.
16 Westbourne Park Villas.

DITTY*

(E. L. G.)

Beneath a knap where flown
    Nestlings play,
Within walls of weathered stone,
    Far away
From the files of formal houses,   5
By the bough the firstling browses,
Lives a Sweet: no merchants meet,
No man barters, no man sells
    Where she dwells.

Upon that fabric fair   10
    'Here is she!'
Seems written everywhere
    Unto me.
But to friends and nodding neighbours,
Fellow-wights in lot and labours,   15
Who descry the times as I,
No such lucid legend tells
    Where she dwells.

Should I lapse to what I was
    Ere we met;   20
(Such will not be, but because
    Some forget

Place W. P. V. *WE, ME; om. all other texts*

DITTY. 10 that] the *Hol.*   fabric] ⟨frontage⟩ *Hol.*   17 lucid legend] ⟨shining
signal⟩ *Hol.*   20 Ere we met;] In days by; *WP98*   21 will not] can not
WP   22 Some forget] Some loves die *WP98*

Let me feign it)—none would notice
That where she I know by rote is
Spread a strange and withering change,   25
Like a drying of the wells
          Where she dwells.

To feel I might have kissed—
          Loved as true—
Otherwhere, nor Mine have missed   30
          My life through,
Had I never wandered near her,
Is a smart severe—severer
In the thought that she is nought,
Even as I, beyond the dells   35
          Where she dwells.

And Devotion droops her glance
          To recall
What bond-servants of Chance
          We are all.   40
I but found her in that, going
On my errant path unknowing,
I did not out-skirt the spot
That no spot on earth excels,
          —Where she dwells!   45

1870.

23 feign] ⟨say⟩ *Hol.*   34 nought,] ~ *Hol.*   37 Devotion] *l.c. Hol.*
44 By the breadth of some few ells *Hol.*   45 —Where] Where *Hol.*   dwells!] ~ .
Hol.

THE SERGEANT'S SONG*

(1803)

When Lawyers strive to heal a breach,
And Parsons practise what they preach;
Then Boney he'll come pouncing down,
And march his men on London town!
    Rollicum-rorum, tol-lol-lorum,   5
    Rollicum-rorum, tol-lol-lay!

When Justices hold equal scales,
And Rogues are only found in jails;
Then Boney he'll come pouncing down,
And march his men on London town!   10
    Rollicum-rorum, &c.

When Rich Men find their wealth a curse,
And fill therewith the Poor Man's purse;
Then Boney he'll come pouncing down,
And march his men on London town!   15
    Rollicum-rorum, &c.

THE SERGEANT'S SONG. *Trumpet-Major [first and fourth stanzas in first edition (1880); second and third added 1881]*
   1 Lawyers] *l.c. TM*   2 Parsons] *l.c. TM*   3 Then little Boney he'll pounce down, *TM*; Then Little Boney he'll pounce down, *WP*   6 -lay!] ∼. *TM, Hol.*   7 Justices] *l.c. TM*   8 Rogues] *l.c. TM*   9 *as line 3*
12 Rich Men] *l.c. TM*   13 Poor Man's] *l.c. TM*   14 *as line 3*
15 town!] ∼. *Hol.*

When Husbands with their Wives agree,
And Maids won't wed from modesty;
Then Boney he'll come pouncing down,
And march his men on London town!   20
    Rollicum-rorum, tol-lol-lorum,
    Rollicum-rorum, tol-lol-lay!

1878.

VALENCIENNES*

(1793)

By Corp'l Tullidge: in *The Trumpet-Major*

(Wessex Dialect)

IN MEMORY OF S. C. (PENSIONER). DIED 184–

We trenched, we trumpeted and drummed,
And from our mortars tons of iron hummed
    Ath'art the ditch, the month we bombed
        The Town o' Valencieën.

'Twas in the June o' Ninety-dree   5
(The Duke o' Yark our then Commander beën)
    The German Legion, Guards, and we
        Laid siege to Valencieën.

17 Husbands . . . Wives] *l.c. TM*   18 Maids] *l.c. TM*   19 *as line 3*
22 -lay!] ~. *Hol.*

VALENCIENNES. *Headnotes* in] *Vide Hol.*; *see WP*   (Wessex Dialect) *WE, ME*] *om. all other*
texts   IN . . . 184-] In memory of ⟨Corporal C—⟩ S. C. Died 184-. *Hol.*
    1 We bugled, trumpeted, and drummed, *Hol.*

This was the first time in the war
That French and English spilled each other's gore;   10
—Few dreamt how far would roll the roar
Begun at Valencieën!

'Twas said that we'd no business there
A-topperèn the French for disagreën;
However, that's not my affair—   15
We were at Valencieën.

Such snocks and slats, since war began
Never knew raw recruit or veteràn:
Stone-deaf therence went many a man
Who served at Valencieën.   20

Into the streets, ath'art the sky,
A hundred thousand balls and bombs were fleën;
And harmless townsfolk fell to die
Each hour at Valencieën!

And, sweatèn wi' the bombardiers,   25
A shell was slent to shards anighst my ears:
—'Twas nigh the end of hopes and fears
For me at Valencieën!

They bore my wownded frame to camp,
And shut my gapèn skull, and washed en cleän,   30
And jined en wi' a zilver clamp
Thik night at Valencieën.

'We've fetched en back to quick from dead;
But never more on earth while rose is red
Will drum rouse Corpel!' Doctor said   35
O' me at Valencieën.

10 spilled] spilt *Hol.*   11 —God knows what year will ⟨end⟩ still the roar *Hol.*;
—God knows what year will end the roar *WP98*   14 A-topperèn ⟨o⟩ the *Hol.*
17 snocks and slats,] devillish din, *Hol.*   19 therence went] ⟨for life⟩ therence
walked *Hol.*   25 bombardiers,] ~ *Hol.*   26 A shell was rent to rags anigh
mine ears: *Hol.*   27 nigh] near *Hol.*   34 while] ⟨wil⟩ *Hol.*

'Twer true. No voice o' friend or foe
Can reach me now, or any livèn beën;
And little have I power to know
    Since then at Valencieën!   40

I never hear the zummer hums
O' bees; and don' know when the cuckoo comes;
But night and day I hear the bombs
    We threw at Valencieën. . . .

As for the Duke o' Yark in war,   45
There may be volk whose judgment o' en is meän;
But this I say—he was not far
    From great at Valencieën.

O' wild wet nights, when all seems sad,
My wownds come back, as though new wownds I'd had;   50
But yet—at times I'm sort o' glad
    I fout at Valencieën.

Well: Heaven wi' its jasper halls
Is now the on'y Town I care to be in. . . .
Good Lord, if Nick should bomb the walls   55
    As we did Valencieën!

                      1878-1897.

37 foe] ~, *Hol.*   40 Valencieën!] ~. *Hol.*   46 may be] be some *WP*
volk] folk *Hol.*   47 he] 'a *WP*   49 sad,] ~ *Hol.*   51 at times]
⟨sometimes⟩*Hol.*

SAN SEBASTIAN*

(*August* 1813)

WITH THOUGHTS OF SERGEANT M—— (PENSIONER), WHO DIED 185-

'Why, Sergeant, stray on the Ivel Way,
As though at home there were spectres rife?
From first to last 'twas a proud career!
And your sunny years with a gracious wife
    Have brought you a daughter dear.   5

'I watched her to-day; a more comely maid,
As she danced in her muslin bowed with blue,
Round a Hintock maypole never gayed.'
—'Aye, aye; I watched her this day, too,
    As it happens,' the Sergeant said.   10

'My daughter is now', he again began,
'Of just such an age as one I knew
When we of the Line, the Forlorn-hope van,
On an August morning—a chosen few—
    Stormed San Sebastian.   15

SAN SEBASTIAN. *Headnote* WITH . . . 185-] In memory of Sergeant M—. Died 184-. *Hol.*
  4 sunny] ⟨placid⟩ *Hol.*   6 watched] ⟨marked⟩ *Hol.*   9 —'Aye,]
"—∼; *Hol.*   watched] ⟨marked⟩ *Hol.*   13 Line, the Forlorn-hope *CP*]
Line, in the Foot-Guard *WP98*; Line and Forlorn-hope *WP03*; Line—the Forlorn-
hope *WE*

'She's a score less three; so about was *she*—
The maiden I wronged in Peninsular days. . . . .
You may prate of your prowess in lusty times,
But as years gnaw inward you blink your bays,
    And see too well your crimes!   20

'We'd stormed it at night, by the flapping light
Of burning towers, and the mortar's boom:
We'd topped the breach; but had failed to stay,
For our files were misled by the baffling gloom;
    And we said we'd storm by day.   25

'So, out of the trenches, with features set,
On that hot, still morning, in measured pace,
Our column climbed; climbed higher yet,
Past the fauss'bray, scarp, up the curtain-face,
    And along the parapet.   30

'From the battered hornwork the cannoneers
Hove crashing balls of iron fire;
On the shaking gap mount the volunteers
In files, and as they mount expire
    Amid curses, groans, and cheers.   35

'Five hours did we storm, five hours re-form,
As Death cooled those hot blood pricked on;
Till our cause was helped by a woe within:
They were blown from the summit we'd leapt upon,
    And madly we entered in.   40

'On end for plunder, 'mid rain and thunder
That burst with the lull of our cannonade,

---

21 flapping light] vlanker-light *WP*   23 topped] scaled *Hol.*   24 baffling]
⟨hovering⟩ ⟨grisly⟩ *Hol.*   26 with] their *Hol.*   32 Hove crashing]
⟨Heaved bursting⟩ *Hol.*   33 shaking gap] quaking breach *Hol.*
36 re-form,] ∼ *Hol.*   37 ⟨As whom Courage advanced were by Death
withdrawn;⟩ As Death cooled ⟨each⟩ those hot blood pricked on; *Hol.*   38 within:]
∼; *Hol.*   39 were blown] swerved *Hol.*; swayed *WP*   40 madly we] ⟨we
madly⟩ *Hol.*   41 'On end for] "Intent on *Hol.*

We vamped the streets in the stifling air—
Our hunger unsoothed, our thirst unstayed—
  And ransacked the buildings there.   45

'From the shady vaults of their walls of white
We rolled rich puncheons of Spanish grape,
Till at length, with the fire of the wine alight,
I saw at a doorway a fair fresh shape—
  A woman, a sylph, or sprite.   50

'Afeard she fled, and with heated head
I pursued to the chamber she called her own;
—When might is right no qualms deter,
And having her helpless and alone
  I wreaked my will on her.   55

'She raised her beseeching eyes to me,
And I heard the words of prayer she sent
In her own soft language. . . . Fatefully
I copied those eyes for my punishment
  In begetting the girl you see!   60

'So, to-day I stand with a God-set brand
Like Cain's, when he wandered from kindred's ken. . . .
I served through the war that made Europe free;
I wived me in peace-year. But, hid from men,
  I bear that mark on me.   65

'Maybe we shape our offspring's guise
From fancy, or we know not what,
And that no deep impression dies,—
For the mother of my child is not
  The mother of her eyes.   70

---

43 vamped] thridded *Hol.*   45 ransacked] ⟨ravaged⟩ *Hol.*   46 "Down
the stony steps of the house-fronts white *WP*   51 'Afeard] "Dismayed *Hol.*
55 will] lust *WP98*   58 Fatefully] Seemingly *WP*   61 'So,] "∼; *Hol.*
63 war] ⟨wars⟩ *Hol.*   made] ⟨set⟩ *Hol.*   66–70 *om. WP*   66 shape]
draw *WE*   offspring's] children's *WE*   67 we know] one knows *WE*

'And I nightly stray on the Ivel Way
As though at home there were spectres rife;
I delight me not in my proud career;
And 'tis coals of fire that a gracious wife
Should have brought me a daughter dear!'   75

THE STRANGER'S SONG*

(As sung by MR. CHARLES CHARRINGTON in the play of *The Three Wayfarers*)

O my trade it is the rarest one,
        Simple shepherds all—
    My trade is a sight to see;
For my customers I tie, and take 'em up on high,
    And waft 'em to a far countree!   5

My tools are but common ones,
        Simple shepherds all—
    My tools are no sight to see:
A little hempen string, and a post whereon to swing,
    Are implements enough for me!   10

To-morrow is my working day,
        Simple shepherds all—
    To-morrow is a working day for me:
For the farmer's sheep is slain, and the lad who did it ta'en,
    And on his soul may God ha' mer-cy!   15

---

71 Way] ⟨*l.c.*⟩ *Hol.*   74 'tis] ⟨it's⟩ *Hol.*

THE STRANGER'S SONG. In 'The Three Strangers', *Longman's Magazine* (March 1883);
Wessex Tales (1888); *The Three Wayfarers* [play] (1893). *MS1 (LM)* Berg
    Headnote *om. LM, WT, TW*
    2 all—] ~, *MS1*   4 'em] them *LM, TW*   high,] ~ *Hol.*   5 'em]
them *TW*
5a–b   Hee-hee!
                            And waft them to a far countree. *added TW*
7 all—] ~, *MS1*   8 see:] ~; *MS1*   10 me!] ~. *MS1, TW*
10a–b   Hee-hee!
                            Are implements enough for me. *added TW*
12 all—] ~ *MS1*   13 me:] ~ *MS1*   15 mer-cy!] ⟨mercee⟩ *MS1*
15a–b   Hee-hee!
                            And on his soul may God ha' mer-cy! *added TW*

THE BURGHERS*

(17—)

The sun had wheeled from Grey's to Dammer's Crest,
And still I mused on that Thing imminent:
At length I sought the High-street to the West.

The level flare raked pane and pediment
And my wrecked face, and shaped my nearing friend   5
Like one of those the Furnace held unshent.

'I've news concerning her,' he said. 'Attend.
They fly to-night at the late moon's first gleam:
Watch with thy steel: two righteous thrusts will end

Her shameless visions and his passioned dream.   10
I'll watch with thee, to testify thy wrong—
To aid, maybe.— Law consecrates the scheme.'

I started, and we paced the flags along
Till I replied: 'Since it has come to this
I'll do it! But alone. I can be strong.'   15

THE BURGHERS. *Title* The ⟨Three⟩ Burghers *Hol.*   *Headnote* (Casterbridge: 17—) *WE*,
SP; *place del. DCM4*
    5 wrecked *WP*, *CP*, *DCM4*] worn *WE*   6 Like one who walked the Furnace-fire
unshent. *Hol.*   9 thrusts] strokes *Hol.*   10 shameless] lawless *Hol.*
12 Law] ⟨Love⟩ *Hol.*   consecrates] sanctifies *Hol.*   15 it!] ~. *Hol.*

Three hours past Curfew, when the Froom's mild hiss
Reigned sole, undulled by whirr of merchandize,
From Pummery-Tout to where the Gibbet is,

I crossed my pleasaunce hard by Glyd'path Rise,
And stood beneath the wall. Eleven strokes went,   20
And to the door they came, contrariwise,

And met in clasp so close I had but bent
My lifted blade on either to have let
Their two souls loose upon the firmament.

But something held my arm. 'A moment yet   25
As pray-time ere you wantons die!' I said;
And then they saw me. Swift her gaze was set

With eye and cry of love illimited
Upon her Heart-king. Never upon me
Had she thrown look of love so thoroughsped! . . .   30

At once she flung her faint form shieldingly
On his, against the vengeance of my vows;
The which o'erruling, her shape shielded he.

Blanked by such love, I stood as in a drowse,
And the slow moon edged from the upland nigh,   35
My sad thoughts moving thuswise: 'I may house

And I may husband her, yet what am I
But licensed tyrant to this bonded pair?
Says Charity, Do as ye would be done by.' . . .

Hurling my iron to the bushes there,   40
I bade them stay. And, as if brain and breast
Were passive, they walked with me to the stair.

18 is,] ~ *Hol.*   19 Glyd' path] ⟨Glyd Lybbeth⟩ *Hol.*   23 on either]
upon them *WP*   31 A't once] And then *Hol.*   36 thuswise:] thiswise:
Hol.   40 Hurling] Flinging *Hol.*   there,] ~ *Hol.*, *WE*, *SP*   41 And,]
~ *Hol.*

Inside the house none watched; and on we prest
Before a mirror, in whose gleam I read
Her beauty, his,—and mine own mien unblest;   45

Till at her room I turned. 'Madam,' I said,
'Have you the wherewithal for this? Pray speak.
Love fills no cupboard. You'll need daily bread.'

'We've nothing, sire,' she lipped; 'and nothing seek.
'Twere base in me to rob my lord unware;   50
Our hands will earn a pittance week by week.'

And next I saw she had piled her raiment rare
Within the garde-robes, and her household purse,
Her jewels, her least lace of personal wear;

And stood in homespun. Now grown wholly hers,   55
I handed her the gold, her jewels all,
And him the choicest of her robes diverse.

'I'll take you to the doorway in the wall,
And then adieu,' I told them. 'Friends, withdraw.'
They did so; and she went—beyond recall.   60

And as I paused beneath the arch I saw
Their moonlit figures—slow, as in surprise—
Descend the slope, and vanish from the haw.

'"Fool," some will say,' I thought.—'But who is wise,
Save God alone, to weigh my reasons why?'   65
—'Hast thou struck home?' came with the boughs' night-sighs.

It was my friend. 'I have struck well. They fly,
But carry wounds that none can cicatrize.'
—'Not mortal?' said he. 'Lingering—worse,' said I.

45 his,—] ∼; *Hol.*   mine own mien] my own face *SP*   47 speak.] ∼; *Hol.*
49 she lipped; *CP, DCM4*] said she; *WP, WE*   52 next] then *Hol.*   she had]
she'd *WP*   54 her least] and least *WP*   55 hers,] ∼ *Hol.*   59 adieu,']
cap. Hol.   told] to *WP*   63 from *DCM3*] on *all other texts*   64 thought.—
CP, DCM4] ∼. *WP, WE*   68 none] naught *Hol.*   69 —"Mortal?" said he.
"Remorseful—worse," said I. *CP19 only*

LEIPZIG*

(1813)

SCENE: *The Master-tradesmen's Parlour at the Old Ship Inn, Casterbridge. Evening.*

'Old Norbert with the flat blue cap—
    A German said to be—
Why let your pipe die on your lap,
    Your eyes blink absently?'

—'Ah!... Well, I had thought till my cheek was wet   5
    Of my mother—her voice and mien
When she used to sing and pirouette,
    And tap the tambourine

'To the march that yon street-fiddler plies:
    She told me 'twas the same   10
She'd heard from the trumpets, when the Allies
    Burst on her home like flame.

LEIPZIG. *Headnote* SCENE: ... *Evening.*] Interior of the Old Ship Inn, Casterbridge. Evening. *Hol.*
    4 eyes] ⟨eyes⟩ eye *Hol.*   7 pirouette,] ~ *Hol.*   8 tap] touse
WP   9 plies:] ⟨plays⟩ *Hol.*   11 trumpets, when] trumpets of *Hol.*
12 When their troops to her city came. *Hol.*; Her city overcame. *WP*

'My father was one of the German Hussars,
    My mother of Leipzig; but he,
Being camped here, fetched her at close of the wars,   15
    And a Wessex lad reared me.

'And as I grew up, again and again
    She'd tell, after trilling that air,
Of her youth, and the battles on Leipzig plain
    And of all that was suffered there! . . .   20

'—'Twas a time of alarms. Three Chiefs-at-arms
    Combined them to crush One,
And by numbers' might, for in equal fight
    He stood the matched of none.

'Carl Schwarzenberg was of the plot,   25
    And Blücher, prompt and prow,
And Jean the Crown-Prince Bernadotte:
    Buonaparte was the foe.

'City and plain had felt his reign
    From the North to the Middle Sea,   30
And he'd now sat down in the noble town
    Of the King of Saxony.

'October's deep dew its wet gossamer threw
    Upon Leipzig's lawns, leaf-strewn,
Where lately each fair avenue   35
    Wrought shade for summer noon.

'To westward two dull rivers crept
    Through miles of marsh and slough,
Whereover a streak of whiteness swept—
    The Bridge of Lindenau.   40

15 Being] Long *WP*   camped] ⟨in barracks⟩ quartered *Hol.*; quartered *WP*, *WE12*, *CP*
wars,] ∼ *Hol.*   20 there! . . .] ∼ . . . *Hol.*   25 Schwarzenberg]
Schwartzenburg *WP98*

33–6   October's deep dews ⟨sprent old⟩ sprinkled Leipzig's purlieus
                  And ramparts of ashlar hewn,
              Beneath whose fronts fair avenues
                  Made eve of afternoon. *Hol.*

'Hard by, in the City, the One, care-tossed,
  Sat pondering his shrunken power;
And without the walls the hemming host
  Waxed denser every hour.

'He had speech that night on the morrow's designs   45
  With his chiefs by the bivouac fire,
While the belt of flames from the enemy's lines
  Flared nigher him yet and nigher.

'Three rockets then from the girdling trine
  Told, "Ready!" As they rose   50
Their flashes seemed his Judgment-Sign
  For bleeding Europe's woes.

''Twas seen how the French watch-fires that night
  Glowed still and steadily;
And the Three rejoiced, for they read in the sight   55
  That the One disdained to flee. . . .

'—Five hundred guns began the affray
  On next day morn at nine;
Such mad and mangling cannon-play
  Had never torn human line.   60

'Around the town three battles beat,
  Contracting like a gin;
As nearer marched the million feet
  Of columns closing in.

'The first battle nighed on the low Southern side;   65
  The second by the Western way;
The nearing of the third on the North was heard:
  —The French held all at bay.

---

41 care-tossed] care-crossed *Hol.*   42 Sat pondering] Gloomed over *WP, WE*
shrunken power;] narrowing powers; *Hol.*   43 hemming] encircling *Hol.*
44 every hour.] with the hours. *Hol.*   47 belt] zone *Hol.*   49 rockets]
sky-signs *Hol.*; sky-lights *WP, CP*   51 flashes] lightnings *Hol.*   Judgment-
Sign] *l.c. Hol.*   54 steadily;] ~, *Hol.*   55 rejoiced,] ~; *Hol.*
62 Contracting] Constricting *Hol.*   63 As] And *Hol.*   million] myriad *Hol.*

'Against the first band did the Emperor stand;
   Against the second stood Ney;   70
Marmont against the third gave the order-word:
   —Thus raged it throughout the day.

'Fifty thousand sturdy souls on those trampled plains and knolls,
   Who met the dawn hopefully,
And were lotted their shares in a quarrel not theirs,   75
   Dropt then in their agony.

'"O," the old folks said, "ye Preachers stern!
   O so-called Christian time!
When will men's swords to ploughshares turn?
   When come the promised prime?" . . .   80

'—The clash of horse and man which that day began,
   Closed not as evening wore;
And the morrow's armies, rear and van,
   Still mustered more and more.

'From the City towers the Confederate Powers   85
   Were eyed in glittering lines,
And up from the vast a murmuring passed
   As from a wood of pines.

'"'Tis well to cover a feeble skill
   By numbers' might!" scoffed He;   90
"But give me a third of their strength, I'd fill
   Half Hell with their soldiery!"

'All that day raged the war they waged,
   And again dumb night held reign,
Save that ever upspread from the dank death-bed   95
   A miles-wide pant of pain.

72 —Thus raged] Thus was *Hol.*   73 'Fifty] "Sixty *Hol.*   sturdy] harmless
Hol.   trampled] girdling *Hol.*   75 theirs,] ~ *Hol.*   77 Preachers] *l.c.*
Hol.   79 swords] spears *Hol.*   81 began,] ~ *Hol.*   83 van,] ~
Hol.   86 eyed] marked *Hol.*   90 By numbers!' scoffed He, *Hol.*; By
numbers!' scoffed He; *WP*   91 strength,] ⟨strength⟩ force, *Hol.*   94 again
dumb] another hushed *Hol.*   95 dank] wide *Hol.*; dark *WP*   96 A miles-
wide pant] Dull monotones *Hol.*

'Hard had striven brave Ney, the true Bertrand,
   Victor, and Augereau,
Bold Poniatowski, and Lauriston,
   To stay their overthrow;   100

'But, as in the dream of one sick to death
   There comes a narrowing room
That pens him, body and limbs and breath,
   To wait a hideous doom,

'So to Napoleon, in the hush   105
   That held the town and towers
Through these dire nights, a creeping crush
   Seemed borne in with the hours.

'One road to the rearward, and but one,
   Did fitful Chance allow;   110
'Twas where the Pleiss' and Elster run—
   The Bridge of Lindenau.

'The nineteenth dawned. Down street and Platz
   The wasted French sank back,
Stretching long lines across the Flats   115
   And on the bridge-way track;

'When there surged on the sky an earthen wave,
   And stones, and men, as though
Some rebel churchyard crew updrave
   Their sepulchres from below.   120

'To Heaven is blown Bridge Lindenau;
   Wrecked regiments reel therefrom;
And rank and file in masses plough
   The sullen Elster-Strom.

'A gulf was Lindenau; and dead   125
   Were fifties, hundreds, tens;

100 overthrow;] ~, *Hol.*   107 these] ⟨the⟩ *Hol.*   nights,] ~; *Hol.*
108 borne in] nearing *Hol.*; inborne *WP*   109 road . . . rearward,] track from the
cincture, *Hol.*   111 run—] run *Hol.*   113 Down] ⟨Down⟩ By *Hol.*
114 wasted] writhing *Hol.*

And every current rippled red
    With Marshals' blood and men's.

'The smart Macdonald swam therein,
    And barely won the verge;   130
Bold Poniatowski plunged him in
    Never to re-emerge.

'Then stayed the strife. The remnants wound
    Their Rhineward way pell-mell;
And thus did Leipzig City sound   135
    An Empire's passing bell;

'While in cavalcade, with band and blade,
    Came Marshals, Princes, Kings;
And the town was theirs. . . . Ay, as simple maid,
    My mother saw these things!   140

'And whenever those notes in the street begin,
    I recall her, and that far scene,
And her acting of how the Allies marched in,
    And her tap of the tambourine!'

128 Marshals' *WE20*] Marshal's *WP, CP, WE13*   129 therein,] ~ *Hol.*
135 City] *l.c. Hol.*   141 begin,] ~ *Hol.*   142 her,] ~; *Hol.*   144 To
the touse of her tambourine!" *Hol.*   tap of] touse of *WP*; tap on *WE*

THE PEASANT'S CONFESSION*

'Si le maréchal Grouchy avait été rejoint par l'officier que Napoléon lui avait expédié la veille à dix heures du soir, toute question eût disparu. Mais cet officier n'était point parvenu à sa destination, ainsi que le maréchal n'a cessé de l'affirmer toute sa vie, et il faut l'en croire, car autrement il n'aurait eu aucune raison pour hésiter. Cet officier avait-il été pris? avait-il passé à l'ennemi? C'est ce qu'on a toujours ignoré.'

THIERS: *Histoire du Consulat et de l'Empire.* 'Waterloo.'

Good Father! . . . It was eve in middle June,
    And war was waged anew
By great Napoleon, who for years had strewn
    Men's bones all Europe through.

Three nights ere this, with columned corps he'd crossed   5
    The Sambre at Charleroi,
To move on Brussels, where the English host
    Dallied in Parc and Bois.

The yestertide we'd heard the gloomy gun
    Growl through the long-sunned day   10
From Quatre-Bras and Ligny; till the dun
    Twilight suppressed the fray;

Albeit therein—as lated tongues bespoke—
    Brunswick's high heart was drained,
And Prussia's Line and Landwehr, though unbroke,   15
    Stood cornered and constrained.

And at next noon-time Grouchy slowly passed
    With thirty thousand men:
We hoped thenceforth no army, small or vast,
    Would trouble us again.   20

My hut lay deeply in a vale recessed,
    And never a soul seemed nigh
When, reassured at length, we went to rest—
    My children, wife, and I.

THE PEASANT'S CONFESSION. *Headnote Histoire* . . . 'Waterloo.'] *Histoire de l'Empire. WP, CP*
  1 It was] 'Twas an *WP, WE*   7 ⟨And drawn him toward the waiting⟩ *Hol.*
8 ⟨By Frasnes and Plancenoit.⟩ *Hol.*   10 Growl] Roar *Hol.*   11 the dun]
anon *Hol.*   12 Twilight suppressed] Silence enwrapt *Hol.*   fray;] ~. *Hol.*
13-16 *om. Hol.*   19 vast,] ~ *Hol.*   21 lay] stood *Hol.*   vale]
⟨wood⟩ *Hol.*   22 nigh] ~ ⟨,⟩ *Hol.*   23 When,] ⟨And⟩ *Hol.*

But what was this that broke our humble ease? 25
    What noise, above the rain,
Above the dripping of the poplar trees
    That smote along the pane?

—A call of mastery, bidding me arise,
    Compelled me to the door, 30
At which a horseman stood in martial guise—
    Splashed—sweating from every pore.

Had I seen Grouchy! Yes? What track took he?
    Could I lead thither on?—
Fulfilment would ensure much gold for me, 35
    Perhaps more gifts anon.

'I bear the Emperor's mandate,' then he said,
    'Charging the Marshal straight
To strike between the double host ahead
    Ere they co-operate, 40

'Engaging Blücher till the Emperor put
    Lord Wellington to flight,
And next the Prussians. This to set afoot
    Is my emprise to-night.'

I joined him in the mist; but, pausing, sought 45
    To estimate his say.
Grouchy had made for Wavre; and yet, on thought,
    I did not lead that way.

I mused: 'If Grouchy thus and thus be told,
    The crash comes sheer hereon; 50
My farm is stript. While, as for gifts of gold,
    Money the French have none.

25 that] ⟨which⟩ *Hol.*   29 —A] A *Hol.*   31 At which] Whereat *Hol.*
32 from] ⟨in⟩ at *Hol.*   33 Grouchy!] ∼? *WP, WE*   What] Which *WP, WE*
34 thither on?—] thenceward on? *Hol.*   35 much gold for me,] gold pieces three,
WP, WE   36 Perhaps] Perchance *WP*   49 and thus be told,] instructed
be, *WP*   50 crash] clash *WP, CP*   sheer] straight *Hol.*   51 gifts of
gold,] pieces three, *WP*

'Grouchy unwarned, moreo'er, the English win,
　　And mine is left to me—
They buy, not borrow.'—Hence did I begin   55
　　To lead him treacherously.

And as we edged Joidoigne with cautious view,
　　Dawn pierced the humid air;
And still I easted with him, though I knew
　　Never marched Grouchy there.   60

Near Ottignies we passed, across the Dyle
　　(Lim'lette left far aside),
And thence direct toward Pervez and Noville
　　Through green grain, till he cried:

'I doubt thy conduct, man! no track is here—   65
　　I doubt thy gagèd word!'
Thereat he scowled on me, and prancing near,
　　He pricked me with his sword.

---

57 By Joidoigne, near to east, as we ondrew, *WP*   58 air;] ~, *Hol.*   59 And
eastward faced I with him, though I knew *WP, WE*   61 Dyle] ~, *Hol.*
65 man!] ⟨hind⟩ *Hol.*   67 Thereon he scowled at me, *Hol.*   prancing] pranced
me *WP*   68 He] And *WP*

'Nay, Captain, hold! We skirt, not trace the course
    Of Grouchy,' said I then: 70
'As we go, yonder went he, with his force
    Of thirty thousand men.'

—At length noon struck; when west, from Saint-John's-Mound,
    A hoarse artillery boomed,
And from Saint-Lambert's upland, chapel-crowned,   75
    The Prussian squadrons loomed.

Then leaping to the wet wild path we had kept,
    'My mission fails!' he cried;
'Too late for Grouchy now to intercept,
    For, peasant, you have lied!'   80

He turned to pistol me. I sprang, and drew
    The sabre from his flank,
And 'twixt his nape and shoulder, ere he knew,
    I struck, and dead he sank.

I hid him deep in nodding rye and oat—   85
    His shroud green stalks and loam;
His requiem the corn-blade's husky note—
    And then I hastened home. . . .

—Two armies writhe in coils of red and blue,
    And brass and iron clang   90
From Goumont, past the front of Waterloo,
    To Pap'lotte and Smohain.

The Guard Imperial wavered on the height;
    The Emperor's face grew glum;
'I sent', he said, 'to Grouchy yesternight,   95
    And yet he does not come!'

73 struck;] nighed; *WP, CP*   77 Then to the wayless wet gray ground he leapt; *WP*
81 ⟨He made to seize his sword.⟩ *Hol.*   turned] ∼, *Hol.*   82 sabre] ⟨weapon⟩
Hol.   86 loam;] ∼: *Hol.*   87 corn-blade's] ⟨corn-beard's⟩ *Hol.*
91 Goumont,] ∼ *Hol.*   Waterloo,] ∼ *Hol.*

'Twas then, Good Father, that the French espied,
　　Streaking the summer land,
The men of Blücher. But the Emperor cried,
　　'Grouchy is now at hand!'   100

And meanwhile Vand'leur, Vivian, Maitland, Kempt,
　　Met d'Erlon, Friant, Ney;
But Grouchy—mis-sent, blamed, yet blame-exempt—
　　Grouchy was far away.

By even, slain or struck, Michel the strong,   105
　　Bold Travers, Dnop, Delord,
Smart Guyot, Reil-le, l'Heriter, Friant,
　　Scattered that champaign o'er.

Fallen likewise wronged Duhesme, and skilled Lobau
　　Did that red sunset see;   110
Colbert, Legros, Blancard! . . . . And of the foe
　　Picton and Ponsonby;

With Gordon, Canning, Blackman, Ompteda,
　　L'Estrange, Delancey, Packe,
Grose, D'Oyly, Stables, Morice, Howard, Hay,   115
　　Von Schwerin, Watzdorf, Boek,

Smith, Phelips, Fuller, Lind, and Battersby,
　　And hosts of ranksmen round . . . . .
Memorials linger yet to speak to thee
　　Of those that bit the ground!   120

The Guards' last column yielded; dykes of dead
　　Lay between vale and ridge,
As, thinned yet closing, faint yet fierce, they sped
　　In packs to Genappe Bridge.

Safe was my stock; my capple cow unslain;   125
    Intact each cock and hen;
But Grouchy far at Wavre all day had lain,
    And thirty thousand men.

O Saints, had I but lost my earing corn
    And saved the cause once prized!   130
O Saints, why such false witness had I borne
    When late I'd sympathized! . . .

So now, being old, my children eye askance
    My slowly dwindling store,
And crave my mite; till, worn with tarriance,   135
    I care for life no more.

To Almighty God henceforth I stand confessed,
    And Virgin-Saint Marie;
O Michael, John, and Holy Ones in rest,
    Entreat the Lord for me!   140

---

125 capple] milkwhite *Hol.*   130 prized!] ~; *Hol.*   137 confessed,] ~
Hol.

THE ALARM*

(Traditional)

IN MEMORY OF ONE OF THE WRITER'S FAMILY WHO WAS A VOLUNTEER DURING
THE WAR WITH NAPOLEON

In a ferny byway
Near the great South-Wessex Highway,
A homestead raised its breakfast-smoke aloft;
The dew-damps still lay steamless, for the sun had made no
    skyway,
      And twilight cloaked the croft.   5

It was almost past conceiving
Here, where woodbines hung inweaving,
That quite closely hostile armaments might steer,
Save from seeing in the porchway a fair woman mutely
    grieving,
      And a harnessed Volunteer.   10

In haste he'd flown there
To his comely wife alone there,
While marching south hard by, to still her fears,
For she soon would be a mother, and few messengers were
    known there
      In these campaigning years.   15

THE ALARM. *Headnote* (traditional)] (1804) / *vide* "The Trumpet Major" *Hol.*; (1803) / *See "The Trumpet Major"* WP
    2 Highway,] ~ *Hol.*   6 'Twas hard to realize on *WP*   7 Hitherside the snug horizon *Hol.*; This snug side the mute horizon *WP*   8 quite closely] beyond it *WP*   9 seeing] this, that *Hol.*   mutely grieving,] weep with eyes on *WP*; wept with eyes on *Hol.*   10 And a] A *WP*   Volunteer.] *l.c. Hol.*   12 there,] ~ *Hol.*   13 ⟨In leave-time scantly given,⟩ *Hol.*

'Twas time to be Good-bying,
Since the assembly-hour was nighing
In royal George's town at six that morn;
And betwixt its wharves and this retreat were ten good miles of
    hieing
        Ere ring of bugle-horn. 20

'I've laid in food, Dear,
And broached the spiced and brewed, Dear;
And if our July hope should antedate,
Let the chore-wench mount and gallop by the halterpath and
    wood, Dear,
        And fetch assistance straight. 25

'As for Buonaparte, forget him;
He's not like to land! But let him,
Those strike with aim who strike for wives and sons!
And the war-boats built to float him; 'twere but wanted to
    upset him
        A slat from Nelson's guns! 30

'But, to assure thee,
And of creeping fears to cure thee,
If he *should* be rumoured anchoring in the Road,
Drive with the nurse to Kingsbere; and let nothing thence allure
    thee
        Till we have him safe-bestowed. 35

'Now, to turn to marching matters:—
I've my knapsack, firelock, spatters,
Crossbelts, priming-horn, stock, bay'net, blackball, clay,
Pouch, magazine, and flint-box that at every quick-step
    clatters;
        . . . My heart, Dear; that must stay!' 40

17 Since] For *Hol.*   18 In regal Budmouth Town *Hol.*   19 its wharves]
the port *Hol.*   21 Dear,] ⟨*l.c.*⟩ *Hol.*   22 spiced and] cask of *Hol.*
24 The lad will mount and gallop by the cut through Yalbury Wood, Dear, *Hol.*   chore-
wench] char-wench *WP, CP*   34 Drive under tilt to Weatherb'ry: let *Hol.*
35 we have] we've *WP*   36 'Now,]" ~; *Hol.*   38 clay,] ~; *Hol.*
39 and] flints, *WP*

—With breathings broken
Farewell was kissed unspoken,
And they parted there as morning stroked the panes;
And the Volunteer went on, and turned, and twirled his glove
    for token,
        And took the coastward lanes.   45

When above He'th Hills he found him,
He saw, on gazing round him,
The Barrow-Beacon burning—burning low,
As if, perhaps, enkindled ever since he'd homeward bound
    him;
        And it meant: Expect the Foe!   50

Leaving the byway,
He entered on the highway,
Where cars and chariots fared them fast inland;
'He's anchored, Soldier!' shouted some: 'God save thee,
    marching thy way,
        Th'lt front him on the strand!'   55

43 panes;] ~ : *Hol.*   44 Volunteer] *l.c. Hol.*   token,] ~ ; *Hol.*
46 him,] ~ *Hol.*   48 Rain-Barrow's Beacon *Hol.*   49 enkindled]
uplighted *WP*   52 He entered on] And following swift *WP*   53 *WE20*]
Cars and chariots met he, hasting hot inland; *Hol.*; Car and chariot met he, faring fast inland;
WP; Where were cars and chariots, faring fast inland; *WE12, CP*   54 "He's landed,
Soldier!" cried the throng. *Hol.*   55 strand!'] ⟨*cap.*⟩ *Hol.*

He slowed; he stopped; he paltered
    Awhile with self, and faltered,
'Why courting misadventure shoreward roam?
To Molly, surely! Seek the woods with her till times have
        altered;
        Charity favours home.   60

'Else, my denying
    He'd come she'll read as lying—
Think the Barrow-Beacon must have met my eyes—
That my words were not unwareness, but deceit of her, while
        vying
        In deeds that jeopardize.   65

'At home is stocked provision,
    And to-night, without suspicion,
We might bear it with us to a covert near;
Such sin, to save a childing wife, would earn it Christ's
        remission,
        Though none forgive it here!'   70

While he stood thinking,
    A little bird, perched drinking
Among the crowfoot tufts the river bore,
Was tangled in their stringy arms, and fluttered, almost sinking
        Near him, upon the moor.   75

He stepped in, reached, and seized it,
    And, preening, had released it
But that a thought of Holy Writ occurred,
And Signs Divine ere battle, till it seemed him Heaven had
        pleased it
        As guide to send the bird.   80

---

56 Stressed for his Dear he ⟨faltered⟩ paltered *Hol.*   57 ⟨As sharp with self he
paltered:⟩ *Hol.*   faltered,] ~: *Hol.*   62 He'd] He would *WP*   she'll] may
Hol.   63 She will think the Beacon *Hol.*   eyes—] ~; *Hol.*   64 unware-
ness,] my un-wit, *Hol.*   vying] trying *WP*   65 In deeds that] My life to *WP*
70 here!] ~. *Hol.*   71 While thus he, thinking, *WP*   72 perched] quick
WP   73 bore,] ~ *Hol.*   74 almost] well-nigh *WP*   75 Near him,]
 Hard by, *Hol.*   moor.] *cap. Hol.*   79 battle,] *cap. Hol.*

'O Lord, direct me! . . . .
    Doth Duty now expect me
To march a-coast, or guard my weak ones near?
Give this bird a flight according, that I thence learn to elect
        me
        The southward or the rear.'   85

    He loosed his clasp; when, rising,
    The bird—as if surmising—
Bore due to southward, crossing by the Froom,
And Durnover Great Field and Fort, the soldier clear
        advising—
        Prompted he deemed by Whom.   90

    Then on he panted
    By grim Mai-Don, and slanted
Up the steep Ridge-way, hearkening between whiles;
Till, nearing coast and harbour, he beheld the shore-line
        planted
        With Foot and Horse for miles.   95

    Mistrusting not the omen,
    He gained the beach, where Yeomen,
Militia, Fencibles, and Pikemen bold,
With Regulars in thousands, were enmassed to meet the
        Foemen,
        Whose fleet had not yet shoaled.   100

    Captain and Colonel,
    Sere Generals, Ensigns vernal,
Were there; of neighbour-natives, Michel, Smith,
Meggs, Bingham, Gambier, Cunningham, to face the said
        nocturnal
        Swoop on their land and kith.   105

---

84 learn] know *WP*   85 southward] ~, *Hol.*   90 deemed] knew *Hol.*; wist
WP; read *WE*   91 Then] ~, *Hol.*   92 By grim Mai-don,] Through
Casterbridge, *Hol.*   93 between] betwixt *WP, WE*   94 harbour,] ~ *Hol.*
96 omen,] ~ *Hol.*   97 beach,] ⟨Port⟩ *Hol.*   102 vernal,] ~ *Hol.*
103 among them Stickland, Mitchell, Smith, *Hol.*   104 to face the said] roused by
the said *Hol.*; roused by the hued *WP*   105 land . . . kith.] *caps. Hol.*

But Buonaparte still tarried;
His project had miscarried;
At the last hour, equipped for victory,
The fleet had paused; his subtle combinations had been parried
    By British strategy.   110

Homeward returning
Anon, no beacons burning,
No alarms, the Volunteer, in modest bliss,
Te Deum sang with wife and friends: 'We praise Thee, Lord,
    discerning
    That Thou hast helped in this!'   115

HER DEATH AND AFTER*

The summons was urgent: and forth I went—
By the way of the Western Wall, so drear
On that winter night, and sought a gate,
    Where one, by Fate,
    Lay dying that I held dear.   5

And there, as I paused by her tenement,
And the trees shed on me their rime and hoar,
I thought of the man who had left her lone—
    Him who made her his own
    When I loved her, long before.   10

The rooms within had the piteous shine
That home-things wear when there's aught amiss;
From the stairway floated the rise and fall
    Of an infant's call,
    Whose birth had brought her to this.   15

---

106 tarried;] ~, *Hol.*   110 British] English *Hol.*   113 Volunteer,] *l.c. Hol.*

HER DEATH AND AFTER. 1 'Twas a death-bed summons, *WP*   urgent: *CP, DCM4*] ~,
WE   went— *CP, DCM4*] ~ *WP, WE*   2 Western] ⟨Roman⟩ *Hol.*
3 gate, *CP, DCM4*] ~— *WP, WE*   4 Where one,] The home, *WP*   Fate,] ~
Hol.   5 Of one I had long held dear. *WP*   12 That] ⟨Which⟩ *Hol.*
when . . . amiss;] which the housewife miss: *Hol.*; which the housewife miss; *WP98*
13 rise and] ⟨rise and⟩ feeble *Hol.*

Her life was the price she would pay for that whine—
For a child by the man she did not love.
'But let that rest for ever,' I said,
    And bent my tread
  To the bedchamber above.   20

She took my hand in her thin white own,
And smiled her thanks—though nigh too weak—
And made them a sign to leave us there;
    Then faltered, ere
  She could bring herself to speak.   25

'Just to see you—before I go—he'll condone
Such a natural thing now my time's not much—
When Death is so near it hustles hence
    All passioned sense
  Between woman and man as such!   30

'My husband is absent. As heretofore
The City detains him. But, in truth,
He has not been kind. . . . I will speak no blame,
    But—the child is lame;
  O, I pray she may reach his ruth!   35

'Forgive past days—I can say no more—
Maybe had we wed you would now repine! . . .
But I treated you ill. I was punished. Farewell!
    —Truth shall I tell?
  Would the child were yours and mine!   40

'As a wife I was true. But, such my unease
That, could I insert a deed back in Time,
I'd make her yours, to secure your care;
    And the scandal bear,
  And the penalty for the crime!'   45

17 love.] ~ : *Hol.*   20 bedchamber] chamber up *WP*   23 there; *Hol.*] ~
WP; ~ , *WE, CP*   26 'Just] " 'Twas *WP*   you—] ~ *WP, WE*   35 reach]
⟨win⟩ *Hol.*   37 if we'd wedded you'd *WP, WE*   41 I was *WP, CP,*
DCM4] I've been *WE*   43 care;] ~ , *Hol.*   45 penalty] ⟨punishment⟩ *Hol.*
crime!'] ~ ." *Hol.*

—When I had left, and the swinging trees
Rang above me, as lauding her candid say,
Another was I. Her words were enough:
     Came smooth, came rough,
    I felt I could live my day.   50

Next night she died; and her obsequies
In the Field of Tombs where the earthworks frowned
Had her husband's heed. His tendance spent,
     I often went
    And pondered by her mound.   55

All that year and the next year whiled,
And I still went thitherward in the gloam;
But the Town forgot her and her nook,
     And her husband took
    Another Love to his home.   60

And the rumour flew that the lame lone child
Whom she wished for its safety child of mine,
Was treated ill when offspring came
     Of the new-made dame,
    And marked a more vigorous line.   65

46 —When] ~ *Hol.*   49 rough,] ~ *Hol.*   52 Tombs, by the Via
renowned, *WP*   57 gloam] ⟨gloom⟩ *Hol.*   62 she] she'd *Hol.*   mine,]
~ *Hol.*   64 dame,] *cap. Hol.*

A smarter grief within me wrought
Than even at loss of her so dear,
That the being whose soul my soul suffused
    Had a child ill-used,
    While I dared not interfere!   70

One eve as I stood at my spot of thought
In the white-stoned Garth, brooding thus her wrong,
Her husband neared; and to shun his nod
    By her hallowed sod
    I went from the tombs among   75

To the Cirque of the Gladiators which faced—
That haggard mark of Imperial Rome,
Whose Pagan echoes mock the chime
    Of our Christian time
    From its hollows of chalk and loam.   80

The sun's gold touch was scarce displaced
From the vast Arena where men had bled,
When her husband followed; bowed; half-passed
    With lip upcast;
    Then halting sullenly said: 85

'It is noised that you visit my first wife's tomb.
Now, I gave her an honoured name to bear
While living, when dead. So I've claim to ask
    By what right you task
    My patience by vigiling there?   90

67 dear,] ~; *WP*; ~ *CP*   68 That] Dead *WP*   suffused] ~, *WP*
69 Had a] Her *WP*   70 I helpless to interfere! *WP, WE*   72 *WP, CP, DCM4*]
Garth with these brooding glooms, *WE*   white-stoned] Holy *Hol.*   73 nod *WE,*
CP23] view *WP, CP19*   74 In ⟨her dear purlieu⟩ the hallowed mew *Hol.*   sod
WE, CP23] mew *WP, CP19*   75 the tombs among *WP, CP, DCM4*] among the
tombs *WE*   79 time *SP, CP23*] ~: *WP*; ~; *WE*; ~— *CP19*   80 *CP20,*
WE20] It was void, and I inward clomb. *WP*; And I drew to its bank and clomb. *WE12*; From
its hollows of turf and loam. *SP*; And I drew to its bank, and clomb. *CP19*   81 *CP,*
DCM4] Scarce had night the sun's gold touch displaced *WP*; Scarce night the sun's gold
touch displaced *PE*; The sun's gold touch was just displaced *WE*   82 From the vast
Rotund and the neighbouring dead *WP*   had *DCM3*] once *all other texts*   83 half-
passed *DCM4*] ~ ⟨;⟩, *Hol.*; ~, *WP*   85 Then halting *CP, DCM4*] Then, halting,
WP, WE   said:] ~:— *Hol.*   86 tomb.] ~: *Hol.*   89 *WP, WE12, CP,*
DCM4] Your right to task *SP, DCM1, WE20*   90 vigiling *WP, CP, DCM4*]
darkling *WE, SP*

'There's decency even in death, I assume;
Preserve it, sir, and keep away;
For the mother of my first-born you
    Show mind undue!
  —Sir, I've nothing more to say.'   95

A desperate stroke discerned I then—
God pardon—or pardon not—the lie;
She had sighed that she wished (lest the child should pine
    Of slights) 'twere mine,
  So I said: 'But the father I.   100

'That you thought it yours is the way of men;
But I won her troth long ere your day:
You learnt how, in dying, she summoned me?
    'Twas in fealty.
  —Sir, I've nothing more to say,   105

'Save that, if you'll hand me my little maid,
I'll take her, and rear her, and spare you toil.
Think it more than a friendly act none can;
    I'm a lonely man,
  While you've a large pot to boil.   110

'If not, and you'll put it to ball or blade—
To-night, to-morrow night, anywhen—
I'll meet you here. . . . But think of it,
    And in season fit
  Let me hear from you again.'   115

—Well, I went away, hoping; but nought I heard
Of my stroke for the child, till there greeted me
A little voice that one day came
    To my window-frame
  And babbled innocently: 120

92 sir,] *cap. Hol.*   93 The mother she of my firstborn, you *Hol.*   94 mind
undue!] zest undue *Hol.*   95 In haunting her grave, I say." *Hol.* 105 —Sir,]
~; *Hol.*   107 toil.] ~; *Hol.*   116 —Well,] ~: *Hol.* 118 that]
which *Hol.*   120 innocently:] ~:— *Hol.*

'My father who's not my own, sends word
I'm to stay here, sir, where I belong!'
Next a writing came: 'Since the child was the fruit
    Of your lawless suit,
    Pray take her, to right a wrong.'   125

And I did. And I gave the child my love,
And the child loved me, and estranged us none.
But compunctions loomed; for I'd harmed the dead
    By what I said
    For the good of the living one.   130

—Yet though, God wot, I am sinner enough,
And unworthy the woman who drew me so,
Perhaps this wrong for her darling's good
    She forgives, or would,
    If only she could know!   135

122 sir,] *cap. Hol.*   belong!'] ~." *Hol.*   124 lawless suit,] passions brute, *WP98*
129 I *CP, DCM4*] I'd *WP, WE*   131 —Yet] ~ *Hol.*

THE DANCE AT THE PHŒNIX*

To Jenny came a gentle youth
    From inland leazes lone,
His love was fresh as apple-blooth
    By Parrett, Yeo, or Tone.
And duly he entreated her   5
To be his tender minister,
    And take him for her own.

Now Jenny's life had hardly been
    A life of modesty;
And few in Casterbridge had seen   10
    More loves of sorts than she
From scarcely sixteen years above;
Among them sundry troopers of
    The King's-Own Cavalry.

But each with charger, sword, and gun,   15
    Had bluffed the Biscay wave;
And Jenny prized her rural one
    For all the love he gave.
She vowed to be, if they were wed,
His honest wife in heart and head   20
    From bride-ale hour to grave.

THE DANCE AT THE PHŒNIX. 1 Jenny] Nelly *Hol. throughout*   2 inland leazes lone,]
Wessex leazes lone; *Hol.*   3 ⟨His love for her was bright as blooth⟩ *Hol.*   4 ⟨In
Ivel gardens grown.⟩ *Hol.*   7 take him for] call him aye *WP*   8 Now] Fair
WP, WE12   10 At Casterbridge experience keen *WP*   11 Of many loves
had she *WP*   15 gun,] ~ *Hol.*   16 Had gone across the wave; *Hol.*
17 prized] ⟨loved⟩ *Hol.*   rural] gentle *WP, WE*   21 bride-ale] ⟨bridal⟩ *Hol.*

Wedded they were. Her husband's trust
    In Jenny knew no bound,
And Jenny kept her pure and just,
    Till even malice found   25
No sin or sign of ill to be
In one who walked so decently
    The duteous helpmate's round.

Two sons were born, and bloomed to men,
    And roamed, and were as not: 30
Alone was Jenny left again
    As ere her mind had sought
A solace in domestic joys,
And ere the vanished pair of boys
    Were sent to sun her cot.   35

She numbered near to sixty years,
    And passed as elderly,
When, on a day, with flushing fears,
    She learnt from shouts of glee,
And shine of swords and thump of drum,   40
Her early loves from war had come,
    The King's-Own Cavalry.

She turned aside, and bowed her head
    Anigh Saint Peter's door;
'Alas for chastened thoughts!' she said;   45
    'I'm faded now, and hoar,
And yet those notes—they thrill me through,
And those gay forms move me anew
    As they moved me of yore!' . . .

'Twas Christmas, and the Phœnix Inn   50
    Was lit with tapers tall,

27 decently] carefully *Hol.*   29 born,] ~ *Hol.*   and bloomed to men,] ⟨to manhood grew,⟩ and grew to men, *Hol.*   31 again] ⟨anew⟩ *Hol.*   35 sun] light *Hol.*
36 near to sixty] more than fifty *Hol.*; near on sixty *WP, CP*   38 When, in the street, with ⟨sudden⟩ ⟨flushing⟩ flush of fears, *Hol.*; When, in the street, with flush of fears, *WP*
39 One day discovered she *Hol.*; ~ , *WP*   40 And] From *WP*   thump] throb *Hol.*   drum,] ~ *Hol.*   44 Saint Peter's] ⟨the Guildhall⟩ *Hol.*   48 move me anew] ⟨my soul bedew⟩ *Hol.*   49 As in the years *WP*; As I was moved *WE*

For thirty of the trooper men
  Had vowed to give a ball
As 'Theirs' had done ('twas handed down)
When lying in the self-same town   55
  Ere Buonaparté's fall.

That night the throbbing 'Soldier's Joy',
  The measured tread and sway
Of 'Fancy-Lad' and 'Maiden Coy',
  Reached Jenny as she lay   60
Beside her spouse; till springtide blood
Seemed scouring through her like a flood
  That whisked the years away.

She rose, arrayed, and decked her head
  Where the bleached hairs grew thin;   65
Upon her cap two bows of red
  She fixed with hasty pin;
Unheard descending to the street
She trod the flags with tune-led feet,
  And stood before the Inn.   70

Save for the dancers', not a sound
  Disturbed the icy air;
No watchman on his midnight round
  Or traveller was there;
But over All-Saints', high and bright,   75
Pulsed to the music Sirius white,
  The Wain towards Bullstake Square.

She knocked, but found her further stride
  Checked by a sergeant's call:

---

54 'twas] 'twas *Hol.*; fame *WP98*   59 Coy',] ~" *Hol.*   61 springtide]
⟨springtime⟩ *Hol.*   62 scouring] rushing *Hol.*   64 arrayed,] ⟨dressed⟩
Hol.; and rayed, *WP*   65 To hide her ringlets thin; *WP98*   grew] ran *WP03, PE*
66 She pranked her cap ⟨with ribbons⟩ with bows of red, *Hol.*   67 And ⟨set
gay bows⟩ stuck rosettes therein; *Hol.*   68 street *Hol., CP*] ~ , *WP, WE*
69 tune-led feet,] footing fleet, *Hol.*   74 there;] ~ : *Hol.*   75 ⟨All-Saints'
belfry-light⟩ *Hol.*   77 towards] ⟨o'er⟩ *Hol.*; by *WP, CP*   79 sergeant's
call: *DCM3*] sergeant tall: *all other texts*

'Gay Granny, whence come you?' he cried;   80
    'This is a private ball.'
—'No one has more right here than me!
Ere you were born, man,' answered she,
    'I knew the regiment all!'

'Take not the lady's visit ill!'   85
    The steward said; 'for, see,
We lack sufficient partners still,
    So, prithee let her be!'
They seized and whirled her 'mid the maze,
And Jenny felt as in the days   90
    Of her immodesty.

Hour chased each hour, and night advanced;
    She sped as shod with wings;
Each time and every time she danced—
    Reels, jigs, poussettes, and flings: 95
They cheered her as she soared and swooped,
(She had learnt ere art in dancing drooped
    From hops to slothful swings).

The favourite Quick-step 'Speed the Plough'—
    (Cross hands, cast off, and wheel)—   100
'The Triumph', 'Sylph', 'The Row-dow-dow',
    Famed 'Major Malley's Reel',
'The Duke of York's', 'The Fairy Dance',
'The Bridge of Lodi' (brought from France),
    She beat out, toe and heel.   105

The 'Fall of Paris' clanged its close,
    And Peter's chimed to four,
When Jenny, bosom-beating, rose
    To seek her silent door.

80 cried;] ~, *Hol.*   85 ⟨"Turn not, turn not the lady back!"⟩ *Hol.*   86 Upspoke
the steward free, *WP*   87 ⟨"Sufficient partners still we lack⟩ *Hol.*   We] "We *WP*
88 prithee] pri'thee *Hol.*   95 ⟨Jigs, hornpipes,⟩ Reels, ⟨country-dances,⟩
allemandes, and flings: *Hol.*   96 soared] ⟨swirled⟩ *Hol.*   97 ⟨(For she had
learnt ere dancing drooped⟩ *Hol.*   (She had] (She'd *WP, WE*   99-105 *om. Hol.*
106 clanged] trilled *Hol.*   107 chimed to *DCM3*] chime told *WP*; chime went
WE, CP   108 bosom-beating,] bosom-bursting, *Hol.*

They tiptoed in escorting her,   110
Lest stroke of heel or clink of spur
    Should break her goodman's snore.

The fire that lately burnt fell slack
    When lone at last was she;
Her nine-and-fifty years came back;   115
    She sank upon her knee
Beside the durn, and like a dart
A something arrowed through her heart
    In shoots of agony.

Their footsteps died as she leant there,   120
    Lit by the morning star
Hanging above the moorland, where
    The aged elm-rows are;
As overnight, from Pummery Ridge
To Maembury Ring and Standfast Bridge   125
    No life stirred, near or far.

Though inner mischief worked amain,
    She reached her husband's side;
Where, toil-weary, as he had lain
    Beneath the patchwork pied   130
When with lax longings she had crept
Therefrom at midnight, still he slept
    Who did in her confide.

A tear sprang as she turned and viewed
    His features free from guile;   135
She kissed him long, as when, just wooed,
    She chose his domicile.

110 in escorting] ⟨as they convoyed⟩ Hol.   113 lately] late had WP
114 was] stood WP   115 five and fifty Hol.   back;] ∼, Hol.
117 beside the durn,] ⟨Before her gate;⟩ ⟨Against the durn;⟩ Beside the durn; Hol.
120 leant] ⟨lay⟩ Hol.   124 As overnight,] ⟨And, as erstwhile,⟩ Hol.; And, as
o'ernight, WP   125 Standfast] Friary Hol.   127 ⟨She strove, though
heart-blood ebbed amain,⟩ Hol.   mischief] ⟨anguish⟩ Hol.   128 ⟨And reached
her husband's side;⟩ She crawled to her bed side; Hol.   131 When yestereve
she'd thenceward crept, Hol.; When yestereve she'd forthward crept, WP; When forthward
yestereve she crept, CP   132 And as unwitting, still he slept WP, CP

She felt she would give more than life
To be the single-hearted wife
   That she had been erstwhile. . . .   140

Time wore to six. Her husband rose
   And struck the steel and stone;
He glanced at Jenny, whose repose
   Seemed deeper than his own.
With dumb dismay, on closer sight,   145
He gathered sense that in the night,
   Or morn, her soul had flown.

When told that some too mighty strain
   For one so many-yeared
Had burst her bosom's master-vein,   150
   His doubts remained unstirred.
His Jenny had not left his side
Betwixt the eve and morning-tide:
   —The King's said not a word.

Well! times are not as times were then,   155
   Nor fair ones half so free;
And truly they were martial men,
   The King's-Own Cavalry.
And when they went from Casterbridge
And vanished over Mellstock Ridge,   160
   'Twas saddest morn to see.

138 ⟨Her breast throbbed death⟩ Death neighboured now; yet, ⟨less for⟩ more than life, *Hol.*; Death menaced now; yet less for life *WP*; She felt she could have given her life *PE* 139 *PE, WE, CP*] She ⟨wished than⟩ craved that she were still the wife *Hol.*; She wished than that she were the wife *WP*   140 erstwhile....] ~. *WP, WE*   146 night,] ~ *Hol.*   149 many-yeared] heavy-yeared *Hol.*   150 heart's intensest vein, *Hol.*   155 Well!] ~: *Hol.*   157 men,] ~ *Hol.*   160 Ridge,] ~ *Hol.*

THE CASTERBRIDGE CAPTAINS*

(Khyber Pass, 1842)

A TRADITION OF J. B. L——, T. G. B——, AND J. L——

Three captains went to Indian wars,
    And only one returned:
Their mate of yore, he singly wore
    The laurels all had earned.

At home he sought the ancient aisle   5
    Wherein, untrumped of fame,
The three had sat in pupilage,
    And each had carved his name.

The names, rough-hewn, of equal size,
    Stood on the panel still;   10
Unequal since.—' 'Twas theirs to aim,
    Mine was it to fulfil!'

—'Who saves his life shall lose it, friends!'
    Outspake the preacher then,
Unweeting he his listener, who   15
    Looked at the names again.

THE CASTERBRIDGE CAPTAINS. *Headnote* A . . . J. L——] In memory of L——, B——, and ⟨L——, of Casterbridge⟩ L——. *Hol.*
    4 The bays that all had earned. *Hol.*   5 At home he entered All-Saints' aisle, *Hol.*   9 names, rough-hewn,] ⟨characters,⟩ *Hol.*   13 —'Who] "Who *Hol.*   14 Outspake] Outspoke *Hol.*

That he had come, and they had been stayed,
  Was but the chance of war:
Another chance, and they had been here,
  And he had lain afar.   20

Yet saw he something in the lives
  Of those who had ceased to live
That sphered them with a majesty
  Which living failed to give.

Transcendent triumph in return   25
  No longer lit his brain;
Transcendence rayed the distant urn
  Where slept the fallen twain.

17 they had been stayed] they'd been stayed, *WP, WE*   18 Was] 'Twas *WP*
19 they had been] they'd sat *WP, WE*   22 who had] who'd *WP, WE*
23 That marked them with a majesty *Hol.*; That rounded them with majesty *WP98*
26 ⟨His heart no longer knew;⟩ *Hol.*   27 distant] ⟨distant⟩ lonely *Hol.*
28 ⟨Above the other two⟩ *Hol.*   fallen] distant *Hol.*

A SIGN-SEEKER*

I mark the months in liveries dank and dry,
　　The noontides many-shaped and hued;
　　I see the nightfall shades subtrude,
And hear the monotonous hours clang negligently by.

I view the evening bonfires of the sun　　　　　　　5
　　On hills where morning rains have hissed;
　　The eyeless countenance of the mist
Pallidly rising when the summer droughts are done.

I have seen the lightning-blade, the leaping star,
　　The cauldrons of the sea in storm,　　　　　　10
　　Have felt the earthquake's lifting arm,
And trodden where abysmal fires and snow-cones are.

I learn to prophesy the hid eclipse,
　　The coming of eccentric orbs;
　　To mete the dust the sky absorbs,　　　　　　15
To weigh the sun, and fix the hour each planet dips.

I witness fellow earth-men surge and strive;
　　Assemblies meet, and throb, and part;
　　Death's sudden finger, sorrow's smart;
—All the vast various moils that mean a world alive.　　20

A SIGN-SEEKER. 1 months] *cap. Hol.*　　　2 noontides] Day-tides *Hol.*; day-tides *WP98*
3 I know the nod of Night subdued, *Hol.*　　　4 hours] *cap. Hol.*　　　5 sun] *cap. Hol.*
8 mist] *cap. Hol.*　　　9 lightning-blade,] *cap. Hol.*　　star,] *cap. Hol.*　　　10 sea]
cap. Hol.　　　11 earthquake's] *cap. Hol.*　　　12 fires] *cap. Hol.*　　snow-cones] *cap.*
Hol.　　13 eclipse,] *cap. Hol.*　　　14 orbs;] ⟨*l.c.*⟩ *cap. Hol.*　　　16 sun,]
cap. Hol.　　planet] *cap. Hol.*　　　19 sudden] soothing *WP*　　sorrow's smart;]
⟨Dolour's⟩ Sorrow's dart; *Hol.*　　20 moils] *cap. Hol.*

But that I fain would wot of shuns my sense—
   Those sights of which old prophets tell,
   Those signs the general word so well,
As vouchsafed their unheed, denied my long suspense.

In graveyard green, where his pale dust lies pent   25
   To glimpse a phantom parent, friend,
   Wearing his smile, and 'Not the end!'
Outbreathing softly: that were blest enlightenment;

Or, if a dead Love's lips, whom dreams reveal
   When midnight imps of King Decay   30
   Delve sly to solve me back to clay,
Should leave some print to prove her spirit-kisses real;

Or, when Earth's Frail lie bleeding of her Strong,
   If some Recorder, as in Writ,
   Near to the weary scene should flit   35
And drop one plume as pledge that Heaven inscrolls
    the wrong.

—There are who, rapt to heights of trancelike trust,
   These tokens claim to feel and see,
   Read radiant hints of times to be—
Of heart to heart returning after dust to dust.   40

Such scope is granted not to lives like mine . . .
   I have lain in dead men's beds, have walked
   The tombs of those with whom I had talked,
Called many a gone and goodly one to shape a sign,

21 wot of] ⟨prospect⟩ *Hol.*   24 Vouchsafed to their unheed, denied my
watchings tense. *WP98*; Vouchsafed to their unheed, denied my long suspense. *WP03, WE*
25 In graveyard green, behind his monument *WP*   29 dead] lost *Hol.*
32 real;] ~ . *Hol.*   36 pledge that Heaven inscrolls] sign Heaven registers *Hol.*
37 —There] ~ *Hol.*   rapt to heights] blest with store *Hol.*   trancelike] stoic *Hol.*
trancéd *WP, WE*   41 Such gift is granted not my lot indign . . . *Hol.*; Such scope is
granted not my powers indign . . . *WP98*   43 I had] I'd *WP*

And panted for response. But none replies;   45
   No warnings loom, nor whisperings
   To open out my limitings,
And Nescience mutely muses: When a man falls he lies.

MY CICELY*

(17—)

'Alive?'—And I leapt in my wonder,
   Was faint of my joyance,
And grasses and grove shone in garments
   Of glory to me.

'She lives, in a plenteous well-being,   5
   To-day as aforetime;
The dead bore the name—though a rare one—
   The name that bore she.'

She lived . . . I, afar in the city
   Of frenzy-led factions,   10
Had squandered green years and maturer
   In bowing the knee

46 loom,] ⟨fall,⟩ *Hol.*

MY CICELY. *Headnote* (17—)] *om. Hol.*
  6 aforetime;] aforehand; *WP, CP*   7 though] not *Hol.*   8 The name
that] That whilom *Hol.*

To Baals illusive and specious,
  Till chance had there voiced me
That one I loved vainly in nonage   15
  Had ceased her to be.

The passion the planets had scowled on,
  And change had let dwindle,
Her death-rumour smartly relifted
  To full apogee.   20

I mounted a steed in the dawning
  With acheful remembrance,
And made for the ancient West Highway
  To far Exonb'ry.

Passing heaths, and the House of Long Sieging,   25
  I neared the thin steeple
That tops the fair fane of Poore's olden
  Episcopal see;

And, changing anew my blown bearer,
  I traversed the downland   30
Whereon the bleak hill-graves of Chieftains
  Bulge barren of tree;

And still sadly onward I followed
  That Highway the Icen,
Which trails its pale riband down Wessex   35
  By lynchet and lea.

Along through the Stour-bordered Forum,
  Where Legions had wayfared,

16 ceased her] ⟨late ceased⟩ *Hol.*   17 on,] ∼ *Hol.*   25 heaths,] *cap. Hol.*
27 That] ⟨Which⟩ *Hol.*   olden] ancient *Hol.*   29 blown bearer,] onbearer, *WP*
30 traversed] thridded *Hol.*   downland] *cap. Hol.*   33 followed] travelled *Hol.*
34 That highway Icenian, *Hol.*   36 By] O'er *WP*
37–48 *one quatrain in Hol. as follows*:
              By Egdon and Casterbridge ⟨straightly⟩ bore I,
                  Where Legions had wayfared,
              ⟨I followed, to mourn and entomb her⟩
              To tomb her I deemed sent to silence
                  ⟨Whose star had darked He.⟩
              By will of the Three.

And where the slow river-face glasses
　Its green canopy, 40

And by Weatherbury Castle, and thencefrom
　Through Casterbridge held I
Still on, to entomb her my mindsight
　Saw stretched pallidly.

No highwayman's trot blew the night-wind 45
　To me so life-weary,
But only the creak of a gibbet
　Or waggoners' jee.

Triple-ramparted Maidon gloomed grayly
　Above me from southward, 50
And north the hill-fortress of Eggar,
　And square Pummerie.

The Nine-Pillared Cromlech, the Bride-streams,
　The Axe, and the Otter
I passed, to the gate of the city 55
　Where Exe scents the sea;

Till, spent, in the graveacre pausing,
　I learnt 'twas not *my* Love
To whom Mother Church had just murmured
　A last lullaby. 60

—'Then, where is the Canon's kinswoman,
　My friend of aforetime?'—
I asked, and disguised my heart-heavings
　And new ecstasy.

39 river-face glasses] river upglasses *WP*　　41 thencefrom] therence *WP98*
42 *PE, WE, CP*] Through Casterbridge, bore I, *WP*　　43 To tomb her whose light,
in my deeming, *WP*　　mindsight] vision *PE, WE*　　44 *PE, WE, CP*] Extinguished
had He. *WP*　　47 the gibbets *WP*; the gibbet *WE*　　53 Bride-streams,]
Bredy, *Hol.*　　57 pausing,] ~ *Hol.*　　58 *my*] rom. *WP*　　61 —'Then,]
'Then, *Hol.*　　is] dwells *WP, CP*　　63 ('Twas hard to repress my heart-heavings
WP　　and disguised] to disguise *CP*　　64 ecstasy.] ~.) *WP*

'She wedded.'—'Ah!'—'Wedded beneath her—　　　65
　　She keeps the stage-hostel
Ten miles hence, beside the great Highway—
　　The famed Lions-Three.

'Her spouse was her lackey—no option
　　'Twixt wedlock and worse things;　　　70
A lapse over-sad for a lady
　　Of her pedigree!'

I shuddered, said nothing, and wandered
　　To shades of green laurel:
More ghastly than death were these tidings　　　75
　　Of Life's irony!

For riding down hither I'd halted
　　Awhile at the Lions,
And her—her whose name had once opened
　　My heart as a key—　　　80

I'd looked on, unknowing, and witnessed
　　Her jests with the tapsters,
Her liquor-fired face, her thick accents
　　In naming her fee.

'O God, why this seeming derision!'　　　85
　　I cried in my anguish:
'O once Loved, O fair Unforgotten—
　　That Thing—meant it thee!

'Inurned and at peace, lost but sainted,
　　Were grief I could compass;　　　90
Depraved—'tis for Christ's poor dependent
　　A cruel decree!'

68 The ⟨Old Holly-Tree⟩ famed Fleur-de-Lis. *Hol.*　　　75 Too ghastly had grown
those first tidings *WP*　　　76 So brightsome of blee! *WP*　　　Life's] *l.c. CP*
77 For, on my track hither, I'd halted *Hol.*; For, on my ride hither, I'd halted *WP*; For, on
my ride down I had halted *CP*　　　78 Lions,] ⟨Holly⟩ Hostel, *Hol.*　　　81 I'd ⟨talked
with,⟩ looked on, unweeting, and noted *Hol.*　　　I'd] I had *CP19 only*　　　85 seeming
derision!'] hocus satiric!" *WP98*　　　87 ⟨O, once loved, O woman corrupted⟩ *Hol.*
once . . . fair] *caps. Hol.*　　　88 ⟨Can That Thing be ye⟩ *Hol.*

I backed on the Highway; but passed not
    The hostel. Within there
Too mocking to Love's re-expression   95
    Was Time's repartee!

Uptracking where Legions had wayfared,
    By cromlechs unstoried,
And lynchets, and sepultured Chieftains,
    In self-colloquy,   100

A feeling stirred in me and strengthened
    That *she* was not my Love,
But she of the garth, who lay rapt in
    Her long reverie.

And thence till to-day I persuade me   105
    That this was the true one;
That Death stole intact her young dearness
    And innocency.

Frail-witted, illuded they call me;
    I may be. Far better   110
To dream than to own the debasement
    Of sweet Cicely.

Moreover I rate it unseemly
    To hold that kind Heaven
Could work such device—to her ruin   115
    And my misery.

So, lest I disturb my choice vision,
    I shun the West Highway,
Even now, when the knaps ring with rhythms
    From blackbird and bee;   120

94 hostel.] ⟨Holly⟩ Hostel. *Hol.*   98 cromlechs] *cap. Hol.*   103 But] ⟨By⟩
Hol.   107 Death stole] Time ⟨took⟩ stole *Hol.*   dearness] sweetness *Hol.*
108 innocency] ⟨lightsome blue⟩ innocent 'ee. *Hol.*   110 Far] 'Tis *WP*
112 Cicely] ⟨?Naomi?⟩ *Hol.*   117 vision,] ∼ *Hol.*   119 knaps] *cap. Hol.*
ring with rhythms] ⟨thrill with singings⟩ *Hol.*   120 From] ⟨Of⟩ *Hol.*

And feel that with slumber half-conscious
   She rests in the church-hay,
Her spirit unsoiled as in youth-time
   When lovers were we.

HER IMMORTALITY

Upon a noon I pilgrimed through
   A pasture, mile by mile,
Unto the place where last I saw
   My dead Love's living smile.

And sorrowing I lay me down   5
   Upon the heated sod:
It seemed as if my body pressed
   The very ground she trod.

I lay, and thought; and in a trance
   She came and stood thereby—   10
The same, even to the marvellous ray
   That used to light her eye.

121 slumber] ⟨slumbers⟩ *Hol.*

HER IMMORTALITY. 1 pilgrimed] wayfared *Hol.*   3 I last saw *WP*
10 thereby—] me by— *WP*

'You draw me, and I come to you,
  My faithful one,' she said,
In voice that had the moving tone   15
  It bore ere she was wed.

'Seven years have circled since I died:
  Few now remember me;
My husband clasps another bride;
  My children's love has she.   20

'My brethren, sisters, and my friends
  Care not to meet my sprite:
Who prized me most I did not know
  Till I passed down from sight.'

I said: 'My days are lonely here;   25
  I need thy smile alway:
I'll use this night my ball or blade,
  And join thee ere the day.'

A tremor stirred her tender lips,
  Which parted to dissuade: 30
'That cannot be, O friend,' she cried;
  'Think, I am but a Shade!

'A Shade but in its mindful ones
  Has immortality;
By living, me you keep alive,   35
  By dying you slay me.

'In you resides my single power
  Of sweet continuance here;
On your fidelity I count
  Through many a coming year.'   40

---

13 you,] ~ *Hol.*   14 said,] ~ *Hol.*   16 *CP23*] It bore ere life had sped.
Hol.; It bore in maidenhead. *WP98*; It bore ere breath had fled. *WP03, CP19*; Of days ere she
was wed. *WE*   17 She said: "'Tis seven years since I died: *WP*   20 My
children mothers she. *WP98*   26 need] ⟨crave⟩ *Hol.*   29 stirred] passed
Hol.   32 'Think,] ~; *Hol.*   Shade!] ⟨*l.c.*⟩ *Hol.*   35 By living you
keep me alive, *Hol.*

—I started through me at her plight,
    So suddenly confessed:
Dismissing late distaste for life,
    I craved its bleak unrest.

'I will not die, my One of all!—   45
    To lengthen out thy days
I'll guard me from minutest harms
    That may invest my ways!'

She smiled and went. Since then she comes
    Oft when her birth-moon climbs,   50
Or at the seasons' ingresses,
    Or anniversary times;

But grows my grief. When I surcease,
    Through whom alone lives she,
Her spirit ends its living lease,   55
    Never again to be!

41 —I] ~ *Hol.*   43 life,] ~ *Hol.*   52 Or August's still noon-times; *Hol.*
55 Ceases my Love, her words, her ways, *WP*; Ceases my Love's terrestrial lease, *WE*
56 be!] ~. *Hol.*

THE IVY-WIFE*

I longed to love a full-boughed beech
    And be as high as he:
I stretched an arm within his reach,
    And signalled unity.
But with his drip he forced a breach,   5
    And tried to poison me.

I gave the grasp of partnership
    To one of other race—
A plane: he barked him strip by strip
    From upper bough to base;   10
And me therewith; for gone my grip,
    My arms could not enlace.

In new affection next I strove
    To coll an ash I saw,
And he in trust received my love;   15
    Till with my soft green claw
I cramped and bound him as I wove . . .
    Such was my love: ha-ha!

By this I gained his strength and height
    Without his rivalry.   20
But in my triumph I lost sight
    Of afterhaps. Soon he,
Being bark-bound, flagged, snapped, fell outright,
    And in his fall felled me!

A MEETING WITH DESPAIR

As evening shaped I found me on a moor
    Sight shunned to entertain:
The black lean land, of featureless contour,
    Was like a tract in pain.

THE IVY-WIFE. 3 reach,] ~; *Hol.*   11 grip,] ~ *Hol.*   13 strove] clove
Hol.   14 To coll an] To a smooth *Hol.*   16 Till] ~ ⟨,⟩ *Hol.*   claw] ~
⟨,⟩ *Hol.*   17 I choked him as I wove and wove . . . *Hol.*   22 afterhaps.]
afterclaps. *Hol.*   23 Being dead, decayed, *Hol.*

A MEETING WITH DESPAIR. *Headnote* ⟨(Egdon Heath)⟩ *Hol.*
  2 Which sight could scarce sustain: *WP*

'This scene, like my own life,' I said, 'is one   5
    Where many glooms abide;
Toned by its fortune to a deadly dun—
    Lightless on every side.'

I glanced aloft and halted, pleasure-caught
    To see the contrast there: 10
The ray-lit clouds gleamed glory; and I thought,
    'There's solace everywhere!'

Then bitter self-reproaches as I stood
    I dealt me silently
As one perverse—misrepresenting Good   15
    In graceless mutiny.

Against the horizon's dim-discernèd wheel
    A form rose, strange of mould:
That he was hideous, hopeless, I could feel
    Rather than could behold.   20

'''Tis a dead spot, where even the light lies spent
    To darkness!' croaked the Thing.
'Not if you look aloft!' said I, intent
    On my new reasoning.

'Yea—but await awhile!' he cried. 'Ho-ho!—   25
    Now look aloft and see!'
I looked. There, too, sat night: Heaven's radiant show
    Had gone that heartened me.

UNKNOWING

When, soul in soul reflected,
We breathed an æthered air,
When we neglected
All things elsewhere,

---

12 "Ah—solace everywhere!" *CP19 only*   21 dead] drear *Hol.*   25 "Yes
—should you wait *Hol.*   26 Look now *WP, WE*   27 There too sat night. *Hol.*
28 Had gone; and gone had he. *Hol.*; Had gone. Then chuckled he. *WP*

And left the friendly friendless
To keep our love aglow,
  We deemed it endless . . .
  —We did not know!   5

When panting passion-goaded,
We planned to hie away,   10
  But, unforeboded,
  All the long day
The storm so pierced and pattered
That none could up and go,
  Our lives seemed shattered . . .   15
  —We did not know!

When I found you helpless lying,
And you waived my long misprise,
  And swore me, dying,
  In phantom-guise   20
To wing to me when grieving,
And touch away my woe,
  We kissed, believing . . .
  —We did not know!

But though, your powers outreckoning,   25
You tarry dead and dumb,
  Or scorn my beckoning,
  And will not come:
And I say, 'Why thus inanely
Brood on her memory so!'   30
  I say it vainly—
  I feel and know!

UNKNOWING. 9 When, by mad passion goaded, *WP*   12 *WE, CP23*] The storm-
shafts gray *WP*; The livelong day *CP19*   13 *CP23*] So heavily down-pattered *WP*;
Wild storms so pierced and pattered *WE*; Wild storm so pierced and pattered *CP19*
14 up and] thenceward *Hol.*; forthward *WP*   17 you *CP, DCM4*] ~ , *WP, WE*
18 long] deep *WP*   26 tarry] hold you *WP*   28 come: *CP, DCM4*] ~;
WP, WE   29 "'Twere mood ungainly *WP*   30 Brood on] To store *WP*
so!' *CP, DCM4*] ~:" *WP, WE*   31 vainly—] ~ *Hol.*

FRIENDS BEYOND*

William Dewy, Tranter Reuben, Farmer Ledlow late at
    plough,
    Robert's kin, and John's, and Ned's,
And the Squire, and Lady Susan, lie in Mellstock
    churchyard now!

'Gone,' I call them, gone for good, that group of local
    hearts and heads;
    Yet at mothy curfew-tide,   5
And at midnight when the noon-heat breathes it back
    from walls and leads,

They've a way of whispering to me—fellow-wight who
    yet abide—
    In the muted, measured note
Of a ripple under archways, or a lone cave's stillicide:

'We have triumphed: this achievement turns the bane to
    antidote,   10
    Unsuccesses to success,
Many thought-worn eves and morrows to a morrow free
    of thought.

'No more need we corn and clothing, feel of old terrestrial
    stress;
    Chill detraction stirs no sigh;
Fear of death has even bygone us: death gave all that we
    possess.'   15

W. D.—'Ye mid burn the old bass-viol that I set such
    value by.'
Squire.—'You may hold the manse in fee,
    You may wed my spouse, may let my children's memory
    of me die.'

FRIENDS BEYOND. 11 success,] ~ ⟨:⟩, *Hol.*   12 thought-worn] ⟨fevered⟩ *Hol.*
to] ⟨bring⟩ *Hol.*   13 'No more need we] "Nought we need of *Hol.*   feel]
know *Hol.*   16 old] wold *WP*   value] ⟨value⟩ *Hol.*; vallie *WP*   18 my
children's memory of me may decry." *WP*

Lady S.—'You may have my rich brocades, my laces; take each
   household key;
      Ransack coffer, desk, bureau;   20
   Quiz the few poor treasures hid there, con the letters kept
      by me.'

Far.—'Ye mid zell my favourite heifer, ye mid let the charlock
      grow,
      Foul the grinterns, give up thrift.'
Far. Wife.—'If ye break my best blue china, children, I shan't
      care or ho.'

All.—'We've no wish to hear the tidings, how the people's
      fortunes shift;   25
      What your daily doings are;
   Who are wedded, born, divided; if your lives beat slow or
      swift.

'Curious not the least are we if our intents you make or
      mar,
      If you quire to our old tune,
   If the City stage still passes, if the weirs still roar afar.'   30

—Thus, with very gods' composure, freed those crosses
      late and soon
      Which, in life, the Trine allow
   (Why, none witteth), and ignoring all that haps beneath
      the moon,

   William Dewy, Tranter Reuben, Farmer Ledlow late at
      plough,
      Robert's kin, and John's, and Ned's,   35
   And the Squire, and Lady Susan, murmur mildly to me
      now.

19 *Lady S.*— Hol., CP] *Lady.*— *WP, WE*   have] ⟨keep⟩ *Hol.*   22 *Far.*—]
Farmer.— *Hol.*   zell] sell *Hol.*   24 *Far. Wife.*—] *Wife.*— *WP, WE*
30 ⟨If the rooks still drown the chiming⟩ *Hol.*   32 allow] ~ ⟨—⟩ *Hol.*

TO OUTER NATURE

Show thee as I thought thee
When I early sought thee,
   Omen-scouting,
   All undoubting
Love alone had wrought thee—   5

Wrought thee for my pleasure,
Planned thee as a measure
   For expounding
   And resounding
Glad things that men treasure.   10

O for but a moment
Of that old endowment—
   Light to gaily
   See thy daily
Iris-hued embowment!   15

But such readorning
Time forbids with scorning—
   Makes me see things
   Cease to be things
They were in my morning.   20

TO OUTER NATURE. *Title* To External Nature *Hol.*
  3 Sorrow-scouting, *Hol.*   4 Never doubting *Hol.*   6 my] our *Hol.*
10 that men treasure.] 〈for our leisure.〉 〈in our leisure.〉 *Hol.*   15 Iris-hued]
Irisèd *WP*

Fad'st thou, glow-forsaken,
Darkness-overtaken!
  Thy first sweetness,
  Radiance, meetness,
None shall re-awaken.   25

Why not sempiternal
Thou and I? Our vernal
  Brightness keeping,
  Time outleaping;
Passed the hodiernal!   30

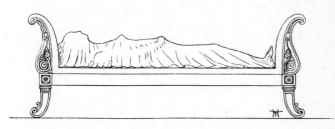

THOUGHTS OF PHENA*

At News of Her Death

Not a line of her writing have I,
  Not a thread of her hair,
No mark of her late time as dame in her dwelling, whereby
  I may picture her there;
And in vain do I urge my unsight   5
  To conceive my lost prize
At her close, whom I knew when her dreams were upbrim-
    ming with light,
  And with laughter her eyes.

21 Fad'st] Fadest *CP19 only*   22 Darkness overtaken; *Hol.*

THOUGHTS OF PHENA. *Title* T——a. *Hol.*; Thoughts of Ph——a *WP98*; At News of a Woman's Death *SP*   *Headnote* ⟨(Died 1890.)⟩ *Hol.*
  3 No mark of her late time, ⟨her dwelling, her lattice,⟩ ⟨her dwelling, her bower,⟩ her bower, her lattice, whereby *Hol.*   4 picture] image *Hol.*   7 At] In *Hol.*

What scenes spread around her last days,
    Sad, shining, or dim?   10
Did her gifts and compassions enray and enarch her sweet
      ways
    With an aureate nimb?
Or did life-light decline from her years,
    And mischances control
Her full day-star; unease, or regret, or forebodings, or fears   15
    Disennoble her soul?

Thus I do but the phantom retain
    Of the maiden of yore
As my relic; yet haply the best of her—fined in my brain
    It may be the more   20
That no line of her writing have I,
    Nor a thread of her hair,
No mark of her late time as dame in her dwelling, whereby
    I may picture her there.

                      March 1890.

MIDDLE-AGE ENTHUSIASMS*

To M. H.

We passed where flag and flower
    Signalled a jocund throng;
We said: 'Go to, the hour
    Is apt!'—and joined the song;
And, kindling, laughed at life and care,   5
Although we knew no laugh lay there.

---

10 Sad, sharp, or serene? *Hol.*   11 Did the Fates and Affections combine to embow
her sweet ways *Hol.*   12 With an irisèd sheen *Hol.*   17 ⟨Thus I have but
the vision to clasp⟩ Thus I do but the vision retain *Hol.*   19 brain] ⟨grasp⟩ *Hol.*
23 No mark of her late time, ⟨her life at her dwelling,⟩ ⟨her life in her bower,⟩ her bower,
her lattice, whereby *Hol.*   24 picture] image *Hol.*

We walked where shy birds stood
Watching us, wonder-dumb;
Their friendship met our mood;
We cried: 'We'll often come: 10
We'll come morn, noon, eve, everywhen!'
—We doubted we should come again.

We joyed to see strange sheens
Leap from quaint leaves in shade;
A secret light of greens   15
They'd for their pleasure made.
We said: 'We'll set such sorts as these!'
—We knew with night the wish would cease.

'So sweet the place,' we said,
'Its tacit tales so dear,   20
Our thoughts, when breath has sped,
Will meet and mingle here!' . . .
'Words!' mused we. 'Passed the mortal door,
Our thoughts will reach this nook no more.'

IN A WOOD*

From *The Woodlanders*

Pale beech and pine so blue,
     Set in one clay,
Bough to bough cannot you
     Live out your day?
When the rains skim and skip,   5
Why mar sweet comradeship,
Blighting with poison-drip
     Neighbourly spray?

MIDDLE-AGE ENTHUSIASMS. 13 sheens] ⟨gleams⟩ *Hol.*   17 set such sorts] plant such growths *Hol.*   24 This nook ⟨can⟩ will know our thoughts no more.' *Hol.*

IN A WOOD. *Headnote* From] *vide Hol.*; See *WP*; om. SP
  1 pine so blue,] pine-tree blue, *WP*   4 Live] Bide *WP*   5 skip,] ~ *Hol.*
7 poisoned drip *Hol.*

Heart-halt and spirit-lame,
  City-opprest,   10
Unto this wood I came
  As to a nest;
Dreaming that sylvan peace
Offered the harrowed ease—
Nature a soft release   15
  From men's unrest.

But, having entered in,
  Great growths and small
Show them to men akin—
  Combatants all!   20
Sycamore shoulders oak,
Bines the slim sapling yoke,
Ivy-spun halters choke
  Elms stout and tall.

Touches from ash, O wych,   25
  Sting you like scorn!
You, too, brave hollies, twitch
  Sidelong from thorn.
Even the rank poplars bear
Lothly a rival's air,   30
Cankering in blank despair
  If overborne.

Since, then, no grace I find
  Taught me of trees,
Turn I back to my kind,   35
  Worthy as these.
There at least smiles abound,
There discourse trills around,
There, now and then, are found
  Life-loyalties.   40

1887: 1896.

13 Dreaming] Deeming *Hol.*   14 Offered my soul release— *Hol.*
15 release] surcease *Hol.*   16 To man's unrest. *Hol.*   18 ⟨These groves
recall⟩ *Hol.*   19 Show them] ⟨Trees are⟩ *Hol.* 22 sapling] ⟨saplings⟩
Hol.   30 Lothly *CP20, WE20*] Illy *WP, WE12, CP19*; Poorly *SP*
31 blank] black *WP, CP*   37 at least] ⟨a few⟩ *Hol.* abound,] ⟨are found,⟩ *Hol.*
39 now and then,] ⟨too, sometimes⟩ now and then *Hol.*

TO A LADY

Offended by a Book of the Writer's

Now that my page is exiled,—doomed, maybe,
Never to press thy cosy cushions more,
Or wake thy ready Yeas as heretofore,
Or stir thy gentle vows of faith in me:

Knowing thy natural receptivity,   5
I figure that, as flambeaux banish eve,
My sombre image, warped by insidious heave
Of those less forthright, must lose place in thee.

So be it. I have borne such. Let thy dreams
Of me and mine diminish day by day,   10
And yield their space to shine of smugger things;
Till I shape to thee but in fitful gleams,
And then in far and feeble visitings,
And then surcease. Truth will be truth alway.

TO A MOTHERLESS CHILD

Ah, child, thou art but half thy darling mother's;
    Hers couldst thou wholly be,
My light in thee would outglow all in others;
    She would relive to me.
But niggard Nature's trick of birth   5
    Bars, lest she overjoy,
Renewal of the loved on earth
    Save with alloy.

TO A LADY. *Title* To Lady——. *Hol.*   *Subtitle* Offended by something the Author had
written. *Hol.*
    1 is exiled,—] upcloses, *WP*; is exiled, *WE*   5 receptivity,] susceptivity
Hol.   11 yield] ⟨give⟩ cede *Hol.*   14 alway.] ~! *Hol.*

TO A MOTHERLESS CHILD. *Title* To an Orphan Child *WP*   *Subtitle* A Whimsey *WP*; *om.*
Hol.
    1 child,] *cap. Hol.*   2 be,] ~ *Hol.*   7 loved] *cap. Hol.*

The Dame has no regard, alas, my maiden,
    For love and loss like mine—   10
No sympathy with mindsight memory-laden;
    Only with fickle eyne.
To her mechanic artistry
    My dreams are all unknown,
And why I wish that thou couldst be   15
    But One's alone!

NATURE'S QUESTIONING*

When I look forth at dawning, pool,
    Field, flock, and lonely tree,
    All seem to gaze at me
Like chastened children sitting silent in a school;

Their faces dulled, constrained, and worn,   5
    As though the master's way
    Through the long teaching day
Had cowed them till their early zest was overborne.

Upon them stirs in lippings mere
    (As if once clear in call,   10
    But now scarce breathed at all)—
'We wonder, ever wonder, why we find us here!

'Has some Vast Imbecility,
    Mighty to build and blend,
    But impotent to tend,   15
Framed us in jest, and left us now to hazardry?

12 eyne.] ~! *Hol.*   16 alone!] ~. *Hol.*

NATURE'S QUESTIONING. 3 All seem] ⟨Seem⟩ *Hol.*   gaze] look *WP98*   4 children]
~, *Hol.*   6 way] ways *WP, CP*   7 day] days *WP, CP*   8 Their
first terrestrial zest had chilled and overborne. *WP*   9 And on them stirs, *WP,*
WE   mere] ~ — *Hol.*   11 all)—] ~) *Hol.*

'Or come we of an Automaton
　　Unconscious of our pains? . . .
　　Or are we live remains
Of Godhead dying downwards, brain and eye now gone?　　20

'Or is it that some high Plan betides,
　　As yet not understood,
　　Of Evil stormed by Good,
We the Forlorn Hope over which Achievement strides?'

Thus things around. No answerer I. . . .　　25
　　Meanwhile the winds, and rains,
　　And Earth's old glooms and pains
Are still the same, and Life and Death are neighbours nigh.

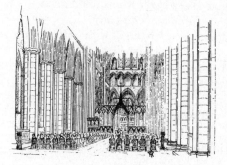

THE IMPERCIPIENT

(At a Cathedral Service)

That with this bright believing band
　　I have no claim to be,
That faiths by which my comrades stand
　　Seem fantasies to me,
And mirage-mists their Shining Land,　　5
　　Is a strange destiny.

28 *WE, CP23*] and gladdest Life dawns but to die. *Hol.*; and gladdest Life Death neighbours nigh. *WP*; and Death and glad Life neighbour nigh. *CP19*

THE IMPERCIPIENT. *Title* 〈The Agnostic〉 *Hol.*　　*Headnote* (Evensong; —— Cathedral.) *Hol.*

　1 with] from *WP*　　2 An outcast I should be, *WP*　　5 And 〈mirage-myth〉 mirage-mist their Happy Land, *Hol.*　　6 strange] drear *WP*

Why thus my soul should be consigned
    To infelicity,
Why always I must feel as blind
    To sights my brethren see,   10
Why joys they have found I cannot find,
    Abides a mystery.

Since heart of mine knows not that ease
    Which they know; since it be
That He who breathes All's Well to these   15
    Breathes no All's-Well to me,
My lack might move their sympathies
    And Christian charity!

I am like a gazer who should mark
    An inland company   20
Standing upfingered, with, 'Hark! hark!
    The glorious distant sea!'
And feel, 'Alas, 'tis but yon dark
    And wind-swept pine to me!'

Yet I would bear my shortcomings   25
    With meet tranquillity,
But for the charge that blessed things
    I'd liefer not have be.
O, doth a bird beshorn of wings
    Go earth-bound wilfully!   30

.   .   .   .   .   .

Enough. As yet disquiet clings
    About us. Rest shall we.

---

7 thus my] ⟨my sad⟩ *Hol.*   10 To bliss my neighbours see; *Hol.*   11 they
have] they've *WP, CP*   15 He who] ⟨Whatso⟩ *Hol.*   17 lack] loss *Hol.*
18a-f *Hol. only*:   But ah, they love me not, although
        I treat them tenderly,
    And while I bear with them they go
        To no such ⟨pains⟩ length with me,
    Because—to match their sight I show
        An incapacity.
21 'Hark! hark!] "Hark; Hark; *Hol.*   26 meet tranquillity,] ⟨equanimity,⟩ *Hol.*
28 I'd rather ⟨not have be.⟩ to unbe. *Hol.*; I'd liefer have unbe. *WP*   29 beshorn
WE20] deprived *WP, WE12, CP*; ⟨beclipt⟩ beshorn *DCM1*   30 wilfully!] ~? *Hol.*
31 disquiet] confusion *Hol.*   32 About us. We shall see. *Hol.*

AT AN INN*

When we as strangers sought
　　Their catering care,
Veiled smiles bespoke their thought
　　Of what we were.
They warmed as they opined　　　　　　5
　　Us more than friends—
That we had all resigned
　　For love's dear ends.

And that swift sympathy
　　With living love　　　　　　　　　10
Which quicks the world—maybe
　　The spheres above,
Made them our ministers,
　　Moved them to say,
'Ah, God, that bliss like theirs　　　　15
　　Would flush our day!'

And we were left alone
　　As Love's own pair;
Yet never the love-light shone
　　Between us there!　　　　　　　　20
But that which chilled the breath
　　Of afternoon,
And palsied unto death
　　The pane-fly's tune.

The kiss their zeal foretold,　　　　　25
　　And now deemed come,
Came not: within his hold
　　Love lingered numb.
Why cast he on our port
　　A bloom not ours?　　　　　　　　30
Why shaped us for his sport
　　In after-hours?

AT AN INN. 2 catering] sheltering *Hol.*　　　8 love's] *cap. Hol.*　　　11 world]
⟨earth⟩ *Hol.*　　　12 ⟨all earths above,⟩ *Hol.*　　　15 Ah,] ~ *Hol.*
20 there! *WP, CP, DCM4*] ~; *Hol.*; ~, *WE*　　　30 bloom] ⟨flush⟩ *Hol.*

As we seemed we were not
        That day afar,
And now we seem not what   35
        We aching are.
O severing sea and land,
        O laws of men,
Ere death, once let us stand
        As we stood then!   40

THE SLOW NATURE

(An Incident of Froom Valley)

'Thy husband—poor, poor Heart!—is dead—
        Dead, out by Moreford Rise;
A bull escaped the barton-shed,
        Gored him, and there he lies!'

—'Ha, ha—go away! 'Tis a tale, methink,   5
        Thou joker Kit!' laughed she.
'I've known thee many a year, Kit Twink,
        And ever hast thou fooled me!'

—'But, Mistress Damon—I can swear
        Thy goodman John is dead!   10
And soon th'lt hear their feet who bear
        His body to his bed.'

So unwontedly sad was the merry man's face—
        That face which had long deceived—
That she gazed and gazed; and then could trace 15
        The truth there; and she believed.

39 ⟨Give us, ere death, to stand⟩ ⟨Let us, ere death, once stand⟩ *Hol.*

THE SLOW NATURE. 4 him,] ~; *Hol.*   5 —'Ha,] "Ha, *Hol.*   9 —'But,]
"But *Hol.*   10 Thy] ⟨Your⟩ *Hol.*

She laid a hand on the dresser-ledge,
  And scanned far Egdon-side;
And stood; and you heard the wind-swept sedge
  And the rippling Froom; till she cried: 20

'O my chamber's untidied, unmade my bed,
  Though the day has begun to wear!
"What a slovenly hussif!" it will be said,
  When they all go up my stair!'

She disappeared; and the joker stood   25
  Depressed by his neighbour's doom,
And amazed that a wife struck to widowhood
  Thought first of her unkempt room.

But a fortnight thence she could take no food,
  And she pined in a slow decay;   30
While Kit soon lost his mournful mood
  And laughed in his ancient way.

                    1894.

18 And glanced at ⟨the far hill-side⟩ far Egdon-side; *Hol.*   21 chamber's]
⟨ro[om's?]⟩ *Hol.*   26 doom,] ∼; *Hol.*   27 a wife struck to] ⟨the wife in
her⟩ a wife struck in *Hol.*   29 take] ⟨eat⟩ *Hol.*   32 ancient] ⟨wonted⟩
Hol.

IN A EWELEAZE NEAR WEATHERBURY

The years have gathered grayly
　　Since I danced upon this leaze
With one who kindled gaily
　　Love's fitful ecstasies!
But despite the term as teacher,　　　　5
　　I remain what I was then
In each essential feature
　　Of the fantasies of men.

Yet I note the little chisel
　　Of never-napping Time　　　　10
Defacing wan and grizzel
　　The blazon of my prime.
When at night he thinks me sleeping
　　I feel him boring sly
Within my bones, and heaping　　　　15
　　Quaintest pains for by-and-by.

Still, I'd go the world with Beauty,
　　I would laugh with her and sing,
I would shun divinest duty
　　To resume her worshipping.　　　　20
But she'd scorn my brave endeavour,
　　She would not balm the breeze
By murmuring 'Thine for ever!'
　　As she did upon this leaze.

　　　　　　　　　　1890.

IN A EWELEAZE NEAR WEATHERBURY. *Title* In a Eweleaze *SP*
　　1 have gathered] ⟨are legion⟩ *Hol.*　　grayly] ⟨?grimly?⟩ ~, *Hol.*　　　　3 kindled]
⟨here learnt⟩ *Hol.*　　gaily] ⟨?⟩ daily *Hol.*　　　　5 teacher,] ~ *Hol., SP*
7 each essential] ⟨many a mental⟩ *Hol.*　　　8 ⟨And in fervours hid from men.⟩ *Hol.*
9 note] mark *Hol.*　　　10 never-napping] never nodding *Hol.*　　　11 Defacing]
⟨Bescraping⟩ *Hol.*　　wan *CP, DCM4*] ghast *WP, WE*　　　17 Beauty,] ⟨*l.c.*⟩ *Hol.*
19 divinest] *cap. Hol.*　　23 With "Love, I'm thine for ever!" *Hol.*

THE BRIDE-NIGHT FIRE*

Or, The Fire at Tranter Sweatley's

(Wessex Dialect)

They had long met o' Zundays—her true love and she—
And at junketings, maypoles, and flings;
But she bode wi' a thirtover uncle, and he
Swore by noon and by night that her goodman should be
Naibour Sweatley—a wight often weak at the knee   5
From taking o' sommat more cheerful than tea—
Who tranted, and moved people's things.

She cried, 'O pray pity me!' Nought would he hear;
Then with wild rainy eyes she obeyed.
She chid when her Love was for vanishing wi' her: 10
The pa'son was told, as the season drew near
To throw over pu'pit the names of the pair
As fitting one flesh to be made.

The wedding-day dawned and the morning drew on;
The couple stood bridegroom and bride;   15
The evening was passed, and when midnight had gone
The feasters horned, 'God save the King', and anon
The twain took their home-along ride.

THE BRIDE-NIGHT FIRE. *Gentleman's Magazine*, Nov. 1875 [*for text see Appendix C*]; Lionel
Johnson, *The Art of Thomas Hardy* (1894), pp. lix-lxiv. *MS1* [*in Mrs Hardy's hand*] (*ATH*)
Bancroft
    Title WE20] The Fire at Tranter Sweatley's *GM, ATH, WP*; The Bride-Night Fire
WE12, CP   *Headnote* (Wessex Dialect) *WE*] A Wessex Ballad *GM*; A Wessex Ballad/By
Thomas Hardy (written 1867). / (Printed, by permission, from the original MS.) / (*NB*— A
bowdlerized version of this ballad appeared in *The Gentleman's Magazine* for November
1875.] *ATH*; *om. WP*; (A Wessex Tradition) *CP*
    1 Zundays—] Sundays— *GM, ATH*   3 bode] dwelt *GM, ATH*   thirtover]
crabbed old *GM, MS1, ATH*   uncle,] ⟨uncle⟩ nuncle, *MS1*; nuncle, *ATH, Hol.*
4 goodman] husband *GM, ATH*   5 wight often] man often *GM, ATH*; ⟨man
often⟩ gaffer oft *Hol.*; gaffer oft *WP*   10 vanishing *WE*] clinking off *GM, ATH*,
WP, CP   11 pa'son] passon *GM*   near,] ~ *Hol.*   12 throw] ⟨fling⟩
Hol.   pu'pit] pulpit *GM, ATH*; ⟨the⟩ pulpit *MS1*   pair] peäir *ATH, WP*
13 one] woone *ATH*   17 feasters horned,] folks horned out *GM, ATH, Hol.*; folks
horned out, *WP*   18 *WE*] To their home the pair gloomily hied. *GM, ATH*; The
twain homealong gloomily hied. *Hol.*; The two home-along gloomily hied. *WP*; The pair
took their homealong ride. *CP*

The lover Tim Tankens mourned heart-sick and lear
    To be thus of his darling deprived: 20
He roamed in the dark ath'art field, mound, and mere,
And, a'most without knowing it, found himself near
The house of the tranter, and now of his Dear,
    Where the lantern-light showed 'em arrived.

The bride sought her chamber so calm and so pale   25
    That a Northern had thought her resigned;
But to eyes that had seen her in tide-times of weal,
Like the white cloud o' smoke, the red battlefield's vail,
    That look spak' of havoc behind.

The bridegroom yet loitered a beaker to drain,   30
    Then reeled to the linhay for more,
When the candle-snoff kindled some chaff from his grain—
Flames spread, and red vlankers, wi' might and wi' main,
    And round beams, thatch, and chimley-tun roar.

Young Tim away yond, rafted up by the light,   35
    Through brimbles and underwood tears,
Till he comes to the orchet, when crooping from sight
In the lewth of a codlin-tree, bivering wi' fright,
Wi' on'y her night-rail to cover her plight,
    His lonesome young Barbree appears.   40

---

19 Tim] Sim *GM throughout*; ⟨*Sim*⟩ Tim *MS1 throughout*   lear *WE*] drear *GM*, *ATH*, *WP*; leer *CP*   21 ath'art] around *GM*   24 Where the moving lights showed they'd arrived. *GM*, *ATH*   25 chamber]chimmer *GM*, *ATH*; cham'mer *Hol.*; cham'er *WP*   27 But] ∼ , *Hol.*   seen] zeed *ATH*   tide-times] seasons *GM*, *ATH*, *Hol.*   of] o' *ATH*, *Hol.*   28 o'] of *GM*   29 spak'] told *GM* 30 loitered *GM*, *WE*] laitered *ATH*, *WP*, *CP*   32 some] the *GM*, *ATH*; ⟨the⟩ *Hol.*   grain—] ∼ ⟨,⟩— *Hol.*   33 Flames sprout and rush upwards *GM*, *MS1*; spread and rush upwards *ATH*   spread,] ∼ ⟨,⟩ *Hol.*   34 And round] Around *CP*   35 Young Sim in the distance, aroused by the light, *GM*; Young Tim away yander, aroused by the light, *ATH*; Young Tim away ⟨yander⟩ yonder, aroused by the light *Hol.*   36 brimbles] brimble *WP*   tears,] ∼ *MS1*   37 when crooping from sight] where slap in his sight, *GM*, *ATH*; when crooping thereright *WP* 38 Beneath a bowed codlin-tree, trimbling wi' fright, *GM*, *ATH*   39 In an old coat she'd found on a scarecrow bedight, *GM*; Wi' nought but her shimmy 'tween her and the night, *ATH*; Wi' ⟨nought but⟩ on'y her night-rail to screen her from sight, *Hol.*; Wi' on'y her night-rail to screen her from sight, *WP*   40 lonesome] gentle *GM*, *ATH*; litsome *Hol.*   Barbree] Barbara *GM*

Her cold little figure half-naked he views
    Played about by the frolicsome breeze,
Her light-tripping totties, her ten little tooes,
All bare and besprinkled wi' Fall's chilly dews,
While her great gallied eyes through her hair hanging loose   45
    Shone as stars through a tardle o' trees.

She eyed him; and, as when a weir-hatch is drawn,
    Her tears, penned by terror afore,
With a rushing of sobs in a shower were strawn,
Till her power to pour 'em seemed wasted and gone   50
    From the heft o' misfortune she bore.

'O Tim, my *own* Tim I must call 'ee—I will!
    All the world has turned round on me so!
Can you help her who loved 'ee, though acting so ill?
Can you pity her misery—feel for her still?   55
When worse than her body so quivering and chill
    Is her heart in its winter o' woe!

'I think I mid almost ha' borne it,' she said,
    'Had my griefs one by one come to hand;
But O, to be slave to thik husbird for bread,   60
And then, upon top o' that, driven to wed,
And then, upon top o' that, burnt out o' bed,
    Is more than my nater can stand!'

Like a lion within him Tim's spirit outsprung—
    (Tim had a great soul when his feelings were wrung)—   65
    'Feel for 'ee, dear Barbree?' he cried;

41 *WE*] Her form in these cold mildewed tatters he views, *GM*; ⟨Her form in this scrimped scrap o' clothing⟩ *MS1*; Her cold little buzzoms half naked he views *ATH*; Her cold little buzzom half naked he views *Hol.*   cold] cwold *WP, CP*   45 gallied] frightened *GM, ATH*   hair hanging] ringlets so *GM, ATH*; ringlets ⟨so⟩ let *Hol.*   46 Shone as] Shone like *GM*; Sheened like *ATH, Hol.*; Sheened as *WP*   tardle] tangle *GM, ATH* o'] of *GM*   47 him; *GM, CP, WE*] en; *ATH, WP*   48 afore] before *GM* 49 With] Wi' *GM, ATH*   shower] torrent *GM, MS1*   51 o'] of *GM, ATH* 53 has] hev *GM, ATH*; ha' *WP*   54 ⟨Here's a larry!...O help me,⟩ *Hol.* 57 o'] of *GM, ATH*   58 mid almost ha'] could almost hev *GM, ATH* 60 thik husbird] an uncle *GM, ATH*   64 *WE*] Sim's soul like a lion within him outsprung— *GM*; Tim's soul like a lion within en outsprung— *ATH*; Tim's soul like a lion 'ithin en ⟨upsprung⟩ outsprung— *Hol.*; Tim's soul like a lion 'ithin en outsprung— *WP* him] en *CP*   65 wrung)—] ~) *Hol.*   66 Barbree] Barbie *GM*

And his warm working-jacket then straightway he flung
Round about her, and bending his back, there she clung
Like a chiel on a gipsy, her figure uphung
　　By the sleeves that he tightly had tied.   70

Over piggeries, and mixens, and apples, and hay,
　　They lumpered straight into the night;
And finding erelong where a bridle-path lay,
Lit on Tim's house at dawn, only seen on their way
By a naibour or two who were up wi' the day;   75
　　But who gathered no clue to the sight.

Then tender Tim Tankens he searched here and there
　　For some garment to clothe her fair skin;
But though he had breeches and waistcoats to spare,
He had nothing quite seemly for Barbree to wear,   80
Who, half shrammed to death, stood and cried on a chair
　　At the caddle she found herself in.

There was one thing to do, and that one thing he did,
　　He lent her some clothes of his own,
And she took 'em perforce; and while swiftly she slid   85
Them upon her Tim turned to the winder, as bid,
Thinking, 'O that the picter my duty keeps hid
　　To the sight o' my eyes mid be shown!'

---

67 And] Then *GM, ATH*; ⟨Then⟩ *Hol.*   then straightway he flung] about her he flung,
GM, ATH, WP   68 *WE*] Made a back, horsed her up, till behind him she clung:
GM, ATH; ∼*WP*; Round about her, and horsed her by jerks, till she clung *CP*
69 gipsy,] ∼ *Hol.*   her figure uphung] her round figure hung *GM*   70 As the
two sleeves before him he tied. *GM*; As the two sleeves afore him he tied. *ATH, Hol.*; By the
sleeves that around her he tied. *WP*   72 lumpered] stumbled *GM, ATH*
73 erelong] at length *GM, ATH*; ⟨at length⟩ bylong *Hol.*; bylong *WP*   bridle-path]
halter-path *WP, CP*   74–94 *GM condenses to 15 lines: see Appendix C.*
74 *WE*] By dawn reached Tim's house, only seed on ⟨the⟩ their way *MS1*; By dawn reached
Tim's house, only zeed on their way *ATH*; By dawn reached Tim's house, on'y zeed on their
way *Hol.*; At dawn reached Tim's house, on'y seen on their way *WP*; Sighted Tim's house by
dawn, on'y seen on their way *CP*   75 ⟨In round bedazed spectacles glared every
way⟩ *MS1*   76 who] they *ATH, WP*   79 waistcoats] weskets *ATH*
spare,] ∼ *Hol.*   81 shrammed] scrammed *ATH, Hol.*   on] in *MS1*
84 some clothes] these clouts *ATH*; some clouts *WP*   85 swiftly] in 'em *ATH,*
Hol.   86 Tim turned to the winder, as modesty bid, *ATH, WP*   88 mid]
might *MS1*

In the tallet he stowed her; there huddied she lay,
   Shortening sleeves, legs, and tails to her limbs;   90
But most o' the time in a mortal bad way,
Well knowing that there'd be the divel to pay
If 'twere found that, instead o' the elements' prey,
   She was living in lodgings at Tim's.

'Where's the tranter?' said men and boys; 'where can he be?'   95
   'Where's the tranter?' said Barbree alone.
'Where on e'th is the tranter?' said everybod-y:
They sifted the dust of his perished roof-tree,
   And all they could find was a bone.

Then the uncle cried, 'Lord, pray have mercy on me!'   100
   And in terror began to repent.
But before 'twas complete, and till sure she was free,
Barbree drew up her loft-ladder, tight turned her key—
Tim bringing up breakfast and dinner and tea—
   Till the news of her hiding got vent.   105

Then followed the custom-kept rout, shout, and flare
Of a skimmity-ride through the naibourhood, ere
   Folk had proof of old Sweatley's decay.

---

89 huddied] huddled *ATH*; hidied *Hol.*   lay,] ~ *Hol.*   90 Shortening] Suiting
ATH, Hol.   limbs;] ~, *Hol.*   91 o'] of *ATH*   mortal bad] terrible *ATH,*
Hol.   92 divel] devil *ATH, Hol.*   93 If 'twere] When 'twas *GM*; If 'twas
ATH   elements'] elements *MS1*; element's *CP*   prey,] ~ *Hol.*   95 he] ⟨he⟩
er *Hol.*; er *WP*   96 Barbree] Barbie *GM*; ⟨Barbee⟩ *MS1*   97 e'th] earth
GM, ATH; arth *MS1*   tranter?] ~! *GM, MS1*   99 bone.] ~! *GM, MS1*
100 ⟨uncle⟩ nuncle *MS1*; nuncle *ATH, Hol.*   101 terror] sorrow *GM*   repent.
WP, CP] ~: *MS1, Hol.*   103 Barbree] Barbie *GM*; ⟨Barbee⟩ *MS1*   key—] ~
⟨,⟩—*Hol.*   104 Sim handing in breakfast, and dinner, and tea—*GM*
105 Till the crabbed man gied his consent. *GM*; Till one morning they packed up, and went.
MS1   106 Then] There *Hol.*
106–13 *MS1 reads:*
        There was skimmity-riding wi' rout, shout, and flare,
        In Weatherbury, Droose, and out Egdon way, ere
           They had proof of old Sweatley's decay:
        The Mellstock and Yalbury folk stood in a stare
        (The trantor ⟨owned⟩ had houses and commonage there),
        But little did Tim and his ⟨Barbee⟩ Barbaree care,
           In the country out west far away.
(*ATH* 106–8 = *MS1, except* 107 Droose,] Drouse,; *ATH* 109–13 = *established text. For*
GM see Appendix C.)   107 skimmington-ride *WP*   108 of old *GM, Hol.,*
WE] o' wold *WP, CP*   decay.] ~: *Hol.*

Whereupon decent people all stood in a stare,
Saying Tim and his lodger should risk it, and pair: 110
So he took her to church. An' some laughing lads there
Cried to Tim, 'After Sweatley!' She said, 'I declare
    I stand as a maiden to-day!'

                              Written 1866; *printed* 1875.

HEIRESS AND ARCHITECT*

For A. W. Blomfield

She sought the Studios, beckoning to her side
An arch-designer, for she planned to build.
He was of wise contrivance, deeply skilled
In every intervolve of high and wide—
    Well fit to be her guide.   5

        'Whatever it be,'
        Responded he,
With cold, clear voice, and cold, clear view,
'In true accord with prudent fashionings
For such vicissitudes as living brings,   10
And thwarting not the law of stable things,
        That will I do.'

    'Shape me', she said, 'high halls with tracery
And open ogive-work, that scent and hue
Of buds, and travelling bees, may come in through,   15
The note of birds, and singings of the sea,
        For these are much to me.'

        'An idle whim!'
        Broke forth from him
Whom nought could warm to gallantries: 20

---

110 An'] And *ATH*
    Date Written, 1867: printed 1874. *Hol.*

HEIRESS AND ARCHITECT. *Headnote* To A. W. B. *Hol.*; For A. W. B. *WP, WE12, CP19*
    8 cold clear voice and cold clear view, *Hol.*   13 "Shape me," she said, "a pile of
light degree *Hol.*   14 With open lattice-work, *Hol.*

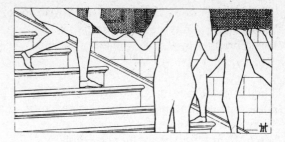

'Cede all these buds and birds, the zephyr's call,
And scents, and hues, and things that falter all,
And choose as best the close and surly wall,
    For winters freeze.'

'Then frame', she cried, 'wide fronts of crystal glass,   25
That I may show my laughter and my light—
Light like the sun's by day, the stars' by night—
Till rival heart-queens, envying, wail, "Alas,
    Her glory!" as they pass.'

    'O maid misled!'   30
    He sternly said
Whose facile foresight pierced her dire;
'Where shall abide the soul when, sick of glee,
It shrinks, and hides, and prays no eye may see?
Those house them best who house for secrecy,   35
    For you will tire.'

'A little chamber, then, with swan and dove
Ranged thickly, and engrailed with rare device
Of reds and purples, for a Paradise
Wherein my Love may greet me, I my Love,   40
    When he shall know thereof?'

    'This, too, is ill,'
    He answered still,
The man who swayed her like a shade.

25 glass,] ~, ⟨"⟩ *Hol.*   28 "Alas,] '~ *Hol.*   31 said *Hol., CP*] ~, *WP,*
WE   32 facile] ⟨eye of⟩ *Hol.*   dire;] ~: *Hol.*   37 chamber,] ~ *Hol.*
44 ⟨The man whose mien no fancy rayed:⟩ *Hol.*

'An hour will come when sight of such sweet nook   45
Would bring a bitterness too sharp to brook,
When brighter eyes have won away his look;
    For you will fade.'

Then said she faintly: 'O, contrive some way—
Some narrow winding turret, quite mine own,   50
To reach a loft where I may grieve alone!
It is a slight thing; hence do not, I pray,
    This last dear fancy slay!'

    'Such winding ways
    Fit not your days,'   55
Said he, the man of measuring eye;
'I must even fashion as the rule declares,
To wit: Give space (since life ends unawares)
To hale a coffined corpse adown the stairs;
    For you will die.'   60

1867.
8 Adelphi Terrace.

THE TWO MEN

There were two youths of equal age,
Wit, station, strength, and parentage;
They studied at the selfsame schools,
And shaped their thoughts by common rules.

One pondered on the life of man,   5
His hopes, his ending, and began
To rate the Market's sordid war
As something scarce worth living for.

'I'll brace to higher aims,' said he,
'I'll further Truth and Purity;
Thereby to mend the mortal lot
And sweeten sorrow. Thrive I not,

'Winning their hearts, my kind will give
Enough that I may lowly live,
And house my Love in some dim dell,
For pleasing them and theirs so well.'

Idly attired, with features wan,
In secret swift he laboured on:
Such press of power had brought much gold
Applied to things of meaner mould.

Sometimes he wished his aims had been
To gather gains like other men;
Then thanked his God he'd traced his track
Too far for wish to drag him back.

He looked out from his loft one day
To where his slighted garden lay;
Nettles and hemlock hid each lawn,
And every flower was starved and gone.

He fainted in his heart, whereon
He rose, and sought his plighted one,
Resolved to loose her bond withal,
Lest she should perish in his fall.

He met her with a careless air,
As though he'd ceased to find her fair,
And said: 'True love is dust to me;
I cannot kiss: I tire of thee!'

13 hearts,] ~ *Hol.*   15 dim] ⟨snug⟩ *Hol.*   17 wan,] ~ *Hol.*
24 So far no wish could drag him back. *Hol.*   25 looked out] lookèd *WP*; looked
down *CP*   26 slighted] ⟨ruined⟩ *Hol.*   27 hid each lawn,] ⟨strove
thereon,⟩ *Hol.*   28 starved] ⟨dead⟩ *Hol.*   31 ⟨Resolved to strain her
strength no more,⟩ *Hol.*   32 ⟨And free her from the troth she swore.⟩ *Hol.*
34 find] ⟨deem⟩ ⟨read⟩ *Hol.*

(That she might scorn him was he fain,
To put her sooner out of pain;
For angered love breathes quick and dies,
When famished love long lingering lies.)   40

Once done, his soul was so betossed,
It found no more the force it lost:
Hope was his only drink and food,
And hope extinct, decay ensued.

And, living long so closely penned,   45
He had not kept a single friend;
He dwindled thin as phantoms be,
And drooped to death in poverty. . .

Meanwhile his schoolmate had gone out
To join the fortune-finding rout;   50
He liked the winnings of the mart,
But wearied of the working part.

He turned to seek a privy lair,
Neglecting note of garb and hair,
And day by day reclined and thought   55
How he might live by doing nought.

'I plan a valued scheme,' he said
To some. 'But lend me of your bread,
And when the vast result looms nigh,
In profit you shall stand as I.'   60

Yet they took counsel to restrain
Their kindness till they saw the gain;
And, since his substance now had run,
He rose to do what might be done.

37 was he fain,] ⟨thus he feigned⟩ *Hol.*   38 pain;] ∼: *Hol.*   39 angered]
incensed *WP*   40 ⟨long lingering⟩ *Hol.*; a-lingering *WP*   41 soul] ⟨mind⟩
Hol.   betossed,] ∼ *Hol.*   44 extinct,] ∼ *Hol.*   49 Meanwhile]
Meantime *WP, CP*   50 rout;] ∼, *Hol.*   53 to seek] ⟨and sought⟩ *Hol.*
54 garb] ⟨beard⟩ *Hol.*   57 scheme,'] ∼" *Hol.*   59 looms] ⟨draws⟩ *Hol.*
nigh,] ∼ *Hol.*   64 do] ⟨find⟩ ⟨learn⟩ *Hol.*

He went unto his Love by night,   65
And said: 'My Love, I faint in fight:
Deserving as thou dost a crown,
My cares shall never drag thee down.'

(He had descried a maid whose line
Would hand her on much corn and wine,   70
And held her far in worth above
One who could only pray and love.)

But this Fair read him; whence he failed
To do the deed so blithely hailed;
He saw his projects wholly marred,   75
And gloom and want oppressed him hard;

Till, living to so mean an end,
Whereby he'd lost his every friend,
He perished in the pauper sty
Where his old mate lay dying nigh.   80

And moralists, reflecting, said,
As 'dust to dust' anon was read
And echoed from each coffin-lid,
'These men were like in all they did.'

1866.
16 Westbourne Park Villas.

---

70 on] down *Hol.*   73 Fair] ⟨one⟩ *Hol.*   74 deed] ⟨thing⟩ *Hol.*
78 Whereby he'd lost] ⟨He lost thereby⟩ *Hol.*   79 ⟨A pauper soon he sank to die,⟩
Hol.; He perished in a pauper sty, *WP*   80 ⟨His mate the pauper dead hard by.⟩
Hol.; His mate the dying pauper nigh. *WP*   81 moralists,] ⟨standers-by,⟩ *Hol.*
82 anon was] in burial *WP*   83 And] Was *WP*   84 *italics, del. Hol.*
    Place WE, ME

LINES*

Spoken by Miss ADA REHAN at the Lyceum Theatre, July 23, 1890, at a performance on behalf
of Lady Jeune's Holiday Fund for City Children

Before we part to alien thoughts and aims,
Permit the one brief word the occasion claims:
—When mumming and grave motives are allied,
Perhaps an Epilogue is justified.

Our under-purpose has, in truth, to-day   5
Commanded most our musings; least the play:
A purpose futile but for your good-will,
Swiftly responsive to the cry of ill:
A purpose all too limited!—to aid
Frail human flowerets, sicklied by the shade,   10
In winning some short spell of upland breeze,
Or strengthening sunlight on the level leas.

Who has not marked, where the full cheek should be,
Incipient lines of lank flaccidity,
Lymphatic pallor where the pink should glow,   15
And where the throb of transport, pulses low?—
Most tragical of shapes from Pole to Line,
O wondering child, unwitting Time's design,
Why should Man add to Nature's quandary,
And worsen ill by thus immuring thee?   20

                              [no stanza break]

LINES. *Pall Mall Gazette*, 23 July 1890 [lines 13-24, 31-4]; *Dorset County Chronicle*, 31 July
1890. *MS1* (Mrs Jeune's copy) RLP; *MS2* (?*DCC*?) HRC
     Headnote Spoken by Miss Ada Rehan / On behalf of Mrs. Jeune's Holiday Fund / for poor
city children: / Written by Thomas Hardy. *MS1, MS2*
     1 aims,] ~ *MS1, MS2, DCC*   2 brief] ⟨brief⟩ frank *MS2*
3 mumming] feigning *MS1*   motives] projects *MS1, MS2, DCC, WP*   allied,] ~
MS1, MS2   4 ⟨Perhaps an epilogue is⟩ A brief unmasking may be *MS2*
Epilogue] *l.c. MS1, DCC*   5 has, in truth,] *commas om. MS1*   7 good-will,
MS1, WE] ~ *MS2, WP, CP*   8 Swiftly] Promptly *MS1, MS2, DCC, Hol.*
ill:] ~. *MS1, MS2, DCC*   9 limited!—] ~! .... *MS1*   10 Frail] Pale
MS1, ⟨Pale⟩ *MS2*   11 breeze,] ~ *MS1, MS2, DCC*   12 And
strengthening sunlight over level leas. *MS1*   or] And *MS2*   13 be,] ~ *MS1,
MS2*   14 Incipient] The incipient *MS1, MS2, PMG*   15 glow,] ~
MS2   16 low?—] ~? *MS1, MS2*   17 Line,] ~ *MS1*   18 child,]
~ *MS1, MS2*   unwitting] unweeting *MS1, MS2, PMG, DCC*   design,] ~!— *MS1,
DCC*   19 Man] *l.c. MS1, MS2, PMG, DCC, Hol.*; Art *WP, CP19*   Nature's]
l.c. MS2   quandary,] cruelty, *MS1, MS2, PMG, DCC, Hol.*

—That races do despite unto their own,
That Might supernal do indeed condone
Wrongs individual for the general ease,
Instance the proof in victims such as these.
Launched into thoroughfares too thronged before,   25
Mothered by those whose protest is 'No more!'
Vitalized without option: who shall say
That did Life hang on choosing—Yea or Nay—
They had not scorned it with such penalty,
And nothingness implored of Destiny?   30

And yet behind the horizon smile serene
The down, the cornland, and the stretching green—
Space—the child's heaven: scenes which at least ensure
Some palliative for ills they cannot cure.

Dear friends—now moved by this poor show of ours   35
To make your own long joy in buds and bowers
For one brief while the joy of infant eyes,
Changing their urban murk to paradise—
You have our thanks!—may your reward include
More than our thanks, far more: their gratitude.   40

Savile Club. *Midnight, July* 1890.

21 *PE*] If Nature can do despite to her own, *MS1, MS2, PMG, DCC; variant line del. Hol.*;
—That races can do despite to their own, *WP*   22 That Might] If might *MS1*,
MS2, PMG, DCC; ⟨If might⟩ *Hol.*   23 ease.] ~ *MS1*   24 Draw we the
proof from instances like these. *PMG*; Draw we the proof from ⟨instances like⟩ victims such
as these. *MS2*; Draw we the proof from victims such as these. *MS1*   25 Launched
into cabins to [*unfinished line, uncancelled*] *MS1*   thoroughfares too thronged] ⟨domiciles
surcharged⟩ *MS2*   26 is] ~, *MS2, DCC*   28 That] ~, *MS2*   —Yea
or Nay—] *l.c. MS1, MS2, DCC; commas for dashes MS2*   29 penalty,] ~ *MS1*,
MS2   30 Destiny?] *l.c. MS1, MS2, DCC*   31 smile] ⟨smiles⟩ *MS2*
32 cornland,] ~ *MS1*   stretching] ⟨village⟩ *Hol.*   34 ills *MS1, MS2, PMG,*
DCC, WE] ill *WP, CP*   35 friends—] ~ ⟨,⟩— *Hol.*   37 brief] short *MS2*
eyes,] ~ *MS1, MS2*   38 paradise—] ~ ⟨,⟩— *Hol.*   39 thanks!—] ~!
MS1; ~!... *MS2, DCC*   may] *cap. MS1, MS2*   40 thanks,] ~— *MS1*
    Place | date Savile Club. July 20, 1890 *MS1*; *om. MS2, WP*

'I LOOK INTO MY GLASS'*

I look into my glass,
And view my wasting skin,
And say, 'Would God it came to pass
My heart had shrunk as thin!'

For then, I, undistrest   5
By hearts grown cold to me,
Could lonely wait my endless rest
With equanimity.

But Time, to make me grieve,
Part steals, lets part abide;   10
And shakes this fragile frame at eve
With throbbings of noontide.

'I LOOK INTO MY GLASS'. *MS1* Bancroft
  1 glass,] *cap. MS1*   6 hearts grown cold] friendships lost *Hol.*
10 abide;] ~ , *Hol.*   12 noontide.] noon tide. *Hol.*

POEMS OF THE PAST
AND THE PRESENT

CONTENTS

IMITATIONS, ETC.—

RETROSPECT—

PREFACE*

HEREWITH I tender my thanks to the editors and proprietors of the *Times*, the *Morning Post*, the *Daily Chronicle*, the *Westminster Gazette*, *Literature*, the *Graphic*, *Cornhill*, *Sphere*, and other papers, for permission to reprint from their pages such of the following pieces of verse as have already been published. 5

As was said of *Wessex Poems*, of the subject-matter of this volume much is dramatic or impersonative even where not explicitly so. And that portion which may be regarded as individual comprises a series of feelings and fancies written down in widely differing moods and circumstances, and at various dates; it will probably be 10 found, therefore, to possess little cohesion of thought or harmony of colouring. I do not greatly regret this. Unadjusted impressions have their value, and the road to a true philosophy of life seems to lie in humbly recording diverse readings of its phenomena as they are forced upon us by chance and change. 15

T. H.

August 1901.

PREFACE. 6 As . . . *Poems*,] *om. PP, CP*   of the . . . volume] ⟨⟨⟨Most⟩⟩ Much of the subject-matter of this volume⟩ ⟨Of the subject-matter of this volume which is not in narrative form,⟩ *Hol.*; Of the subject-matter of this volume which is in other than narrative form, *PP*; Of the subject-matter of this volume—even that which is in other than narrative form—*CP*   7 impersonative] personative *Hol.*   even . . . so] ⟨both in presentation and in philosophy.⟩ *Hol.*   8 And that] Moreover, that *PP, CP*   9-10 differing . . . circumstances] ⟨differing circumstances⟩ *Hol.*   10 dates; it will probably] ⟨dates. They may⟩ *Hol.*; dates. It will probably *PP, CP*   11-12 cohesion . . . colouring.] ⟨cohesion or harmony.⟩ *Hol.*   12-13 this. . . . road] ⟨this fault, as it may be considered, since the road⟩ ⟨this fault, as it may be considered. The road⟩ *Hol.*   13 lie] ⟨lie not a little⟩ *Hol.*   14 diverse readings] ⟨divergent impressions⟩ *Hol.* phenomena] ⟨meaning⟩ *Hol.*   14-15 are forced] ⟨occur⟩ *Hol.*

V.R. 1819-1901

A Reverie

The mightiest moments pass uncalendared,
  And when the Absolute
In backward Time pronounced the deedful word
  Whereby all life is stirred:
'Let one be born and throned whose mould shall constitute   5
The norm of every royal-reckoned attribute,'
  No mortal knew or heard.

But in due days the purposed Life outshone—
  Serene, sagacious, free;
—Her waxing seasons bloomed with deeds well done,   10
  And the world's heart was won . . .
Yet may the deed of hers most bright in eyes to be
Lie hid from ours—as in the All-One's thought lay she—
  Till ripening years have run.

Sunday Night,
27th January 1901.

v. R. 1819-1901. *Times*, 29 Jan. 1901
    1 Moments the mightiest *PP*   3 In backward Time pronounced] In Time agone
outgave *T*; ⟨In the dim Backward gave⟩ ⟨In Time agone outgave⟩ *Hol.*; In backward Time
outgave *PP*   6 royal-reckoned] royal-rated *T*; ⟨royal-rated⟩ *Hol.*   9 free;]
∼ — *Hol.*   10 its fourscore cycles beamed *T*; ⟨Its fourscore ⟨⟨zodiacs⟩⟩ cycles
beamed⟩ *Hol.*   —Her] Her *Hol.*
    Date January 1901 *T*

WAR POEMS

EMBARCATION*

(Southampton Docks: October, 1899)

Here, where Vespasian's legions struck the sands,
And Cerdic with his Saxons entered in,
And Henry's army leapt afloat to win
Convincing triumphs over neighbour lands,

Vaster battalions press for further strands,   5
To argue in the selfsame bloody mode
Which this late age of thought, and pact, and code,
Still fails to mend.—Now deckward tramp the bands,

Yellow as autumn leaves, alive as spring;
And as each host draws out upon the sea   10
Beyond which lies the tragical To-be,
None dubious of the cause, none murmuring,

Wives, sisters, parents, wave white hands and smile,
As if they knew not that they weep the while.

DEPARTURE

(Southampton Docks: October, 1899)

While the far farewell music thins and fails,
And the broad bottoms rip the bearing brine—
All smalling slowly to the gray sea-line—
And each significant red smoke-shaft pales,

EMBARCATION. *Daily Chronicle,* 25 Oct. 1899
   Title 'The Departure' *DC*   *Headnote date om. SP*
  8 —Now shipped each war-troop stands, *DC; variant line del. Hol.*   10 each]
the *DC*

DEPARTURE. *Headnote date om. SP*

Keen sense of severance everywhere prevails,   5
Which shapes the late long tramp of mounting men
To seeming words that ask and ask again:
'How long, O striving Teutons, Slavs, and Gaels

Must your wroth reasonings trade on lives like these,
That are as puppets in a playing hand? —   10
When shall the saner softer polities
Whereof we dream, have sway in each proud land
And patriotism, grown Godlike, scorn to stand
Bondslave to realms, but circle earth and seas?'

THE COLONEL'S SOLILOQUY

(Southampton Docks: October, 1899)

'The quay recedes. Hurrah! Ahead we go! . . .
It's true I've been accustomed now to home,
And joints get rusty, and one's limbs may grow
        More fit to rest than roam.

'But I can stand as yet fair stress and strain;   5
There's not a little steel beneath the rust;
My years mount somewhat, but here's to't again!
        And if I fall, I must.

'God knows that for myself I have scanty care;
Past scrimmages have proved as much to all;   10
In Eastern lands and South I have had my share
        Both of the blade and ball.

---

5 Keen] ⟨A⟩ *Hol.*   6 long] ⟨loud⟩ *Hol.*   8 striving *PP, CP, DCM4*]
ruling *WE*   9 trade] ⟨feed⟩ *Hol.*   11 polities] ⟨enquiries⟩ *Hol.*
12 have sway *WE, CP20*] ⟨take sha[pe] form⟩ *Hol.*; have play *PP, CP19*   proud] ⟨fair⟩
Hol.   land *CP, DCM4*] ~, *Hol. PP, WE*

THE COLONEL'S SOLILOQUY. 5 fair] ⟨some⟩ *Hol.*   9 I have] I've *PP*   11 I have]
I've *PP*

'And where those villains ripped me in the flitch
With their old iron in my early time,
I'm apt at change of wind to feel a twitch,   15
    Or at a change of clime.

'And what my mirror shows me in the morning
Has more of blotch and wrinkle than of bloom;
My eyes, too, heretofore all glasses scorning,
    Have just a touch of rheum. . . .   20

'Now sounds "The Girl I've left behind me", —Ah,
The years, the ardours, wakened by that tune!
Time was when, with the crowd's farewell "Hurrah!"
    'Twould lift me to the moon.

'But now it's late to leave behind me one   25
Who if, poor soul, her man goes underground,
Will not recover as she might have done
    In days when hopes abound.

'She's waving from the wharfside, palely grieving,
As down we draw. . . . Her tears make little show,   30
Yet now she suffers more than at my leaving
    Some twenty years ago!

'I pray those left at home will care for her!
I shall come back; I have before; though when
The Girl you leave behind you is a grandmother,   35
    Things may not be as then.'

15 wind] ⟨moon⟩ *Hol.*   28 days] ⟨years⟩ *Hol.*   32 twenty] ⟨thirty⟩ *Hol.*
ago! *Hol., CP*] ~ . *PP, WE*   34 shall] ⟨may⟩ *Hol.*   though] ⟨but⟩ *Hol.*
35 grandmother,] ~ *Hol.*

THE GOING OF THE BATTERY*

Wives' Lament

(*Casterbridge: November 2, 1899*)

I

O it was sad enough, weak enough, mad enough—
Light in their loving as soldiers can be—
First to risk choosing them, leave alone losing them
Now, in far battle, beyond the South Sea! . . .

II

—Rain came down drenchingly; but we unblenchingly   5
Trudged on beside them through mirk and through mire,
They stepping steadily—only too readily!—
Scarce as if stepping brought parting-time nigher.

III

Great guns were gleaming there, living things seeming
      there,
Cloaked in their tar-cloths, upmouthed to the night;   10
Wheels wet and yellow from axle to felloe,
Throats blank of sound, but prophetic to sight.

IV

Gas-glimmers drearily, blearily, eerily
Lit our pale faces outstretched for one kiss,
While we stood prest to them, with a last quest to them   15
Not to court perils that honour could miss.

THE GOING OF THE BATTERY. *Graphic*, 11 Nov. 1899
    Headnotes Wives' Lament] Wives' Voices: *G*; *om. SP*   (*Casterbridge* . . . 1899)]
[November 2, 1899. Late at night, in rain and in darkness, the 73rd Battery, R. F. A., left
Dorchester Barracks for the War in South Africa, marching on foot to the railway station,
where their guns were already entrained.] *G*; *date only PP, CP*
    1–4 *om. G, SP*   1 weak enough] ⟨that we were⟩ ⟨bad enough⟩ *Hol.*
3 leave] ⟨let⟩ *Hol.*   5 came down] ⟨drifted⟩ *Hol.*   10 upmouthed]
upnosed *G*   13 Lamplight all drearily blinking and blearily *G*   eerily] ∼, *Hol.*

V

Sharp were those sighs of ours, blinded these eyes of ours,
When at last moved away under the arch
All we loved. Aid for them each woman prayed for them,
Treading back slowly the track of their march.   20

VI

Someone said: 'Nevermore will they come: evermore
Are they now lost to us.' O it was wrong!
Though may be hard their ways, some Hand will guard their
     ways,
Bear them through safely, in brief time or long.

VII

—Yet, voices haunting us, daunting us, taunting us,   25
Hint in the night-time when life beats are low
Other and graver things . . . Hold we to braver things,
Wait we, in trust, what Time's fulness shall show.

AT THE WAR OFFICE, LONDON*

(*Affixing the Lists of Killed and Wounded: December,* 1899)

I

Last year I called this world of gaingivings
The darkest thinkable, and questioned sadly
If my own land could heave its pulse less gladly,
So charged it seemed with circumstance that brings
     The tragedy of things.   5

17-20 *om. G*   23 Though may be] Howsoe'er *G*   28 show.] know. *G*

AT THE WAR OFFICE. *Sphere*, 27 Jan. 1900 [*facsimile of MS1*]; *Lest We Forget*, ed. H. B. Elliott
(London: 1915). *MS1* (*S*) HRC
     Title At the War Office *MS1, S*; The War-Shadow *LWF*   *Headnote* After a Bloody
Battle *MS1, S; om. LWF*
     3. gladly,] ~ — *MS1, S*   4 that brings] whence springs *S, PP*

II

Yet at that censured time no heart was rent
Or feature blanched of parent, wife, or daughter
By hourly posted sheets of scheduled slaughter;
Death waited Nature's wont; Peace smiled unshent
    From Ind to Occident.   10

A CHRISTMAS GHOST-STORY*

South of the Line, inland from far Durban,
A mouldering soldier lies—your countryman.
Awry and doubled up are his gray bones,
And on the breeze his puzzled phantom moans
Nightly to clear Canopus: 'I would know   5
By whom and when the All-Earth-gladdening Law
Of Peace, brought in by that Man Crucified,
Was ruled to be inept, and set aside?
And what of logic or of truth appears
In tacking "Anno Domini" to the years?   10
Near twenty-hundred liveried thus have hied,
But tarries yet the Cause for which He died.'

                    Christmas-eve, 1899.

---

7 parent, wife,] ~ ~ *MS1, S*   daughter] ~, *Hol.*   8 posted] blazoned *MS1, S,*
PP, WE scheduled] listed *MS1, S, PP, WE*   slaughter;] ~: *MS1, S*   9 wont;]
~: *MS1, S*   Peace smiled unshent] men came and went *S*   10 Abroad, at home,
unshent. *S.*

A CHRISTMAS GHOST-STORY. *Westminster Gazette,* 23 Dec. 1899
  Headnote ⟨December, 1899⟩ *Hol.*
  2 There lies—be he or not your countryman—*WG*; ⟨There lies (be he or not your
countryman)⟩ *Hol.*   3 A fellow-mortal. Riddled are his bones, *WG*; *variant line del.*
Hol.   4 And on] But 'mid *WG*; And ⟨mid⟩ on *Hol.*   5 Nightly to clear
Canopus—fain to know *WG*   7 That Man Crucified,] Some-One crucified, *WG*
9–12 *om. WG*   12 Cause] ⟨?⟩ *Hol.*   He] ⟨*l.c.*⟩ *Hol.*
  Date om. WG; December 23, 1899 *Hol.*

DRUMMER HODGE

I

They throw in Drummer Hodge, to rest
    Uncoffined—just as found:
His landmark is a kopje-crest
    That breaks the veldt around;
And foreign constellations west   5
    Each night above his mound.

II

Young Hodge the Drummer never knew—
    Fresh from his Wessex home—
The meaning of the broad Karoo,
    The Bush, the dusty loam,
And why uprose to nightly view   10
    Strange stars amid the gloam.

III

Yet portion of that unknown plain
    Will Hodge for ever be;
His homely Northern breast and brain   15
    Grow to some Southern tree,
And strange-eyed constellations reign
    His stars eternally.

DRUMMER HODGE. *Literature*, 25 Nov. 1899
   Title The Dead Drummer *L, PP*   *Headnote* ['One of the Drummers killed was a native
of a village near Casterbridge.'] *L*
   3 kopje-crest] *cap. L, Hol.*   4 veldt] *cap. L, Hol.*   16 Grow to some *CP,*
DCM4] Grow up a *L, PP, WE*

A WIFE IN LONDON*

(*December*, 1899)

I

She sits in the tawny vapour
    That the Thames-side lanes have uprolled,
    Behind whose webby fold on fold
Like a waning taper
    The street-lamp glimmers cold.   5

A messenger's knock cracks smartly,
    Flashed news is in her hand
    Of meaning it dazes to understand
Though shaped so shortly:
    He—has fallen—in the far South Land. . . .   10

II

'Tis the morrow; the fog hangs thicker,
    The postman nears and goes:
    A letter is brought whose lines disclose
By the firelight flicker
    His hand, whom the worm now knows: 15

Fresh—firm—penned in highest feather—
    Page-full of his hoped return,
    And of home-planned jaunts by brake and burn
In the summer weather,
    And of new love that they would learn.   20

A WIFE IN LONDON. *Subtitles preceding first stanza*: i ⟨Overnight.⟩ ⟨The Eve⟩ The Tragedy.
Hol.; I. The Tragedy *PP*   *preceding third stanza*: ii ⟨Next Day.⟩ ⟨The Morrow⟩ The
Irony. *Hol.*; II. The Irony *PP*
  1 She sits] ⟨I sit⟩ *Hol.*   2 Thames-side] City *PP*   7 her] ⟨my⟩
Hol.   hand] ~⟨,⟩ *Hol.*   11 'Tis the morrow;] ⟨It is morning⟩ *Hol.*
20 they] ⟨we⟩ *Hol.*

THE SOULS OF THE SLAIN*

I

The thick lids of Night closed upon me
    Alone at the Bill
    Of the Isle by the Race—
    Many-caverned, bald, wrinkled of face—
And with darkness and silence the spirit was on me   5
    To brood and be still.

II

No wind fanned the flats of the ocean,
    Or promontory sides,
    Or the ooze by the strand,
    Or the bent-bearded slope of the land,   10
Whose base took its rest amid everlong motion
    Of criss-crossing tides.

III

Soon from out of the Southward seemed nearing
    A whirr, as of wings
    Waved by mighty-vanned flies,   15
    Or by night-moths of measureless size,
And in softness and smoothness well-nigh beyond hearing
    Of corporal things.

IV

And they bore to the bluff, and alighted—
    A dim-discerned train   20
    Of sprites without mould,
    Frameless souls none might touch or might hold—
On the ledge by the turreted lantern, far-sighted
    By men of the main.

THE SOULS OF THE SLAIN. *Cornhill*, April 1900. *MS1*, *P1*, *P2* (*C*) Adams
  1 thick lids of] thick lid of *C*; ⟨lids of the⟩ *Hol*.   5 was] came *C*
6 brood] stand, *MS1*, *P1*   7 fanned] whipped *MS1*, *P1*; ⟨whipped⟩ *P2*   flats]
⟨ooze⟩ *P2*   9 ooze] spawls *MS1*; sprawls *P1*; spawls *P2*, *C*   13 Soon] ~,
MS1-*C*   15 mighty-vanned] mammoth-vanned *MS1*, *P1*   16 night-
moths] night-birds *C*; night-birds night-moths *Hol*. [*neither del*.]   22 Frameless]
Loosened *MS1*, *P1*   might ... might] could ... could *MS1*, *P1*   23 ledge]
brow *MS1*, *P1*   turreted] ⟨uppermost⟩ *MS1*   lantern,] beacon, *MS1*, *P1*

V

And I heard them say 'Home!' and I knew them   25
    For souls of the felled
        On the earth's nether bord
    Under Capricorn, whither they'd warred,
And I neared in my awe, and gave heedfulness to them
        With breathings inheld.   30

VI

Then, it seemed, there approached from the northward
    A senior soul-flame
        Of the like filmy hue:
    And he met them and spake: 'Is it you,
O my men?' Said they, 'Aye! We bear homeward and hearth-
        ward
        To feast on our fame!'   35

VII

'I've flown there before you,' he said then:
    'Your households are well;
        But—your kin linger less
    On your glory and war-mightiness   40
Than on dearer things.'—'Dearer?' cried these from the dead
        then,
        'Of what do they tell?'

VIII

'Some mothers muse sadly, and murmur
    Your doings as boys—
        Recall the quaint ways   45
    Of your babyhood's innocent days.
Some pray that, ere dying, your faith had grown firmer,
        And higher your joys.

28 Under] Beneath *MS1, P1*   34 them] ~, *MS1–C*   spoke:] spoke: *MS1, P1;*
⟨spoke:⟩ *P2*   you,] ~ *MS1*   35 men?] ~?"—*MS1*   36 feast on] list
to *C, PP*   fame!'] ~." *MS1, P1*   39 less] not *MS1, P1*   40 On
your glory. In chamber and cot *MS1, P1;* On your glory ⟨amid their distress⟩ *P2*
41 Than on dearer things.'—'Dearer?'] Echo other things." — "Other?" *MS1, P1;* Than on
other things." "Other?" *P2, C;* Than on ⟨further⟩ ⟨other⟩ dearer things." ⟨"Further⟩
⟨Other⟩ Dearer?" *Hol.*   43 sadly,] ⟨softly⟩ *MS1*   46 days.] ~, *MS1*

IX

'A father broods: "Would I had set him
   To some humble trade,
   And so slacked his high fire,   50
   And his passionate martial desire;
And told him no stories to woo him and whet him
   To this dire crusade!"'

X

'And, General, how hold out our sweethearts,   55
   Sworn loyal as doves?'
   —'Many mourn; many think
It is not unattractive to prink
Them in sables for heroes. Some fickle and fleet hearts
   Have found them new loves.'   60

XI

'And our wives?' quoth another resignedly,
   'Dwell they on our deeds?'
   —'Deeds of home; that live yet
Fresh as dew—deeds of fondness or fret;
Ancient words that were kindly expressed or unkindly,   65
   These, these have their heeds.'

XII

—'Alas! then it seems that our glory
   Weighs less in their thought
   Than our old homely acts,
And the long-ago commonplace facts   70
Of our lives—held by us as scarce part of our story,
   And rated as nought!'

---

52 desire;] ~, *C*　　53 And told *CP, DCM4*] And had told *C*; ⟨And had told⟩ *Hol.*;
Had told *PP, WE*　　55 'And,] "—*MS1*　　57 "—Many mourn . . . And some
think *MS1, P1*; "Many mourn . . . Many think *P2, C*; —'Many] " ~ *Hol.*　　59 heroes.]
~ . . . *MS1–C*　　62 'Dwell they on] ⟨Glow they at⟩ *MS1*　　63 —'Deeds]
'⟨—⟩ Deeds *P1*; "Deeds *Hol.*　　64 dew—] new— *C, PP, WE*　　66 ⟨These
have most of their heeds."⟩ *MS1*　　67 —'Alas! then] "Alas! then, *MS1–C*; "Alas!
then *Hol.*　　69 old] small *C*; ⟨small⟩ *Hol.*　　71 story,] ~ *MS1–C*

XIII

Then bitterly some: 'Was it wise now
    To raise the tomb-door
    For such knowledge? Away!'
But the rest: 'Fame we prized till to-day;   75
Yet that hearts keep us green for old kindness we prize now
    A thousand times more!'

XIV

Thus speaking, the trooped apparitions
    Began to disband   80
    And resolve them in two:
Those whose record was lovely and true
Bore to northward for home: those of bitter traditions
    Again left the land,

XV

And, towering to seaward in legions,   85
    They paused at a spot
    Overbending the Race—
That engulphing, ghast, sinister place—
Whither headlong they plunged, to the fathomless regions
    Of myriads forgot.   90

XVI

And the spirits of those who were homing
    Passed on, rushingly,
    Like the Pentecost Wind;
And the whirr of their wayfaring thinned
And surceased on the sky, and but left in the gloaming   95
    Sea-mutterings and me.

December 1899.

75 Away!'] ~!"...MS1-C   82 lovely] goodly MS1, P1   84 land,] ~.
MS1   89 plunged,] ~ MS1-C   93 the] a MS1, P1   94 thinned]
~, MS1-C   96 Sea-mutterings] ⟨Sea-moanings⟩ MS1

SONG OF THE SOLDIERS' WIVES
AND SWEETHEARTS*

I

At last! In sight of home again,
    Of home again;
No more to range and roam again
    As at that bygone time?
No more to go away from us   5
    And stay from us?—
Dawn, hold not long the day from us,
    But quicken it to prime!

II

Now all the town shall ring to them,
    Shall ring to them,   10
And we who love them cling to them
    And clasp them joyfully;
And cry, 'O much we'll do for you
    Anew for you,
Dear Loves!—aye, draw and hew for you,   15
    Come back from oversea.'

III

Some told us we should meet no more,
    Yea, meet no more!—
Should wait, and wish, but greet no more
    Your faces round our fires;   20
That, in a while, uncharily
    And drearily
Men gave their lives—even wearily,
    Like those whom living tires.

SONG OF THE SOLDIERS' WIVES. *Morning Post*, 30 Nov. 1900; *Khaki*, Mar. 1915
   Title Song of the Soldiers' Wives *PP*; Hope-Song of the Soldiers' Sweethearts and Wives *K*
   1 At last!] ~? *MP, Hol.*; Some day! *K*   7 the] that *K*   9 Now] ⟨Then⟩ *Hol.*; Then *K*   17-24 *om. K*   18 Should meet no more; *MP, PP* 20 round] by *MP*

IV

And now you are nearing home again,   25
    Dears, home again;
No more, may be, to roam again
    As at that bygone time,
Which took you far away from us
    To stay from us;   30
Dawn, hold not long the day from us,
    But quicken it to prime!

THE SICK BATTLE-GOD*

I

In days when men found joy in war,
A God of Battles sped each mortal jar;
    The peoples pledged him heart and hand,
    From Israel's land to isles afar.

II

His crimson form, with clang and chime,   5
Flashed on each murk and murderous meeting-time,
    And kings invoked, for rape and raid,
    His fearsome aid in rune and rhyme.

III

On bruise and blood-hole, scar and seam,
On blade and bolt, he flung his fulgid beam: 10
    His haloes rayed the very gore,
    And corpses wore his glory-gleam.

---

25 O you'll be nearing home again, *K*   28 time,] ~ *MP, Hol.*   29 far]
all *MP*

THE SICK BATTLE-GOD. *Title* The Sick God *PP, CP19*
  1 found joy in] had joy of *PP*   2 God] *l.c. Hol.*   3 hand,] ~ *Hol.*

IV

Often an early King or Queen,
And storied hero onward, caught his sheen;
'Twas glimpsed by Wolfe, by Ney anon,   15
And Nelson on his blue demesne.

V

But new light spread. That god's gold nimb
And blazon have waned dimmer and more dim;
Even his flushed form begins to fade,
Till but a shade is left of him.   20

VI

That modern meditation broke
His spell, that penmen's pleadings dealt a stroke,
Say some; and some that crimes too dire
Did much to mire his crimson cloak.

VII

Yea, seeds of crescent sympathy   25
Were sown by those more excellent than he,
Long known, though long contemned till then—
The gods of men in amity.

VIII

Souls have grown seers, and thought outbrings
The mournful many-sidedness of things   30
With foes as friends, enfeebling ires
And fury-fires by gaingivings!

IX

He rarely gladdens champions now;
They do and dare, but tensely—pale of brow;
And would they fain uplift the arm   35
Of that weak form they know not how.

---

13 ⟨Duly the sworded British Queen,⟩ *Hol.*   14 hero] ⟨heroes⟩ *Hol.*   caught]
knew *PP*   sheen;] ⟨mien;⟩ *Hol.*   15 glimpsed] ⟨glimpsed⟩ ⟨eyed⟩
Hol.   by Ney anon,] ⟨and Wellington,⟩ ⟨Washington,⟩ *Hol.*   anon,] ∼ — *Hol.*
17 spread.] shone. *PP01 only*   22 penman's pleadings] ⟨rigid reasonings⟩ ⟨written
reasonings⟩ *Hol.*   25 crescent] crescive *PP, WE*   33 rarely gladdens]
scarce impassions *PP*   36 weak] faint *PP*

X

Yet wars arise, though zest grows cold;
Wherefore, at times, as if in ancient mould
   He looms, bepatched with paint and lath;
   But never hath he seemed the old!   40

XI

Let men rejoice, let men deplore,
The lurid Deity of heretofore
   Succumbs to one of saner nod;
   The Battle-god is god no more.

38 times, as if] whiles, as 'twere *PP*   39 bepatched] ⟨out-eked⟩ *Hol.*   paint]
⟨rag⟩ *Hol.*   42 lurid Deity] ⟨Power predominant⟩ *Hol.*   43 saner]
⟨newer⟩ ⟨nobler⟩ *Hol.*

POEMS OF PILGRIMAGE*

GENOA AND THE MEDITERRANEAN*

(*March*, 1887)

O epic-famed, god-haunted Central Sea,
Heave careless of the deep wrong done to thee
When from Torino's track I saw thy face first flash on me.

And multimarbled Genova the Proud,
Gleam all unconscious how, wide-lipped, up-browed,   5
I first beheld thee clad—not as the Beauty but the Dowd.

Out from a deep-delved way my vision lit
On housebacks pink, green, ochreous—where a slit
Shoreward 'twixt row and row revealed the classic blue
    through it.

And thereacross waved fishwives' high-hung smocks,   10
Chrome kerchiefs, scarlet hose, darned underfrocks;
Often since when my dreams of thee, O Queen, that frippery
    mocks:

Whereat I grieve, Superba! . . . Afterhours
Within Palazzo Doria's orange bowers
Went far to mend these marrings of thy soul-subliming
    powers.   15

But, Queen, such squalid undress none should see,
Those dream-endangering eyewounds no more be
Where lovers first behold thy form in pilgrimage to thee.

GENOA. 3 ⟨When from nigh Torino's trackway-term thy face first flashed on me.⟩ *Hol.*
4 Genova] Genoa *CP19 only*   9 classic] ⟨historic⟩ ⟨historied⟩ *Hol.*
12 Since when too oft *PP*

SHELLEY'S SKYLARK

(*The neighbourhood of Leghorn: March*, 1887)

Somewhere afield here something lies
In Earth's oblivious eyeless trust
That moved a poet to prophecies—
A pinch of unseen, unguarded dust:

The dust of the lark that Shelley heard,   5
And made immortal through times to be;—
Though it only lived like another bird,
And knew not its immortality.

Lived its meek life; then, one day, fell—
A little ball of feather and bone;   10
And how it perished, when piped farewell,
And where it wastes, are alike unknown.

Maybe it rests in the loam I view,
Maybe it throbs in a myrtle's green,
Maybe it sleeps in the coming hue   15
Of a grape on the slopes of yon inland scene.

Go find it, faeries, go and find
That tiny pinch of priceless dust,
And bring a casket silver-lined,
And framed of gold that gems encrust;   20

And we will lay it safe therein,
And consecrate it to endless time;
For it inspired a bard to win
Ecstatic heights in thought and rhyme.

SHELLEY'S SKYLARK. *MS1* BL Ashley MS 4164
   Headnote March] ⟨April⟩ *Hol.*   1 afield] ⟨around⟩ *Hol.*   5 that]
⟨that⟩ ⟨which⟩ *Hol.*   7 Though it] ⟨Yet which⟩ ⟨But which⟩ *Hol.*
14 throbs in a] ⟨tingles in⟩ *Hol.*   15 sleeps] ⟨swells⟩ *Hol.*   18 pinch]
speck *Hol.*   22 time;] ∼, *MS1*   24 Ecstatic heights] ⟨Heights
unsurpassed⟩ *Hol.*

IN THE OLD THEATRE, FIESOLE*

(*April*, 1887)

I traced the Circus whose gray stones incline
Where Rome and dim Etruria interjoin,
Till came a child who showed an ancient coin
That bore the image of a Constantine.

She lightly passed; nor did she once opine   5
How, better than all books, she had raised for me
In swift perspective Europe's history
Through the vast years of Cæsar's sceptred line.

For in my distant plot of English loam
'Twas but to delve, and straightway there to find   10
Coins of like impress. As with one half blind
Whom common simples cure, her act flashed home
In that mute moment to my opened mind
The power, the pride, the reach of perished Rome.

ROME

ON THE PALATINE*

(*April*, 1887)

We walked where Victor Jove was shrined awhile,
And passed to Livia's rich red mural show,
Whence, thridding cave and Criptoportico,
We gained Caligula's dissolving pile.

IN THE OLD THEATRE. 'Mr. Thomas Hardy's New Poems', *Academy*, 23 Nov. 1901
   3 came] ⟨neared⟩ *Hol.*   an] ⟨some⟩ *Hol.*   11 impress. *A, PPo2, WE, CP*]
⟨impress.⟩ ⟨gravure.⟩ impress. *Hol.*; gravure. *PPo1*   13 mute] ⟨brief⟩ *Hol.*
14 *A, PPo2, WE, CP*] ⟨The power, the pride, the reach⟩ ⟨The world-imprinting power⟩
The power, the pride, the reach, *Hol.*; The world-imprinting power *PPo1*

ROME: ON THE PALATINE. 4 pile.] ∼; *Hol.*

And each ranked ruin tended to beguile   5
The outer sense, and shape itself as though
It wore its marble gleams in pristine glow
Of scenic frieze and pompous peristyle.

When lo, swift hands, on strings nigh overhead,
Began to melodize a waltz by Strauss: 10
It stirred me as I stood, in Cæsar's house,
Raised the old routs Imperial lyres had led,

And blended pulsing life with lives long done,
Till Time seemed fiction, Past and Present one.

ROME

BUILDING A NEW STREET IN THE ANCIENT QUARTER*

(*April*, 1887)

These umbered cliffs and gnarls of masonry
Outskeleton Time's central city, Rome;
Whereof each arch, entablature, and dome
Lies bare in all its gaunt anatomy.

And cracking frieze and rotten metope   5
Express, as though they were an open tome
Top-lined with caustic monitory gnome;
'Dunces, Learn here to spell Humanity!'

And yet within these ruins' very shade
The singing workmen shape and set and join   10
Their frail new mansion's stuccoed cove and quoin
With no apparent sense that years abrade,
Though each rent wall their feeble works invade
Once shamed all such in power of pier and groin.

---

7 gleams in] hues, its *PP*; gleams, its *CP*   12 ⟨Raised the old routs Imperial viols had sped.⟩ ⟨Waked the old whirls Imperial lyres had led.⟩ *Hol.*

ROME: BUILDING A NEW STREET. *Title* Rome. Building a New Street in the Ancient Quarter. *Hol.*
    2 Time's central city,] ⟨the Mistress-city,⟩ *Hol.*   7 caustic] ⟨iterate⟩ *Hol.*
8 'Dunces] ⟨"Dunces,⟩ ⟨"Readers:⟩ *Hol.*   11 frail] ⟨gay⟩ *Hol.*

ROME

THE VATICAN: SALA DELLE MUSE*

(1887)

I sat in the Muses' Hall at the mid of the day,
And it seemed to grow still, and the people to pass away,
And the chiselled shapes to combine in a haze of sun,
Till beside a Carrara column there gleamed forth One.

She looked not this nor that of those beings divine,   5
But each and the whole—an essence of all the Nine;
With tentative foot she neared to my halting-place,
A pensive smile on her sweet, small, marvellous face.

'Regarded so long, we render thee sad?' said she.
'Not you,' sighed I, 'but my own inconstancy!   10
I worship each and each; in the morning one,
And then, alas! another at sink of sun.

'To-day my soul clasps Form; but where is my troth
Of yesternight with Tune: can one cleave to both?'
—'Be not perturbed,' said she. 'Though apart in fame,   15
As I and my sisters are one, those, too, are the same.'

—'But my love goes further—to Story, and Dance,
    and Hymn,
The lover of all in a sun-sweep is fool to whim—
Is swayed like a river-weed as the ripples run!'
—'Nay, wooer, thou sway'st not. These are but phases of one;   20

'And that one is I; and I am projected from thee,
One that out of thy brain and heart thou causest to be—
Extern to thee nothing. Grieve not, nor thyself becall,
Woo where thou wilt; and rejoice thou canst love at all!'

ROME: THE VATICAN. *Title* ⟨In⟩ Rome. / The Vatican. Sala delle Muse. *Hol.*
    5 looked not] was nor *PP*   9 thee] ⟨you⟩ *Hol.*   12 alas!] ∼, *Hol.*
sink of sun.] ⟨set of sun!⟩ *Hol.*   14 Tune:] ⟨Song:⟩ ⟨Sound⟩ Tune; *Hol.*
17 —But] But *Hol.*   love goes] loves go *PP*   Story,] ⟨Colour,⟩ *Hol.*
19 run!'] ∼!"— *Hol.*   20 —'Nay,] "Nay, *Hol.*   thou sway'st] ⟨you sway⟩
Hol.   wooer, *WE20, CP23, DCM4*] wight, *PP, WE12, CP19*   22 causest to]
⟨hast compassed to⟩ *Hol.*   24 all!'] ∼." *Hol.*

ROME

AT THE PYRAMID OF CESTIUS
NEAR THE GRAVES OF SHELLEY AND KEATS*

(1887)

Who, then, was Cestius,
And what is he to me?—
Amid thick thoughts and memories multitudinous
One thought alone brings he.

I can recall no word   5
Of anything he did;
For me he is a man who died and was interred
To leave a pyramid

Whose purpose was exprest
Not with its first design,   10
Nor till, far down in Time, beside it found their rest
Two countrymen of mine.

Cestius in life, maybe,
Slew, breathed out threatening;
I know not. This I know: in death all silently   15
He does a finer thing,

In beckoning pilgrim feet
With marble finger high
To where, by shadowy wall and history-haunted street,
Those matchless singers lie. . . .   20

—Say, then, he lived and died
That stones which bear his name
Should mark, through Time, where two immortal
            Shades abide;
It is an ample fame.

ROME: AT THE PYRAMID. *MS1* BL Ashley MS 4165
  Title ⟨In⟩ Rome. At the Pyramid of Cestius. / Near the Graves of Shelley and Keats. *Hol.*
Headnote (April, 1887) *Hol.*
  1 Who, then, was] ⟨Who was⟩ *Hol.*   7 a man] ⟨but one⟩ *Hol.*   10 with]
⟨in⟩ *Hol.*   12 mine.] ~. . . . *MS1*   14 Slew,] ⟨Slew,⟩ ⟨Scourged,⟩ *Hol.*
16 finer *CP, DCM4*] sweeter *Hol.*; kindlier *PP*; rarer *WE*   19 street,] ~ *Hol.*
23 mark,] ⟨point,⟩ *Hol.*

LAUSANNE*

In Gibbon's Old Garden: 11-12 p.m.

June 27, 1897

(The 110th anniversary of the completion of the *Decline and Fall* at the same hour and place)

A spirit seems to pass,
Formal in pose, but grave withal and grand:
He contemplates a volume in his hand,
And far lamps fleck him through the thin acacias.

Anon the book is closed,   5
With 'It is finished!' And at the alley's end
He turns, and when on me his glances bend
As from the Past comes speech—small, muted, yet composed.

'How fares the Truth now?—Ill?
—Do pens but slily further her advance?   10
May one not speed her but in phrase askance?
Do scribes aver the Comic to be Reverend still?

'Still rule those minds on earth
At whom sage Milton's wormwood words were hurled:
"*Truth like a bastard comes into the world*   15
Never without ill-fame to him who gives her birth"?'

ZERMATT*

To the Matterhorn

(*June-July,* 1897)

Thirty-two years since, up against the sun,
Seven shapes, thin atomies to lower sight,

LAUSANNE. *Title* ⟨At⟩ Lausanne. *Hol.*   *Headnote* anniversary . . . completion] *caps. Hol.*
  2 *WE, CP23*] grave and grand withal: *PP, CP19*   3 contemplates] ⟨glances from⟩ *Hol.*   a volume in his hand,] a volume stout and tall, *PP, CP19*; a writing in his hand, *WE*   5 book is *PP, CP, DCM1*] leaves are *WE*   7 when] soon *PP* bend] ∼; *PP*   8 As from the Past] And, as from earth, *PP*   speech—] ⟨words—⟩ *Hol.* 15 *world*] ∼, *Hol.*

ZERMATT. *Title* ⟨To the Matterhorn⟩ *Hol. table of contents*
  2 thin atomies to] ⟨scarce traceable by⟩ *Hol.*

Labouringly leapt and gained thy gabled height,
And four lives paid for what the seven had won.

They were the first by whom the deed was done,   5
And when I look at thee, my mind takes flight
To that day's tragic feat of manly might,
As though, till then, of history thou hadst none.

Yet ages ere men topped thee, late and soon
Thou didst behold the planets lift and lower;   10
Saw'st, maybe, Joshua's pausing sun and moon,
And the betokening sky when Cæsar's power
Approached its bloody end: yea, even that Noon
When darkness filled the earth till the ninth hour.

THE BRIDGE OF LODI*

(*Spring*, 1887)

I

When of tender mind and body
    I was moved by minstrelsy,
And that air 'The Bridge of Lodi'
    Brought a strange delight to me.

II

In the battle-breathing jingle   5
    Of its forward-footing tune
I could see the armies mingle,
    And the columns crushed and hewn

---

5 the deed] ⟨that deed⟩ *Hol.*   10 Thou didst behold] ⟨Thou'st watch'd each
⟨⟨night⟩⟩ ⟨⟨year⟩⟩ night⟩ *Hol.*; Thou watch'dst each night *PP*   11 Saw'st,
maybe,] Thou gleam'dst to *PP*   12 And the betokening] And brav'dst the tokening
PP   Cæsar's] Caesars *Hol.*   13 even] saw'st *PP*

THE BRIDGE OF LODI. *Headnote* (*Visited 23 April, 1887: Battle fought May 10, 1796*) *Hol.*
    2 minstrelsy,] ⟨melody,⟩ *Hol.*   3 air] strain *PP*   8 crushed] cleft *PP*,
CP19

III

On that far-famed spot by Lodi
    Where Napoleon clove his way   10
To his fame, when like a god he
    Bent the nations to his sway.

IV

Hence the tune came capering to me
    While I traced the Rhone and Po;
Nor could Milan's Marvel woo me   15
    From the spot englamoured so.

V

And to-day, sunlit and smiling,
    Here I stand upon the scene,
With its saffron walls, dun tiling,
    And its meads of maiden green,   20

VI

Even as when the trackway thundered
    With the charge of grenadiers,
And the blood of forty hundred
    Splashed its parapets and piers. . . .

VII

Any ancient crone I'd toady   25
    Like a lass in young-eyed prime,
Could she tell some tale of Lodi
    At that moving mighty time.

VIII

So, I ask the wives of Lodi
    For traditions of that day;   30
But alas! not anybody
    Seems to know of such a fray.

9 spot by] ⟨Bridge of⟩ *Hol.*   15 Marvel] ⟨*l.c.*⟩ *Hol.*   17 smiling,] ~ *Hol.*
23 blood of forty] ⟨Austrian twenty⟩ *Hol.*   24 Splashed its] ⟨Fell by⟩ *Hol.*
28 moving mighty] ⟨rare romantic⟩ *Hol.*   30 day;] ~ : *Hol.*   31 alas!]
~ ; *Hol.*

IX

And they heed but transitory
    Marketings in cheese and meat,
Till I judge that Lodi's story   35
    Is extinct in Lodi's street.

X

Yet while here and there they thrid them
    In their zest to sell and buy,
Let me sit me down amid them
    And behold those thousands die. . . .   40

XI

—Not a creature cares in Lodi
    How Napoleon swept each arch,
Or where up and downward trod he,
    Or for his outmatching march!

XII

So that wherefore should I be here,   45
    Watching Adda lip the lea,
When the whole romance to see here
    Is the dream I bring with me?

XIII

And why sing 'The Bridge of Lodi'
    As I sit thereon and swing,   50
When none shows by smile or nod he
    Guesses why or what I sing? . . .

XIV

Since all Lodi, low and head ones,
    Seem to pass that story by,
It may be the Lodi-bred ones   55
    Rate it truly, and not I.

44 outmatching] memorial *PP* march! *Hol.*, *CP23*] *cap! PP*, *CP19*; ~ . *WE*   45 here,]
~ *Hol.*   46 lip] ⟨lick⟩ *Hol.*   53 ⟨Since the Lodi borough head ones,⟩ *Hol.*

XV

Once engrossing Bridge of Lodi,
  Is thy claim to glory gone?
Must I pipe a palinody,
  Or be silent thereupon?   60

XVI

And if here, from strand to steeple,
  Be no stone to fame the fight,
Must I say the Lodi people
  Are but viewing war aright? . . .

XVII

Nay; I'll sing 'The Bridge of Lodi'—   65
  That long-loved, romantic thing,
Though none show by smile or nod he
  Guesses why and what I sing!

ON AN INVITATION TO THE UNITED STATES

I

My ardours for emprize nigh lost
Since Life has bared its bones to me,
I shrink to seek a modern coast
Whose riper times have yet to be;
Where the new regions claim them free   5
From that long drip of human tears
Which peoples old in tragedy
Have left upon the centuried years.

---

59 palinody,] ~ *Hol.*   64 war] crime *PP, WE*

ON AN INVITATION. *New York Times Saturday Review of Books and Art*, 21 Sept. 1901
   1 ardours] ardor *NYT*   emprize] surprise *NYT*   2 Life] *l.c. NYT* ⟨Since
Being showed its seams to me,⟩ *Hol.*   3 seek] see *NYT*   4 times have]
time has *NYT*   5 them] men *NYT*   7 ⟨Which nations old in agony⟩ *Hol.*
8 the] their *NYT*   ⟨Have shed elsewhere ⟨⟨these⟩⟩ ?some? thousand years.⟩ *Hol.*

II

For, wonning in these ancient lands,
Enchased and lettered as a tomb,   10
And scored with prints of perished hands,
And chronicled with dates of doom,
Though my own Being bear no bloom
I trace the lives such scenes enshrine,
Give past exemplars present room,   15
And their experience count as mine.

9 wonning] ⟨haunting⟩ *Hol.*   lands,] ∼ ⟨—⟩ *Hol.*   10 as] ⟨as⟩ ⟨like⟩ *Hol.*
13 Being] *l.c. NYT*; ⟨budding⟩ *Hol.*   14 scenes] spots *NYT*; ⟨spots⟩ *Hol.*
15 exemplars] examples *NYT*

MISCELLANEOUS POEMS

THE MOTHER MOURNS*

When mid-autumn's moan shook the night-time,
    And sedges were horny,
And summer's green wonderwork faltered
    On leaze and in lane,

I fared Yell'ham-Firs way, where dimly   5
    Came wheeling around me
Those phantoms obscure and insistent
    That shadows unchain.

Till airs from the needle-thicks brought me
    A low lamentation,   10
As though from a tree-god disheartened,
    Perplexed, or in pain.

And, heeding, it awed me to gather
    That Nature herself there
Was breathing in aërie accents,   15
    With dirgelike refrain,

Weary plaint that Mankind, in these late days,
    Had grieved her by holding
Her ancient high fame of perfection
    In doubt and disdain. . . .   20

—'I had not proposed me a Creature
    (She soughed) so excelling
All else of my kingdom in compass
    And brightness of brain

THE MOTHER MOURNS. 1 -autumn's] *cap. Hol.*   3 summer's] *cap. Hol.*
5 ⟨I went Yell'ham-Wood way,⟩ *Hol.*   9 needle-thicks] needle-boughs *WE12*
11 though from] 'twere of *PP*   15 aërie] ⟨Aeolic⟩ *Hol.*   16 With
dirgelike] ⟨A dirge-like⟩ *Hol.*; With dirgeful *PP*   17 Weary plaint] ⟨Setting forth⟩
Hol.   days,] ~ *Hol.*   21 Creature] ⟨*l.c.*⟩ *Hol.*   24 brain] ~, *Hol.*

'As to read my defects with a god-glance,   25
  Uncover each vestige
Of old inadvertence, annunciate
  Each flaw and each stain!

'My purpose went not to develop
  Such insight in Earthland;   30
Such potent appraisements affront me,
  And sadden my reign!

'Why loosened I olden control here
  To mechanize skywards,
Undeeming great scope could outshape in 35
  A globe of such grain?

'Man's mountings of mind-sight I checked not,
  Till range of his vision
Now tops my intent, and finds blemish
  Throughout my domain.   40

'He holds as inept his own soul-shell—
  My deftest achievement—
Contemns me for fitful inventions
  Ill-timed and inane:

'No more sees my sun as a Sanct-shape,   45
  My moon as the Night-queen,
My stars as august and sublime ones
  That influences rain:

'Reckons gross and ignoble my teaching,
  Immoral my story,   50
My love-lights a lure, that my species
  May gather and gain.

---

30 ⟨On Earth such in-seeing;⟩ *Hol.* 31 me,] ∼ *Hol.* 36 ⟨This narrow champaign!⟩ *Hol.* grain?] ∼! *Hol.* 39 Now tops] Has topped *PP, WE* finds] found *PP* 45 a Sanct-shape,] ⟨a God-shape,⟩ ⟨the Godhead,⟩ *Hol.* 46 Night-queen,] ⟨Sky-queen,⟩ *Hol.*

'"Give me", he has said, "but the matter
    And means the gods lot her,
My brain could evolve a creation   55
    More seemly, more sane."

—'If ever a naughtiness seized me
    To woo adulation
From creatures more keen than those crude ones
    That first formed my train—   60

'If inly a moment I murmured,
    "The simple praise sweetly,
But sweetlier the sage"—and did rashly
    Man's vision unrein,

'I rue it! . . . His guileless forerunners,   65
    Whose brains I could blandish,
To measure the deeps of my mysteries
    Applied them in vain.

'From them my waste aimings and futile
    I subtly could cover;   70
"Every best thing", said they, "to best purpose
    Her powers preordain."—

'No more such! . . . My species are dwindling,
    My forests grow barren,
My popinjays fail from their tappings,   75
    My larks from their strain.

'My leopardine beauties are rarer,
    My tusky ones vanish,
My children have aped mine own slaughters
    To quicken my wane.   80

'Let me grow, then, but mildews and mandrakes,
    And slimy distortions,
Let nevermore things good and lovely
    To me appertain;

56 sane."] ∼' . . . . *Hol.*   57 —'If] "If *Hol.*   61 ⟨a moment I⟩ ⟨I
momently⟩ *Hol.*   63 sweetlier] ⟨sweeter⟩ *Hol.*   72 preordain."—] ∼.'
Hol.   84 appertain;] ∼ ⟨!⟩; *Hol.*

'For Reason is rank in my temples,   85
    And Vision unruly,
And chivalrous laud of my cunning
    Is heard not again!'

'I SAID TO LOVE'

I said to Love,
'It is not now as in old days
When men adored thee and thy ways
    All else above;
Named thee the Boy, the Bright, the One   5
Who spread a heaven beneath the sun,'
    I said to Love.

I said to him,
'We now know more of thee than then;
We were but weak in judgment when,   10
    With hearts abrim,
We clamoured thee that thou would'st please
Inflict on us thine agonies,'
    I said to him.

I said to Love,   15
'Thou art not young, thou art not fair,
No elfin darts, no cherub air,
    Nor swan, nor dove
Are thine; but features pitiless,
And iron daggers of distress,'   20
    I said to Love.

---

86 Vision] ⟨Visions⟩ *Hol.*

'I SAID TO LOVE'. 3 ways] ~ — *CP19 only*   4 Set none above; *CP19 only*
5 Boy,] ⟨Blest,⟩ *Hol.*   6 heaven] *cap. Hol.*   17 No elfin darts,] ⟨Thou
hast no plume,⟩ *Hol.*; No faery darts, *PP*   19 ⟨But features wry and reasonless,⟩
Hol.   20 iron daggers] ⟨hidden vials⟩ *Hol.*

'Depart then, Love! . . .
—Man's race shall perish, threatenest thou,
Without thy kindling coupling-vow?
The age to come the man of now   25
        Know nothing of?—
We fear not such a threat from thee;
We are too old in apathy!
Mankind shall cease.—So let it be,'
        I said to Love.

A COMMONPLACE DAY*

The day is turning ghost,
And scuttles from the kalendar in fits and furtively,
        To join the anonymous host
Of those that throng oblivion; ceding his place, maybe,
        To one of like degree.   5

I part the fire-gnawed logs,
Rake forth the embers, spoil the busy flames, and lay the ends
        Upon the shining dogs;
Further and further from the nooks the twilight's stride
        extends,
        And beamless black impends.   10

Nothing of tiniest worth
Have I wrought, pondered, planned; no one thing asking
        blame or praise,
        Since the pale corpse-like birth
Of this diurnal unit, bearing blanks in all its rays—
        Dullest of dull-hued Days!   15

---

23 perish, threatenest thou,] end, does threaten thou? *PP*   24 *line om. PP*

A COMMONPLACE DAY. 2 kalendar] *cap. Hol.*   4 throng] ⟨crowd⟩ *Hol.*
7 forth] ⟨out⟩ *Hol.*   14 rays—] ∼ ⟨,⟩— *Hol.*   15 ⟨Flattest of flat-
pitched days.⟩ *Hol.*   Days!] ∼. *Hol.*

Wanly upon the panes
The rain slides as have slid since morn my colourless
     thoughts; and yet
Here, while Day's presence wanes,
And over him the sepulchre-lid is slowly lowered and set,
He wakens my regret.   20

Regret—though nothing dear
That I wot of, was toward in the wide world at his prime,
     Or bloomed elsewhere than here,
To die with his decease, and leave a memory sweet, sublime,
Or mark him out in Time. . . .   25

—Yet, maybe, in some soul,
In some spot undiscerned on sea or land, some impulse rose,
     Or some intent upstole
Of that enkindling ardency from whose maturer glows
The world's amendment flows;   30

But which, benumbed at birth
By momentary chance or wile, has missed its hope to be
     Embodied on the earth;
And undervoicings of this loss to man's futurity
May wake regret in me.   35

AT A LUNAR ECLIPSE

Thy shadow, Earth, from Pole to Central Sea,
Now steals along upon the Moon's meek shine
In even monochrome and curving line
Of imperturbable serenity.

16 ⟨Upon the window-panes⟩ *Hol.*   17 The] ⟨Slow⟩ *Hol.*   19 ⟨And on
him Time the sepulchre-lid begins to lower and set,⟩ *Hol.*   20 ⟨Something awakes
regret.⟩ *Hol.*   21 ⟨Though nought to stir emotion⟩ *Hol.*   23 ⟨Nor scene
on earth or ocean⟩ *Hol.*   24 ⟨Has lapsed with him, to write his memory sweet, sad,
or sublime,⟩ *Hol.*   29 enkindling ardency] ⟨fine luminescence⟩ *Hol.*   from
whose] ⟨from whose⟩ ⟨in its⟩ *Hol.*

AT A LUNAR ECLIPSE. 3 curving] ⟨arched⟩ *Hol.*

How shall I link such sun-cast symmetry   5
With the torn troubled form I know as thine,
That profile, placid as a brow divine,
With continents of moil and misery?

And can immense Mortality but throw
So small a shade, and Heaven's high human scheme   10
Be hemmed within the coasts yon arc implies?

Is such the stellar gauge of earthly show,
Nation at war with nation, brains that teem,
Heroes, and women fairer than the skies?

THE LACKING SENSE

SCENE.—*A sad-coloured landscape, Waddon Vale*

I

'O Time, whence comes the Mother's moody look amid her
    labours,
  As of one who all unwittingly has wounded where she
    loves?
Why weaves she not her world-webs to according lutes and
    tabors,
  With nevermore this too remorseful air upon her face,
    As of angel fallen from grace?'   5

II

—'Her look is but her story: construe not its symbols keenly:
  In her wonderworks yea surely has she wounded where she
    loves.
The sense of ills misdealt for blisses blanks the mien most
    queenly,
  Self-smitings kill self-joys; and everywhere beneath the sun
    Such deeds her hands have done.'   10

8 moil] ⟨moan⟩ *Hol.*   11 ⟨Be hemmed in what that puny arc implies?⟩ ⟨Be girded
by the coasts yon arc implies?⟩ *Hol.*   coasts] ⟨ball⟩ *Hol.*   13 brains] ⟨Thoughts⟩
Brains *Hol.*; Brains *PP01*

THE LACKING SENSE. 5 grace?'] ~?"— *Hol.*   7 yea surely] most truly *PP01, PP02*
8 ills misdealt for blisses blanks] ⟨ill outleaping good may quell⟩ ⟨ills misdealt for weals
may quell⟩ *Hol.*

III

—'And how explains thy Ancient Mind her crimes upon her
    creatures,
  These fallings from her fair beginnings, woundings where
    she loves,
Into her would-be perfect motions, modes, effects, and
    features
  Admitting cramps, black humours, wan decay, and baleful
    blights,
        Distress into delights?' 15

IV

—'Ah! knowest thou not her secret yet, her vainly veiled
    deficience,
  Whence it comes that all unwittingly she wounds the lives
    she loves?
That sightless are those orbs of hers?—which bar to her
    omniscience
  Brings those fearful unfulfilments, that red ravage through
    her zones
        Whereat all creation groans. 20

V

'She whispers it in each pathetic strenuous slow endeavour,
  When in mothering she unwittingly sets wounds on what
    she loves;
Yet her primal doom pursues her, faultful, fatal is she ever;
  Though so deft and nigh to vision is her facile finger-touch
    That the seers marvel much. 25

VI

'Deal, then, her groping skill no scorn, no note of malediction;
  Not long on thee will press the hand that hurts the lives it
    loves;

---

11 —'And] "And *Hol.*   thy Ancient] ⟨the Moveless⟩ *Hol.*   13 Into] ⟨Into⟩
⟨Against⟩ *Hol.*   14 Admitting] ⟨Distilling⟩ ⟨Inweaving⟩ *Hol.*   15 into]
⟨into⟩ ⟨amid⟩ *Hol.*   16 —'Ah!] "Ah— *Hol.*   knowest thou] ⟨know you⟩ *Hol.*;
know'st thou *PP, WE*   23 faultful,] ⟨faulty,⟩ ⟨flagrant,⟩ *Hol.*   25 much.]
~! *Hol.*   26 'Deal, then,] ⟨"Accord⟩ "Deal, then *Hol.*   27 press] ⟨bear⟩
Hol.

And while she plods dead-reckoning on, in darkness of
    affliction,
Assist her where thy creaturely dependence can or may,
    For thou art of her clay.'   30

TO LIFE

O Life with the sad seared face,
    I weary of seeing thee,
And thy draggled cloak, and thy hobbling pace,
    And thy too-forced pleasantry!

I know what thou would'st tell   5
    Of Death, Time, Destiny—
I have known it long, and know, too, well
    What it all means for me.

But canst thou not array
    Thyself in rare disguise,   10
And feign like truth, for one mad day,
    That Earth is Paradise?

I'll tune me to the mood,
    And mumm with thee till eve;
And maybe what as interlude   15
    I feign, I shall believe!

DOOM AND SHE

I

There dwells a mighty pair—
    Slow, statuesque, intense—
    Amid the vague Immense:
None can their chronicle declare,
    Nor why they be, nor whence.   5

28 plods] dares *PP, CP19*   29 can or may,] gives thee room, *PP01 only*
30 clay.] womb. *PP01 only*

TO LIFE. 16 feign] ⟨mumm⟩ *Hol.*

DOOM AND SHE. 2 intense—] ⟨immense—⟩ *Hol.*

II

Mother of all things made,
Matchless in artistry,
Unlit with sight is she.—
And though her ever well-obeyed
Vacant of feeling he.   10

III

The Matron mildly asks—
A throb in every word—
'Our clay-made creatures, lord,
How fare they in their mortal tasks
Upon Earth's bounded bord?   15

IV

'The fate of those I bear,
Dear lord, pray turn and view,
And notify me true;
Shapings that eyelessly I dare
Maybe I would undo.   20

V

'Sometimes from lairs of life
Methinks I catch a groan,
Or multitudinous moan,
As though I had schemed a world of strife,
Working by touch alone.'   25

VI

'World-weaver!' he replies,
'I scan all thy domain;
But since nor joy nor pain
It lies in me to recognize,
Thy questionings are vain.   30

6 made,] ~ *Hol.*   16 bear,] ⟨bare,⟩ *Hol.*   22 groan,] ~ *Hol*
24 strife,] ~ *Hol.*   26 'World-weaver!'] "~," *Hol.*   29 Doth my clear
substance recognize, *PP* recognize,] ~ *Hol.*   30 *WE, CP23*] I read thy realms
in vain. *PP, CP19*

VII

'World-weaver! what *is* Grief?
And what are Right, and Wrong,
And Feeling, that belong
To creatures all who owe thee fief?
Why is Weak worse than Strong?' . . .   35

VIII

—Unanswered, curious, meek,
She broods in sad surmise. . . .
—Some say they have heard her sighs
On Alpine height or Polar peak
When the night tempests rise.   40

THE PROBLEM*

Shall we conceal the Case, or tell it—
    We who believe the evidence?
Here and there the watch-towers knell it
    With a sullen significance,
Heard of the few who listen intently with strained and eager
        and reaching sense.   5

Hearts that are happiest hold not by it;
    Better we let, then, the old view reign;
Since there is peace in that, why decry it?
    Since there is comfort, why disdain?
Note not the pigment so long as the painting determines
        humanity's joy and pain!   10

31 Grief?] ⟨*l.c.,*⟩ ~?— *Hol.*   32 Wrong,] ~ ⟨?—⟩, *Hol.*   34 fief?] ~?—
Hol.   35 What worse is Weak than Strong?" . . . *PP*   36 —Unanswered,
WE, CP23] —Unlightened, *PP*; So, baffled, *CP19*   curious,] ⟨yearning,⟩ *Hol.*
38 Some say they] ⟨Times have I⟩ *Hol.*   39 ⟨On High-Stoy Hill or Pilsdon Peak⟩
⟨On Pilsdon Pen or Lewsdon Peak⟩ *Hol.*   peak] *cap. Hol.*   40 rise.] ~ ⟨!⟩. *Hol.*

THE PROBLEM. 1 Case,] ⟨truth⟩ *Hol.*   2 believe] ⟨have read⟩ *Hol.*   evidence?]
~?— *Hol.*   5 hearken intently and carry an eagerly upstrained sense. *PP, CP*
7 Better we hence let the old view reign; *CP19 only*   8 that,] it, *PP, WE*
10 *WE, CP20*] ⟨Never the substance, but ⟨⟨always⟩⟩ ever the seeming⟩ *Hol.*; Note not the
pigment the while that the painting *PP*; Note not the pigment, then, in that the painting
CP19 only

THE SUBALTERNS

I

'Poor wanderer,' said the leaden sky,
    'I fain would lighten thee,
But there are laws in force on high
    Which say it must not be.'

II

—'I would not freeze thee, shorn one,' cried   5
    The North, 'knew I but how
To warm my breath, to slack my stride;
    But I am ruled as thou.'

III

—'To-morrow I attack thee, wight,'
    Said Sickness. 'Yet I swear   10
I bear thy little ark no spite,
    But am bid enter there.'

IV

—'Come hither, Son,' I heard Death say;
    'I did not will a grave
Should end thy pilgrimage to-day,   15
    But I, too, am a slave!'

V

We smiled upon each other then,
    And life to me had less
Of that fell look it wore ere when
    They owned their passiveness.   20

THE SUBALTERNS. 'Mr. Thomas Hardy's New Poems', *Academy*, 23 Nov. 1901
    3 are *CP20, WE20*] be *PP, WE12, CP19*   16 slave!'] ~ ." *Hol.*   18 had
WE, CP20] wore *PP, CP19*   19 of that fell look *WE, CP23*] ⟨That drear contour⟩
Hol.; That fell contour *PP*; Of that fell guise *CP19*

THE SLEEP-WORKER

When wilt thou wake, O Mother, wake and see—
As one who, held in trance, has laboured long
By vacant rote and prepossession strong—
The coils that thou hast wrought unwittingly;

Wherein have place, unrealized by thee,   5
Fair growths, foul cankers, right enmeshed with wrong,
Strange orchestras of victim-shriek and song,
And curious blends of ache and ecstasy?—

Should that morn come, and show thy opened eyes
All that Life's palpitating tissues feel,   10
How wilt thou bear thyself in thy surprise?—

Wilt thou destroy, in one wild shock of shame,
Thy whole high heaving firmamental frame,
Or patiently adjust, amend, and heal?

THE BULLFINCHES

Brother Bulleys, let us sing
From the dawn till evening!—
For we know not that we go not
When to-day's pale pinions fold
Where they be that sang of old.   5

When I flew to Blackmoor Vale,
Whence the green-gowned faeries hail,
Roosting near them I could hear them
Speak of queenly Nature's ways,
Means, and moods,—well known to fays.   10

THE SLEEP-WORKER. 2 As] ⟨⟨⟩ As *Hol*.   3 vacant rote and] automatic *PP01, PP02*
strong—] ~ ⟨⟩⟩ — *Hol*.   5 have place,] ⟨commix,⟩ *Hol*.   7 orchestras]
⟨symphonies⟩ ⟨operas⟩ *Hol*.   9 morn *PP, CP, DCM4*] day *WE*   10 that
Life's] ⟨thy tribes'⟩ *Hol*.

THE BULLFINCHES. 4 ⟨Ere the day's white wings upfold⟩ *Hol*.   to-day's *WE, CP23*] the
day's *PP, CP19*   5 Where they be that *WE, CP23*] ⟨Where they be who⟩ *Hol*;
Unto those who *PP*; Where those be that *CP19*   old.] ~! *Hol*.   8 Roosting]
⟨Fruiting⟩ *Hol*.   9 queenly] Mother *Hol*.

All we creatures, nigh and far
(Said they there), the Mother's are;
Yet she never shows endeavour
To protect from warrings wild
Bird or beast she calls her child.

15

Busy in her handsome house
Known as Space, she falls a-drowse;
Yet, in seeming, works on dreaming,
While beneath her groping hands
Fiends make havoc in her bands.

20

How her hussif'ry succeeds
She unknows or she unheeds,
All things making for Death's taking!
—So the green-gowned faeries say
Living over Blackmoor way.

25

Come then, brethren, let us sing,
From the dawn till evening!—
For we know not that we go not
When to-day's pale pinions fold
Where they sleep that sang of old.

30

GOD-FORGOTTEN

I towered far, and lo! I stood within
The presence of the Lord Most High,
Sent thither by the sons of earth, to win
Some answer to their cry.

11 creatures,] ~ *Hol.*   nigh] ⟨near⟩ *Hol.*   far] ~, *Hol.*   13 shows] ⟨makes⟩ *Hol.*   17 falls] ⟨falls⟩ ⟨fell⟩ *Hol.*   18 in seeming,] ⟨⟨⟩ in seeming ⟨⟩⟩, *Hol.*   23 taking!] ~!.... *Hol.*   24 —So] So *Hol.*   26 brethren,] ⟨bulleys,⟩ *Hol.*   sing,] ~ *Hol.*   29 to-day's] the day's *PP, CP*   pale pinions fold] ⟨white wings upfold⟩ *Hol.*   30 ⟨Where they be⟩ *Hol.*; Unto those who *PP*; Where those be that *CP*

GOD-FORGOTTEN. 1 lo!] ~, *Hol.*   Most High,] ⟨*l.c.*⟩ *Hol.*   3 earth,] *cap. CP*

—'The Earth, sayest thou? The Human race?   5
    By Me created? Sad its lot?
Nay: I have no remembrance of such place:
    Such world I fashioned not.'—

—'O Lord, forgive me when I say
    Thou spakest the word that made it all.'—   10
'The Earth of men—let me bethink me. . . . Yea!
    I dimly do recall

'Some tiny sphere I built long back
    (Mid millions of such shapes of mine)
So named . . . It perished, surely—not a wrack   15
    Remaining, or a sign?

'It lost my interest from the first,
    My aims therefor succeeding ill;
Haply it died of doing as it durst?'—
    'Lord, it existeth still.'—   20

'Dark, then, its life! For not a cry
    Of aught it bears do I now hear;
Of its own act the threads were snapt whereby
    Its plaints had reached mine ear.

'It used to ask for gifts of good,   25
    Till came its severance self-entailed,
When sudden silence on that side ensued,
    And has till now prevailed.

'All other orbs have kept in touch;
    Their voicings reach me speedily: 30
Thy people took upon them overmuch
    In sundering them from me!

5 —'The] "The *Hol.*   sayest] say'st *PP, WE*   Human] ⟨*l.c.*⟩ *Hol.*   9 —'O
Lord,] "O Lord *Hol.*   10 *WE12, CP23*] spak'st the word, and mad'st *PP*; spakest
the word, and madest *CP19*; spakest the word and made *WE20*   13 built] framed
PP01, PP02   back] ~, *Hol.*

'And it is strange—though sad enough—
Earth's race should think that one whose call
Frames, daily, shining spheres of flawless stuff   35
    Must heed their tainted ball! . . .

'But sayest it is by pangs distraught,
And strife, and silent suffering?—
Sore grieved am I that injury should be wrought
    Even on so poor a thing!   40

'Thou shouldst have learnt that *Not to Mend*
For Me could mean but *Not to Know:*
Hence, Messengers! and straightway put an end
    To what men undergo.' . . .

Homing at dawn, I thought to see   45
One of the Messengers standing by.
—O childish thought! . . . Yet still it comes to me
    When trouble hovers nigh.

THE BEDRIDDEN PEASANT TO AN UNKNOWING GOD*

Much wonder I—here long low-laid—
    That this dead wall should be
Betwixt the Maker and the made,
    Between Thyself and me!

For, say one puts a child to nurse,   5
    He eyes it now and then
To know if better it is, or worse,
    And if it mourn, and when.

37 "But say'st thou 'tis *PP*   distraught,] ~ ⟨?⟩, *Hol.*   39 Sore] Deep *PP*
40 poor] ⟨mean⟩ *Hol.*   41 shouldst] should'st *PP*   42 Me] ⟨*l.c.*⟩ *Hol.*
43 put] ⟨make⟩ *Hol.*   44 undergo.' . . .] ~!" . . . *Hol.*   47 —O] Oh,
Hol. —Oh, *PP, CP*   thought! . . .] hope! . . . *Hol.*   still] oft *PP*; often *CP*
48 hovers] ⟨neighbours⟩ ⟨tokens⟩ ⟨borders⟩ *Hol.*

THE BEDRIDDEN PEASANT. 'Mr. Thomas Hardy's New Poems', *Academy*, 23 Nov. 1901
    Title ⟨A Peasant's Philosophy⟩ *Hol.*   Unknowing] Unknown *CP19 only*
    7 it is,] 'tis *PP*

But Thou, Lord, givest men their day
    In helpless bondage thus   10
To Time and Chance, and seem'st straightway
    To think no more of us!

That some disaster cleft Thy scheme
    And tore it wide apart,
So that no cry can cross, I deem;   15
    For Thou art mild of heart,

And wouldst not shape and shut us in
    Where voice can not be heard:
Plainly Thou meantest we should win
    Thy succour by a word.   20

Might but Thy sense flash down the skies
    Like man's from clime to clime,
Thou wouldst not let me agonize
    Through my remaining time;

But, seeing how much Thy creatures bear—   25
    Lame, starved, or maimed, or blind—
Wouldst heal the ills with quickest care
    Of me and all my kind. . . .

Since, making not these things to be,
    These things Thou dost not know,   30
I'll praise Thee as were shown to me
    The mercies Thou wouldst show!

---

9 giv'st us men our day *PP, CP23*; givest us men our day *CP19*   12 us!] ∼ . *Hol.*
13 cleft] ⟨maimed⟩ *Hol.*   scheme] ∼ , *Hol.*   14 it] us *A, PP, CP*
16 mild] broad *A*; ⟨broad⟩ *Hol.*   17 wouldst] would'st *A, PP*   19 'Tis
plain Thou meant'st that *A, PP*; Plainly Thou meant'st that *CP*   23 wouldst]
would'st *A, PP*   me] ⟨us⟩ *Hol.*   24 my] ⟨our⟩ *Hol.*   26 starved,]
⟨halt⟩ *Hol.*   27 Wouldst] Thou'dst *A, PP*   28 kind. . . .] ∼ . *A, PP, CP*
29 ⟨Sure, then, that Thou dost not make be⟩ *Hol.*; Then, since Thou mak'st not these
things be, *A, PP, CP*   30 ⟨These things, but such unknow,⟩ *Hol.*; But these things
dost not know, *A, PP, CP*   32 mercies] ⟨mercy⟩ *Hol.*   wouldst] would'st *A, PP*

BY THE EARTH'S CORPSE

I

'O Lord, why grievest Thou?—
Since Life has ceased to be
Upon this globe, now cold
As lunar land and sea,
And humankind, and fowl, and fur   5
Are gone eternally,
All is the same to Thee as ere
They knew mortality.'

II

'O Time,' replied the Lord,
'Thou readest me ill, I ween;   10
Were all *the same*, I should not grieve
At that late earthly scene,
Now blestly past—though planned by me
With interest close and keen!—
Nay, nay: things now are *not* the same   15
As they have earlier been.

III

'Written indelibly
On my eternal mind
Are all the wrongs endured
By Earth's poor patient kind,   20
Which my too oft unconscious hand
Let enter undesigned.
No god can cancel deeds foredone,
Or thy old coils unwind!

IV

'As when, in Noë's days,   25
I whelmed the plains with sea,

BY THE EARTH'S CORPSE. 2 Life] ⟨*l.c.*⟩ *Hol.*   5 *no commas Hol.*
10 readest] read'st *PP, WE*   16 ⟨As ere the world had been.⟩ *Hol.*
19 wrongs] ⟨pangs⟩ *Hol.*   24 coils] *cap. Hol.*   26 plains] ⟨world⟩ *Hol.*

So at this last, when flesh
And herb but fossils be,
And, all extinct, their piteous dust
Revolves obliviously,   30
That I made Earth, and life, and man,
It still repenteth me!'

MUTE OPINION*

I

I traversed a dominion
Whose spokesmen spake out strong
Their purpose and opinion
Through pulpit, press, and song.
I almost failed to note there   5
A large-eyed few, and dumb,
Who thought not as those thought there
That stirred the heat and hum.

II

When as a Shade, beholding
That land in lifetime trode,   10
To learn if its unfolding
Fulfilled its clamoured code,
I saw, in web unbroken,
Its history outwrought
Not as the loud had spoken,   15
But as the mute had thought.

MUTE OPINION. 'Mr. Thomas Hardy's New Poems', *Academy*, 23 Nov. 1901
    2 spokesmen] ⟨peoples⟩ ⟨people⟩ *Hol.*   spake] spoke *A*; ⟨spoke⟩ ⟨voiced⟩ ⟨gave⟩
Hol.   3 Their] ⟨Their⟩ ⟨Its⟩ *Hol.*   purpose] ⟨?purport?⟩ *Hol.*
4 press,] ⟨print,⟩ *Hol.*   5 I almost failed] I scarce had means *A, PP, CP*
9 When as] When, grown *A, PP, CP*   15 had] has *A, Hol.*   16 mute]
dumb *A, Hol.*

TO AN UNBORN PAUPER CHILD*

I

Breathe not, hid Heart: cease silently,
And though thy birth-hour beckons thee,
Sleep the long sleep:
The Doomsters heap
Travails and teens around us here,   5
And Time-wraiths turn our songsingings to fear.

II

Hark, how the peoples surge and sigh,
And laughters fail, and greetings die:
Hopes dwindle; yea,
Faiths waste away,   10
Affections and enthusiasms numb;
Thou canst not mend these things if thou dost come.

III

Had I the ear of wombèd souls
Ere their terrestrial chart unrolls,
And thou wert free   15
To cease, or be,
Then would I tell thee all I know,
And put it to thee: Wilt thou take Life so?

IV

Vain vow! No hint of mine may hence
To theeward fly: to thy locked sense   20
Explain none can
Life's pending plan:
Thou wilt thy ignorant entry make
Though skies spout fire and blood and nations quake.

TO AN UNBORN PAUPER CHILD. 'Mr. Thomas Hardy's New Poems', *Academy*, 23 Nov. 1901
    Title ⟨To an Unborn Child⟩ *Hol.*   *Epigraph* "She must go to the ⟨Union⟩ Union-
house to have her baby." ⟨*Casterbridge*⟩ *Petty Sessions. Hol.*
  2 thee,] ∼ *Hol.*   3 sleep:] ∼; *Hol.*   6 ⟨our songsingings⟩
⟨festivity⟩ *Hol.*   8 die:] ∼; *Hol.*   9 yea,] ∼ *Hol.*   11 numb;]
∼, *Hol.*   13 ear of wombèd] circuit of all *A*; ⟨circuit of all⟩ ⟨circuit of sealed⟩ *Hol.*
14 chart] ⟨page⟩ *Hol.*   22 pending] dismal *A, Hol.*

V

Fain would I, dear, find some shut plot   25
Of earth's wide wold for thee, where not
One tear, one qualm,
Should break the calm.
But I am weak as thou and bare;
No man can change the common lot to rare.   30

VI

Must come and bide. And such are we—
Unreasoning, sanguine, visionary—
That I can hope
Health, love, friends, scope
In full for thee; can dream thou wilt find   35
Joys seldom yet attained by humankind!

TO FLOWERS FROM ITALY IN WINTER

Sunned in the South, and here to-day;
—If all organic things
Be sentient, Flowers, as some men say,
What are your ponderings?

How can you stay, nor vanish quite   5
From this bleak spot of thorn,
And birch, and fir, and frozen white
Expanse of the forlorn?

Frail luckless exiles hither brought!
Your dust will not regain   10
Old sunny haunts of Classic thought
When you shall waste and wane;

---

26 wold] world *A*   30 No man can move the stony gods to spare! *A; variant line del.*
Hol.   32 sanguine,] ⟨fatuous,⟩ *Hol.*   35 thou wilt *CP, DCM4*] thou'lt *PP,*
WE, DCM3   36 seldom] ⟨seldom⟩ ⟨never⟩ *Hol.*   yet] ⟨here⟩ *Hol.*

TO FLOWERS FROM ITALY. 9 Frail] ⟨Poor⟩ *Hol.*   10 ⟨When you shall rot and rust,⟩
Hol.   12 ⟨Will never hold your dust,⟩ *Hol.*

But mix with alien earth, be lit
With frigid Boreal flame,
And not a sign remain in it
To tell man whence you came.

15

ON A FINE MORNING

I

Whence comes Solace?—Not from seeing
What is doing, suffering, being,
Not from noting Life's conditions,
Nor from heeding Time's monitions;
But in cleaving to the Dream,
And in gazing at the gleam
Whereby gray things golden seem.

5

II

Thus do I this heyday, holding
Shadows but as lights unfolding,
As no specious show this moment
With its iriséd embowment;
But as nothing other than
Part of a benignant plan;
Proof that earth was made for man.

10

February 1899.

TO LIZBIE BROWNE*

I

Dear Lizbie Browne,
Where are you now?
In sun, in rain?—
Or is your brow
Past joy, past pain,
Dear Lizbie Browne?

5

---

13 ⟨But alien icy precincts lit⟩ *Hol.*
Hol.

16 man] men *PP, WE*   came.] ~!

ON A FINE MORNING. 1 Not] ⟨*l.c.*⟩ *Hol.*
Hol.; irisèd *PP*; iridized *WE12*; iris-hued *CP*

11 iriséd *DCM1, WE20*] ⟨iridesced⟩

II

Sweet Lizbie Browne,
How you could smile,
How you could sing!—
How archly wile   10
In glance-giving,
Sweet Lizbie Browne!

III

And, Lizbie Browne,
Who else had hair
Bay-red as yours,   15
Or flesh so fair
Bred out of doors,
Sweet Lizbie Browne?

IV

When, Lizbie Browne,
You had just begun   20
To be endeared
By stealth to one,
You disappeared,
My Lizbie Browne!

V

Ay, Lizbie Browne,   25
So swift your life,
And mine so slow,
You were a wife
Ere I could show
Love, Lizbie Browne.   30

VI

Still, Lizbie Browne,
You won, they said,
The best of men
When you were wed. . . .
Where went you then,   35
O Lizbie Browne?

TO LIZBIE BROWNE. 7 Browne, *SP*] ~ *all other texts*   10 archly] ⟨you would⟩ *Hol.*
15 as] ⟨like⟩ *Hol.*

VII

Dear Lizbie Browne,
I should have thought,
'Girls ripen fast,'
And coaxed and caught   40
You ere you passed,
Dear Lizbie Browne!

VIII

But, Lizbie Browne,
I let you slip;
Shaped not a sign;   45
Touched never your lip
With lip of mine,
Lost Lizbie Browne!

IX

So, Lizbie Browne,
When on a day   50
Men speak of me
As not, you'll say,
'And who was he?'—
Yes, Lizbie Browne!

SONG OF HOPE

O sweet To-morrow!—
    After to-day
    There will away
This sense of sorrow.
Then let us borrow   5
Hope, for a gleaming
Soon will be streaming,
    Dimmed by no gray—
    No gray!

50 When] ⟨If⟩ *Hol.*

SONG OF HOPE. *Title* ⟨Young Hope/(Song.)⟩ *Hol.*
    8 ⟨Under the gray—⟩ *Hol.*   9 ⟨The gray!⟩ *Hol.*

While the winds wing us   10
Sighs from The Gone,
Nearer to dawn
Minute-beats bring us;
When there will sing us
Larks of a glory   15
Waiting our story
Further anon—
Anon!

Doff the black token,
Don the red shoon,   20
Right and retune
Viol-strings broken;
Null the words spoken
In speeches of rueing,
The night cloud is hueing,   25
To-morrow shines soon—
Shines soon!

THE WELL-BELOVED*

I went by star and planet shine
Towards my Dear's abode
At Jordon, there to make her mine
When the next noon-tide glowed.

I edged the ancient hill and wood   5
Beside the Ikling Way,
Near where the Pagan temple stood
In the world's earlier day.

And as I quick and quicker walked
On gravel and on green,   10
I sang to sky, and tree, or talked
Of her I called my queen.

THE WELL-BELOVED. 1 went] wayed *PP*   2 *WE, DCM3*] Towards the dear one's
home *PP, CP*   3 Jordon, *WE, DCM3*] Kingsbere, *PP, CP*   4 noon-tide
glowed. *WE, DCM3*] sun upclomb. *PP, CP*   7 Near] Nigh *PP, CP*

—'O faultless is her dainty form,
    And luminous her mind;
She is the God-created norm
    Of perfect womankind!'   15

A shape whereon one star-blink gleamed
    Slid softly to my side,
A woman's; and her motion seemed
    The motion of my bride.   20

And yet methought she'd drawn the while
    Adown the ancient leaze,
Where once were pile and peristyle
    For men's idolatries.

—'O maiden lithe and lone, what may   25
    Thy name and lineage be,
Who so resemblest by this ray
    My darling?—Art thou she?'

The Shape: 'Thy bride remains within
    Her father's grange and grove.'   30
—'Thou speakest rightly,' I broke in,
    'Thou art not she I love.'

—'Nay: though thy bride remains inside
    Her father's walls,' said she,
'The one most dear is with thee here,   35
    For thou dost love but me.'

Then I: 'But she, my only choice,
    Is now at Jordon Grove?'
Again her soft mysterious voice:
    'I am thy only Love.'   40

---

17 star-blink] ⟨star-mote⟩ *Hol.*   18 Slid softly to my side *WE*] Glode ⟨softly⟩
smoothly by my side, *Hol.*; Glode softly by my side, *PP, CP19*; Slid softly by my side, *CP23*
21 the while] erstwhile *PP, CP*   22 Adown] Out from *CP*   23 were]
⟨were⟩ ⟨stood⟩ *Hol.*   24 men's] Love's *CP19 only*   25 maiden] *cap. Hol.*
28 she?'] ∼?" ⟨—⟩ *Hol.*   29 The Shape: 'Thy] ⟨"Thy morrow's⟩ *Hol.*
Shape:] *l.c. Hol.*   30 grove.'] ∼." ⟨—⟩ *Hol.*   32 love.'] ∼." ⟨—⟩ *Hol.*
36 me.'] ∼."— *Hol.*   38 Jordon] Kingsbere *PP, CP*   40 Love.'] ∼."—
Hol.

Thus still she vouched, and still I said,
  'O sprite, that cannot be!' . . .
It was as if my bosom bled,
  So much she troubled me.

The sprite resumed: 'Thou hast transferred   45
  To her dull form awhile
My beauty, fame, and deed, and word,
  My gestures and my smile.

'O fatuous man, this truth infer,
  Brides are not what they seem;   50
Thou lovest what thou dreamest her;
  I am thy very dream!'

—'O then,' I answered miserably,
  Speaking as scarce I knew,
'My loved one, I must wed with thee   55
  If what thou say'st be true!'

She, proudly, thinning in the gloom:
  'Though, since troth-plight began,
I've ever stood as bride to groom,
  I wed no mortal man!'   60

Thereat she vanished by the lane
  Adjoining Budmouth town,
Near where, men say, once stood the Fane
  To Venus, on the Down.

—When I arrived and met my bride   65
  Her look was pinched and thin,
As if her soul had shrunk and died,
  And left a waste within.

---

52 dream!'] ~!" ⟨—⟩ *Hol.*   56 say'st] sayest *CP*   59 I've] I have
CP   60 man!'] ~." *Hol.*   61 lane] Cross *PP*   62 That, entering
Kingsbere town, *PP*; Adjoining Kingsbere town, *CP*   63 The two long lanes form,
near the fosse *PP*   64 ⟨Below the Camp and Down.⟩ *Hol.*; Below the faneless
Down. *PP*

HER REPROACH*

Con the dead page as 'twere live love: press on!
Cold wisdom's words will ease thy track for thee;
Aye, go; cast off sweet ways, and leave me wan
To biting blasts that are intent on me.

But if thy object Fame's far summits be,   5
Whose inclines many a skeleton overlies
That missed both dream and substance, stop and see
How absence wears these cheeks and dims these eyes!

It surely is far sweeter and more wise
To water love, than toil to leave anon   10
A name whose glory-gleam will but advise
Invidious minds to eclipse it with their own,

And over which the kindliest will but stay
A moment, musing, 'He, too, had his day!'

16 Westbourne Park Villas
1867.

THE INCONSISTENT

I say, 'She was as good as fair!'
    When standing by her mound;
'Such passing sweetness', I declare,
    'No longer treads the ground.'
I say, 'What living Love can catch   5
    Her bloom and bonhomie,
And what in later maidens match
    Her olden warmth to me!'

HER REPROACH. 1 love:] ~; *Hol.*   4 biting] ⟨howling⟩ *Hol.*   6 overlies]
o'erlies *PP*   7 stop] ~, *Hol.*   12 eclipse *WE, CP23*] quench *PP*; dull
CP19
    Place/date] Westbourne Park Villas, 1867. *PP, CP*

THE INCONSISTENT. 1 fair!'] ~," *PP, WE*   7 later] ⟨modern⟩ *Hol.*; newer *PP*;
recent *CP*

—There stands within yon vestry-nook
   Where bonded lovers sign,   10
Her name upon a faded book
   With one that is not mine.
To him she breathed the tender vow
   She once had breathed to me,
But yet I say, 'O Love, even now   15
   Would I had died for thee!'

A BROKEN APPOINTMENT*

   You did not come,
And marching Time drew on, and wore me numb.—
Yet less for loss of your dear presence there
Than that I thus found lacking in your make
That high compassion which can overbear   5
Reluctance for pure lovingkindness' sake
Grieved I, when, as the hope-hour stroked its sum,
   You did not come.

   You love not me,
And love alone can lend you loyalty;   10
—I know and knew it. But, unto the store
Of human deeds divine in all but name,
Was it not worth a little hour or more
To add yet this: Once you, a woman, came
To soothe a time-torn man; even though it be   15
   You love not me?

'BETWEEN US NOW'

   Between us now and here—
     Two thrown together
  Who are not wont to wear
    Life's flushest feather—

14 breathed] ⟨made⟩ *Hol.*   15 ⟨But yet "O Love," I whisper now⟩ *Hol.*
Love,] *l.c. PP*

A BROKEN APPOINTMENT. 6 Reluctance] ⟨Averseness⟩ *Hol.*   7 sum,] ~ *Hol.*
10 lend you] ⟨move your⟩ *Hol.*   14 Once you, *CP, DCM4*] ⟨Once, here,⟩ *Hol.*;
Once, you, *PP, WE*   15 time-torn] ⟨soul-sad⟩ *Hol.*

Who see the scenes slide past,5
The daytimes dimming fast,
Let there be truth at last,
Even if despair.

So thoroughly and long
Have you now known me,10
So real in faith and strong
Have I now shown me,
That nothing needs disguise
Further in any wise,
Or asks or justifies15
A guarded tongue.

Face unto face, then, say,
Eyes my own meeting,
Is your heart far away,
Or with mine beating?20
When false things are brought low,
And swift things have grown slow,
Feigning like froth shall go,
Faith be for aye.

'HOW GREAT MY GRIEF'

(Triolet)

How great my grief, my joys how few,
Since first it was my fate to know thee!
—Have the slow years not brought to view
How great my grief, my joys how few,
Nor memory shaped old times anew,5
Nor lovingkindness helped to show thee
How great my grief, my joys how few,
Since first it was my fate to know thee?

'BETWEEN US NOW'. 18 my] mine *PP, WE, CP19*

'HOW GREAT MY GRIEF'. *Title* ⟨His Love brings little Pleasure⟩ *Hol.*
1 few,] ∼ *Hol.* 2 thee!] ∼!— *Hol.* 3 —Have] Have *Hol.*
7 few,] ∼ *Hol.*

'I NEED NOT GO'*

I need not go
Through sleet and snow
To where I know
She waits for me;
She will tarry me there   5
Till I find it fair,
And have time to spare
From company.

When I've overgot
The world somewhat,   10
When things cost not
Such stress and strain,
Is soon enough
By cypress sough
To tell my Love   15
I am come again.

And if some day,
When none cries nay,
I still delay
To seek her side,   20
(Though ample measure
Of fitting leisure
Await my pleasure)
She will not chide.

What—not upbraid me   25
That I delayed me,
Nor ask what stayed me
So long? Ah, no !—
New cares may claim me,
New loves inflame me,   30
She will not blame me,
But suffer it so.

'I NEED NOT GO'. 4 me;] ~: *Hol.*   5 tarry] wait *PP, CP19*   11 cost not]
wear not *PP01 only*   16 I am] I'm *Hol.*   17 day,] ~ *Hol.*   18 cries]
⟨says⟩ *Hol.*   20 side,] ~ *Hol.*   26 I delayed] ⟨I have delayed⟩ *Hol.*
28 So long?] ⟨From her?⟩ *Hol.*   32 ⟨But let me go.⟩ *Hol.*   so.] ~ ⟨!⟩. *Hol.*

THE COQUETTE, AND AFTER*

(Triolets)

I

For long the cruel wish I knew
That your free heart should ache for me,
While mine should bear no ache for you;
For, long—the cruel wish!—I knew
How men can feel, and craved to view   5
My triumph—fated not to be
For long! . . . The cruel wish I knew
That your free heart should ache for me!

II

At last one pays the penalty—
The woman—women always do.   10
My farce, I found, was tragedy
At last!—One pays the penalty
With interest when one, fancy-free,
Learns love, learns shame. . . . Of sinners two
At last *one* pays the penalty—   15
The woman—women always do!

A SPOT

In years defaced and lost,
Two sat here, transport-tossed,
Lit by a living love
The wilted world knew nothing of:
Scared momently   5
By gaingivings,
Then hoping things
That could not be.

THE COQUETTE. 3 bear] ⟨feel⟩ *Hol.*

A SPOT. 2 transport-tossed,] ⟨trouble-tossed,⟩ *Hol.*   4 wilted] ⟨weltering⟩
⟨frigid⟩ *Hol.*

Of love and us no trace
Abides upon the place;   10
The sun and shadows wheel,
Season and season sereward steal;
Foul days and fair
Here, too, prevail,
And gust and gale   15
As everywhere.

But lonely shepherd souls
Who bask amid these knolls
May catch a faery sound
On sleepy noontides from the ground: 20
'O not again
Till Earth outwears
Shall love like theirs
Suffuse this glen!'

LONG PLIGHTED

Is it worth while, dear, now,
To call for bells, and sally forth arrayed
For marriage-rites—discussed, decried, delayed
So many years?

Is it worth while, dear, now,   5
To stir desire for old fond purposings,
By feints that Time still serves for dallyings,
Though quittance nears?

Is it worth while, dear, when
The day being so far spent, so low the sun,   10
The undone thing will soon be as the done,
And smiles as tears?

12 sereward] ⟨onward⟩ *Hol.*   17 lonely shepherd] ⟨supersubtle⟩ *Hol.*
18 bask] ⟨muse⟩ ⟨doze⟩ *Hol.*   20 On sleepy noontides] ⟨At eves of murmurings⟩
⟨On warm still noontides⟩ *Hol.*

LONG PLIGHTED. 6 desire] ⟨regrets⟩ *Hol.*   ⟨old vain purposings⟩ ⟨fond once-hoped-for
things⟩ *Hol.*   purposings,] ~ *Hol.*   8 Though] ⟨When⟩ *Hol.*

Is it worth while, dear, when
Our cheeks are worn, our early brown is gray;
When, meet or part we, none says yea or nay,   15
   Or heeds, or cares?

Is it worth while, dear, since
We still can climb old Yell'ham's wooded mounds
Together, as each season steals its rounds
   And disappears?   20

Is it worth while, dear, since
As mates in Mellstock churchyard we can lie,
Till the last crash of all things low and high
   Shall end the spheres?

THE WIDOW BETROTHED*

I passed the lodge and avenue
   To her fair tenement,
And sunset on her window-panes
   Reflected our intent.

The creeper on the gable nigh   5
   Was fired to more than red,
And when I came to halt thereby,
   'Bright as my joy!' I said.

Of late days it had been her aim
   To meet me in the hall;   10
Now at my footsteps no one came,
   And no one to my call.

---

18 ⟨We still can roam in Yell'ham, climb the mounds⟩ *Hol.*   19 Together,] ⟨Of
Egdon,⟩ *Hol.*   steals] ⟨glides⟩ *Hol.*   22 lie,] ~ *Hol.*

THE WIDOW BETROTHED. *Title* The Widow *PP*
   1 By Mellstock Lodge and Avenue *PP*   2 Towards her door I went, *PP*

Again I knocked, and tardily
   An inner tread was heard,
And I was shown her presence then   15
   With a mere answering word.

She met me, and but barely took
   My proffered warm embrace;
Preoccupation weighed her look,
   And hardened her sweet face.   20

'To-morrow—could you—would you call?
   Abridge your present stay?
My child is ill—my one, my all!—
   And can't be left to-day.'

And then she turns, and gives commands   25
   As I were out of sound,
Or were no more to her and hers
   Than any neighbour round. . . .

—As maid I loved her; but one came
   And pleased, and coaxed, and wooed,   30
And when in time he wedded her
   I deemed her gone for good.

He won, I lost her; and my loss
   I bore I know not how;
But I do think I suffered then   35
   Less wretchedness than now.

For Time, in taking him, unclosed
   An unexpected door
Of bliss for me, which grew to seem
   Far surer than before. . . .   40

14 tread] step *PP*   16 a mere] scarce an *PP*   21 would you call?] ⟨could
you come?⟩ *Hol.*   22 ⟨I hardly now can stay.⟩ *Hol.*   Abridge] Make brief *PP*;
Shorten *WE*   23 ⟨My child has sickened—and I ⟨⟨would⟩⟩ must⟩ *Hol.*
24 ⟨Fain not leave him to-day!"⟩ ⟨Not leave him lone to-day!"⟩ *Hol.*   to-day.'] ~!"
Hol.   25 commands] ⟨command⟩ *Hol.*   29 loved] wooed *PP*   but]
cap. Hol.   30 And coaxed her heart away, *PP*   32 good.] aye. *PP*
34 know] knew *Hol.*   37 unclosed] had oped *PP*

Yet in my haste I overlooked
  When secondly I sued
That then, as not at first, she had learnt
  The call of motherhood. . . .

Her word is steadfast, and I know   45
  How firmly pledged are we:
But a new love-claim shares her since
  She smiled as maid on me!

AT A HASTY WEDDING

(Triolet)

If hours be years the twain are blest,
For now they solace swift desire
By bonds of every bond the best,
If hours be years. The twain are blest
Do eastern stars slope never west,   5
Nor pallid ashes follow fire:
If hours be years the twain are blest,
For now they solace swift desire.

THE DREAM-FOLLOWER

A dream of mine flew over the mead
  To the halls where my old Love reigns;
And it drew me on to follow its lead:
  And I stood at her window-panes;

41-4 *om. PP*   46 How firmly pledged] ⟨That plighted fast⟩ *Hol.*; That plighted firm *PP*; That firmly pledged *WE*   47 ⟨But she has found ⟨⟨new⟩⟩ ⟨⟨fresh⟩⟩ new interests since⟩ *Hol.*; But she has caught new love-calls since *PP*

AT A HASTY WEDDING. 'A Changed Man', *Sphere*, 21 Apr. 1900
  3 By lifelong ties that tether zest *S*   5 stars] suns *S*

THE DREAM-FOLLOWER. 4 -panes;] ∼: *Hol.*

And I saw but a thing of flesh and bone   5
  Speeding on to its cleft in the clay;
And my dream was scared, and expired on a moan,
  And I whitely hastened away.

HIS IMMORTALITY*

I

I saw a dead man's finer part
Shining within each faithful heart
Of those bereft. Then said I: 'This must be
  His immortality.'

II

I looked there as the seasons wore,   5
And still his soul continuously bore
A life in theirs. But less its shine excelled
  Than when I first beheld.

III

His fellow-yearsmen passed, and then
In later hearts I looked for him again;   10
And found him—shrunk, alas! into a thin
  And spectral mannikin.

IV

Lastly I ask—now old and chill—
If aught of him remain unperished still;
And find, in me alone, a feeble spark,   15
  Dying amid the dark.

February 1899.

8 whitely] ⟨palely⟩ *Hol.*

HIS IMMORTALITY. 'Mr. Thomas Hardy's New Poems', *Academy*, 23 Nov. 1901
  3 must] ⟨must⟩ ⟨may⟩ *Hol.*   5 I looked there on a later day, *A*; ⟨*variant line del.*⟩ *Hol.*   6 And still his soul outshaped, as when in clay, *A*; *variant line del. Hol.*
bore] upbore *PP*   7 A life] Its life *A*, *PP*   11 alas!] ~, *Hol.*
13 old] aged *A*; ⟨aged⟩ *Hol.*

THE TO-BE-FORGOTTEN*

I

I heard a small sad sound,
And stood awhile among the tombs around:
'Wherefore, old friends,' said I, 'are you distrest,
     Now, screened from life's unrest?'

II

     —'O not at being here;
But that our future second death is near;   5
When, with the living, memory of us numbs,
     And blank oblivion comes!

III

     'These, our sped ancestry,
Lie here embraced by deeper death than we;   10
Nor shape nor thought of theirs can you descry
     With keenest backward eye.

IV

     'They count as quite forgot;
They are as men who have existed not;
Theirs is a loss past loss of fitful breath;   15
     It is the second death.

V

     'We here, as yet, each day
Are blest with dear recall; as yet, can say
We hold in some soul loved continuance
     Of shape and voice and glance.   20

THE TO-BE-FORGOTTEN. *Headnote* ⟨(In Stourcastle Churchyard.)⟩ *Hol.*   *Epigraph*
⟨"Neither have they any more a reward, for the memory of them is forgotten."⟩ *Hol.*
    1 small] ⟨thin⟩ *Hol.*   2 among] amid *PP*   3 you] ye *PP*
4 unrest?] ~?"— *Hol.*   6 near;] drear; *PP*   9 "Those who our
⟨forbears⟩ grandsires be *Hol.*; "Those who our grandsires be *PP, WE*   11 can you]
canst thou *PP*   thought of theirs] ⟨sound of them⟩ *Hol.*   12 keenest backward]
⟨spirit-ear or⟩ *Hol.*   13 count] bid *PP*   18 can say] alway *PP*
19 In some soul hold a loved continuance *PP*

VI

'But what has been will be—
First memory, then oblivion's swallowing sea;
Like men foregone, shall we merge into those
　　Whose story no one knows.

VII

'For which of us could hope   25
To show in life that world-awakening scope
Granted the few whose memory none lets die,
　　But all men magnify?

VIII

'We were but Fortune's sport;
Things true, things lovely, things of good report   30
We neither shunned nor sought . . . We see our bourne,
　　And seeing it we mourn.'

WIVES IN THE SERE

I

Never a careworn wife but shows,
　　If a joy suffuse her,
Something beautiful to those
　　Patient to peruse her,
Some one charm the world unknows   5
　　Precious to a muser,
Haply what, ere years were foes,
　　Moved her mate to choose her.

---

22 swallowing] turbid *PP*   23 men foregone,] ⟨friends before,⟩ *Hol.*   shall we merge into] we join us unto *PPo1, PPo2*   24 story] ⟨earthtime⟩ *Hol.*
　　Date ⟨Feb. 9. ⟨⟨?1889?⟩⟩ 1899?⟩ *Hol.*

WIVES IN THE SERE. *Tatler*, 31 July 1901. *MS1* (*T*) Bancroft
　　4 her,] ~— *MS1, T*   5 unknows] ~, *MS1, T, Hol.*   6 muser,] ~;
MS1, T

II

But, be it a hint of rose
    That an instant hues her,   10
Or some early light or pose
    Wherewith thought renews her—
Seen by him at full, ere woes
    Practised to abuse her—
Sparely comes it, swiftly goes,   15
    Time again subdues her.

THE SUPERSEDED

I

As newer comers crowd the fore,
    We drop behind.
—We who have laboured long and sore
    Times out of mind,
And keen are yet, must not regret   5
    To drop behind.

II

Yet there are some of us who grieve
    To go behind;
Staunch, strenuous souls who scarce believe
    Their fires declined,
And know none spares, remembers, cares   10
    Who go behind.

III

'Tis not that we have unforetold
    The drop behind;
We feel the new must oust the old   15
    In every kind;
But yet we think, must we, must *we*,
    Too, drop behind?

12 her—] ~ ⟨,⟩— *Hol.*   14 her—] ~ ⟨,⟩— *Hol.*

THE SUPERSEDED. *May Book.* Compiled by Mrs Aria in aid of Charing Cross Hospital (London: 1901)
    1 fore,] ~ *MB, Hol.*   2 behind.] ~.... *MB, Hol.*   3 —We] We *MB, Hol.*   7 some of us *WE, CP23*] of us some *MB, PP, CP19*   11 cares, remembers, spares *MB, PP*   16 kind;] ~, *MB, Hol.*

AN AUGUST MIDNIGHT

I

A shaded lamp and a waving blind,
And the beat of a clock from a distant floor:
On this scene enter—winged, horned, and spined—
A longlegs, a moth, and a dumbledore;
While 'mid my page there idly stands   5
A sleepy fly, that rubs its hands . . .

II

Thus meet we five, in this still place,
At this point of time, at this point in space.
—My guests besmear my new-penned line,
Or bang at the lamp and fall supine.   10
'God's humblest, they!' I muse. Yet why?
They know Earth-secrets that know not I.

Max Gate, 1899.

THE CAGED THRUSH FREED AND HOME AGAIN

(Villanelle)

'Men know but little more than we,
Who count us least of things terrene,
How happy days are made to be!

'Of such strange tidings what think ye,
O birds in brown that peck and preen?   5
Men know but little more than we!

'When I was borne from yonder tree
In bonds to them, I hoped to glean
How happy days are made to be,

AN AUGUST MIDNIGHT. 1 lamp] ~, *Hol.*   5 'mid] mid *Hol.*   9 —My] My
Hol.   besmear] parade *PP, WE*   line,] ink, *PP*   10 ⟨Or bang at the lamp,
and whirl, and sink.⟩ *Hol.*; Or bang at the lamp-glass, whirl, and sink. *PP*; Or bang at the
lamp, and sink supine. *WE*   11 ⟨Life's meanest creatures they. —Yet why?⟩
Hol.   muse.] ⟨think⟩ muse.— *Hol.*   12 ⟨earth-secrets⟩ ⟨life-secrets⟩
earth-secrets *Hol.*

THE CAGED THRUSH FREED. 4 ye,] ~ *Hol.*   5 that] ⟨who⟩ *Hol.*

'And want and wailing turned to glee;   10
Alas, despite their mighty mien
Men know but little more than we!

'They cannot change the Frost's decree,
They cannot keep the skies serene;
How happy days are made to be   15

'Eludes great Man's sagacity
No less than ours, O tribes in treen!
Men know but little more than we
How happy days are made to be.'

BIRDS AT WINTER NIGHTFALL*

(Triolet)

Around the house the flakes fly faster,
And all the berries now are gone
From holly and cotoneaster
Around the house. The flakes fly!—faster
Shutting indoors that crumb-outcaster   5
We used to see upon the lawn
Around the house. The flakes fly faster,
And all the berries now are gone!

Max Gate. 1900.

THE PUZZLED GAME-BIRDS*

(Triolet)

They are not those who used to feed us
When we were young—they cannot be—
These shapes that now bereave and bleed us?
They are not those who used to feed us,

11 Alas,] ~! *Hol.*

BIRDS AT WINTER NIGHTFALL. *Place all texts*   *Date DCM1 only*

THE PUZZLED GAME-BIRDS. *Title* The Battue *WE*
4 us,] ~,— *Hol., PP, WE*

For did we then cry, they would heed us.   5
—If hearts can house such treachery
They are not those who used to feed us
When we were young—they cannot be!

WINTER IN DURNOVER FIELD*

SCENE.—*A wide stretch of fallow ground recently sown with wheat, and frozen to iron hardness. Three large birds walking about thereon, and wistfully eyeing the surface. Wind keen from northeast: sky a dull grey.*

(Triolet)

Rook.—Throughout the field I find no grain;
  The cruel frost encrusts the cornland!
Starling.—Aye: patient pecking now is vain
  Throughout the field, I find . . .
Rook.—   No grain!
Pigeon.—Nor will be, comrade, till it rain,   5
  Or genial thawings loose the lorn land
  Throughout the field.
Rook.—   I find no grain:
  The cruel frost encrusts the cornland!

THE LAST CHRYSANTHEMUM

Why should this flower delay so long
  To show its tremulous plumes?
Now is the time of plaintive robin-song,
  When flowers are in their tombs.

Through the slow summer, when the sun   5
  Called to each frond and whorl
That all he could for flowers was being done,
  Why did it not uncurl?

5 〈And would, at least, fair terms concede us?—〉 *Hol.*; For would they not fair terms concede us? *PP, WE* 6 —If] 〈If〉 *Hol.*

WINTER IN DURNOVER FIELD. 5 be,] ~ *Hol.*

THE LAST CHRYSANTHEMUM. 5 slow] 〈long〉 *Hol.*

It must have felt that fervid call
Although it took no heed,   10
Waking but now, when leaves like corpses fall,
And saps all retrocede.

Too late its beauty, lonely thing,
The season's shine is spent,
Nothing remains for it but shivering   15
In tempests turbulent.

Had it a reason for delay,
Dreaming in witlessness
That for a bloom so delicately gay
Winter would stay its stress?   20

—I talk as if the thing were born
With sense to work its mind;
Yet it is but one mask of many worn
By the Great Face behind.

THE DARKLING THRUSH*

I leant upon a coppice gate
When Frost was spectre-gray,
And Winter's dregs made desolate
The weakening eye of day.
The tangled bine-stems scored the sky   5
Like strings of broken lyres,
And all mankind that haunted nigh
Had sought their household fires.

The land's sharp features seemed to be
The Century's corpse outleant,   10
His crypt the cloudy canopy,
The wind his death-lament.

20 stress?] ∼?. . . . *Hol.*   21 —I] I *Hol.*   22 mind;] ∼, *Hol.*
23 Yet it is] ⟨Alas, 'tis⟩ ⟨When it is⟩ *Hol.*

THE DARKLING THRUSH. *Graphic*, 29 Dec. 1900. *MS1* (*G*) Adams
  Title By the Century's Deathbed *G*
  1 coppice] paddock *G*   2 Frost was] shades were *G*   5 bine-stems]
twig-lines *MS1*   6 of *WE, CP23*] from *PP, CP19*   11 His] Its *MS1*
12 his] its *MS1*

The ancient pulse of germ and birth
   Was shrunken hard and dry,
And every spirit upon earth   15
   Seemed fervourless as I.

At once a voice arose among
   The bleak twigs overhead
In a full-hearted evensong
   Of joy illimited;   20
An aged thrush, frail, gaunt, and small,
   In blast-beruffled plume,
Had chosen thus to fling his soul
   Upon the growing gloom.

So little cause for carolings   25
   Of such ecstatic sound
Was written on terrestrial things
   Afar or nigh around,
That I could think there trembled through
   His happy good-night air   30
Some blessed Hope, whereof he knew
   And I was unaware.

31 December 1900.

THE COMET AT YELL'HAM*

I

It bends far over Yell'ham Plain,
   And we, from Yell'ham Height,
Stand and regard its fiery train,
   So soon to swim from sight.

---

14 Was shrunken, hard, and dry, *MS1, G*   16 fervourless] ⟨promiseless⟩
morrowless *MS1*   17 arose *WE, CP23*] outburst *PP*; burst forth *CP19*
20 illimited;] ∼. *MS1, G*   21 gaunt,] thin, *G*
   Date *DCM3*] *om. G*; The Century's End, ⟨1899.⟩ 1900. *Hol.*; *December* 1900 *PP, CP,*
WE

THE COMET AT YELL'HAM. *Title* The Comet at Yalbury or Yell'ham *PP, WE, CP19*

II

It will return long years hence, when   5
    As now its strange swift shine
Will fall on Yell'ham; but not then
    On face of mine or thine.

MAD JUDY

When the hamlet hailed a birth
    Judy used to cry:
When she heard our christening mirth
    She would kneel and sigh.
She was crazed, we knew, and we   5
Humoured her infirmity.

When the daughters and the sons
    Gathered them to wed,
And we like-intending ones
    Danced till dawn was red,
She would rock and mutter, 'More   10
Comers to this stony shore!'

When old Headsman Death laid hands
    On a babe or twain,
She would feast, and by her brands
    Sing her songs again.   15
What she liked we let her do,
Judy was insane, we knew.

A WASTED ILLNESS

(Overheard)

Through vaults of pain,
Enribbed and wrought with groins of ghastliness,
I passed, and garish spectres moved my brain
    To dire distress.

8 On that sweet ⟨face⟩ form of thine. *Hol.*; On that sweet form of thine. *PP, CP*

MAD JUDY. 6 infirmity.] ⟨sad fantasy.⟩ *Hol.*; aberrancy. *PP01, PP02*   12 stony]
⟨sunless⟩ *Hol.*   14 babe or twain,] ⟨neighbour swain,⟩ *Hol.*

A WASTED ILLNESS. *Headnote WE20*

And hammerings,   5
And quakes, and shoots, and stifling hotness, blent
With webby waxing things and waning things
        As on I went.

        'Where lies the end
To this foul way?' I asked with weakening breath.   10
Thereon ahead I saw a door extend—
        The door to Death.

        It loomed more clear:
'At last!' I cried. 'The all-delivering door!'
And then, I knew not how, it grew less near   15
        Than theretofore.

        And back slid I
Along the galleries by which I came,
And tediously the day returned, and sky,
        And life—the same.   20

        And all was well:
Old circumstance resumed its former show,
And on my head the dews of comfort fell
        As ere my woe.

        I roam anew,   25
Scarce conscious of my late distress. . . . And yet
Those backward steps to strength I cannot view
        Without regret.

        For that dire train
Of waxing shapes and waning, passed before,   30
And those grim chambers, must be ranged again
        To reach that door.

---

12 Death] *l.c. Hol.*, *PP*   23 comfort] ⟨kindness⟩ *Hol.*   27 to strength]
through pain *PP*   31 chambers] aisles *PP*   ranged] traversed *PP*

A MAN

(In Memory of H. of M.)

I

In Casterbridge there stood a noble pile,
Wrought with pilaster, bay, and balustrade
In tactful times when shrewd Eliza swayed.—
    On burgher, squire, and clown
It smiled the long street down for near a mile.   5

II

But evil days beset that domicile;
The stately beauties of its roof and wall
Passed into sordid hands. Condemned to fall
    Were cornice, quoin, and cove,
And all that art had wove in antique style.   10

III

Among the hired dismantlers entered there
One till the moment of his task untold.
When charged therewith he gazed, and answered bold:
    'Be needy I or no,
I will not help lay low a house so fair!   15

IV

'Hunger is hard. But since the terms be such—
No wage, or labour stained with the disgrace
Of wrecking what our age cannot replace
    To save its tasteless soul—
I'll do without your dole. Life is not much!'   20

V

Dismissed with sneers he backed his tools and went,
And wandered workless; for it seemed unwise
To close with one who dared to criticize
    And carp on points of taste:
Rude men should work where placed, and be content.   25

A MAN. 2 balustrade] ~, *Hol.*   6 domicile;] ~, *Hol.*   10 in] ⟨of⟩ *Hol.*
12 untold.] ~; *Hol.*   13 When] Being *Hol.*   answered] ⟨spoke out⟩ *Hol.*
16 hard.] ⟨keen.⟩ *Hol.*   be] ⟨are⟩ *Hol.*   25 To work where they were placed
rude men were meant. *PP, WE*

VI

Years whiled. He aged, sank, sickened, and was not:
And it was said, 'A man intractable
And curst is gone.' None sighed to hear his knell,
  None sought his churchyard-place;
His name, his rugged face, were soon forgot.   30

VII

The stones of that fair hall lie far and wide,
And but a few recall its ancient mould;
Yet when I pass the spot I long to hold
  As truth what fancy saith:
'His protest lives where deathless things abide!'   35

THE DAME OF ATHELHALL*

I

'Dear! Shall I see thy face', she said,
  'In one brief hour?
And away with thee from a loveless bed
To a far-off sun, to a vine-wrapt bower,
And be thine own unseparated,   5
  And challenge the world's white glower?'

II

She quickened her feet, and met him where
  They had predesigned:
And they clasped, and mounted, and cleft the air
Upon whirling wheels; till the will to bind   10
Her life with his made the moments there
  Efface the years behind.

---

26 whiled.] ⟨passed⟩ wore *Hol.*   27 intractable] ⟨untractable⟩ *Hol.*
28 curst] ⟨gross⟩ *Hol.*   34 As] ⟨It⟩ *Hol.*

THE DAME OF ATHELHALL. *Title* ⟨The Return to Athels-Hall⟩ *Hol. table of contents*
  1 'Dear!] "SOUL! *PP*   4 vine-wrapt] ⟨vine-laced⟩ *Hol.*

III

Miles slid, and the port appeared in view
   As they sped on;
When slipping its bond the bracelet flew   15
From her fondled arm. Replaced anon,
Its cameo of the abjured one drew
   Her musings thereupon.

IV

The gaud with his image once had been
   A gift from him: 20
And so it was that its carving keen
Refurbished memories wearing dim,
Which set in her soul a twinge of teen,
   And a tear on her lashes' brim.

V

'I may not go!' she at length outspake,   25
   'Thoughts call me back—
I would still lose all for your dear, true sake;
My heart is thine, friend! But my track
Home—home to Athel I must take
   To hinder household wrack!'   30

VI

He was wroth. And they parted, weak and wan;
   And he left the shore;
His ship diminished, was low, was gone;
And she heard in the waves as the daytide wore,
And read in the leer of the sun that shone,   35
   That they parted for evermore.

---

13 ⟨Mile upon mile, two, three-score grew⟩ *Hol.*; Miles slid, and the sight of the port
upgrew *PP*; Miles slid, and the port uprose to view *CP*   15 bond] ⟨spring⟩ *Hol.*
19 his image] ⟨its portrait⟩ *Hol.*   22 Refurbished] ⟨Awakened⟩ *Hol.*
23 ⟨Did stir her soul with a touch of teen,⟩ *Hol.*   Which] ⟨That⟩ *Hol.*   twinge] throe
PP   25 outspake,] upspake, *PP, WE*   27 dear, true] dear dear *Hol.*; dear,
dear *PP, WE*   29 *DCMI*] ⟨I straightway henceward home must take⟩ I home to
⟨Athels-hall⟩ Athelhall must take *Hol.*; I home to Athelhall must take *PP*; Home, home to
Athelhall I must take *CP*; Home—home to Athelhall I must take *WE*   31 He was
wroth. And] He appealed. But *PP*   32 ⟨Upon the shore;⟩ *Hol.*   35 read]
⟨saw⟩ *Hol.*

VII

She homed as she came, at the dip of eve
    On Athel Coomb
Regaining the Hall she had sworn to leave.
The house was soundless as a tomb,   40
And she stole to her chamber, there to grieve
    Lone, kneeling, in the gloom.

VIII

From the lawn without rose her husband's voice
    To one his friend:
'Another her Love, another my choice,   45
Her going is good. Our conditions mend;
In a change of mates we shall both rejoice;
    I hoped that it thus might end!

IX

'A due divorce; she will make him hers,
    And I wed mine.   50
So Time rights all things in long, long years—
Or rather she, by her bold design!
I admire a woman no balk deters:
    She has blessed my life, in fine.

X

'I shall build new rooms for my new true bride,   55
    Let the bygone be:
By now, no doubt, she has crossed the tide
With the man to her mind. Far happier she
In some warm vineland by his side
    Than ever she was with me.'   60

---

37 homed] ⟨returned⟩ *Hol.*   at] ⟨*cap.*⟩ *Hol.*   dip] ⟨fall⟩ *Hol.*   38 ⟨On roof
and room⟩ ⟨On Athel's Coomb⟩ *Hol.*   39 ⟨She regained the walls⟩ *Hol.*
leave.] ~ . . . *Hol., PP*   41 stole to] entered *PP*   49 due] quick *PP,*
CP   51 long,] ~ *Hol.*   58 to] ⟨of⟩ *Hol.*

THE SEASONS OF HER YEAR

I

Winter is white on turf and tree,
    And birds are fled;
But summer songsters pipe to me,
    And petals spread,
For what I dreamt of secretly   5
    His lips have said!

II

O 'tis a fine May morn, they say,
    And blooms have blown;
But wild and wintry is my day,
    My songbirds moan;   10
For he who vowed leaves me to pay
    Alone—alone!

THE MILKMAID*

Under a daisied bank
There stands a rich red ruminating cow,
    And hard against her flank
A cotton-hooded milkmaid bends her brow.

The flowery river-ooze   5
Uplifts and falls; the milk purrs in the pail;
    Few pilgrims but would choose
The peace of such a life in such a vale.

The maid breathes words—to vent,
It seems, her sense of Nature's scenery, 10
    Of whose life, sentiment,
And essence, very part itself is she.

THE SEASONS OF HER YEAR. *Title* ⟨The Pathetic Fallacy⟩ *Hol.*
    9 wild] ⟨chill⟩ *Hol.*   10 My birds make moan; *PP, CP19*

THE MILKMAID. 6 Uplifts] Upheaves *PP, CP*   10 Nature's] *l.c. Hol.*

She throws a glance of pain,
And, at a moment, lets escape a tear;
Is it that passing train,   15
Whose alien whirr offends her country ear?—

Nay! Phyllis does not dwell
On visual and familiar things like these;
What moves her is the spell
Of inner themes and inner poetries: 20

Could but by Sunday morn
Her gay new gown come, meads might dry to dun,
Trains shriek till ears were torn,
If Fred would not prefer that Other One.

THE LEVELLED CHURCHYARD*

'O Passenger, pray list and catch
    Our sighs and piteous groans,
Half stifled in this jumbled patch
    Of wrenched memorial stones!

'We late-lamented, resting here,   5
    Are mixed to human jam,
And each to each exclaims in fear,
    "I know not which I am!"

'The wicked people have annexed
    The verses on the good;   10
A roaring drunkard sports the text
    Teetotal Tommy should!

---

13 throws] ⟨gives⟩ *Hol.*; bends *PP, CP*   15 Is it] ⟨Alas—⟩ *Hol.*   train,] ~
⟨—⟩, *Hol.*   16 Whose alien whirr] ⟨Its ugliness⟩ ⟨Whose alien air⟩ *Hol.*
ear?—] ⟨~!—⟩ *Hol.*   18 visual] neighbouring *Hol.*   20 Of other themes
and other poetries: *Hol.*   21 Could she ⟨by⟩ next Sunday morn *Hol.*
22 ⟨Get her new frock,⟩ Sport silk attire, the meads might dry to dun, *Hol.*

THE LEVELLED CHURCHYARD. *Headnote* ⟨(W——e Minster.)⟩ *Hol.*
    4 wrenched] ⟨smashed⟩ *Hol.*

'Where we are huddled none can trace,
 And if our names remain,
They pave some path or porch or place   15
 Where we have never lain!

'Here's not a modest maiden elf
 But dreads the final Trumpet,
Lest half of her should rise herself,
 And half some sturdy strumpet!   20

'From restorations of Thy fane,
 From smoothings of Thy sward,
From zealous Churchmen's pick and plane,
 Deliver us O Lord! Amen!'

1882.

THE RUINED MAID

'O 'Melia, my dear, this does everything crown!
Who could have supposed I should meet you in Town?
And whence such fair garments, such prosperi-ty?'—
'O didn't you know I'd been ruined?' said she.

—'You left us in tatters, without shoes or socks,   5
Tired of digging potatoes, and spudding up docks;
And now you've gay bracelets and bright feathers three!'—
'Yes: that's how we dress when we're ruined,' said she.

—'At home in the barton you said "thee" and "thou",
And "thik oon", and "theäs oon", and "t'other"; but now   10
Your talking quite fits 'ee for high compa-ny!'—
'A polish is gained with one's ruin,' said she.

13 are huddled] ⟨were lying⟩ Hol.   14 remain,] ~ Hol.   15 porch or
place WE, CP20] ⟨outer place⟩ Hol.; p——ing place PP, CP19   17 Here's] There's
PP   20 ⟨And all the rest a strumpet!⟩ Hol.   sturdy WE, CP20] local PP, CP19
21 Thy] ⟨cap.⟩ l.c. Hol.   24 Amen!'] ~." Hol.
  Date About 1882. Hol.

THE RUINED MAID. 1 dear,] cap. Hol.   crown!] ~!— Hol.   2 Town?] ~! Hol.
4 O] ~, Hol.   5 ⟨"I left ee⟩ Hol.   6 Tired of digging] ⟨A-digging⟩ Hol.
7 bracelets] ⟨slippers⟩ Hol.   bright] ⟨white⟩ Hol.   12 'A] ⟨"Sich⟩ Hol.;
"Some PP, CP

—'Your hands were like paws then, your face blue and bleak,
But now I'm bewitched by your delicate cheek,
And your little gloves fit as on any la–dy!'—   15
'We never do work when we're ruined,' said she.

—'You used to call home-life a hag-ridden dream,
And you'd sigh, and you'd sock; but at present you seem
To know not of megrims or melancho-ly!'—
'True. One's pretty lively when ruined,' said she.   20

—'I wish I had feathers, a fine sweeping gown,
And a delicate face, and could strut about Town!'—
'My dear—a raw country girl, such as you be,
Cannot quite expect that. You ain't ruined,' said she.

Westbourne Park Villas, 1866.

THE RESPECTABLE BURGHER ON 'THE HIGHER CRITICISM'

Since Reverend Doctors now declare
That clerks and people must prepare
To doubt if Adam ever were;
To hold the flood a local scare;
To argue, though the stolid stare,   5
That everything had happened ere
The prophets to its happening sware;
That David was no giant-slayer,
Nor one to call a God–obeyer
In certain details we could spare,   10
But rather was a debonair
Shrewd bandit, skilled as banjo–player:

---

20 ⟨That's the advantage of ruin,"⟩ ⟨That's one advantage of ruin,"⟩ ⟨There is some value in ruin,"⟩ *Hol.*; There's an advantage in ruin," *PP*   21 —'I] "I *Hol.*   23 'My dear—a] ⟨"Ah-ha.— A⟩ "Ah-no!— A *Hol.*   24 Cannot quite expect that.] ⟨Isn't equal to sich.⟩ *Hol.*; Isn't equal to that. *PP*

Place/date: Westbourne Park Villas, ⟨1867.⟩ 1866. *Hol.*

THE RESPECTABLE BURGHER. 4 To] ⟨And⟩ *Hol.*   flood] *cap. Hol.*   8 giant-] *cap. Hol.*   10 we could] ⟨shame shall⟩ *Hol.*

That Solomon sang the fleshly Fair,
And gave the Church no thought whate'er;
That Esther with her royal wear,   15
And Mordecai, the son of Jair,
And Joshua's triumphs, Job's despair,
And Balaam's ass's bitter blare;
Nebuchadnezzar's furnace-flare,
And Daniel and the den affair,   20
And other stories rich and rare,
Were writ to make old doctrine wear
Something of a romantic air:
That the Nain widow's only heir,
And Lazarus with cadaverous glare   25
(As done in oils by Piombo's care)
Did not return from Sheol's lair:
That Jael set a fiendish snare,
That Pontius Pilate acted square,
That never a sword cut Malchus' ear;   30
And (but for shame I must forbear)
That — — did not reappear! . . .
—Since thus they hint, nor turn a hair,
All churchgoing will I forswear,
And sit on Sundays in my chair,   35
And read that moderate man Voltaire.

ARCHITECTURAL MASKS

I

There is a house with ivied walls,
And mullioned windows worn and old,
And the long dwellers in those halls
Have souls that know but sordid calls,
And daily dote on gold.   5

---

16 Mordecai,] ~ *Hol.*   25 glare] ⟨stare⟩ *Hol.*   28 Jael set] ⟨Jael's was⟩
Hol.   31 ⟨And—(but I really must forbear!)⟩ *Hol.*   33 —Since] Since
Hol.   they hint,] ⟨they'll hold,⟩ ⟨they'll vow,⟩ *Hol.*

ARCHITECTURAL MASKS. 1 walls,] ~ *Hol.*   2 old,] ~: *Hol.*   5 dote on]
⟨dream of⟩ dote on *Hol.*; dream of *PP01*

II

In blazing brick and plated show
Not far away a 'villa' gleams,
And here a family few may know,
With book and pencil, viol and bow,
    Lead inner lives of dreams.   10

III

The philosophic passers say,
'See that old mansion mossed and fair,
Poetic souls therein are they:
And O that gaudy box! Away,
    You vulgar people there.'   15

THE TENANT-FOR-LIFE

The sun said, watching my watering-pot:
    'Some morn you'll pass away;
These flowers and plants I parch up hot—
    Who'll water them that day?

'Those banks and beds whose shape your eye   5
    Has planned in line so true,
New hands will change, unreasoning why
    Such shape seemed best to you.

'Within your house will strangers sit,
    And wonder how first it came;   10
They'll talk of their schemes for improving it,
    And will not mention your name.

'They'll care not how, or when, or at what
    You sighed, laughed, suffered here,
Though you feel more in an hour of the spot   15
    Than they will feel in a year.

8 know,] ~ *Hol.*   12 fair,] ~; *Hol.*   14 Away,] ~ *Hol.*

'As I look on at you here, now,
    Shall I look on at these;
But as to our old times, avow
    No knowledge—hold my peace! ...   20

'O friend, it matters not, I say;
    Bethink ye, I have shined
On nobler ones than you, and they
    Are dead men out of mind!'

THE KING'S EXPERIMENT*

It was a wet wan hour in spring,
And Nature met King Doom beside a lane,
Wherein Hodge tramped, all blithely ballading
    The Mother's smiling reign.

'Why warbles he that skies are fair   5
And coombs alight', she cried, 'and fallows gay,
When I have placed no sunshine in the air
    Or glow on earth to-day?'

''Tis in the comedy of things
That such should be,' returned the one of Doom;   10
'Charge now the scene with brightest blazonings,
    And he shall call them gloom.'

She gave the word: the sunbeams broke,
All Froomside shone, the hedgebirds raised a strain;
And later Hodge, upon the midday stroke,   15
    Returned along the lane,

Low murmuring: 'O this bitter scene,
And thrice accurst horizon hung with gloom!
How deadly like this sky, these fields, these treen,
    To trappings of the tomb!'   20

THE TENANT-FOR-LIFE. 24 mind!'] ~ ." *Hol.*

THE KING'S EXPERIMENT. 1 It was] ⟨It was⟩ ⟨During⟩ *Hol.*   2 ⟨The Mother met
King Doom by Long-ash Lane,⟩ *Hol.*   3 tramped, *WE, CP20*] trudged, *PP, CP19*
4 The Mother's] ⟨Of Nature's⟩ *Hol.*   5 fair] ~ ⟨,⟩ *Hol.*   10 Doom;] ~ ,
Hol.   13 sunbeams broke,] sun outbroke, *PP, WE*   14 Froomside]
⟨Blackmoor⟩ *Hol.*   strain; *WE, CP23*] song; *PP, CP19*   15 stroke,] ~ *Hol.*
16 along the lane, *WE, CP23*] the lane along, *PP, CP19*   18 horizon] ⟨horizons⟩
Hol.

The Beldame then: 'The fool and blind!
Such mad perverseness who may apprehend?'—
'Nay; there's no madness in it; thou shalt find
        Thy law there,' said her friend.

'When Hodge went forth 'twas to his Love,   25
To make her, ere this eve, his wedded prize,
And Earth, despite the heaviness above,
        Was bright as Paradise.

'But I sent on my messenger,
With cunning arrows poisonous and keen,   30
To take forthwith her laughing life from her,
        And dull her little een,

'And white her cheek, and still her breath,
Before her buoyant Hodge had reached her side;
So, when he came, he clasped her but in death,   35
        And never as his bride.

'And there's the humour, as I said;
Thy dreary dawn he saw as gleaming gold,
And in thy glistening green and radiant red
        Funereal gloom and cold.'   40

THE TREE

An Old Man's Story

I

Its roots are bristling in the air
Like some mad Earth-god's spiny hair;
The loud south-wester's swell and yell
Smote it at midnight, and it fell.
        Thus ends the tree   5
        Where Some One sat with me.

---

29 messenger,] ~ *Hol.*   30 keen,] ~ *Hol.*   34 Before her *DCM1*] Ere her
too *all other texts*

THE TREE. 3 south-wester's] *cap. Hol.*   6 Some One] Someone *Hol.*

II

Its boughs, which none but darers trod,
A child may step on from the sod,
And twigs that earliest met the dawn
Are lit the last upon the lawn.   10
        Cart off the tree
        Beneath whose trunk sat we!

III

Yes, there we sat: she cooed content,
And bats ringed round, and daylight went;
The gnarl, our seat, is wrenched and sunk,   15
Prone that queer pocket in the trunk
        Where lay the key
        To her pale mystery.

IV

I said to her: 'I found a scrawl,
My Love, within this pocket hole   20
Years back, not meant to meet my eye;
I glanced thereat, and let it lie:
        The words were three—
        "*Beloved, I agree.*"

V

'Who placed it here; to what request   25
It gave assent, I never guessed.
Some prayer of some hot heart, no doubt,
To some coy maiden hereabout,
        Just as, maybe,
        With you, Sweet Heart, and me.'   30

VI

She waited, till with quickened breath
She spoke, as one who banisheth

---

9 met] ⟨meet⟩ *Hol.*   19 "Years back, within this pocket-hole *PP, CP*
20 I found, my Love, a hurried scrawl *PP, CP*   21 Meant not for me, ⟨to her⟩ at
length said I; *Hol.*; Meant not for me, at length said I; *PP, CP*

Reserves that lovecraft heeds so well,
To ease some mighty wish to tell:
    ''Twas I', said she,   35
    'Who wrote thus clinchingly.

VII

'My lover's wife—aye, wife!—knew nought
Of what we felt, and bore, and thought. . . .
He'd said: "*I wed with thee or die:*
She stands between, 'tis true. But why?   40
    Do thou agree,
    And—she shall cease to be."

VIII

'How I held back, how love supreme
Involved me madly in his scheme
Why should I say? . . . I wrote assent   45
(You found it hid) to his intent. . . .
    She—*died.* . . . But he
    Came not to wed with me.

IX

'O shrink not, Love!—Had these eyes seen
But once thine own, such had not been!   50
But we were strangers. . . . Thus the plot
Cleared passion's path.—Why came he not
    To wed with me? . . .
    He wived the gibbet-tree.'

X

—Under that oak of heretofore   55
Sat Sweetheart mine with me no more:
By many a Fiord, and Strom, and Fleuve
Have I since wandered. . . . Soon, for love,
    Distraught went she—
    'Twas said for love of me.   60

39 *die*:] ~; *Hol.*   52 not] ~⟨?⟩ *Hol.*   54 gibbet-tree.'] ⟨gallows-tree."⟩
Hol.   55 —Under] Under *Hol.*

HER LATE HUSBAND

(King's-Hintock, 182-.)

'No—not where I shall make my own;
　　But dig his grave just by
The woman's with the initialed stone—
　　As near as he can lie—
After whose death he seemed to ail,　　　　　5
　　Though none considered why.

'And when I also claim a nook,
　　And your feet tread me in,
Bestow me, in my maiden name,
　　Among my kith and kin,　　　　　　　10
That strangers gazing may not dream
　　I did a husband win.'

'Widow, your wish shall be obeyed;
　　Though, thought I, certainly
You'd lay him where your folk are laid,　　15
　　And your grave, too, will be,
As custom hath it; you to right,
　　And on the left hand he.'

'Aye, sexton; such the Hintock rule,
　　And none has said it nay;　　　　　　20
But now you find a native here
　　Eschews that ancient way . . .
And it may be, some Christmas night,
　　When angels walk, they'll say:

'"O strange interment! Civilized lands　　25
　　Afford few types thereof;
Here is a man who takes his rest
　　Beside his very Love,
Beside the one who was his wife
　　In our sight up above!"'　　　　　　30

HER LATE HUSBAND. 3 stone—] ~, *Hol.*　　　4 lie—] ~, *Hol.*　　　7 nook,]
~ *Hol.*　　　9 in my maiden] under my old *PP*　　　14 Though I thought certainly
Hol.　　　19 sexton;] *cap. Hol.*　　　21 you find] it haps *PP*　　native] ⟨dweller⟩
Hol.　　　30 In our sight] ⟨By our laws⟩ *Hol.*

THE SELF-UNSEEING*

Here is the ancient floor,
Footworn and hollowed and thin,
Here was the former door
Where the dead feet walked in.

She sat here in her chair,   5
Smiling into the fire;
He who played stood there,
Bowing it higher and higher.

Childlike, I danced in a dream;
Blessings emblazoned that day;   10
Everything glowed with a gleam;
Yet we were looking away!

IN TENEBRIS*

I

'Percussus sum sicut foenum, et aruit cor meum.'—Ps. ci.

Wintertime nighs;
But my bereavement-pain
It cannot bring again:
    Twice no one dies.

Flower-petals flee;   5
But, since it once hath been,
No more that severing scene
    Can harrow me.

Birds faint in dread:
I shall not lose old strength   10
In the lone frost's black length:
    Strength long since fled!

THE SELF-UNSEEING. *Title* ⟨Unregarding⟩ *Hol.*
    9 Childlike,] ∼ *Hol.*

IN TENEBRIS I. *Title* ⟨De Profundis⟩ ⟨In Tenebris⟩ *Hol.*; De Profundis *PP*
    5 ⟨Flowers will soon flee:⟩ *Hol.*   7 severing] ⟨parting⟩ *Hol.*

Leaves freeze to dun;
But friends can not turn cold
This season as of old   15
For him with none.

Tempests may scath;
But love can not make smart
Again this year his heart
Who no heart hath.   20

Black is night's cope;
But death will not appal
One who, past doubtings all,
Waits in unhope.

IN TENEBRIS*

II

'Considerabam ad dexteram, et videbam; et non erat qui cognosceret me. . . . Non est qui requirat animam meam.'—Ps. cxli.

When the clouds' swoln bosoms echo back the shouts of the
      many and strong
That things are all as they best may be, save a few to be right
      ere long,
And my eyes have not the vision in them to discern what to
      these is so clear,
The blot seems straightway in me alone; one better he were
      not here.

The stout upstanders say, All's well with us: ruers have nought
      to rue!   5
And what the potent say so oft, can it fail to be somewhat true?

23 all,] ~ *Hol.*

IN TENEBRIS II. *Title* ⟨De Profundis⟩ ⟨In Tenebris⟩ *Hol.*; De Profundis *PP*   *Epigraph*
⟨"Quare fremuerunt gentes, et populi meditati sunt inania?" Ps. II.⟩ *Hol.*
      3 what to these is] demonstration *PP01 only*   4 ⟨and I ⟨⟨wish⟩⟩ would that I
were not here!⟩ *Hol.*   here.] ~! *Hol.*   5 ⟨The breezy bevies say, All's
well with us: why then should others rue!⟩ *Hol.*   say, *PP, CP, DCM4*] chime, *WE*
6 potent] ⟨vigorous⟩ *Hol.*   say so oft, *PP, CP, DCM4*] so often say, *WE*

Breezily go they, breezily come; their dust smokes around
    their career,
Till I think I am one born out of due time, who has no calling
    here.

Their dawns bring lusty joys, it seems; their evenings all that
    is sweet;
Our times are blessed times, they cry: Life shapes it as is most
    meet,   10
And nothing is much the matter; there are many smiles to a
    tear;
Then what is the matter is I, I say. Why should such an one be
    here? . . .

Let him in whose ears the low-voiced Best is killed by the
    clash of the First,
Who holds that if way to the Better there be, it exacts a full
    look at the Worst,
Who feels that delight is a delicate growth cramped by
    crookedness, custom, and fear,   15
Get him up and be gone as one shaped awry; he disturbs the
    order here.

1895-96.

IN TENEBRIS*

III

'Heu mihi, quia incolatus meus prolongatus est! Habitavi cum habitantibus Cedar;
multum incola fuit anima mea.'—Ps. cxix.

There have been times when I well might have passed and the
    ending have come—

7 ⟨Cheerily go they, cheerily come; their fame stretches far and near,⟩ ⟨their dust clouds the
far and near,⟩ *Hol.*   8 time,] ~ *Hol.*   calling] ⟨right to be⟩ ⟨vocation⟩ *Hol.*
9 eves exultance sweet, *PP, CP19*   12 ⟨Good God, why should I be here! . . . .⟩
Hol.   here? . . .] ~! . . . *Hol.*   13 Let him] ⟨Maybe all⟩ ⟨Haply⟩ *Hol.*   in] to
PP, CP19   is killed] seems stilled *PP, CP19*   14 holds] ⟨hold⟩ *Hol.*
15 feels] ⟨feel⟩ *Hol.*   16 Get him] ⟨Should⟩ *Hol.*   one] ⟨men⟩ *Hol.*   he
disturbs the order] ⟨or as weird ghosts wandering⟩ ⟨unwished, unwanted⟩ *Hol.*   here.]
~! *Hol.*

IN TENEBRIS III. *Title* ⟨De Profundis⟩ ⟨In Tenebris⟩ *Hol.*; De Profundis *PP*

Points in my path when the dark might have stolen on me,
    artless, unrueing—
Ere I had learnt that the world was a welter of futile doing:
Such had been times when I well might have passed, and the
    ending have come!

Say, on the noon when the half-sunny hours told that April
    was nigh,   5
And I upgathered and cast forth the snow from the crocus-
    border,
Fashioned and furbished the soil into a summer-seeming
    order,
Glowing in gladsome faith that I quickened the year thereby.

Or on that loneliest of eves when afar and benighted we
    stood,
She who upheld me and I, in the midmost of Egdon together,   10
Confident I in her watching and ward through the blackening
    heather,
Deeming her matchless in might and with measureless scope
    endued.

Or on that winter-wild night when, reclined by the chimney-
    nook quoin,
Slowly a drowse overgat me, the smallest and feeblest of folk
    there,
Weak from my baptism of pain; when at times and anon I
    awoke there—   15
Heard of a world wheeling on, with no listing or longing to
    join.

Even then! while unweeting that vision could vex or that
    knowledge could numb,
That sweets to the mouth in the belly are bitter, and tart, and
    untoward,

2 artless] ⟨passive⟩ *Hol.*   10 She who upheld] ⟨One who bestead⟩ *Hol.*
15 at times and anon] ⟨bestirring myself⟩ *Hol.*   16 ⟨longing or listing⟩ *Hol.*
17 Even then! while unweeting] ⟨Aye, when unknowing⟩ *Hol.*   18 ⟨Witless that
fruits of this life show them bitter, and black, and untoward,⟩ *Hol.*

Then, on some dim-coloured scene should my briefly raised
    curtain have lowered,
Then might the Voice that is law have said 'Cease!' and the
    ending have come.   20

                          1896.

THE CHURCH-BUILDER*

I

The church projects a battled shade
    Over the moon-lit sward;
The church; my gift; whereto I paid
    My all in hand and hoard:
        Lavished my gains   5
        With stintless pains
    To glorify the Lord.

II

I squared the broad foundations in,
    Set ashlared masonry;
I moulded mullions thick and thin,   10
    Hewed fillet and ogee:
        I circleted
        Each sculptured head
    With nimb and canopy.

III

I called in many a craftsmaster   15
    To fix emblazoned glass,
To figure Cross and Sepulchre
    On dossal, boss, and brass.
        My gold all spent,
        My jewels went   20
    To gem the cups of Mass.

THE CHURCH-BUILDER. *Title* ⟨Nisi Dominus Frustra⟩ *Hol.*

  1 projects] ⟨flings forth⟩ ⟨outflings⟩ *Hol.*; flings forth *PP, CP*   2 moon-lit]
moon-blanched *PP, CP*   8 in,] ~ *PP, CP*   9 Set] Of *PP, CP*
11 ogee:] ~. *Hol.*   15 in] ⟨down⟩ *Hol.*

IV

I borrowed deep to carve the screen
  And raise the ivoried Rood;
I parted with my small demesne
  To make my owings good.   25
     Heir-looms unpriced
     I sacrificed,
  Until debt-free I stood.

V

So closed the task. 'Deathless the Creed
  Here substanced!' said my soul: 30
'I heard me bidden to this deed,
  And straight obeyed the call.
     Illume this fane,
     That not in vain
  I build it, Lord of all!'   35

VI

But, as it chanced me, then and there
  Did dire misfortunes burst;
My home went waste for lack of care,
  My sons rebelled and curst;
     Till I confessed   40
     That aims the best
  Were looking like the worst.

VII

Enkindled by my votive work
  No burning faith I find;
The deeper thinkers sneer and smirk,   45
  And give my toil no mind;
     From nod and wink
     I read they think
  That I am fool and blind.

27 sacrificed,] ~ *Hol.*

VIII

My gift to God seems futile, quite;   50
The world moves as erstwhile;
And powerful Wrong on feeble Right
Tramples in olden style.
        My faith burns down,
        I see no crown;   55
But Cares, and Griefs, and Guile.

IX

So now, the remedy? Yea, this:
I gently swing the door
Here, of my fane—no soul to wis—
And cross the patterned floor   60
        To the rood-screen
        That stands between
The nave and inner chore.

X

The rich red windows dim the moon,
But little light need I;   65
I mount the prie-dieu, lately hewn
From woods of rarest dye;
        Then from below
        My garment, so,
I draw this cord, and tie   70

XI

One end thereof around the beam
Midway 'twixt Cross and truss:
I noose the nethermost extreme,
And in ten seconds thus
        I journey hence—   75
        To that land whence
No rumour reaches us.

---

52 Wrong . . . Right] *l.c. PP*   57 this:] ~⟨—⟩ *Hol.*   65 I;] ~:
Hol.

XII

Well: Here at dawn they'll light on one
    Dangling in mockery
Of what he spent his substance on   80
    Blindly and uselessly! . . .
        'He might', they'll say,
        'Have built, some way,
        A cheaper gallows-tree!'

THE LOST PYX*

A Mediæval Legend

Some say the spot is banned; that the pillar Cross-and-Hand
    Attests to a deed of hell;
But of else than of bale is the mystic tale
    That ancient Vale-folk tell.

Ere Cernel's Abbey ceased hereabout there dwelt a priest,   5
    (In later life sub-prior
Of the brotherhood there, whose bones are now bare
    In the field that was Cernel choir).

One night in his cell at the foot of yon dell
    The priest heard a frequent cry: 10
'Go, father, in haste to the cot on the waste,
    And shrive a man waiting to die.'

Said the priest in a shout to the caller without,
    'The night howls, the tree-trunks bow;
One may barely by day track so rugged a way,   15
    And can I then do so now?'

78 dawn] morn *PP, CP*

THE LOST PYX. *Sphere*, 22 Dec. 1900. *MS1 (S)* Adams; *P1 (S)* HRC
    Subtitle om. S
    1 Cross-and-Hand] ⟨Christ-in-Hand⟩ *MS1*; ⟨cross-and-hand⟩ *P1*   2 hell;]
cap. MS1, S   8 choir] *cap. MS1-S*   11 father,] *cap. MS1, S*   waste,]
~ *MS1-S, Hol.*

No further word from the dark was heard,
    And the priest moved never a limb;
And he slept and dreamed; till a Visage seemed
    To frown from Heaven at him.   20

In a sweat he arose; and the storm shrieked shrill,
    And smote as in savage joy;
While High-Stoy trees twanged to Bubb-Down Hill,
    And Bubb-Down to High-Stoy.

There seemed not a holy thing in hail,   25
    Nor shape of light or love,
From the Abbey north of Blackmore Vale
    To the Abbey south thereof.

Yet he plodded thence through the dark immense,
    And with many a stumbling stride   30
Through copse and briar climbed nigh and nigher
    To the cot and the sick man's side.

When he would have unslung the Vessels hung
    To his arm in the steep ascent,
He made loud moan: the Pyx was gone   35
    Of the Blessed Sacrament.

Then in dolorous dread he beat his head:
    'No earthly prize or pelf
Is the thing I've lost in tempest tossed,
    But the Body of Christ Himself!'   40

He thought of the Visage his dream revealed,
    And turned towards whence he came,
Hands groping the ground along foot-track and field,
    And head in a heat of shame.

---

19 dreamed;] $\langle\sim\rangle$ $\sim$, *P1*   20 To] $\langle$The$\rangle$ *MS1*   24 And Bubb-Down
Hill to Stoy. *WE12 only*   33 hung] uphung *PP, CP*   35 moan:] $\sim$; *MS1-S*
37 dolourous] dolour and *MS1-S*

Till here on the hill, betwixt vill and vill,   45
    He noted a clear straight ray
Stretching down from the sky to a spot hard by,
    Which shone with the light of day.

And gathered around the illumined ground
    Were common beasts and rare,   50
All kneeling at gaze, and in pause profound
    Attent on an object there.

'Twas the Pyx, unharmed mid the circling rows
    Of Blackmore's hairy throng,
Whereof were oxen, sheep, and does,   55
    And hares from the brakes among;

And badgers grey, and conies keen,
    And squirrels of the tree,
And many a member seldom seen
    Of Nature's family.   60

The ireful winds that scoured and swept
    Through coppice, clump, and dell,
Within that holy circle slept
    Calm as in hermit's cell.

Then the priest bent likewise to the sod   65
    And thanked the Lord of Love,
And Blessed Mary, Mother of God,
    And all the saints above.

And turning straight with his priceless freight,
    He reached the dying one,   70
Whose passing sprite had been stayed for the rite
    Without which bliss hath none.

And when by grace the priest won place,
    And served the Abbey well,
He reared this stone to mark where shone   75
    That midnight miracle.

45 Till here] And here, *MS1–S*   hill,] ~ *MS1–S, Hol.*   vill,] ~ *P1, S, Hol.*
47 by,] ~ *Hol.*   52 Attent on] Attent to *MS1*; ⟨Attent to⟩ Intent on *P1*; Attent
to   *S*   53 mid *Hol., WE*] 'mid *PP, CP*   56 among;] ~ , *Hol.*
67 Mary,] ~ *MS1, Hol.*   69 freight,] ~ *MS1–S, Hol.*

TESS'S LAMENT

I

I would that folk forgot me quite,
 Forgot me quite!
I would that I could shrink from sight,
 And no more see the sun.
Would it were time to say farewell,   5
To claim my nook, to need my knell,
Time for them all to stand and tell
 O' my day's work as done.

II

Ah! dairy where I lived so long,
 I lived so long;   10
Where I would rise up stanch and strong,
 And lie down hopefully.
'Twas there within the chimney-seat
He watched me to the clock's slow beat—
Loved me, and learnt to call me Sweet,   15
 And whispered words to me.

III

And now he's gone; and now he's gone; . . .
 And now he's gone!
The flowers we potted p'rhaps are thrown
 To rot upon the farm.   20
And where we had our supper-fire
May now grow nettle, dock, and briar,
And all the place be mould and mire
 So cozy once and warm.

IV

And it was I who did it all,   25
 Who did it all;
'Twas I who made the blow to fall
 On him who thought no guile.

TESS'S LAMENT. *Title* ⟨A Lament⟩ *Hol. table of contents*; ⟨?⟩ Lament *Hol.*
 1 I] O *Hol.*   3 I] O *Hol.*   8 O'] Of *PP, CP*   14 clock's slow
beat—] ⟨long⟩ slow clock-beat— *Hol.*   15 Sweet,] *l.c. PP*   19 p'rhaps]
⟨p'raps⟩ *Hol.*; perhaps *CP*   22 grow] ⟨grown⟩ *Hol.*

Well, it is finished—past, and he
Has left me to my misery,   30
And I must take my Cross on me
    For wronging him awhile.

V

How gay we looked that day we wed,
    That day we wed!
'May joy be with ye!' all o'm said   35
    A standing by the durn.
I wonder what they say o's now,
And if they know my lot; and how
She feels who milks my favourite cow,
    And takes my place at churn!   40

VI

It wears me out to think of it,
    To think of it;
I cannot bear my fate as writ,
    I'd have my life unbe;
Would turn my memory to a blot,   45
Make every relic of me rot,
My doings be as they were not,
    And leave no trace of me!

THE SUPPLANTER*

I

He bends his travel-tarnished feet
    To where she wastes in clay:
From dawn till eventide he fares
    Along the wintry way;
From dawn till eventide he bears   5
    A wreath of blooms and bay.

---

29 Well,] ~; *Hol.*   35 all o'm] they all *CP*   48 And what they've brought
to me! *PP*; And gone all trace of me! *CP*

THE SUPPLANTER. *Title* ⟨At the Cemetery Lodge⟩ *Hol.*   *Subtitle* A Tale. *PP, CP*
  3 From day-dawn until eve he fares *PP, CP*   5 From day-dawn until eve repairs
PP, CP19; From day-dawn until eve he bears *CP23*   6 *WE, CP23*] Unto ⟨the⟩ her
mound to pray. *Hol.*; Unto her mound to pray. *PP*; Towards her mound to pray. *CP19*

II

'Are these the gravestone shapes that meet
    My forward-straining view?
Or forms that cross a window-blind
    In circle, knot, and queue: 10
Gay forms, that cross and whirl and wind
    To music throbbing through?'—

III

'The Keeper of the Field of Tombs
    Dwells by its gateway-pier;
He celebrates with feast and dance   15
    His daughter's twentieth year:
He celebrates with wine of France
    The birthday of his dear.'—

IV

'The gates are shut when evening glooms:
    Lay down your wreath, sad wight;   20
To-morrow is a time more fit
    For placing flowers aright:
The morning is the time for it;
    Come, wake with us to-night!'—

V

He downs his wreath when entered in,   25
    And sits, and shares their cheer.—
'I fain would foot with you, young man,
    Before all others here;
I fain would foot it for a span
    With such a cavalier!'   30

VI

She coaxes, clasps, nor fails to win
    His first-unwilling hand:

18 dear.'—] ~." *Hol.*   19 evening glooms:] ⟨evening glooms:⟩ ⟨eve englooms:⟩
Hol.   23 morning] ⟨daylight⟩ *Hol.*   25 He grounds his wreath, and
enters in, *PP*; He drops his wreath, and enters in, *CP*   26 cheer.—] ~. *Hol.*
32 first-] ⟨half-⟩ *Hol.*

The merry music strikes its staves,
  The dancers quickly band;
And with the Damsel of the Graves   35
  He duly takes his stand.

VII

'You dance divinely, stranger swain,
  Such grace I've never known.
O longer stay! Breathe not adieu
  And leave me here alone!   40
O longer stay: to her be true
  Whose heart is all your own!'—

VIII

'I mark a phantom through the pane,
  That beckons in despair,
Its mouth drawn down as by a moan—   45
  Her to whom once I sware!'—
'Nay; 'tis the lately carven stone
  Of some strange girl laid there!'—

IX

'I see white flowers upon the floor
  Betrodden to a clot;   50
My wreath were they?'—'Nay; love me much,
  Swear you'll forget me not!
'Twas but a wreath! Full many such
  Are brought here and forgot.' . . .

X

The watches of the night grow hoar,   55
  He wakens with the sun;
'Now could I kill thee here!' he says,
  'For winning me from one

35 Damsel of the Graves CP] l.c. PP, WE   36 He duly] ⟨The young man⟩ Hol.
39 Breathe] ⟨Say⟩ Hol.   42 own!'—] ~!" Hol.   45 Its mouth all drawn
with heavy moan— PP, CP   53 wreath!] ~. Hol.   54 forgot.' . . .] ~."
PP, CP   PP, CP add a line of widely-spaced dots below line 54   56 wakens
with] rises ere PP; wakens ere CP19

Who ever in her living days
Was pure as cloistered nun!' 60

XI

Out from her arms he takes his track
Afar for many a mile,
For evermore to be apart
From her who could beguile
His senses by her burning heart, 65
And win his love awhile. . . .

XII

A year: and he is travelling back
To one who wastes in clay;
From dawn till eventide he fares
Along the wintry way, 70
From dawn till eventide he bears
A wreath of blooms and bay.

XIII

And there he sets him to fulfil
His frustrate first intent:
And lay upon her bed, at last, 75
The offering earlier meant:
When, on his stooping figure, ghast
And haggard eyes are bent.

XIV

'O surely for a little while
You can be kind to me! 80
For do you love her, do you hate,
She knows not—cares not she:
Only the living feel the weight
Of loveless misery!

61 She cowers, and he takes his track *PP*; She cowers; and, rising, roves he then *CP*
66 awhile. . . .] ~ . *PP, CP*   67 A year beholds him wend again *CP*
68 one] her *PP, CP*   69 From day-dawn until eve he fares *PP, CP*
71 From day-dawn until eve repairs *PP, CP*   72 Unto her mound to pray. *PP*;
Towards her mound to pray. *CP*   77 stooping] ⟨bending⟩ *Hol.*

XV

'I own my sin; I've paid its cost,   85
    Being outcast, shamed, and bare:
I give you daily my whole heart,
    Your child my tender care,
I pour you prayers; this life apart
    Is more than I can bear!'   90

XVI

He turns—unpitying, passion-tossed:
    'I know you not!' he cries,
'Nor know your child. I knew this maid,
    But she's in Paradise!'
And he has vanished in the shade   95
    From her beseeching eyes.

---

85 sin;] fault; *Hol.*   88 child *WE, CP23*] babe *PP, CP19*   89 This life apart *WE, CP23*] and aye to part *PP, CP19*   91 ⟨He turns as one whose mind is lost:⟩ He turns remorseless—passion-tossed: *Hol.*; He turns—remorseless, *PP01, PP02*   95 *WE, CP23*] And swiftly in the winter shade *PP, CP19*   96 *WE, CP23*] He breaks from her and flies. *PP, CP19*

IMITATIONS, ETC.

SAPPHIC FRAGMENT*

'Thou shalt be—Nothing.'—OMAR KHAYYÁM.
'Tombless, with no remembrance.'—W. SHAKESPEARE.

Dead shalt thou lie; and nought
Be told of thee or thought,
For thou hast plucked not of the Muses' tree:
And even in Hades' halls
Amidst thy fellow-thralls   5
No friendly shade shall keep thee company!

CATULLUS: XXXI*

(After passing Sirmione, April 1887.)

Sirmio, thou dearest dear of strands
That Neptune strokes in lake and sea,
With what high joy from stranger lands
Doth thy old friend set foot on thee!
Yea, barely seems it true to me   5
That no Bithynia holds me now,
But calmly and assuringly
Around me stretchest homely Thou.

Is there a scene more sweet than when
Our clinging cares are undercast,   10
And, worn by alien moils and men,
The long untrodden sill repassed,
We press the pined for couch at last,
And find a full repayment there?
Then hail, sweet Sirmio; thou that wast,   15
And art, mine own unrivalled Fair!

SAPPHIC FRAGMENT. *Epigraph* ⟨"Neither have they any more a reward, for the memory of
them is forgotten." Eccles. IX. 5.⟩ *Hol.*
    2 Be] ⟨Shall be⟩ *Hol.*   6 shall keep thee] thy shade shall *PP, CP*

CATULLUS: XXXI. 13 pined for] ⟨kindly⟩ pined for *Hol.*; kindly *PP01, PP02*

AFTER SCHILLER*

Knight, a true sister-love
This heart retains;
Ask me no other love,
That way lie pains!

Calm must I view thee come,   5
Calm see thee go;
Tale-telling tears of thine
I must not know!

*   *   *   *

SONG FROM HEINE*

I scanned her picture, dreaming,
Till each dear line and hue
Was imaged, to my seeming,
As if it lived anew.

Her lips began to borrow   5
Their former wondrous smile;
Her fair eyes, faint with sorrow,
Grew sparkling as erstwhile.

Such tears as often ran not
Ran then, my love, for thee;   10
And O, believe I cannot
That thou art lost to me!

AFTER SCHILLER. *CP om. the line of asterisks after last line of text*

SONG FROM HEINE. *Title* ⟨Song. After Heine.⟩ *Hol.*   *Headnote* ⟨Die Heimkehr . . . .⟩ *Hol.*
  1 dreaming,] ∼; *Hol.*   10 love,] *cap. Hol.*   11 And O—believe I can
not *Hol.*   12 art] are *PP*

FROM VICTOR HUGO*

Child, were I king, I'd yield my royal rule,
   My chariot, sceptre, vassal-service due,
My crown, my porphyry-basined waters cool,
My fleets, whereto the sea is but a pool,
   For a glance from you!   5

Love, were I God, the earth and its heaving airs,
   Angels, the demons abject under me,
Vast chaos with its teeming womby lairs,
Time, space, all would I give—aye, upper spheres,
   For a kiss from thee!   10

CARDINAL BEMBO'S EPITAPH ON RAPHAEL*

Here's one in whom Nature feared—faint at such vying—
Eclipse while he lived, and decease at his dying.

FROM VICTOR HUGO. *The Hol. text before revision read:*

After
Victor Hugo

Child, were I King, I'd yield my rule,
Crown, sceptre, vassal-service due,
My chariot, porphyried basins cool,
My fleets, that make the sea a pool,
   For a glance from you!

Love, were I God, the earth and airs,
Angels, the demons under me,
Vast chaos with its womby lairs,
Time, space I'd give—aye, upper spheres,
   For a kiss from thee!

2 vassal-service] ⟨vassal-service⟩ ⟨knee-devotion⟩ *Hol.*   9 space,] ~ — *Hol.*

RETROSPECT

'I HAVE LIVED WITH SHADES'

I

I have lived with Shades so long,
And talked to them so oft,
Since forth from cot and croft
I went mankind among,
    That sometimes they   5
    In their dim style
    Will pause awhile
    To hear my say;

II

And take me by the hand,
And lead me through their rooms   10
In the To-be, where Dooms
Half-wove and shapeless stand:
    And show from there
    The dwindled dust
    And rot and rust   15
    Of things that were.

III

'Now turn,' they said to me
One day: 'Look whence we came,
And signify his name
Who gazes thence at thee.'—   20
    —'Nor name nor race
    Know I, or can,'
    I said, 'Of man
    So commonplace.

'I HAVE LIVED WITH SHADES'. 2 *PP, CP, DCM4*] So long have talked to them, *WE*
3 *PP, CP, DCM4*] Since from the forest's hem *WE*   4 *PP, CP, DCM4*] I sped to
street and throng, *WE*   12 stand:] ~ ; *Hol.*   17 they said *WE, CP23*] ⟨said
they⟩ *Hol.*; spake they *PP, CP19*

IV

'He moves me not at all;   25
I note no ray or jot
Of rareness in his lot,
Or star exceptional.
    Into the dim
    Dead throngs around   30
    He'll sink, nor sound
    Be left of him.'

V

'Yet', said they, 'his frail speech,
Hath accents pitched like thine—
Thy mould and his define   35
A likeness each to each—
    But go! Deep pain,
    Alas, would be
    His name to thee,
    And told in vain!'   40

Feb. 2, 1899.

MEMORY AND I

'O Memory, where is now my Youth,
Who used to say that life was truth?'

'I saw him in a crumbled cot
    Beneath a tottering tree;
That he as phantom lingers there   5
    Is only known to me.'

---

34 ⟨Shows accents pitched like thine?⟩ ⟨Doth it not chord with thine?⟩ *Hol.*
36 each—] ∼ ⟨?⟩— *Hol.*   37 pain, *Clark, WE20*] ∼ *PP, WE12, CP*

MEMORY AND I. 1 Youth] *l.c. PP, CP*   6 ⟨Is known to none but me."⟩ *Hol.*

'O Memory, where is now my Joy,
Who lived with me in sweet employ?'

'I saw him on a lonely lawn,
   Where laughter used to be;
That he as phantom wanders there
   Is known to none but me.'   10

'O Memory, where is now my Hope,
Who charged with deeds my skill and scope?'

'I saw her in a tomb of tomes,   15
   Where dreams are wont to be;
That she as spectre haunteth there
   Is only known to me.'

'O Memory, where is now my Faith,
One time a champion, now a wraith?'   20

'I saw her in a ravaged aisle,
   Bowed down on bended knee;
That her poor ghost outflickers there
   Is known to none but me.'

'O Memory, where is now my Love,   25
That rayed me as a god above?'

'I saw her in an ageing shape
   Where beauty used to be;
That her fond phantom lingers there
   Is only known to me.'   30

---

7 Joy] *l.c. PP, CP*   9 on a lonely lawn,] ⟨in old gardens gray⟩ in gray gardens lone, *Hol.*; in gaunt gardens lone, *PP, CP*   10 laughter] ⟨gayings⟩ *Hol.*
13 Hope] *l.c. PP, CP*   14 ⟨Who fired to deeds my skill and scope?"⟩ ⟨Who flushed my skill and starred my scope?"⟩ *Hol.*   15 her] ⟨him⟩ *Hol.*   19 Faith] *l.c. PP, CP*   21 her] ⟨him⟩ *Hol.*   ravaged] ⟨holy⟩ *Hol.*   22 Bowed down] Sunken *Hol.*   25 Love] *l.c. PP, CP*   27 her in] him by *PP*
29 her] his *PP*

ΑΓΝΩΣΤΩι ΘΕΩι*

Long have I framed weak phantasies of Thee,
  O Willer masked and dumb!
  Who makest Life become,—
As though by labouring all-unknowingly,
  Like one whom reveries numb.   5

How much of consciousness informs Thy will,
  Thy biddings, as if blind,
  Of death-inducing kind,
Nought shows to us ephemeral ones who fill
  But moments in Thy mind.   10

Perhaps Thy ancient rote-restricted ways
  Thy ripening rule transcends;
  That listless effort tends
To grow percipient with advance of days,
  And with percipience mends.   15

For, in unwonted purlieus, far and nigh,
  At whiles or short or long,
  May be discerned a wrong
Dying as of self-slaughter; whereat I
  Would raise my voice in song.   20

ΑΓΝΩΣΤΩι ΘΕΩι. 1 framed] ⟨spun⟩ Hol.   2 ⟨O Unseen Willer dumb!⟩ Hol.
4 By labouring all-unknowingly, maybe, PPo1, PPo2   7 biddings,] ⟨aimings,⟩
Hol.   as if blind,] ⟨as if blind,⟩ ⟨undesigned,⟩ Hol.   8 death-inducing] ⟨self-
destructive⟩ Hol.   11 Perhaps] ⟨Perchance⟩ Haply Hol.; Haply PPo1, PPo2
rote-restricted] ⟨tentative, slow⟩ ⟨tentative, dream-⟩ ⟨automatic⟩ tentative, slow Hol.;
automatic PPo1 only   12 rule] ⟨scope⟩ Hol.   13 listless] ⟨long crass⟩
⟨long rapt⟩ Hol.   19 self-slaughter;] ⟨self-vision;⟩ Hol.   20 Would]
⟨Would⟩ ⟨Do⟩ Would Hol.; Do PPo1, PPo2

TIME'S LAUGHINGSTOCKS
AND OTHER VERSES

CONTENTS

A SET OF COUNTRY SONGS—

PIECES OCCASIONAL AND VARIOUS—

PREFACE

I N collecting the following poems I have to thank the editors and proprietors of the periodicals in which certain of them have appeared for permission to reclaim them.

Now that the miscellany is brought together, some lack of concord in pieces written at widely severed dates, and in contrasting moods and circumstances, will be obvious enough. This I cannot help, but the sense of disconnection, particularly in respect of those lyrics penned in the first person, will be immaterial when it is borne in mind that they are to be regarded, in the main, as dramatic monologues by different characters.

As a whole they will, I hope, take the reader forward, even if not far, rather than backward. I should add that some lines in the early-dated poems have been rewritten, though they have been left substantially unchanged.

T. H.

September 1909.

PREFACE. 1 poems *ME*] poems to form a volume, *TL, WE; comma om. Hol.*   2 certain] some *Hol.*   4–6 together . . . enough.] together a lack of harmony will be apparent in the pieces. *Hol.*   6–8 This I cannot help, and perhaps any ⟨unconvincing effect⟩ sense of discontinuity therefrom, particularly in respect of those lyrics penned in the first person, will be ⟨removed by bearing⟩ accepted when it is borne *Hol.*   11–12 forward rather than backward, even if not far. *Hol.*   12–13 early-dated] earlier *TL09* 13–14 they . . . unchanged.] ⟨their meaning has not been changed.⟩ *Hol.*

TIME'S LAUGHINGSTOCKS

THE REVISITATION*

As I lay awake at night-time
In an ancient country barrack known to ancient cannoneers,
And recalled the hopes that heralded each seeming brave and
    bright time
    Of my primal purple years,

    Much it haunted me that, nigh there,   5
I had borne my bitterest loss—when One who went, came not
    again;
In a joyless hour of discord, in a joyless-hued July there—
    A July just such as then.

    And as thus I brooded longer,
With my faint eyes on the feeble square of wan-lit window
    frame,   10
A quick conviction sprung within me, grew, and grew yet
    stronger,
    That the month-night was the same,

    Too, as that which saw her leave me
On the rugged ridge of Waterstone, the peewits plaining
    round;
And a lapsing twenty years had ruled that—as it were to
    grieve me—   15
    I should near the once-loved ground.

THE REVISITATION. *Fortnightly Review*, 1 Aug. 1904
   Title Time's Laughingstocks *FR*   *Subtitle* A Summer Romance *FR*
  2 cannoneers,] cannoniers, *FR, Hol.*   4 Of] In *FR*; ⟨In⟩ *Hol.*   6 went,]
~⟨,⟩ *Hol.*   again;] ~⟨;—⟩, *Hol.*   7 In a] ⟨After⟩ ⟨Borne⟩ *Hol.*
8 just] there *FR, Hol.*   10 wan-lit] wansome *FR*; ⟨wansome⟩ ⟨wan lit⟩ wansome
Hol.   12 month-night] the night, too, *FR*; ⟨the night, too,⟩ *Hol.*   same,] ~⟨;⟩,
Hol.   13 Ay, as that which *FR*; ⟨Ay, the same that⟩ *Hol.*   14 On the] On
⟨that⟩ *Hol.*   round;] ~.... *FR, Hol.*

Though but now a war-worn stranger
Chance had quartered here, I rose up and descended to the
    yard.
All was soundless, save the troopers' horses tossing at the
    manger,
    And the sentry keeping guard.   20

Through the gateway I betook me
Down the High Street and beyond the lamps, across the
    battered bridge,
Till the country darkness clasped me and the friendly shine
    forsook me,
    And I bore towards the Ridge,

With a dim unowned emotion   25
Saying softly: 'Small my reason, now at midnight, to be
    here . . . .
Yet a sleepless swain of fifty with a brief romantic notion
    May retrace a track so dear.'

Thus I walked with thoughts half-uttered
Up the lane I knew so well, the grey, gaunt, lonely Lane of
    Slyre;   30
And at whiles behind me, far at sea, a sullen thunder muttered
    As I mounted high and higher.

Till, the upper roadway quitting,
I adventured on the open drouthy downland thinly grassed,
While the spry white scuts of conies flashed before me,
    earthward flitting,   35
    And an arid wind went past.

Round about me bulged the barrows
As before, in antique silence—immemorial funeral piles—
Where the sleek herds trampled daily the remains of flint-tipt
    arrows
    Mid the thyme and chamomiles;   40

18 rose up] clothed me *FR*; clothed me⟨,⟩ *Hol.*   26 ⟨I said softly: "This is
foolish,⟩ *Hol.*   here. . . .] ~! . . . *FR*; ~⟨!⟩ . . . *Hol.*   30 grey, gaunt, lonely]
long, gaunt, lonesome *FR*; ⟨long⟩ grey gaunt lonesome *Hol.*   33 Till,] ~ *Hol.*
34 drouthy] ⟨drouth-dried⟩ *Hol.*   36 an arid] a sultry *FR, Hol.*

And the Sarsen stone there, dateless,
On whose breast we had sat and told the zephyrs many a
    tender vow,
Held the heat of yester sun, as sank thereon one fated mateless
    From those far fond hours till now.

Maybe flustered by my presence   45
Rose the peewits, just as all those years back, wailing soft and
    loud,
And revealing their pale pinions like a fitful phosphorescence
    Up against the cope of cloud,

Where their dolesome exclamations
Seemed the voicings of the self-same throats I had heard
    when life was green,   50
Though since that day uncounted frail forgotten generations
    Of their kind had flecked the scene.—

And so, living long and longer
In a past that lived no more, my eyes discerned there,
    suddenly,
That a figure broke the skyline—first in vague contour, then
    stronger,   55
    And was crossing near to me.

Some long-missed familiar gesture,
Something wonted, struck me in the figure's pause to list and
    heed,
Till I fancied from its handling of its loosely wrapping vesture
    That it might be She indeed.   60

'Twas not reasonless: below there
In the vale, had been her home; the nook might hold her even
    yet,
And the downlands were her father's fief; she still might come
    and go there;—
    So I rose, and said, 'Agnette!'

42 On whose breast we had sat] Where of old we'd sat *FR*; ⟨Where of old we'd sat⟩ *Hol.*
44 fond] fair *FR*; ⟨fair⟩ *Hol.*   52 kind] ⟨tribe⟩ *Hol.*

With a little leap, half-frightened,
She withdrew some steps; then letting intuition smother fear
In a place so long-accustomed, and as one whom thought
    enlightened,
    She replied: 'What—*that* voice?—here!'

'Yes, Agnette!—And did the occasion
Of our marching hither make you think I *might* walk where we
    two—'   70
'O, I often come', she murmured with a moment's coy evasion,
    '('Tis not far),—and—think of you.'

Then I took her hand, and led her
To the ancient people's stone whereon I had sat. There now
    sat we;
And together talked, until the first reluctant shyness fled her,   75
    And she spoke confidingly.

'It is *just* as ere we parted!'
Said she, brimming high with joy.—'And when, then, came
    you here, and why?'
'—Dear, I could not sleep for thinking of our trystings when
    twin-hearted.'
    She responded, 'Nor could I.   80

'There are few things I would rather
Than be wandering at this spirit-hour—lone-lived, my
    kindred dead—
On this wold of well-known feature I inherit from my father:
    Night or day, I have no dread . . . .

'O I wonder, wonder whether   85
Any heartstring bore a signal-thrill between us twain or no?—
Some such influence can, at times, they say, draw severed
    souls together.'
    I said, 'Dear, we'll dream it so.'

---

68 *that* voice?—] ⟨Brian—⟩ *Hol.*   69 'Yes,] ⟨"Ay,⟩ *Hol.*   78 when,
then,] ⟨wherefore⟩ *Hol.*   82 be] ⟨come⟩ *Hol.*   83 wold] ⟨fell⟩ *Hol.*
I inherit from] ⟨passed unto me by⟩ *Hol.*   86 bore] sent *FR*; ⟨sent⟩ *Hol.*

Each one's hand the other's grasping,
And a mutual forgiveness won, we sank to silent thought,   90
A large content in us that seemed our rended lives reclasping,
And contracting years to nought.

Till I, maybe overweary
From the lateness, and a wayfaring so full of strain and stress
For one no longer buoyant, to a peak so steep and eery,   95
Sank to slow unconsciousness . . . .

How long I slept I knew not,
But the brief warm summer night had slid when, to my swift
    surprise,
A red upedging sun, of glory chambered mortals view not,
Was blazing on my eyes,   100

From the Milton Woods to Dole-Hill
All the spacious landscape lighting, and around about my feet
Flinging tall thin tapering shadows from the meanest mound
    and mole-hill,
And on trails the ewes had beat.

She was sitting still beside me,   105
Dozing likewise; and I turned to her, to take her hanging
    hand;
When, the more regarding, that which like a spectre shook
    and tried me
In her image then I scanned;

That which Time's transforming chisel
Had been tooling night and day for twenty years, and tooled
    too well,   110
In its rendering of crease where curve was, where was raven,
    grizzle—
Pits, where peonies once did dwell.

93 maybe] ⟨haply⟩ *Hol.*   95 steep] still *FR*   ⟨And bedrowsed by place and meeting so uncustomed, still and eery,⟩ ⟨For one no longer buoyant, and a place so still and eery,⟩ *Hol.*   99 of] in *FR, Hol.*   103 thin tapering] ⟨unwonted⟩ *Hol.*
106 Dozing] Sleeping *FR, Hol.*   107 spectre] phantom *FR*; ⟨phantom⟩ *Hol.*
108 In her shape I straightway scanned; *FR*; ⟨By my seat I straightway scanned;⟩ ⟨In her shape I straightway scanned;⟩ *Hol.*   111 was,] ~, ⟨—⟩ *Hol.*   112 White, where roses *FR*; ⟨White,⟩ Pits, where roses *Hol.*

She had wakened, and perceiving
(I surmise) my sigh and shock, my quite involuntary dismay,
Up she started, and—her wasted figure all throughout it
    heaving—   115
Said, 'Ah, yes: I am *thus* by day!

'Can you really wince and wonder
That the sunlight should reveal you such a thing of skin and
    bone,
As if unaware a Death's-head must of need lie not far under
Flesh whose years out-count your own?   120

'Yes: that movement was a warning
Of the worth of man's devotion!—Yes, Sir, I am *old*,' said she,
'And the thing which should increase love turns it quickly into
    scorning—
And your new-won heart from me!'

Then she went, ere I could call her,   125
With the too proud temper ruling that had parted us before,
And I saw her form descend the slopes, and smaller grow and
    smaller,
Till I caught its course no more . . . .

True; I might have dogged her downward;
—But it *may* be (though I know not) that this trick on us of
    Time   130
Disconcerted and confused me.—Soon I bent my footsteps
    townward,
Like to one who had watched a crime.

Well I knew my native weakness,
Well I know it still. I cherished her reproach like physic-wine,
For I saw in that emaciate shape of bitterness and bleakness   135
A nobler soul than mine.

114 quite] vague *FR*   120 Flesh] One *TL*   124 me!'] ~!". . . . *FR*; ~!"
⟨. . . .⟩ *Hol.*   128 Till I noted it no more.— *FR*; Till I noted it no more. . . . *Hol.*
129 dogged] tracked *FR*; ⟨tracked⟩ *Hol.*   downward;] ~. *FR, Hol.*   132 watched]
seen *FR*; ⟨seen⟩ *Hol.*   134 Well] And *FR*   136 A] ⟨Was⟩ *Hol.*

Did I not return, then, ever?—
Did we meet again?—mend all?—Alas, what greyhead per-
    severes!—
Soon I got the Route elsewhither.—Since that hour I have
    seen her never:
Love is lame at fifty years.   140

A TRAMPWOMAN'S TRAGEDY*

(182-)

I

From Wynyard's Gap the livelong day,
    The livelong day,
We beat afoot the northward way
    We had travelled times before.
The sun-blaze burning on our backs,   5
Our shoulders sticking to our packs,
By fosseway, fields, and turnpike tracks
    We skirted sad Sedge-Moor.

II

Full twenty miles we jaunted on,
    We jaunted on,—   10
My fancy-man, and jeering John,
    And Mother Lee, and I.
And, as the sun drew down to west,
We climbed the toilsome Poldon crest,
And saw, of landskip sights the best,   15
    The inn that beamed thereby.

139 elsewhither.—] ⟨from Casterbridge.—⟩ *Hol.*   that hour] ⟨then⟩ *Hol.*   never:]
~. *FR, Hol.*

A TRAMPWOMAN'S TRAGEDY. *North American Review*, Nov. 1903; *FEH* (1917). *MS1, P1*
(*NAR*) Adams; *P2* (*NAR*) Berg
    Title The Tramp's Tragedy *MS1, P1*; ⟨The Tramp's⟩ *P2*   *Headnote* (The incidents
on which this tale is based occurred in 1827) *NAR*; (1827) *Hol.*
    2 day,] ~ *Hol.*   4 ⟨We'd⟩ *MS1*   9 ⟨we'd⟩ *MS1*   10 ⟨We'd⟩
MS1   on,—] ~, *MS1-NAR, Hol.*   14 toilsome] lofty *MS1, P1*; ⟨lofty⟩
parching *P2*; parching *NAR*   15 saw,] ~⟨—⟩, *MS1*   best,] ~⟨—⟩, *MS1*
16 beamed] stood *NAR*; ⟨stood⟩ *Hol.*

III

For months we had padded side by side,
     Ay, side by side
Through the Great Forest, Blackmoor wide,
     And where the Parret ran.   20
We'd faced the gusts on Mendip ridge,
Had crossed the Yeo unhelped by bridge,
Been stung by every Marshwood midge,
     I and my fancy-man.

IV

Lone inns we loved, my man and I,   25
     My man and I;
'King's Stag', 'Windwhistle' high and dry,
     'The Horse' on Hintock Green,
The cozy house at Wynyard's Gap,
'The Hut' renowned on Bredy Knap,   30
And many another wayside tap
     Where folk might sit unseen.

V

Now as we trudged—O deadly day,
     O deadly day!—
I teased my fancy-man in play   35
     And wanton idleness.
I walked alongside jeering John,
I laid his hand my waist upon;
I would not bend my glances on
     My lover's dark distress.   40

VI

Thus Poldon top at last we won,
     At last we won,
And gained the inn at sink of sun
     Far-famed as 'Marshal's Elm'.

17 ⟨we'd⟩ *MS1*   side,] ~⟨—⟩, *MS1*   18 Ay,] All *TL09*; Close *TL10, FEH*
side] ~, *MS1-NAR*   25 I,] ~ *Hol.*   26 I;] ~, *MS1-NAR, Hol.*
27 *no quotation marks MS1-NAR, Hol.*   28 The "Horse" *MS1-NAR*
30 The "Hut" *MS1-NAR*   renowned] for rest *WE20*   Bredy] Bredy's *MS1-NAR*
Knap,] ~ *Hol.*   37 John,] ~ *Hol.*   44 Far-famed] ⟨Renowned⟩ *MS1*
no quotation marks MS1-NAR, Hol.

Beneath us figured tor and lea,   45
From Mendip to the western sea—
I doubt if finer sight there be
    Within this royal realm.

VII

Inside the settle all a-row—
    All four a-row   50
We sat, I next to John, to show
    That he had wooed and won.
And then he took me on his knee,
And swore it was his turn to be
My favoured mate, and Mother Lee   55
    Passed to my former one.

VIII

Then in a voice I had never heard,
    I had never heard,
My only Love to me: 'One word,
    My lady, if you please!   60
Whose is the child you are like to bear?—
His? After all my months o' care?'
God knows 'twas not! But, O despair!
    I nodded—still to tease.

IX

Then up he sprung, and with his knife—   65
    And with his knife
He let out jeering Johnny's life,
    Yes; there, at set of sun.
The slant ray through the window nigh
Gilded John's blood and glazing eye,   70
Ere scarcely Mother Lee and I
    Knew that the deed was done.

46 western] cap. MS1-NAR, Hol.   50 Ay, all a-row— NAR, Hol.; Ay, all a-row
TL   55 mate,] man, NAR, Hol.   57 I had] I'd NAR   58 I had]
I'd NAR   59 word,] ~ Hol.   60 lady,] cap. MS1-NAR, Hol.; doxy,
TLo9   61 bear?-] ~? MS1   63 God] ⟨—⟩ God MS1
65 knife—] ~, MS1, P1; ~⟨,⟩— P2   66 knife] ~, MS1, P1; ~⟨,⟩ P2
67 life,] ~; MS1-NAR, Hol.   68 set] sink MS1-NAR   70 eye,] ~ Hol.

X

The taverns tell the gloomy tale,
    The gloomy tale,
How that at Ivel-chester jail   75
    My Love, my sweetheart swung;
Though stained till now by no misdeed
Save one horse ta'en in time o' need;
(Blue Jimmy stole right many a steed
    Ere his last fling he flung).   80

XI

Thereaft I walked the world alone,
    Alone, alone!
On his death-day I gave my groan
    And dropt his dead-born child.
'Twas nigh the jail, beneath a tree,   85
None tending me; for Mother Lee
Had died at Glaston, leaving me
    Unfriended on the wild.

XII

And in the night as I lay weak,
    As I lay weak,   90
The leaves a-falling on my cheek,
    The red moon low declined—
The ghost of him I'd die to kiss
Rose up and said: 'Ah, tell me this!
Was the child mine, or was it his?   95
    Speak, that I rest may find!'

XIII

O doubt not but I told him then,
    I told him then,

73 tale,] ~ *Hol.*
80 flung).] ~.) *all texts*
82 alone!] ~! ⟨. . . .⟩ *MS1*
~,⟨—⟩ *MS1*
94 up] ~, *MS1–NAR*
97 O] ~, *MS1–NAR*

76 My man, my lover, *NAR*; ⟨My man, my lover⟩ *Hol.*
81 walked] traipsed *MS1*, *P1*; ⟨traipsed⟩ *P2*
83 groan] ~, *MS1–NAR*   90 weak]
91 cheek,] ~ *Hol.*   92 declined—] ⟨deprest⟩ *P2*
'Ah,] "O *MS1–NAR, Hol.*   96 ⟨find my rest!"⟩ *P2*

That I had kept me from all men
    Since we joined lips and swore.   100
Whereat he smiled, and thinned away
    As the wind stirred to call up day . . .
—'Tis past! And here alone I stray
    Haunting the Western Moor.

                April 1902.

THE TWO ROSALINDS*

I

The dubious daylight ended,
And I walked the Town alone, unminding whither bound and
    why,
As from each gaunt street and gaping square a mist of light
    ascended
And dispersed upon the sky.

II

Files of evanescent faces   5
Passed each other without heeding, in their travail, teen, or
    joy,
Some in void unvisioned listlessness inwrought with pallid
    traces
Of keen penury's annoy.

100 Since faith with him I swore. *MS1, P1*; ⟨faith with him I⟩ *P2*   101 away] ∼,
MS1, P1; ∼⟨,⟩ *P2*   102 to call] ⟨to call⟩ ⟨it called⟩ *MS1*   103 And I
alone now stay *NAR*; And lonely here I stay *Hol.*
    Date om. *MS1*

THE TWO ROSALINDS. *Collier's,* 20 Mar. 1909; 'London Nights by Thomas Hardy. I. The Two
Rosalinds', *English Review,* Apr. 1909. *MS1* (*C*) Adams
    2 unminding] unweeting *C*   6 Passed, unheeding one another *C*   teen,] ∼
Hol.

III

Nebulous flames in crystal cages
Leered as if with discontent at city movement, murk, and
    grime,   10
And as waiting some procession of great ghosts from bygone
    ages
To exalt the ignoble time.

IV

In a colonnade high-lighted,
By a thoroughfare where stern utilitarian traffic dinned,
On a red and white emblazonment of players and parts, I
    sighted   15
The name of 'Rosalind',

V

And her famous mates of 'Arden',
Who observed no stricter customs than 'the seasons' differ-
    ence' bade,
Who lived with running brooks for books in Nature's
    wildwood garden,
And called idleness their trade   20

VI

Now the poster stirred an ember
Still remaining from my ardours of some forty years before,
When the selfsame portal on an eve it thrilled me to remember
A like announcement bore;

VII

And expectantly I had entered,   25
And had first beheld in human mould a Rosalind woo and
    plead,
On whose transcendent figuring my speedy soul had centred
As it had been she indeed . . . .

10 Leered C, WE, CP] Gleamed ER, TL   with] in C   city] cap. MS1   murk,]
mulch, C   13 colonnade] ~, MS1, C   17 'Arden',] "Arden"
MS1, C, ER   18 seasons'] season's MS1, C, ER   bade,] ~ Hol.
22 before,] ~ MS1, C, ER

VIII

So; all other plans discarding,
I resolved on entrance, bent on seeing what I once had seen,   30
And approached the gangway of my earlier knowledge, dis-
    regarding
    The tract of time between.

IX

'The words, sir?' cried a creature
Hovering mid the shine and shade as 'twixt the live world and
    the tomb;
But the well-known numbers needed not for me a text or
    teacher
     To revive and re-illume.   35

X

Then the play . . . . But how unfitted
Was *this* Rosalind!—a mammet quite to me, in memories
    nurst,
And with chilling disappointment soon I sought the street I
    had quitted,
    To re-ponder on the first.   40

XI

The hag still hawked,—I met her
Just without the colonnade. 'So you don't like her, sir?' said
    she.
'Ah—*I* was once that Rosalind!—I acted her—none better—
    Yes—in eighteen sixty-three.

XII

'Thus I won Orlando to me   45
In my then triumphant days when I had charm and
    maidenhood,

---

29 discarding,] ~ *MS1, C, ER, Hol.*   30 resolved on entrance,] now turned
me inward, *C*   31 approached the gangway] pursued the pathway *C*
32 tract] expanse *C, ER, TL*   33 sir?'] *cap. MS1*   34 'twixt the shine
and shade as mid *C, ER, TL*   37 Then the play....] I passed in.... *C*; I was
in... *ER*; ⟨I was in⟩ *Hol.*; In I went..... *TL*   39 quitted,] ~ *MS1, C, ER, Hol.*
42 said] cried *C, ER, Hol.*   43 'Ah—] "Ah, well— *C*   44 sixty-three.]
~! *C, ER, Hol.*   45 'This is how I won him to me *C*   46 then] once *C, ER*

Now some forty years ago.—I used to say, *Come woo me, woo
  me!*'
  And she struck the attitude.

XIII

  It was when I had gone there nightly;
And the voice—though raucous now—was yet the old one.—
  Clear as noon   50
My Rosalind was here . . . . Thereon the band withinside
  lightly
  Beat up a merry tune.

A SUNDAY MORNING TRAGEDY*

(*circa* 186–)

  I bore a daughter flower-fair,
  In Pydel Vale, alas for me;
  I joyed to mother one so rare,
  But dead and gone I now would be.

  Men looked and loved her as she grew,   5
  And she was won, alas for me;
  She told me nothing, but I knew,
  And saw that sorrow was to be.

  I knew that one had made her thrall,
  A thrall to him, alas for me;   10
  And then, at last, she told me all,
  And wondered what her end would be.

47 *no ital. Hol.*   *me!*'] ~!"— *MS1, C*   49 It was when] 'Twas the year *C*
51 This was my Rosalind . . . . As interlude the band withinside lightly *C*; My Rosalind was
here . . . . The band within, as int'ract lightly *ER*

A SUNDAY MORNING TRAGEDY. *English Review*, Dec. 1908. *MS1 (ER)* Huntington Library
  Headnote (186–) *MS1*; (*circa* 1860) *ER, Hol.*
  2 Yea, flower-fair, alas for me; *ER, Hol.*   8 be.] ~: *MS1, ER*   11 all,]
~; *MS1*

She owned that she had loved too well,
Had loved too well, unhappy she,
And bore a secret time would tell, 　　　　15
Though in her shroud she'd sooner be.

I plodded to her sweetheart's door
In Pydel Vale, alas for me:
I pleaded with him, pleaded sore,
To save her from her misery. 　　　　20

He frowned, and swore he could not wed,
Seven times he swore it could not be;
'Poverty's worse than shame', he said,
Till all my hope went out of me.

'I've packed my traps to sail the main'— 　　　25
Roughly he spake, alas did he—
'Wessex beholds me not again,
'Tis worse than any jail would be!'

—There was a shepherd whom I knew,
A subtle man, alas for me: 　　　　30
I sought him all the pastures through,
Though better I had ceased to be.

I traced him by his lantern light,
And gave him hint, alas for me,
Of how she found her in the plight 　　　35
That is so scorned in Christendie.

'Is there an herb. . . .?' I asked. 'Or none?'
Yes, thus I asked him desperately.
'—There is', he said; 'a certain one. . . .'
Would he had sworn that none knew he! 　　　40

15 time] *cap. MS1* 　　　　　　16 Though in her grave she'd gladlier be. *MS1*
17 door] ~, *MS1, ER, Hol.* 　　　　18 Went to his door, alas for me. *ER*; ~: *Hol.*
25 main'—] ~", *MS1, ER*; ~"⟨,⟩— *Hol.* 　　　26 he—] ~. *MS1, ER*
27 'Wessex] "This spot *MS1* 　　29 —There] There *MS1* 　　36 in] by *ER*
39 '—There] "There *MS1, ER* 　　40 that none knew he!] none such to be. *MS1*;
naught such to be! *ER, TL09*

'To-morrow I will walk your way,'
He hinted low, alas for me.—
Fieldwards I gazed throughout next day;
Now fields I never more would see!

The sunset-shine, as curfew strook,   45
As curfew strook beyond the lea,
Lit his white smock and gleaming crook,
While slowly he drew near to me.

He pulled from underneath his smock
The herb I sought, my curse to be—   50
'At times I use it in my flock,'
He said, and hope waxed strong in me.

'''Tis meant to balk ill-motherings'—
(Ill-motherings! Why should they be?)—
'If not, would God have sent such things?'   55
So spoke the shepherd unto me.

That night I watched the poppling brew,
With bended back and hand on knee:
I stirred it till the dawnlight grew,
And the wind whiffled wailfully.   60

'This scandal shall be slain', said I,
'That lours upon her innocency:
I'll give all whispering tongues the lie;'—
But worse than whispers was to be.

'Here's physic for untimely fruit,'   65
I said to her, alas for me,
Early that morn in fond salute;
And in my grave I now would be.

—Next Sunday came, with sweet church chimes,
Next Sunday came, alas for me: 70
I went into her room betimes;
No more may such a Sunday be!

'Mother, instead of rescue nigh,'
She faintly breathed, alas for me,
'I feel as I were like to die,   75
And underground soon, soon should be.'

From church that noon the people walked
In twos and threes, alas for me,
Showed their new raiment—smiled and talked,
Though sackcloth-clad I longed to be.   80

Came to my door her lover's friends,
And cheerly cried, alas for me,
'Right glad are we he makes amends,
For never a sweeter bride can be.'

My mouth dried, as 'twere scorched within,   85
Dried at their words, alas for me:
More and more neighbours crowded in,
(O why should mothers ever be!)

'Ha-ha! Such well-kept news!' laughed they,
Yes—so they laughed, alas for me.   90
'Whose banns were called in church to-day?'—
Christ, how I wished my soul could flee!

'Where is she? O the stealthy miss,'
Still bantered they, alas for me,
'To keep a wedding close as this . . . .'   95
Ay, Fortune worked thus wantonly!

69 chimes, *TL*, *WE*] ~; *Hol.*; ~ *MS1*, *CP*   70 *ER*, *Hol.*, *WE*] ~; *MS1*; In Pydel
Vale, alas for me: *TL*, *CP*   71 betimes;] ~, *MS1*   72 And the wind
whiffled wearily. *MS1*   79 raiment—] ~,— *MS1*, *ER*   90 me.] ~; *MS1*;
~: *ER*, *Hol.*   92 Christ, how I wished I could un-be!— *ER*   93 miss,']
~!" *MS1*   94 Still] So *MS1*   95 this. . . .'] this". . . . *MS1*
96 Ay,] Yes, *MS1*   wantonly!] ~. *Hol.*

'But you are pale—you did not know?'
They archly asked, alas for me.
I stammered, 'Yes—some days—ago,'
While coffined clay I wished to be.   100

''Twas done to please her, we surmise?'
(They spoke quite lightly in their glee)
'Done by him as a fond surprise?'
I thought their words would madden me.

Her lover entered. 'Where's my bird?—   105
My bird—my flower—my picotee?
First time of asking, soon the third!'
Ah, in my grave I well may be.

To me he whispered: 'Since your call—'
So spoke he then, alas for me—   110
'I've felt for her, and righted all.'
—I think of it to agony.

'She's faint to-day—tired—nothing more—'
Thus did I lie, alas for me. . . .
I called her at her chamber door   115
As one who scarce had strength to be.

No voice replied. I went within—
O women! scourged the worst are we. . . .
I shrieked. The others hastened in
And saw the stroke there dealt on me.   120

There she lay—silent, breathless, dead,
Stone-dead she lay—wronged, sinless she!—
Ghost-white the cheeks once rosy-red:
Death had took her. Death took not me.

98 me. *MS1, ER, Hol.*] ~ , *TL, WE, CP*   99 days—] ~ *MS1*   101 her,]
~ *MS1, ER, Hol.*   102 *no parentheses MS1, ER*   103 'Done] "—Done
MS1, ER   107 asking,] ~ — *MS1*   third!'] ~ !"— *MS1*   109 call—']
~"— *MS1, ER, Hol.*   110 me—] ~ , *MS1, ER*; ~ *Hol.*   113 more—']
~"— *MS1, ER, Hol.*   117 within—] ~ ,— *MS1, ER, Hol.*   120 on] to
ER   121 dead,] ~ — *MS1, ER, Hol.*   122 Stone-dead she lay— *Hol., CP,
WE*] In Pydel Vale— *TL*   124 her.] ~ : *MS1, ER, Hol.*

I kissed her colding face and hair, 125
I kissed her corpse—the bride to be!—
My punishment I cannot bear,
But pray God *not* to pity me.

January 1904.

THE HOUSE OF HOSPITALITIES

Here we broached the Christmas barrel,
    Pushed up the charred log-ends;
Here we sang the Christmas carol,
    And called in friends.

Time has tired me since we met here 5
    When the folk now dead were young,
Since the viands were outset here
    And quaint songs sung.

And the worm has bored the viol
    That used to lead the tune, 10
Rust eaten out the dial
    That struck night's noon.

Now no Christmas brings in neighbours,
    And the New Year comes unlit;
Where we sang the mole now labours, 15
    And spiders knit.

Yet at midnight if here walking,
    When the moon sheets wall and tree,
I see forms of old time talking,
    Who smile on me. 20

THE HOUSE OF HOSPITALITIES. *New Quarterly*, Jan. 1909
    2 And up-piled the billet-ends; *NQ*   6 young,] ~,— *Hol.*   17 Yet at
midnight if I walk here *NQ*   walking,] ~ *Hol.*   19 Forms outshape and seem to
talk here, *NQ*   20 Who] And *NQ*

JOHN AND JANE

I

He sees the world as a boisterous place
Where all things bear a laughing face,
And humorous scenes go hourly on,
    Does John.

II

They find the world a pleasant place   5
Where all is ecstasy and grace,
Where a light has risen that cannot wane,
    Do John and Jane.

III

They see as a palace their cottage-place,
Containing a pearl of the human race,   10
A hero, maybe, hereafter styled,
    Do John and Jane with a baby-child.

IV

They rate the world as a gruesome place,
Where fair looks fade to a skull's grimace,—
As a pilgrimage they would fain get done—   15
    Do John and Jane with their worthless son.

THE CURATE'S KINDNESS

A Workhouse Irony

I

I thought they'd be strangers aroun' me,
    But she's to be there!
Let me jump out o' waggon and go back and drown me
    At Pummery or Ten-Hatches Weir.

JOHN AND JANE. 7 wane,] ~ *Hol.*   9 cottage-place,] ~ *Hol.*   11 *no commas Hol.*   13 place,] ~ *Hol.*   14 grimace,—] ~, *Hol.* 15 done—] ~ *Hol.*

THE CURATE'S KINDNESS. 1 aroun'] ⟨around⟩ *Hol.*   me,] ~ *Hol.*   4 Hatches] ~' *Hol.*

II

I thought: 'Well, I've come to the Union—
　　The workhouse at last—
After honest hard work all the week, and Communion
　　O' Zundays, these fifty years past.

III

''Tis hard; but', I thought, 'never mind it:
　　There's gain in the end:
And when I get used to the place I shall find it
　　A home, and may find there a friend.

IV

'Life there will be better than t'other,
　　For peace is assured.
The men in one wing and their wives in another
　　Is strictly the rule of the Board.'

V

Just then our young Pa'son arriving
　　Steps up out of breath
To the side o' the waggon wherein we were driving
　　To Union; and calls out and saith:

VI

'Old folks, that harsh order is altered,
　　Be not sick of heart!
The Guardians they poohed and they pished and they paltered
　　When urged not to keep you apart.

VII

'"It is wrong", I maintained, "to divide them,
　　Near forty years wed."
"Very well, sir. We promise, then, they shall abide them
　　In one wing together," they said.'

---

15 *another*] ~⟨,⟩ *Hol.*　　17 our *Hol., WE, DCM3*] one *TL, CP*　　26 wed."]
~."— *Hol.*　　27 sir.] *cap. Hol.*

VIII

Then I sank—knew 'twas quite a foredone thing
        That misery should be   30
To the end! . . . To get freed of her there was the one thing
        Had made the change welcome to me.

IX

To go there was ending but badly;
        'Twas shame and 'twas pain;
'But anyhow', thought I, 'thereby I shall gladly   35
        Get free of this forty years' chain.'

X

I thought they'd be strangers aroun' me,
        But she's to be there!
Let me jump out o' waggon and go back and drown me
        At Pummery or Ten-Hatches Weir.   40

THE FLIRT'S TRAGEDY

(17—)

Here alone by the logs in my chamber,
        Deserted, decrepit—
Spent flames limning ghosts on the wainscot
        Of friends I once knew—

My drama and hers begins weirdly   5
        Its dumb re-enactment,
Each scene, sigh, and circumstance passing
        In spectral review.

—Wealth was mine beyond wish when I met her—
        The pride of the lowland—   10
Embowered in Tintinhull Valley
        By laurel and yew;

---

37 me,] ~ *Hol.*   39 waggon] ~, *Hol.*

THE FLIRT'S TRAGEDY. 1 chamber,] ~ — *Hol.*   4 knew—] ~, *Hol.*   8 In
⟨gho⟩ spectral *Hol.*

And love lit my soul, notwithstanding
    My features' ill favour,
Too obvious beside her perfections   15
    Of line and of hue.

But it pleased her to play on my passion,
    And whet me to pleadings
That won from her mirthful negations
    And scornings undue.   20

Then I fled her disdains and derisions
    To cities of pleasure,
And made me the crony of idlers
    In every purlieu.

Of those who lent ear to my story,   25
    A needy Adonis
Gave hint how to grizzle her garden
    From roses to rue,

Could his price but be paid for so purging
    My scorner of scornings:
Thus tempted, the lust to avenge me   30
    Germed inly and grew.

I clothed him in sumptuous apparel,
    Consigned to him coursers,
Meet equipage, liveried attendants   35
    In full retinue.

So dowered, with letters of credit
    He wayfared to England,
And spied out the manor she goddessed,
    And handy thereto,   40

Set to hire him a tenantless mansion
    As coign-stone of vantage
For testing what gross adulation
    Of beauty could do.

13 notwithstanding] though misgiving *Hol.*   25 story,] ~ *Hol.*   31 avenge
me] retaliate *TL, WE13*   32 inly] in me *TL, WE13*   40 handy] ⟨nig⟩
Hol.   thereto,] ~ *Hol.*

He laboured through mornings and evens,   45
      On new moons and sabbaths,
By wiles to enmesh her attention
      In park, path, and pew;

And having afar played upon her,
      Advanced his lines nearer,   50
And boldly outleaping conventions,
      Bent briskly to woo.

His gay godlike face, his rare seeming
      Anon worked to win her,
And later, at noontides and night-tides   55
      They held rendezvous.

His tarriance full spent, he departed
      And met me in Venice,
And lines from her told that my jilter
      Was stooping to sue.   60

Not long could be further concealment,
      She pled to him humbly:
'By our love and our sin, O protect me;
      I fly unto you!'

A mighty remorse overgat me,   65
      I heard her low anguish,
And there in the gloom of the *calle*
      My steel ran him through.

A swift push engulphed his hot carrion
      Within the canal there—   70
That still street of waters dividing
      The city in two.

—I wandered awhile all unable
      To smother my torment,
My brain racked by yells as from Tophet   75
      Of Satan's whole crew.

49 her,] ~ *Hol.*   51 conventions,] ~ *Hol.*   57 spent,] ~ *Hol.*
61 concealment,] ~ *Hol.*   69 push] thrust *TL*

A month of unrest brought me hovering
  At home in her precincts,
To whose hiding-hole local story
  Afforded a clue.   80

Exposed, and expelled by her people,
  Afar off in London
I found her alone, in a sombre
  And soul-stifling mew.

Still burning to make reparation   85
  I pleaded to wive her,
And father her child, and thus faintly
  My mischief undo.

She yielded, and spells of calm weather
  Succeeded the tempest;   90
And one sprung of him stood as scion
  Of my bone and thew. . . .

But Time unveils sorrows and secrets,
  And so it befell now:
By inches the curtain was twitched at, 95
  And slowly undrew.

As we lay, she and I, in the night-time,
  We heard the boy moaning:
'O misery mine! My false father
  Has murdered my true!'   100

She gasped: yea, she heard; understood it.
  Next day the child fled us;
And nevermore sighted was even
  A print of his shoe.

Thenceforward she shunned me, and languished; 105
  Till one day the park-pool
Embraced her fair form, and extinguished
  Her eyes' living blue.

79 hiding-hole] ⟨late career⟩ *Hol.*

—So; ask not what blast may account for
        This aspect of pallor,   110
These bones that just prison within them
        Life's poor residue;

But pass by, and leave unregarded
        A Cain to his suffering,
For vengeance too dark on the woman   115
        Whose lover he slew.

THE FARM-WOMAN'S WINTER

I

If seasons all were summers,
        And leaves would never fall,
And hopping casement-comers
        Were foodless not at all,
And fragile folk might be here   5
        That white winds bid depart;
Then one I used to see here
        Would warm my wasted heart!

II

One frail, who, bravely tilling
        Long hours in gripping gusts,   10
Was mastered by their chilling,
        And now his ploughshare rusts.
So savage winter catches
        The breath of limber things,
And what I love he snatches,   15
        And what I love not, brings.

---

111 just prison] ⟨can just cage⟩ *Hol.*   112 residue;] ~, *Hol.*

THE FARM-WOMAN'S WINTER. *Pall Mall Magazine*, Jan. 1905. *MS1 (PM)* Bancroft
    1 all were] were all *PM*   6 depart;] ~, *MS1*   11 chilling,] ~; *MS1*,
PM   15 snatches,] ~ *Hol.*, *TL09*

BEREFT

In the black winter morning
No light will be struck near my eyes
While the clock in the stairway is warning
For five, when he used to rise.
       Leave the door unbarred,   5
       The clock unwound,
       Make my lone bed hard—
       Would 'twere underground!

When the summer dawns clearly,
And the appletree-tops seem alight,   10
Who will undraw the curtain and cheerly
Call out that the morning is bright?

       When I tarry at market
No form will cross Durnover Lea
In the gathering darkness, to hark at   15
Grey's Bridge for the pit-pat o' me.

When the supper crock's steaming,
And the time is the time of his tread,
I shall sit by the fire and wait dreaming
In a silence as of the dead.   20
       Leave the door unbarred,
       The clock unwound,
       Make my lone bed hard—
       Would 'twere underground!

                1901.

SHE HEARS THE STORM

There was a time in former years—
    While my roof-tree was his—
When I should have been distressed by fears
    At such a night as this.

BEREFT. 9 clearly,] ~ *Hol.*   16 o' me.] of me. *Hol.*

SHE HEARS THE STORM. *Title* The Widow's Thought *Hol.*

I should have murmured anxiously,   5
    'The pricking rain strikes cold;
His road is bare of hedge or tree,
    And he is getting old.'

But now the fitful chimney-roar,
    The drone of Thorncombe trees,   10
The Froom in flood upon the moor,
    The mud of Mellstock Leaze,

The candle slanting sooty wick'd,
    The thuds upon the thatch,
The eaves-drops on the window flicked,   15
    The clacking garden-hatch,

And what they mean to wayfarers,
    I scarcely heed or mind;
He has won that storm-tight roof of hers
    Which Earth grants all her kind.   20

AUTUMN IN KING'S HINTOCK PARK*

Here by the baring bough
    Raking up leaves,
Often I ponder how
    Springtime deceives,—
I, an old woman now,   5
    Raking up leaves.

Here in the avenue
    Raking up leaves
Lords' ladies pass in view,
    Until one heaves   10

8 he is] ⟨I am⟩ Hol.   19 He has reached the roof well-known as hers Hol.
20 That Earth provides her kind. Hol.

AUTUMN IN KING'S HINTOCK PARK. Daily Mail Books' Supplement, 17 Nov. 1906. MS1 (DM)
Bancroft
    Title Autumn in my Lord's Park DM; Autumn in the Park TL
    8 leaves,] ~ Hol.   9 Ladies and lords I view, DM   10 Till a sigh
heaves DM

Sighs at life's russet hue,
    Raking up leaves!

Just as my shape you see
    Raking up leaves,
I saw, when fresh and free,
    Those memory weaves
Into grey ghosts by me,
    Raking up leaves.

Yet, Dear, though one may sigh,
    Raking up leaves,
New leaves will dance on high—
    Earth never grieves!—
Will not, when missed am I
    Raking up leaves.

                1901.

15

20

SHUT OUT THAT MOON*

Close up the casement, draw the blind,
    Shut out that stealing moon,
She bears too much the guise she wore
    Before our lutes were strewn
With years-deep dust, and names we read
    On a white stone were hewn.

Step not forth on the dew-dashed lawn
    To view the Lady's Chair,
Immense Orion's glittering form,
    The Less and Greater Bear:
Stay in; to such sights we were drawn
    When faded ones were fair.

5

10

11 At my life's russet hue *DM*   hue,] ~ *Hol.*   12 leaves!] ~. *MS1, DM, Hol.*
13 shape] form *DM*; ⟨form⟩ *Hol.*   14 leaves,] ~ *Hol.*   15 fresh] fair *DM,*
Hol.   17 by] for *DM*   me,] ~ *MS1, Hol.*   19 sigh,] ~ *MS1, Hol.*
22 grieves!—] ~! *MS1, DM*   23 Will] — ~ *MS1, DM*
    Date *om. DM*

SHUT OUT THAT MOON. 2 stealing] sad-shaped *TL09*   3 bears] wears *TL, WE13,*
CP   guise] look *SP*   5 read] ⟨know⟩ *Hol.*   7 forth] out *TL, CP*
10 Less] small *Hol.*; Small *TL09*   Greater] *l.c. Hol.*

Brush not the bough for midnight scents
    That come forth lingeringly,
And wake the same sweet sentiments   15
    They breathed to you and me
When living seemed a laugh, and love
    All it was said to be.

Within the common lamp-lit room
    Prison my eyes and thought;   20
Let dingy details crudely loom,
    Mechanic speech be wrought:
Too fragrant was Life's early bloom,
    Too tart the fruit it brought!

1904.

REMINISCENCES OF A DANCING MAN*

I

Who now remembers Almack's balls—
    Willis's sometime named—
In those two smooth-floored upper halls
    For faded ones so famed?
Where as we trod to trilling sound   5
The fancied phantoms stood around,
    Or joined us in the maze,
Of the powdered Dears from Georgian years,
Whose dust lay in sightless sealed-up biers,
    The fairest of former days.   10

II

Who now remembers gay Cremorne,
    And all its jaunty jills,
And those wild whirling figures born
    Of Jullien's grand quadrilles?

22 wrought:] ~; *Hol.*

REMINISCENCES OF A DANCING MAN. *Collier's*, 27 Mar. 1909; 'London Nights by Thomas
Hardy. II. Reminiscences of a Dancing Man', *English Review*, Apr. 1909. *MS1 (ER)* Yale
    2 sometime] sometimes *C*   9 sightless] eighteen *C*   biers,] ~; *MS1, C, ER*
11 Cremorne,] ~ *MS1, C, ER*

With hats on head and morning coats   15
There footed to his prancing notes
      Our partner-girls and we;
And the gas-jets winked, and the lustres clinked,
And the platform throbbed as with arms enlinked
      We moved to the minstrelsy.   20

III

Who now recalls those crowded rooms
      Of old yclept 'The Argyll',
Where to the deep Drum-polka's booms
      We hopped in standard style?
Whither have danced those damsels now!   25
Is Death the partner who doth moue
      Their wormy chaps and bare?
Do their spectres spin like sparks within
The smoky halls of the Prince of Sin
      To a thunderous Jullien air?   30

THE DEAD MAN WALKING

They hail me as one living,
      But don't they know
That I have died of late years,
      Untombed although?

I am but a shape that stands here,   5
      A pulseless mould,
A pale past picture, screening
      Ashes gone cold.

Not at a minute's warning,
      Not in a loud hour,   10
For me ceased Time's enchantments
      In hall and bower.

24 hopped] swung *TL*   standard] boisterous *C, ER, Hol.*   26 moue]
mowe *MS1*
      Date 1895 *C*

THE DEAD MAN WALKING. 10 Not] Nor *Hol.*   hour,] ~ *Hol.*

There was no tragic transit,
    No catch of breath,
When silent seasons inched me   15
    On to this death. . . .

—A Troubadour-youth I rambled
    With Life for lyre,
The beats of being raging
    In me like fire.   20

But when I practised eyeing
    The goal of men,
It iced me, and I perished
    A little then.

When passed my friend, my kinsfolk,   25
    Through the Last Door,
And left me standing bleakly,
    I died yet more;

And when my Love's heart kindled
    In hate of me,   30
Wherefore I knew not, died I
    One more degree.

And if when I died fully
    I cannot say,
And changed into the corpse-thing   35
    I am to-day;

Yet is it that, though whiling
    The time somehow
In walking, talking, smiling,
    I live not now.   40

14 No] Nor *Hol.*   16 Onward to death . . . . *Hol.*   35 the] ⟨this⟩ *Hol.*
36 to-day;] ~, *Hol.*
    Date 1896 *Hol.*

MORE LOVE LYRICS

1967

In five-score summers! All new eyes,
New minds, new modes, new fools, new wise;
New woes to weep, new joys to prize;

With nothing left of me and you
In that live century's vivid view   5
Beyond a pinch of dust or two;

A century which, if not sublime,
Will show, I doubt not, at its prime,
A scope above this blinkered time.

—Yet what to me how far above?   10
For I would only ask thereof
That thy worm should be my worm, Love!

16 Westbourne Park Villas, 1867.

HER DEFINITION

I lingered through the night to break of day,
Nor once did sleep extend a wing to me,
Intently busied with a vast array
Of epithets that should outfigure thee.

Full-featured terms—all fitless—hastened by,   5
And this sole speech remained: 'That maiden mine!'—
Debarred from due description then did I
Perceive the indefinite phrase could yet define.

1967. *Place* 16 W. P. Villas, 1867. *TL*

HER DEFINITION. 1 day,] ~ *Hol.*   5 Full-featured] Full-feathered *Hol.*

As common chests encasing wares of price
Are borne with tenderness through halls of state,   10
For what they cover, so the poor device
Of homely wording I could tolerate,
Knowing its unadornment held as freight
The sweetest image outside Paradise.

                                              16 Westbourne Park Villas,
                                                    Summer: 1866.

THE DIVISION*

Rain on the windows, creaking doors,
    With blasts that besom the green,
And I am here, and you are there,
    And a hundred miles between!

O were it but the weather, Dear,   5
    O were it but the miles
That summed up all our severance,
    There might be room for smiles.

But that thwart thing betwixt us twain,
    Which nothing cleaves or clears,   10
Is more than distance, Dear, or rain,
    And longer than the years!

                                              1893.

11 Their core their warrant, so the poor device *TL*
    Place Westbourne Park Villas *Hol.*; W. P. V. *TL, WE, CP*

THE DIVISION. *MS1* RLP
    2 blasts] gusts *MS1, Hol.*   green,] ~; *MS1, Hol.*   5 Dear,] *l.c. MS1*
    7 That make our sum of severance *MS1*; ~, *TL*; That made up all our severance, *WE13*
    9 But that dark bar betwixt us, dear *MS1*   thwart thing] dark cloud *Hol.*   twain,]
    〈still〉 *Hol.*   10 Which nothing cloaks or clears, *MS1, Hol.*; Which hides, yet
    reappears, *TL*   11 Is more than storm and distance *MS1*; 〈Is more than storm and
    distance, Dear,〉 *Hol.*   or rain,] 〈and rain,〉 *Hol.*
    Date DCM3] *om. MS1, TL, WE13*; 189- *CP, WE20, DCM2 and 4*

ON THE DEPARTURE PLATFORM

We kissed at the barrier; and passing through
She left me, and moment by moment got
Smaller and smaller, until to my view
    She was but a spot;

A wee white spot of muslin fluff   5
That down the diminishing platform bore
Through hustling crowds of gentle and rough
    To the carriage door.

Under the lamplight's fitful glowers,
Behind dark groups from far and near,   10
Whose interests were apart from ours,
    She would disappear,

Then show again, till I ceased to see
That flexible form, that nebulous white;
And she who was more than my life to me   15
    Had vanished quite. . . .

We have penned new plans since that fair fond day,
And in season she will appear again—
Perhaps in the same soft white array—
    But never as then!   20

—'And why, young man, must eternally fly
A joy you'll repeat, if you love her well?'
—O friend, nought happens twice thus; why,
    I cannot tell!

ON THE DEPARTURE PLATFORM. *MS1* Adams
    4 spot;] ∼, *MS1*; ∼.— *Hol.*   10 near,] ∼ *MS1, WE*   14 That] The *MS1*   that] the *MS1*   15 my life] them all *MS1, Hol.*   17 penned] shaped *MS1, Hol.*   20 then!] ∼. *MS1*   21 —'And] "And *MS1*   fly] die *MS1, Hol.*   22 joy] scene *MS1*; ⟨bliss⟩ *Hol.*   23 —O] O *MS1* why,] ∼ *Hol.*

IN A CATHEDRAL CITY

These people have not heard your name;
No loungers in this placid place
Have helped to bruit your beauty's fame.

The grey Cathedral, towards whose face
Bend eyes untold, has met not yours;　　　　5
Your shade has never swept its base,

Your form has never darked its doors,
Nor have your faultless feet once thrown
A pensive pit-pat on its floors.

Along the street to maids well known　　　10
Blithe lovers hum their tender airs,
But in your praise voice not a tone. . . .

—Since nought bespeaks you here, or bears,
As I, your imprint through and through,
Here might I rest, till my heart shares　　　15
The spot's unconsciousness of you!

　　　　　　　　　　　　　　Salisbury.

'I SAY I'LL SEEK HER'

I say, 'I'll seek her side
　　Ere hindrance interposes';
　　But eve in midnight closes,
And here I still abide.

When darkness wears I see　　　　　5
　　Her sad eyes in a vision;
　　They ask, 'What indecision
Detains you, Love, from me?—

IN A CATHEDRAL CITY. 2 placid] quiet *Hol.*　　　　3 bruit] spread *Hol.*
8 faultless] ⟨pensive⟩ *Hol.*　　　9 A pensive] ⟨The faintest⟩ *Hol.*　　　10 maids
well *TL, CP, DCM4*] maidens *WE*　　　16 you!] ∼. *Hol.*

'I SAY I'LL SEEK HER'. 2 hindrance] peril *TL*　　　3 eve in midnight] ⟨day in darkness⟩
Hol.　　　5 darkness] ⟨midnight⟩ *Hol.*　　　6 sad] great *TL, WE13*　　　vision;]
∼: *Hol.*

'The creaking hinge is oiled,
    I have unbarred the backway,   10
    But you tread not the trackway;
And shall the thing be spoiled?

'Far cockcrows echo shrill,
    The shadows are abating,
    And I am waiting, waiting;   15
But O, you tarry still!'

HER FATHER*

I met her, as we had privily planned,
    Where passing feet beat busily:
She whispered: 'Father is at hand!
    He wished to walk with me.'

His presence as he joined us there   5
    Banished our words of warmth away;
We felt, with cloudings of despair,
    What Love must lose that day.

Her crimson lips remained unkissed,
    Our fingers kept no tender hold,   10
His lack of feeling made the tryst
    Embarrassed, stiff, and cold.

A cynic ghost then rose and said,
    'But is his love for her so small
That, nigh to yours, it may be read   15
    As of no worth at all?

'You love her for her pink and white;
    But what when their fresh splendours close?
His love will last her in despite
    Of Time, and wrack, and foes.'   20

Weymouth.

10 ⟨Unbolted is the backway,⟩ *Hol.*   14 ⟨The darkness is abating,⟩ *Hol.*

HER FATHER. 16 worth] count *TL*
    Place ⟨Weymouth: 1869.⟩ *Hol.*

AT WAKING

When night was lifting,
And dawn had crept under its shade,
  Amid cold clouds drifting
Dead-white as a corpse outlaid,
    With a sudden scare   5
    I seemed to behold
    My Love in bare
    Hard lines unfold.

  Yea, in a moment,
An insight that would not die   10
  Killed her old endowment
Of charm that had capped all nigh,
    Which vanished to none
    Like the gilt of a cloud,
    And showed her but one   15
    Of the common crowd.

  She seemed but a sample
Of earth's poor average kind,
  Lit up by no ample
Enrichments of mien or mind.   20
    I covered my eyes
    As to cover the thought,
    And unrecognize
    What the morn had taught.

  O vision appalling   25
When the one believed-in thing
  Is seen falling, falling,
With all to which hope can cling.
    Off: it is not true;
    For it cannot be   30
    That the prize I drew
    Is a blank to me!

                        Weymouth, 1869.

AT WAKING. 1 lifting,] ~ *Hol.*   5 With a sudden] ⟨With sudden⟩ *Hol.*
10 ⟨Those words she had written awry⟩ *Hol.*   11 endowment] ~ ⟨,⟩ *Hol.*
12 ⟨And gifts that had cheaped all nigh,⟩ *Hol.*   13 Which vanished] ⟨Vanished⟩ *Hol.*

FOUR FOOTPRINTS

Here are the tracks upon the sand
Where stood last evening she and I—
Pressed heart to heart and hand to hand;
The morning sun has baked them dry.

I kissed her wet face—wet with rain,   5
For arid grief had burnt up tears,
While reached us as in sleeping pain
The distant gurgling of the weirs.

'I have married him—yes; feel that ring;
'Tis a week ago that he put it on. . . .   10
A dutiful daughter does this thing,
And resignation succeeds anon!

'But that I body and soul was yours
Ere he'd possession, he'll never know.
He's a confident man. "The husband scores",   15
He says, "in the long run" . . . Now, Dear, go!'

I went. And to-day I pass the spot;
It is only a smart the more to endure;
And she whom I held is as though she were not,
For they have resumed their honeymoon tour.   20

IN THE VAULTED WAY

In the vaulted way, where the passage turned
To the shadowy corner that none could see,
You paused for our parting,—plaintively;
Though overnight had come words that burned
My fond frail happiness out of me.   5

FOUR FOOTPRINTS. 2 ⟨Where we stood last night—she and I—⟩ *Hol.*   11 ⟨Home
pressures rushed me into the thing;⟩ *Hol.*   12 ⟨Well, resignation may come anon!⟩
Hol.   18 smart] pang *TL*   19 not,] ∼: *Hol.*   20 For they] ⟨For
the pair⟩ The pair *Hol.*

IN THE VAULTED WAY. *Title* In the Crypted Way *TL*
    1 vaulted] crypted *TL*   3 ⟨You paused, you remember, to part from me;⟩ You
lingered, to part from me,—wistfully; *Hol.*; You paused to part from me,—plaintively; *TL*,
WE13, *CP19*

And then I kissed you,—despite my thought
That our spell must end when reflection came
On what you had deemed me, whose one long aim
Had been to serve you; that what I sought
Lay not in a heart that could breathe such blame.   10

But yet I kissed you; whereon you again
As of old kissed me. Why, why was it so?
Do you cleave to me after that light-tongued blow?
If you scorned me at eventide, how love then?
The thing is dark, Dear. I do not know.   15

IN THE MIND'S EYE*

That was once her casement,
    And the taper nigh,
Shining from within there
    Beckoned, 'Here am I!'

Now, as then, I see her   5
    Moving at the pane;
Ah; 'tis but her phantom
    Borne within my brain!—

Foremost in my vision
    Everywhere goes she;   10
Change dissolves the landscapes,
    She abides with me.

Shape so sweet and shy, Dear,
    Who can say thee nay?
Never once do I, Dear,   15
    Wish thy ghost away.

6 And then] ⟨But yet⟩ *Hol.*   13 light-tongued] ⟨tongu⟩ hot-tongued *Hol.*
15 The] ⟨That⟩ *Hol.*
    Date 1870 *Hol.*

IN THE MIND'S EYE. *Title DCM2 and 3*] The Phantom *TL, WE, CP* The Face in the Mind's Eye *SP*
    14 nay?] ~! *Hol.*

THE END OF THE EPISODE

Indulge no more may we
In this sweet-bitter pastime:
The love-light shines the last time
    Between you, Dear, and me.

There shall remain no trace   5
Of what so closely tied us,
And blank as ere love eyed us
    Will be our meeting-place.

The flowers and thymy air,
Will they now miss our coming?   10
The dumbles thin their humming
    To find we haunt not there?

Though fervent was our vow,
Though ruddily ran our pleasure,
Bliss has fulfilled its measure,   15
    And sees its sentence now.

Ache deep; but make no moans:
Smile out; but stilly suffer:
The paths of love are rougher
    Than thoroughfares of stones.   20

THE SIGH*

Little head against my shoulder,
Shy at first, then somewhat bolder,
    And up-eyed;
Till she, with a timid quaver,
Yielded to the kiss I gave her;   5
    But, she sighed.

THE END OF THE EPISODE. 4 Dear,] Sweet, *TL*, *WE13*, *CP19*   8 meeting-place.]
trysting-place. *Hol.*   16 sentence] ending *Hol.*

That there mingled with her feeling
Some sad thought she was concealing
    It implied.
—Not that she had ceased to love me,   10
None on earth she set above me;
    But she sighed.

She could not disguise a passion,
Dread, or doubt, in weakest fashion
    If she tried: 15
Nothing seemed to hold us sundered,
Hearts were victors; so I wondered
    Why she sighed.

Afterwards I knew her throughly,
And she loved me staunchly, truly,   20
    Till she died;
But she never made confession
Why, at that first sweet concession,
    She had sighed.

It was in our May, remember;   25
And though now I near November,
    And abide
Till my appointed change, unfretting,
Sometimes I sit half regretting
    That she sighed.   30

'IN THE NIGHT SHE CAME'

I told her when I left one day
That whatsoever weight of care
Might strain our love, Time's mere assault
    Would work no changes there.
And in the night she came to me,   5
    Toothless, and wan, and old,
With leaden concaves round her eyes,
    And wrinkles manifold.

I tremblingly exclaimed to her,
'O wherefore do you ghost me thus!   10
I have said that dull defacing Time
    Will bring no dreads to us.'
'And is that true of *you*?' she cried
    In voice of troubled tune.
I faltered: 'Well . . . I did not think   15
    You would test me quite so soon!'

She vanished with a curious smile,
Which told me, plainlier than by word,
That my staunch pledge could scarce beguile
    The fear she had averred.   20
Her doubts then wrought their shape in me,
    And when next day I paid
My due caress, we seemed to be
    Divided by some shade.

THE CONFORMERS*

    Yes; we'll wed, my little fay,
      And you shall write you mine,
  And in a villa chastely gray
      We'll house, and sleep, and dine.
      But those night-screened, divine,   5
      Stolen trysts of heretofore,
  We of choice ecstasies and fine
      Shall know no more.

    The formal faced cohue
      Will then no more upbraid   10
  With smiting smiles and whisperings two
      Who have thrown less loves in shade.
      We shall no more evade
      The searching light of the sun,
  Our game of passion will be played,   15
      Our dreaming done.

'IN THE NIGHT SHE CAME'. 11 dull] mere *Hol.*   19 ⟨That she regarded with sick
fear⟩ *Hol.*   20 ⟨The staunchness I had averred.⟩ *Hol.*   21 in] ⟨on⟩ *Hol.*

THE CONFORMERS. 3 ⟨And in a cot of brown or gray⟩ *Hol. verso;* ⟨And in a cot of genteel
gray⟩ *Hol.*   5 *no commas Hol.*   6 Stolen dalliances of yore, *Hol.*

We shall not go in stealth
To rendezvous unknown,
But friends will ask me of your health,
And you about my own.   20
When we abide alone,
No leapings each to each,
But syllables in frigid tone
Of household speech.

When down to dust we glide   25
Men will not say askance,
As now: 'How all the country side
Rings with their mad romance!'
But as they graveward glance
Remark: 'In them we lose   30
A worthy pair, who helped advance
Sound parish views.'

THE DAWN AFTER THE DANCE*

Here is your parents' dwelling with its curtained windows
    telling
Of no thought of us within it or of our arrival here;
Their slumbers have been normal after one day more of
    formal
Matrimonial commonplace and household life's mechanic
    gear.

I would be candid willingly, but dawn draws on so chillingly   5
As to render further cheerlessness intolerable now,
So I will not stand endeavouring to declare a day for severing,
But will clasp you just as always—just the olden love avow.

21 alone,] ~ *Hol.*   22 to] ⟨of? af?⟩ *Hol.*   27 ⟨"How these two make the
country side⟩ *Hol.*   28 Rings] ⟨Ring⟩ *Hol.*   29 ⟨As now they say, but
glance⟩ ⟨As now, but graveward glance⟩ *Hol.*   30 Remark:] ⟨And state,⟩ *Hol.*
31 ⟨A sound pair, two in consonance⟩ *Hol.*   32 ⟨With parish views."⟩ *Hol.*

THE DAWN AFTER THE DANCE. 1 parents'] ⟨father's⟩ *Hol.*   5 Be candid would I
willingly, *TL*

Through serene and surly weather we have walked the ways
    together,
And this long night's dance this year's end eve now finishes
    the spell;   10
Yet we dreamt us but beginning a sweet sempiternal spinning
Of a cord we have spun to breaking—too intemperately, too
    well.

Yes; last night we danced I know, Dear, as we did that year ago,
    Dear,
When a new strange bond between our days was formed, and
    felt, and heard;
Would that dancing were the worst thing from the latest to the
    first thing
That the faded year can charge us with; but what avails a   15
    word!

That which makes man's love the lighter and the woman's
    burn no brighter
Came to pass with us inevitably while slipped the shortening
    year. . . .
And there stands your father's dwelling with its blind bleak
    windows telling
That the vows of man and maid are frail as filmy gossamere.   20

                                  Weymouth, 1869.

THE SUN ON THE LETTER

I drew the letter out, while gleamed
The sloping sun from under a roof
Of cloud whose verge rose visibly.

11 we dreamt us] ⟨you dream we are⟩ *Hol.*   13 Dear . . . Dear] *l.c. Hol.*
14 heard;] ∼ : *Hol.*   17 lighter] ∼ , *Hol.*   burn no] ⟨love the⟩ *Hol.*
brighter] ∼ , *Hol.*   19 blind bleak] blank blear *Hol.*; blank bleak *TL*
20 man and] man ⟨to⟩ *Hol.*   frail as filmy gossamere.] flimsy, frail, and insincere. *TL09*;
frail and fitful mouthings mere. *TL10*

THE SUN ON THE LETTER. *Title* ⟨A Discord⟩ *Hol.*

The burning ball flung rays that seemed
Stretched like a warp without a woof   5
Across the levels of the lea

To where I stood, and where they beamed
As brightly on the page of proof
That she had shown her false to me

As if it had shown her true—had teemed   10
With passionate thought for my behoof
Expressed with their own ardency!

THE NIGHT OF THE DANCE

The cold moon hangs to the sky by its horn,
        And centres its gaze on me;
The stars, like eyes in reverie,
Their westering as for a while forborne,
        Quiz downward curiously.   5

Old Robert draws the backbrand in,
        The green logs steam and spit;
The half-awakened sparrows flit
From the riddled thatch; and owls begin
        To whoo from the gable-slit.   10

Yes; far and nigh things seem to know
        Sweet scenes are impending here;
That all is prepared; that the hour is near
For welcomes, fellowships, and flow
        Of sally, song, and cheer;   15

4 burning] red round *Hol.*   8 page] ⟨words⟩ *Hol.*   10 it] she *TL*
true—had] true and *Hol.*   11 thought] ⟨thoughts⟩ *Hol.*

THE NIGHT OF THE DANCE. 1 horn,] ~ *Hol.*   3 in reverie,] that idle be, *TL*
6 draws *TL, CP, DCM4*] drags *Hol.*; hauls *WE*

That spigots are pulled and viols strung;
　　That soon will arise the sound
Of measures trod to tunes renowned;
　　That She will return in Love's low tongue
My vows as we wheel around. 　20

MISCONCEPTION

I busied myself to find a sure
　　Snug hermitage
That should preserve my Love secure
　　From the world's rage;
Where no unseemly saturnals, 　5
　　Or strident traffic-roars,
Or hum of intervolved cabals
　　Should echo at her doors.

I laboured that the diurnal spin
　　Of vanities 　10
Should not contrive to suck her in
　　By dark degrees,
And cunningly operate to blur
　　Sweet teachings I had begun;
And then I went full-heart to her 　15
　　To expound the glad deeds done.

She looked at me, and said thereto
　　With a pitying smile,
'And *this* is what has busied you
　　So long a while? 　20
O poor exhausted one, I see
　　You have worn you old and thin
For naught! Those moils you fear for me
　　My nature revels in!'

MISCONCEPTION. 16 deeds] deed *Hol.* 　19 *this*] rom. *Hol.* 　22 thin] ⟨thin⟩
bare *Hol.* 　23 ⟨For naught! Those ⟨⟨risks⟩⟩ scenes fear you for me?⟩ For naught!
Fear you those things for me? *Hol.* 　24 ⟨I find most pleasure in!"⟩ For little else I
care!" *Hol.*; I find most pleasure in!" *TL, CP*

THE VOICE OF THE THORN

I

When the thorn on the down
Quivers naked and cold,
And the mid-aged and old
Pace the path there to town,
In these words dry and drear   5
It seems to them sighing:
'O winter is trying
To sojourners here!'

II

When it stands fully tressed
On a hot summer day,   10
And the ewes there astray
Find its shade a sweet rest,
By the breath of the breeze
It inquires of each farer:
'Who would not be sharer   15
Of shadow with these?'

III

But by day or by night,
And in winter or summer,
Should I be the comer
Along that lone height,   20
In its voicing to me
Only one speech is spoken:
'Here once was nigh broken
A heart, and by thee.'

FROM HER IN THE COUNTRY

I thought and thought of thy crass clanging town
To folly, till convinced such dreams were ill,

I held my heart in bond, and tethered down
Fancy to where I was, by force of will.

I said: How beautiful are these flowers, this wood,   5
One little bud is far more sweet to me
Than all man's urban shows; and then I stood
Urging new zest for bird, and bush, and tree;

And strove to feel my nature brought it forth
Of instinct, or no rural maid was I;   10
But it was vain; for I could not see worth
Enough around to charm a midge or fly,

And mused again on city din and sin,
Longing to madness I might move therein!

        16 Westbourne Park Villas, 1866.

HER CONFESSION

As some bland soul, to whom a debtor says
'I'll now repay the amount I owe to you,'
In inward gladness feigns forgetfulness
That such a payment ever was his due

(His long thought notwithstanding), so did I   5
At our last meeting waive your proffered kiss
With quick divergent talk of scenery nigh,
By such suspension to enhance my bliss.

And as his looks in consternation fall
When, gathering that the debt is lightly deemed,   10
The debtor makes as not to pay at all,
So faltered I, when your intention seemed

---

7 shows;] ⟨life;⟩ *Hol.*   8 Urging ⟨an⟩ new interest in bird, bush, and tree; *Hol.*
14 Longing still more that I might be therein! *Hol.*
  Place/date Hol.] 16 W. P. V., 1866 *all printed texts*

HER CONFESSION. 1 soul, to] soul (to *Hol.*   2 you,'] you,") *Hol.*   amount] sum
Hol.   12 faltered] also *Hol.*

Converted by my false uneagerness
To putting off for ever the caress.

16 Westbourne Park Villas: 1865–7.

TO AN IMPERSONATOR OF ROSALIND*

Did he who drew her in the years ago—
Till now conceived creator of her grace—
With telescopic sight high natures know,
Discern remote in Time's untravelled space

Your soft sweet mien, your gestures, as do we,   5
And with a copyist's hand but set them down,
Glowing yet more to dream our ecstasy
When his Original should be forthshown?

For, kindled by that animated eye,
Whereto all fairnesses about thee brim,   10
And by thy tender tones, what wight can fly
The wild conviction welling up in him

That he at length beholds woo, parley, plead,
The 'very, very Rosalind' indeed!

8 Adelphi Terrace,
21st April 1867.

TO AN ACTRESS*

I read your name when you were strange to me,
Where it stood blazoned bold with many more;
I passed it vacantly, and did not see
Any great glory in the shape it wore.

Place/date Westbourne Park Villas: 1865–7. *Hol.*; W. P. V., 1865–67 *all printed texts*

TO AN IMPERSONATOR. 3 With that far prescience highest natures know, *Hol.*   5 mien,]
⟨notes,⟩ *Hol.*
    Place CP, WE20] ⟨W. P. V.⟩ *Hol.*   *Date all texts*

TO AN ACTRESS. 4 shape] ⟨tinct⟩ *Hol.*

O cruelty, the insight barred me then! 5
Why did I not possess me with its sound,
And in its cadence catch and catch again
Your nature's essence floating therearound?

Could *that* man be this I, unknowing you,
When now the knowing you is all of me, 10
And the old world of then is now a new,
And purpose no more what it used to be—
A thing of formal journeywork, but due
To springs that then were sealed up utterly?

1867.

THE MINUTE BEFORE MEETING

The grey gaunt days dividing us in twain
Seemed hopeless hills my strength must faint to climb,
But they are gone; and now I would detain
The few clock-beats that part us; rein back Time,

And live in close expectance never closed 5
In change for far expectance closed at last,
So harshly has expectance been imposed
On my long need while these slow blank months passed.

And knowing that what is now about to be
Will all *have been* in O, so short a space! 10
I read beyond it my despondency
When more dividing months shall take its place,
Thereby denying to this hour of grace
A full-up measure of felicity.

1871.

14 then . . . up] were a sealed ⟨book⟩ source *Hol.*; were a sealed source *TL*
Place ⟨Westbourne Park Villas:⟩ *Hol.*

THE MINUTE BEFORE MEETING. 14 A] ⟨The⟩ *Hol.*

HE ABJURES LOVE*

At last I put off love,
    For twice ten years
The daysman of my thought,
    And hope, and doing;
Being ashamed thereof,   5
    And faint of fears
And desolations, wrought
    In his pursuing,

Since first in youthtime those
    Disquietings   10
That heart-enslavement brings
    To hale and hoary,
Became my housefellows,
    And, fool and blind,
I turned from kith and kind   15
    To give him glory.

I was as children be
    Who have no care;
I did not shrink or sigh,
    I did not sicken;   20
But lo, Love beckoned me,
    And I was bare,
And poor, and starved, and dry,
    And fever-stricken.

Too many times ablaze   25
    With fatuous fires,
Enkindled by his wiles
    To new embraces,
Did I, by wilful ways
    And baseless ires,   30
Return the anxious smiles
    Of friendly faces.

HE ABJURES LOVE. 19 shrink] think *TL, WE13*   26 fatuous] sudden *Hol.*

No more will now rate I
　The common rare,
The midnight drizzle dew,   35
　The gray hour golden,
The wind a yearning cry,
　The faulty fair,
Things dreamt, of comelier hue
　Than things beholden! . . .   40

—I speak as one who plumbs
　Life's dim profound,
One who at length can sound
　Clear views and certain.
But—after love what comes?   45
　A scene that lours,
A few sad vacant hours,
　And then, the Curtain.

1883.

37　The wind a jealous cry, *Hol.*; The creak a jealous cry, *TL*   38　The day a care, *Hol.*; The speech a snare, *TL*   39　Things dreamt of as more fair *Hol.*
42　profound,] ~ — *Hol.*   43　can sound] has found *Hol.*   44　Clear] Vast *Hol.*   48　then,] ~ *Hol.*

A SET OF COUNTRY SONGS

LET ME ENJOY*

(Minor Key)

I

Let me enjoy the earth no less
Because the all-enacting Might
That fashioned forth its loveliness
Had other aims than my delight.

II

About my path there flits a Fair,   5
Who throws me not a word or sign;
I'll charm me with her ignoring air,
And laud the lips not meant for mine.

III

From manuscripts of moving song
Inspired by scenes and dreams unknown   10
I'll pour out raptures that belong
To others, as they were my own.

IV

And some day hence, toward Paradise
And all its blest—if such should be—
I will lift glad, afar-off eyes,   15
Though it contain no place for me.

LET ME ENJOY. *Cornhill*, Apr. 1909. *P1* (*C*) Adams
   Headnote Song: Minor Key *C*; *om. SP*
    1 earth] cap. *C*, *Hol*.   7 I will find charm in her ⟨uncare⟩ chill air, *P1*; I will find
charm in her loth air, *C*; I will find charm in her uncare, *TL*   8 laud] ⟨in⟩ *P1*
the] those *C*, *TL*   9 moving song] ⟨lyric strain⟩ *P1*; tender song *C*; rapturous strain
Hol.   10 scenes and dreams] ⟨love to me⟩ *P1*; scenes and souls *TL*, *CP*
unknown *DCM4*] ~, *all other texts*   11 raptures that belong] ⟨songs that
appertain⟩ *P1*; songs that appertain *Hol*.   13 And some day hence, *C*, *WE*, *CP*]
⟨Perhaps some day,⟩ *P1*; Perhaps some day, *TL*   14 ⟨And those therein—blest aye
to be—⟩ *P1*   15 I will lift] ⟨I shall cast⟩ Let me cast *P1*; I will cast *C*; I shall lift *TL*

AT CASTERBRIDGE FAIR*

I

THE BALLAD-SINGER

Sing, Ballad-singer, raise a hearty tune;
Make me forget that there was ever a one
I walked with in the meek light of the moon
   When the day's work was done.

Rhyme, Ballad-rhymer, start a country song;   5
Make me forget that she whom I loved well
Swore she would love me dearly, love me long,
   Then—what I cannot tell!

Sing, Ballad-singer, from your little book;
Make me forget those heart-breaks, achings, fears;   10
Make me forget her name, her sweet sweet look—
   Make me forget her tears.

II

FORMER BEAUTIES

These market-dames, mid-aged, with lips thin-drawn,
   And tissues sere,
Are they the ones we loved in years agone,
   And courted here?

Are these the muslined pink young things to whom   5
   We vowed and swore
In nooks on summer Sundays by the Froom,
   Or Budmouth shore?

Do they remember those gay tunes we trod
   Clasped on the green;   10
Aye; trod till moonlight set on the beaten sod
   A satin sheen?

AT CASTERBRIDGE FAIR: I. THE BALLAD-SINGER. *Cornhill*, Apr. 1902
   Title THE . . . SINGER] At Casterbridge Fair *C*
   11 sweet sweet] ∼ ⟨,⟩ ∼ *Hol.*
   Date ⟨1901⟩ *Hol.*

They must forget, forget! They cannot know
　　What once they were,
Or memory would transfigure them, and show　　　　15
　　Them always fair.

III

AFTER THE CLUB-DANCE

Black'on frowns east on Maidon,
　　And westward to the sea,
But on neither is his frown laden
　　With scorn, as his frown on me!

At dawn my heart grew heavy,　　　　5
　　I could not sip the wine,
I left the jocund bevy
　　And that young man o' mine.

The roadside elms pass by me, —
　　Why do I sink with shame　　　　10
When the birds a-perch there eye me?
　　They, too, have done the same!

IV

THE MARKET-GIRL

Nobody took any notice of her as she stood on the causey kerb,
All eager to sell her honey and apples and bunches of garden herb;
And if she had offered to give her wares and herself with them too
　　　　that day,
I doubt if a soul would have cared to take a bargain so choice away.

III. AFTER THE CLUB-DANCE. 1 Maidon,] ~ *Hol.*　　　4 as] like *TL*　　　5 heavy,]
~ *Hol.*　　　8 Full o' this fault o' mine. *Hol.*

IV. THE MARKET-GIRL. *Venture*, ed. L. Housman and W. S. Maugham (London: 1903). *MS1*
(*V*) Laurence Housman Collection, Somerset County Library.
　　Headnote (Country Song) *V*
　　2 All eager] A-trying *V, TL*　　　3 wares] ~, *MS1, V*　　　too] ~, *MS1, V*

But chancing to trace her sunburnt grace that morning as I
    passed nigh,   5
I went and I said, 'Poor maidy dear !—and will none of the
    people buy?'
And so it began; and soon we knew what the end of it all must be,
And I found that though no others had bid, a prize had been
    won by me.

V

THE INQUIRY

And are ye one of Hermitage—
Of Hermitage, by Ivel Road,
And do ye know, in Hermitage,
A thatch-roofed house where sengreens grow?
And does John Waywood live there still—   5
He of the name that there abode
When father hurdled on the hill
        Some fifteen years ago?

Does he now speak o' Patty Beech,
The Patty Beech he used to—see,   10
Or ask at all if Patty Beech
Is known or heard of out this way?
—Ask ever if she's living yet,
And where her present home may be,
And how she bears life's fag and fret   15
        After so long a day?

In years agone at Hermitage
This faded face was counted fair,
None fairer; and at Hermitage
We swore to wed when he should thrive.   20
But never a chance had he or I,
And waiting made his wish outwear,
And Time, that dooms man's love to die,
        Preserves a maid's alive.

---

6 said, *MS1, V, Hol., WE*] ~ *TL, CP*   maidy] ~ , *MS1, V*   of] o' *MS1, V*
V. THE INQUIRY. 3 Hermitage, *Hol.*] ~ *all other texts*   23 dooms] doom's *Hol.*

VI

A WIFE WAITS*

Will's at the dance in the Club-room below,
    Where the tall liquor-cups foam;
I on the pavement up here by the Bow,
    Wait, wait, to steady him home.

Will and his partner are treading a tune,   5
    Loving companions they be;
Willy before we were married in June,
    Said he loved no one but me;

Said he would let his old pleasures all go
    Ever to live with his Dear.   10
Will's at the dance in the Club-room below,
    Shivering I wait for him here.

VII

AFTER THE FAIR

The singers are gone from the Cornmarket-place
    With their broadsheets of rhymes,
The street rings no longer in treble and bass
    With their skits on the times,
And the Cross, lately thronged, is a dim naked space   5
    That but echoes the stammering chimes.

From Clock-corner steps, as each quarter ding-dongs,
    Away the folk roam
By the 'Hart' and Grey's Bridge into byways and 'drongs',
    Or across the ridged loam;   10
The younger ones shrilling the lately heard songs,
    The old saying, 'Would we were home.'

The shy-seeming maiden so mute in the fair
    Now rattles and talks,
And that one who looked the most swaggering there   15
    Grows sad as she walks,
And she who seemed eaten by cankering care
    In statuesque sturdiness stalks.

And midnight clears High Street of all but the ghosts
    Of its buried burghees,   20
From the latest far back to those old Roman hosts
    Whose remains one yet sees,
Who loved, laughed, and fought, hailed their friends, drank
    their toasts
    At their meeting-times here, just as these!

                              1902.

THE DARK-EYED GENTLEMAN

I

I pitched my day's leazings in Crimmercrock Lane,
To tie up my garter and jog on again,
When a dear dark-eyed gentleman passed there and said,
In a way that made all o' me colour rose-red,
       'What do I see—   5
       O pretty knee!'
And he came and he tied up my garter for me.

II

'Twixt sunset and moonrise it was, I can mind:
Ah, 'tis easy to lose what we nevermore find!—
Of the dear stranger's home, of his name, I knew nought,   10
But I soon knew his nature and all that it brought.
       Then bitterly
       Sobbed I that he
Should ever have tied up my garter for me!

THE DARK-EYED GENTLEMAN. 1 leazings] leaze-nitch *Hol.*   4 rose-red,] up red, *Hol.*
8 mind:] ~; *Hol.*   12 bitterly] bitter-ly *Hol.*

III

Yet now I've beside me a fine lissom lad,   15
And my slip's nigh forgot, and my days are not sad;
My own dearest joy is he, comrade, and friend,
He it is who safe-guards me, on him I depend;
    No sorrow brings he,
    And thankful I be   20
That his daddy once tied up my garter for me!

TO CARREY CLAVEL

You turn your back, you turn your back,
    And never your face to me,
Alone you take your homeward track,
    And scorn my company.

What will you do when Charley's seen   5
    Dewbeating down this way?
—You'll turn your back as now, you mean?
    Nay, Carrey Clavel, nay!

You'll see none's looking; put your lip
    Up like a tulip, so;   10
And he will coll you, bend, and sip:
    Yes, Carrey, yes; I know!

THE ORPHANED OLD MAID

I wanted to marry, but father said, 'No—
'Tis weakness in women to give themselves so;
If you care for your freedom you'll listen to me,
Make a spouse in your pocket, and let the men be.'

18 depend;] ~. *Hol.*   19 he,] ~ *Hol.*

TO CARREY CLAVEL. 10 so;] ~: *Hol.*

I spake on't again and again: father cried,   5
'Why—if you go husbanding, where shall I bide?
For never a home's for me elsewhere than here!'
And I yielded; for father had ever been dear.

But now father's gone, and I feel growing old,
And I'm lonely and poor in this house on the wold,   10
And my sweetheart that was found a partner elsewhere,
And nobody flings me a thought or a care.

THE SPRING CALL

Down Wessex way, when spring's a-shine,
　　The blackbird's 'pret-ty de-urr!'
In Wessex accents marked as mine
　　Is heard afar and near.

He flutes it strong, as if in song   5
　　No R's of feebler tone
Than his appear in 'pretty dear,'
　　Have blackbirds ever known.

Yet they pipe 'prattie deerh!' I glean,
　　Beneath a Scottish sky,   10
And 'pehty de-aw!' amid the treen
　　Of Middlesex or nigh.

While some folk say—perhaps in play—
　　Who know the Irish isle,
'Tis 'purrity dare!' in treeland there   15
　　When songsters would beguile.

THE ORPHANED OLD MAID. 5 cried,] ~; *Hol.*

THE SPRING CALL. *Cornhill*, May 1906; *Dorset Year-Book* (1914–15).
　Title Down Wessex Way *DYB*
　2 'pret-ty] 'purr-ty *C*   4 near.] ne-ar. *Hol.*   7 'pretty dear,'] 'purr-ty
de-urr!' *C*   dear,'] ~" *Hol.*   9 'prattie] 'prittie *C, DYB*   11 de-aw!']
deaw!' *C*

Well: I'll say what the listening birds
    Say, hearing 'pret-ty de-urr!'—
However strangers sound such words,
    That's how we sound them here.   20

Yes, in this clime at pairing time,
    As soon as eyes can see her
At dawn of day, the proper way
    To call is 'pret-ty de-urr!'

JULIE-JANE*

Sing; how 'a would sing!
    How 'a would raise the tune
When we rode in the waggon from harvesting
    By the light o' the moon!

Dance; how 'a would dance!   5
    If a fiddlestring did but sound
She would hold out her coats, give a slanting glance,
    And go round and round.

Laugh; how 'a would laugh!
    Her peony lips would part   10
As if none such a place for a lover to quaff
    At the deeps of a heart.

Julie, O girl of joy,
    Soon, soon that lover he came.
Ah, yes; and gave thee a baby-boy,   15
    But never his name . . . .

—Tolling for her, as you guess;
    And the baby too . . . . 'Tis well.
You knew her in maidhood likewise?—Yes,
    That's her burial bell.   20

18 'pret-ty] 'purr-ty C   19-24 *C sets in single quotation marks*   20 them
here.] 'em *he-urr. C*   23 dawn of] eve or C; ⟨eve or⟩ *Hol.*   24 'pret-ty
de-urr!'] "purr-ty de-urr!"' *C*

'I suppose', with a laugh, she said,
'I should blush that I'm not a wife;
But how can it matter, so soon to be dead,
What one does in life!'

When we sat making the mourning   25
By her death-bed side, said she,
'Dears, how can you keep from your lovers, adorning
In honour of me!'

Bubbling and brightsome eyed!
But now—O never again.   30
She chose her bearers before she died
From her fancy-men.

NEWS FOR HER MOTHER*

I

One mile more is
Where your door is
Mother mine!—
Harvest's coming,
Mills are strumming,   5
Apples fine,
And the cider wrung to-year will be as wine.

II

Yet, not viewing
What's a-doing
Here around   10
Is it thrills me,
And so fills me
That I bound
Like a ball or leaf or lamb along the ground.

NEWS FOR HER MOTHER. *Dorset Year-Book* (1922)
  4-5 *transposed, Hol.*   7 wrung *DYB*] made *all other texts*

III

Tremble not now   15
At your lot now
        Silly soul!
Hosts have sped them
Quick to wed them,
        Great and small,   20
Since the first two sighing half-hearts made a whole.

IV

Yet I wonder,
Will it sunder
        Her from me?
Will she guess that   25
I said 'Yes',—that
        His I'd be,
Ere I thought she might not see him as I see!

V

Old brown gable,
Granary, stable,   30
        Here you are!
O my mother,
Can another
        Ever bar
Mine from thy heart, make thy nearness seem afar?   35

THE FIDDLER

The fiddler knows what's brewing
        To the lilt of his lyric wiles:
The fiddler knows what rueing
        Will come of this night's smiles!

He sees couples join them for dancing,   5
        And afterwards joining for life,
He sees them pay high for their prancing
        By a welter of wedded strife.

THE FIDDLER. 2 wiles:] ∼, *Hol.*

He twangs: 'Music hails from the devil,
    Though vaunted to come from heaven,   10
For it makes people do at a revel
    What multiplies sins by seven.

'There's many a heart now mangled,
    And waiting its time to go,
Whose tendrils were first entangled   15
    By my sweet viol and bow!'

THE HUSBAND'S VIEW

'Can anything avail
Beldame, for hidden grief?—
Listen: I'll tell the tale,
It may bring faint relief!—

'I came where I was not known,   5
In hope to flee my sin;
And walking forth alone
A young man said, "Good e'en."

'In gentle voice and true
He asked to marry me;   10
"You only—only you
Fulfil my dream!" said he.

'We married o' Monday morn,
In the month of hay and flowers;
My cares were nigh forsworn,   15
And perfect love was ours.

'But ere the days are long
Untimely fruit will show;
My Love keeps up his song,
Undreaming it is so.   20

THE HUSBAND'S VIEW. 2 hidden] my hid *TL, CP*   3 tale,] ~ *Hol.*   5 known,]
~ *Hol.*

'And I awake in the night,
And think of months gone by,
And of that cause of flight
Concealed from my Love's eye.

'Discovery borders near,   25
And then! . . . . But something stirred?—
My husband—he is here!
Heaven—has he overheard?'—

'Yes; I have heard, sweet Nan;
I have known it all the time.   30
I am not a particular man;
Misfortunes are no crime:

'And what with our serious need
Of sons for soldiering,
That accident, indeed,   35
To maids, is a useful thing!'

ROSE-ANN

Why didn't you say you was promised, Rose-Ann?
    Why didn't you name it to me,
Ere ever you tempted me hither, Rose-Ann,
    So often, so wearifully?

O why did you let me be near 'ee, Rose-Ann,   5
    Talking things about wedlock so free,
And never by nod or by whisper, Rose-Ann,
    Give a hint that it wasn't to be?

Down home I was raising a flock of stock ewes,
    Cocks and hens, and wee chickens by scores,   10
And lavendered linen all ready to use,
    A-dreaming that they would be yours.

24 Concealed] Hidden TL, CP   25 ⟨Discovery nears me fast,⟩ Hol.
28 Heaven—] God— Hol.   33 serious need] ⟨want of men⟩ Hol.   34 Of
sons for] ⟨For ships and⟩ Hol.; Of youths for TL   35 indeed,] ⟨now and then⟩ Hol.
36 maids,] girls, Hol.   thing!'] ∼." Hol.

Mother said: 'She's a sport-making maiden, my son';
  And a pretty sharp quarrel had we;
O why do you prove by this wrong you have done   15
  That I saw not what mother could see?

Never once did you say you was promised, Rose-Ann,
  Never once did I dream it to be;
And it cuts to the heart to be treated, Rose-Ann,
  As you in your scorning treat me!   20

THE HOMECOMING*

Gruffly growled the wind on Toller downland broad and bare,
And lonesome was the house, and dark; and few came there.

'Now don't ye rub your eyes so red; we're home and have no
    cares;
Here's a skimmer-cake for supper, peckled onions, and some
    pears;
I've got a little keg o' summat strong, too, under stairs: 5
—What, slight your husband's victuals? Other brides can tackle
    theirs!'

The wind of winter mooed and mouthed their chimney like a horn,
And round the house and past the house 'twas leafless and lorn.

'But my dear and tender poppet, then, how came ye to agree
In Ivel church this morning? Sure, therereight you married me!'   10
—'Hoo-hoo!—I don't know—I forgot how strange and far
    'twould be,
An' I wish I was at home again with dear daddee!'

Gruffly growled the wind on Toller downland broad and bare,
And lonesome was the house and dark; and few came there.

THE HOMECOMING. *Graphic*, Christmas Number [23 Nov.] 1903
  Hol. om. ital. throughout; G transposes, to read: 1-20, 33-8, 21-32, 39-48   1 *broad*]
bleak G   3 home] ~, *Hol.*   have] hae *G*   5 summat] sommat *G, Hol.*
6 tackle] welcome *G*   8 *past the house 'twas*] past it all was *G*   11 don't]
don' *G*   strange] dark *G*   13 *broad*] bleak *G*

'I didn't think such furniture as this was all you'd own,   15
And great black beams for ceiling, and a floor o' wretched stone,
And nasty pewter platters, horrid forks of steel and bone,
And a monstrous crock in chimney. 'Twas to me quite un-
        beknown!'

Rattle rattle went the door; down flapped a cloud of smoke,
As shifting north the wicked wind assayed a smarter stroke.   20

'Now sit ye by the fire, poppet; put yourself at ease:
And keep your little thumb out of your mouth, dear, please!
And I'll sing to 'ee a pretty song of lovely flowers and bees,
And happy lovers taking walks within a grove o' trees.'

Gruffly growled the wind on Toller Down, so bleak and bare,   25
And lonesome was the house, and dark; and few came there.

'Now, don't ye gnaw your handkercher; 'twill hurt your little
        tongue,
And if you do feel spitish, 'tis because ye are over young;
But you'll be getting older, like us all, ere very long,
And you'll see me as I am—a man who never did 'ee wrong.'   30

Straight from Whit'sheet Hill to Benvill Lane the blusters pass,
Hitting hedges, milestones, handposts, trees, and tufts of grass.

'Well, had I only known, my dear, that this was how you'd be,
I'd have married her of riper years that was so fond of me.
But since I can't, I've half a mind to run away to sea,   35
And leave 'ee to go barefoot to your d—d daddee!'

Up one wall and down the other—past each window-pane—
Prance the gusts, and then away down Crimmercrock's long lane.

15 I didn' think this ugly furniture was all you'd own, *G*   16 wretched] chilly *G*
17 of] o' *G*   19 *flapped*] *flopped G*   20 *assayed*] *essayed G*
21 ⟨"Well, had I o'ny guessed my dear that this was how you'd be,⟩ *Hol.*   yourself]
yerself *G*   23 bees] ⟨trees⟩ *Hol.*   24 o'] ⟨of⟩ *Hol.*   25 *Down, so*]
Downland G; *Down so Hol.*   27 gnaw] bite *G*   30 am—a man] am, Dear—
one *G*   33 only] on'y *TL, WE*   34 of...of] o'...o' *G*   36 d—d]
dear *G*

'I—I—don't know what to say to't, since your wife I've vowed
    to be;
And as 'tis done, I s'pose here I must bide—poor me!   40
Aye—as you are ki-ki-kind, I'll try to live along with 'ee,
Although I'd fain have stayed at home with dear daddee!'

Gruffly growled the wind on Toller Down, so bleak and bare,
And lonesome was the house and dark; and few came there.

'That's right, my Heart! And though on haunted Toller Down
    we be,   45
And the wind swears things in chimley, we'll to supper merrily!
So don't ye tap your shoe so pettish-like; but smile at me,
And ye'll soon forget to sock and sigh for dear daddee!'

December 1901.

39 since I've vowed your wife to be; *G*; ⟨since I've vowed your wife to be;⟩ *Hol.*
41 you are] you're *G*   43 *Down, so*] *Downland G*; Down so *Hol.*
48 sock] sob *G*
   Date om. G

PIECES OCCASIONAL AND VARIOUS

A CHURCH ROMANCE*

(Mellstock, *circa* 1835)

She turned in the high pew, until her sight
Swept the west gallery, and caught its row
Of music-men with viol, book, and bow
Against the sinking sad tower-window light.

She turned again; and in her pride's despite   5
One strenuous viol's inspirer seemed to throw
A message from his string to her below,
Which said: 'I claim thee as my own forthright!'

Thus their hearts' bond began, in due time signed.
And long years thence, when Age had scared Romance,   10
At some old attitude of his or glance
That gallery-scene would break upon her mind,
With him as minstrel, ardent, young, and trim,
Bowing 'New Sabbath' or 'Mount Ephraim'.

THE RASH BRIDE*

An Experience of the Mellstock Quire

I

We Christmas-carolled down the Vale, and up the Vale, and round
    the Vale,
We played and sang that night as we were yearly wont to do—
A carol in a minor key, a carol in the major D,
Then at each house: 'Good wishes: many Christmas joys to you!'

A CHURCH ROMANCE. *Saturday Review*, 8 Sept. 1906. *MS1* (*SR*) Holmes
  Headnote place om. SR, TL
   1 In the high pew she turned, *SR*   3 viol, book,] ~ ~ *MS1, SR*   4 tower-window-light: *MS1*   8 said:] ~ , *MS1, SR*   13 minstrel,] ~ — *MS1, SR* trim,] ~ — *MS1, SR*

THE RASH BRIDE. *Graphic*, Christmas Number [24 Nov.] 1902
   1 up the Vale, across the Vale, and down the Vale; *G*

II

Next, to the widow's John and I and all the rest drew on. And I   5
Discerned that John could hardly hold the tongue of him for
    joy.
The widow was a sweet young thing whom John was bent on
    marrying,
And quiring at her casement seemed romantic to the boy.

III

'She'll make reply, I trust,' said he, 'to our salute? She must!'
    said he,
'And then I will accost her gently—much to her surprise!—   10
For knowing not I am with you here, when I speak up and call
    her dear
A tenderness will fill her voice, a bashfulness her eyes.'

IV

So, by her window-square we stood; ay, with our lanterns there
    we stood,
And he along with us,—not singing, waiting for a sign;
And when we'd quired her carols three a light was lit and out
    looked she,   15
A shawl about her bedgown, and her colour red as wine.

V

And sweetly then she bowed her thanks, and smiled, and spoke
    aloud her thanks;
When lo, behind her back there, in the room, a man appeared.
I knew him—one from Woolcomb way—Giles Swetman—
    honest as the day,
But eager, hasty; and I felt that some strange trouble neared.   20

5 Next to the widow's—John, and I, and Michael, and the rest. And I *G*   Next,] ~ *Hol.*
7 whom] who *G*   bent] nigh *G*   9 "She'll make reply," at last said he, "to our
salute. She must," said he, *G*   must!'] ~ ," *Hol.*   11 I am] I'm *G*
13 window-square] darkened house *G*   14 waiting] watching *G*   17 And
sweetly then she spoke her thanks, and bowed her thanks, and smiled her thanks; *G*
18 back there,] shoulder, *G*   19 Woolcomb] Ivel *G*

VI

'How comes he there? . . . Suppose', said we, 'she's wed of late!
   Who knows?' said we.
—'She married yester-morning—only mother yet has known
The secret o't!' shrilled one small boy. 'But now I've told, let's
   wish 'em joy!'
A heavy fall aroused us: John had gone down like a stone.

VII

We rushed to him and caught him round, and lifted him, and
   brought him round,   25
When, hearing something wrong had happened, oped the
   window she:
'Has one of you fallen ill?' she asked, 'by these night labours
   overtasked?'
None answered. That she'd done poor John a cruel turn felt we.

VIII

Till up spoke Michael: 'Fie, young dame! You've broke your
   promise, sly young dame,
By forming this new tie, young dame, and jilting John so true, 30
Who trudged to-night to sing to 'ee because he thought he'd
   bring to 'ee
Good wishes as your coming spouse. May ye such trifling rue!'

IX

Her man had said no word at all; but being behind had heard it
   all,
And now cried: 'Neighbours, on my soul I knew not 'twas like
   this!'
And then to her: 'If I had known you'd had in tow not me alone, 35
No wife should you have been of mine. It is a dear bought bliss!'

---

21 "How comes he there?" at length said we. "She wed?" said we. "Who knows?" said we.
G   wed of late! Who] wed!" said we. "Who *TL, WE13, CP19*   23 shrilled]
quoth *G, TL, WE13*   25 We raised him, brought some life to him; and steadied him
and spoke to him, *G*   29 Till up spoke Michael Mail: "Young dame, you've
wronged a loving heart, young dame, *G*   30 By wedding this new man, *G*
31 trudged] came *G*   34 on my soul] scourge it all; *G*   35 had in tow]
promised him— *G*   alone,] ~ *Hol.*

X

She changed death-white, and heaved a cry: we'd never heard
    so grieved a cry
As came from her at this from him: heartbroken quite seemed
    she;
And suddenly, as we looked on, she turned, and rushed; and she
    was gone,
Whither, her husband, following after, knew not; nor knew we.   40

XI

We searched till dawn about the house; within the house,
    without the house,
We searched among the laurel boughs that grew beneath the
    wall,
And then among the crocks and things, and stores for winter
    junketings,
In linhay, loft, and dairy; but we found her not at all.

XII

Then John rushed in: 'O friends,' he said, 'hear this, this, this!'
    and bends his head:
                                   45
'I've—searched round by the—*well*, and find the cover open
    wide!
I am fearful that—I can't say what . . . Bring lanterns, and some
    cords to knot.'
We did so, and we went and stood the deep dark hole beside.

XIII

And then they, ropes in hand, and I—ay, John, and all the band,
    and I
Let down a lantern to the depths—some hundred feet and
    more;
                                   50
It glimmered like a fog-dimmed star; and there, besides its light,
    afar,
White drapery floated, and we knew the meaning that it bore.

37 changed] grew G   40 Whither,] ~ *Hol.*; Where to, G   nor knew] nor did G
41 We searched till dawn—around the house, behind the house, and in the house; G
44 dairy;] outhouse. G   45 Then John rushed in: "O, Will!" he said. "Hear this,"
he said, "Ay, *this*!" he said. G   47 I am] I'm G   48 hole] well G
49 And then in silence they and I—ay, John, and all the quire and I— G   I] ~ —
Hol.   50 more;] ~ .⟨—⟩ *Hol.*   51 its] the G

XIV

The rest is naught . . . We buried her o' Sunday. Neighbours
    carried her;
And Swetman—he who'd married her—now miserablest of
    men,
Walked mourning first; and then walked John; just quivering,
    but composed anon;   55
And we the quire formed round the grave, as was the custom
    then.

XV

Our old bass player, as I recall—his white hair blown—but why
    recall!—
His viol upstrapped, bent figure—doomed to follow her full
    soon—
Stood bowing, pale and tremulous; and next to him the rest of
    us. . . .
We sang the Ninetieth Psalm to her—set to 'Saint Stephen's'
    tune.   60

THE DEAD QUIRE*

I

Beside the Mead of Memories,
Where Church-way mounts to Moaning Hill,
The sad man sighed his phantasies:
    He seems to sigh them still.

II

' 'Twas the Birth-tide Eve, and the hamleteers   5
Made merry with ancient Mellstock zest,
But the Mellstock quire of former years
    Had entered into rest.

56 formed round] drew nigh *G*   57 Our old bass player, I well can mind, his white
hair fluttering, I can mind, *G*   58 His viol unstrapped—ay, sixty years ago it will be
soon! . . . *G*   59 Stood bowing 'twixt the grave and wall; and next to him stood I, and
all. . . . *G*   tremulous;] ⟨piteous;⟩ *Hol.*   60 The ninetieth Psalm we sung to
her— *G*   'Saint Stephen's' *DCM1, WE20, ME*] *no quotation marks all other texts*

THE DEAD QUIRE. *Graphic*, Christmas Number [25 Nov.] 1901
    3 sad] sad *Hol.*; meek *TL*   sighed] spoke *G*   4 sigh] speak *G*   6 zest,]
~ *Hol.*

III

'Old Dewy lay by the gaunt yew tree,
And Reuben and Michael a pace behind,   10
And Bowman with his family
    By the wall that the ivies bind.

IV

'The singers had followed one by one,
Treble, and tenor, and thorough-bass;
And the worm that wasteth had begun   15
    To mine their mouldering place.

V

'For two-score years, ere Christ-day light,
Mellstock had throbbed to strains from these;
But now there echoed on the night
    No Christmas harmonies.   20

VI

'Three meadows off, at a dormered inn,
The youth had gathered in high carouse,
And, ranged on settles, some therein
    Had drunk them to a drowse.

VII

'Loud, lively, reckless, some had grown,   25
Each dandling on his jigging knee
Eliza, Dolly, Nance, or Joan—
    Livers in levity.

VIII

'The taper flames and hearthfire shine
Grew smoke-hazed to a lurid light,   30
And songs on subjects not divine
    Were warbled forth that night.

9 gaunt] great *G*   18 Had Mellstock throbbed *G*   these;] ∼, *Hol.*
27 Eliza, Betsy, Nancy, Joan, *G*   or] and *Hol.*   29 The taper-flame and chimney-
shine *G*   30 Grew hazed with smoke and lurid light; *G*   31 not] scarce *G*

IX

'Yet many were sons and grandsons here
Of those who, on such eves gone by,
At that still hour had throated clear   35
    Their anthems to the sky.

X

'The clock belled midnight; and ere long
One shouted, "Now 'tis Christmas morn;
Here's to our women old and young,
    And to John Barleycorn!"   40

XI

'They drink the toast and shout again:
The pewter-ware rings back the boom,
And for a breath-while follows then
    A silence in the room.

XII

'When nigh without, as in old days,   45
The ancient quire of voice and string
Seemed singing words of prayer and praise
    As they had used to sing:

XIII

'*While shepherds watch'd their flocks by night,—*
Thus swells the long familiar sound   50
In many a quaint symphonic flight—
    To, *Glory shone around.*

XIV

'The sons defined their fathers' tones,
The widow his whom she had wed,
And others in the minor moans   55
    The viols of the dead.

33 many] some *G*   35 throated] voiced out *G*   37 "Midnight resounded;
and ere long *G*   41 "They drink it; and they shout again; *G*   toast *CP, DCM4*]
~, *Hol., TL, WE*   again:] ~; *Hol.*   42 pewter-ware] dresser-ware *G*   boom,]
~ *Hol.*   48 sing: *CP, DCM4*] ~. *Hol. TL, WE*   50 long] once *G*
51 flight—] ~ *Hol.*   52 To,] ~ *Hol.*   53 defined] discerned *G*
tones,] ~ *Hol.*

XV

'Something supernal has the sound
As verse by verse the strain proceeds,
And stilly staring on the ground
    Each roysterer holds and heeds.   60

XVI

'Towards its chorded closing bar
Plaintively, thinly, waned the hymn,
Yet lingered, like the notes afar
    Of banded seraphim.

XVII

'With brows abashed, and reverent tread,   65
The hearkeners sought the tavern door:
But nothing, save wan moonlight, spread
    The empty highway o'er.

XVIII

'While on their hearing fixed and tense
The aerial music seemed to sink,   70
As it were gently moving thence
    Along the river brink.

XIX

'Then did the Quick pursue the Dead
By crystal Froom that crinkles there;
And still the viewless quire ahead   75
    Voiced the old holy air.

XX

'By Bank-walk wicket, brightly bleached,
It passed, and 'twixt the hedges twain,
Dogged by the living; till it reached
    The bottom of Church Lane.   80

58 strain] Quire *G*; quire *Hol.*   proceeds,] ∼ *Hol.*   60 holds] lists *G*
66 hearkeners] listeners *G*   door:] ∼ ; *Hol.*   70 aerial] aethereal *G*
73 Quick ... Dead] ⟨*l.c.*⟩ *Hol.*   74 By flowery Froom that meanders there; *G*
76 Voiced] Tuned *G*   77–80 *om. G, Hol.*

XXI

'There, at the turning, it was heard
Drawing to where the churchyard lay:
But when they followed thitherward
    It smalled, and died away.

XXII

'Each headstone of the quire, each mound,   85
Confronted them beneath the moon;
But no more floated therearound
    That ancient Birth-night tune.

XXIII

'There Dewy lay by the gaunt yew tree,
There Reuben and Michael, a pace behind,   90
And Bowman with his family
    By the wall that the ivies bind. . . .

XXIV

'As from a dream each sobered son
Awoke, and musing reached his door:
'Twas said that of them all, not one   95
    Sat in a tavern more.'

XXV

—The sad man ceased; and ceased to heed
His listener, and crossed the leaze
From Moaning Hill towards the mead—
    The Mead of Memories.   100

1897.

81 "Till, where the cascade's cry is heard, *G*   'There,] "Till, *Hol.*   82 The
music took the churchyard side; *G*   lay:] ~; *Hol.*   84 It paused, and there it
died. *G*   85 headstone] gravestone *TL*   88 Birth-night] Bethlehem *G*
tune.] ~. ⟨. . .⟩ *Hol.*   89-92 *om. G*   91 And] There *Hol.*   94 door:]
~:— *Hol.*   97 sad] sad *Hol.*; meek *TL*
    Date *om. G*

THE CHRISTENING

Whose child is this they bring
    Into the aisle?—
At so superb a thing
The congregation smile
And turn their heads awhile.   5

Its eyes are blue and bright,
    Its cheeks like rose;
Its simple robes unite
Whitest of calicoes
With lawn, and satin bows.   10

A pride in the human race
    At this paragon
Of mortals, lights each face
While the old rite goes on;
But ah, they are shocked anon.   15

What girl is she who peeps
    From the gallery stair,
Smiles palely, redly weeps,
With feverish furtive air
As though not fitly there?   20

'I am the baby's mother;
    This gem of the race
The decent fain would smother,
And for my deep disgrace
I am bidden to leave the place.'   25

'Where is the baby's father?'—
    'In the woods afar.
He says there is none he'd rather
Meet under moon or star
Than me, of all that are.   30

THE CHRISTENING. 14 on;] ~, *Hol.*   15 And they ask its name anon. *Hol.*   But
ah,] But lo, *TL*   26 the] your *Hol.*

'To clasp me in lovelike weather,
    Wish fixing when,
He says: To be together
At will, just now and then,
Makes him the blest of men;   35

'But chained and doomed for life
    To slovening
As vulgar man and wife,
He says, is another thing:
Yea: sweet Love's sepulchring!'   40

                  1904.

A DREAM QUESTION*

'It shall be dark unto you, that ye shall not divine.' Micah iii. 6.

I asked the Lord: 'Sire, is this true
Which hosts of theologians hold,
That when we creatures censure you
For shaping griefs and ails untold
(Deeming them punishments undue)   5
You rage, as Moses wrote of old?

'When we exclaim: "Beneficent
He is not, for he orders pain,
Or, if so, not omnipotent:
To a mere child the thing is plain!"   10
Those who profess to represent
You, cry out: "Impious and profane!"'

He: 'Save me from my friends, who deem
That I care what my creatures say!
Mouth as you list: sneer, rail, blaspheme,   15
O manikin, the livelong day,

31 clasp] see *Hol.*   weather,] ~ *Hol.*   40 sepulchring!'] ~ ." *Hol.*

A DREAM QUESTION. *Title* ⟨An Inquiry⟩ *Hol.*   *Epigraph* "Thy footsteps are not known."—
Ps. LXXVII. 19. *Hol.*
    4 ⟨For scheming griefs and pains untold⟩ *Hol.*

Not one grief-groan or pleasure-gleam
Will you increase or take away.

'Why things are thus, whoso derides,
May well remain my secret still   20
A fourth dimension, say the guides,
To matter is conceivable.
Think some such mystery resides
Within the ethic of my will.'

BY THE BARROWS*

Not far from Mellstock—so tradition saith—
Where barrows, bulging as they bosoms were
Of Multimammia stretched supinely there,
Catch night and noon the tempest's wanton breath,

A battle, desperate doubtless unto death,   5
Was one time fought. The outlook, lone and bare,
The towering hawk and passing raven share,
And all the upland round is called 'The He'th'.

Here once a woman, in our modern age,
Fought singlehandedly to shield a child—   10
One not her own—from a man's senseless rage.
And to my mind no patriots' bones there piled
So consecrate the silence as her deed
Of stoic and devoted self-unheed.

24 ethic] ⟨measure⟩ *Hol.*

BY THE BARROWS. 2 as they bosoms were] ⟨like the paps in air⟩ *Hol.*   4 and] ⟨or⟩
Hol.   5 doubtless unto death,] ⟨to the last spent breath⟩ *Hol.*   death,] ∼ *Hol.*
6 The outlook,] ⟨The spot is⟩ *Hol.*   12 patriots' bones there piled] ⟨clash of
warriors wild⟩ *Hol.*   13 ⟨To save their land, outvalues what did she⟩ *Hol.*
consecrate] ⟨consecrates⟩ *Hol.*   14 ⟨In self-forgetting ⟨⟨woma⟩⟩ stoical bravery.⟩
Hol.

A WIFE AND ANOTHER*

'War ends, and he's returning
  Early; yea,
The evening next to-morrow's!'—
  —This I say
To her, whom I suspiciously survey,   5

Holding my husband's letter
  To her view.—
She glanced at it but lightly,
  And I knew
That one from him that day had reached her too.   10

There was no time for scruple;
  Secretly
I filched her missive, conned it,
  Learnt that he
Would lodge with her ere he came home to me.   15

To reach the port before her,
  And, unscanned,
There wait to intercept them
  Soon I planned:
That, in her stead, *I* might before him stand.   20

So purposed, so effected;
  At the inn
Assigned, I found her hidden:—
  O that sin
Should bear what she bore when I entered in!   25

Her heavy lids grew laden
  With despairs,
Her lips made soundless movements
  Unawares,
While I peered at the chamber hired as theirs.   30

A WIFE AND ANOTHER. 2 yea,] ~ *Hol.*   14 he] she *TL*   15 lodge with
her] tryst with him *TL*

And as beside its doorway,
   Deadly hued,
One inside, one withoutside
   We two stood,
He came—my husband—as she knew he would.   35

No pleasurable triumph
   Was that sight!
The ghastly disappointment
   Broke them quite.
What love was theirs, to move them with such might!   40

'Madam, forgive me!' said she,
   Sorrow bent,
'A child—I soon shall bear him . . . .
   Yes—I meant
To tell you—that he won me ere he went.'   45

Then, as it were, within me
   Something snapped,
As if my soul had largened:
   Conscience-capped,
I saw myself the snarer—them the trapped.   50

'My hate dies, and I promise,
   Grace-beguiled,'
I said, 'to care for you, be
   Reconciled;
And cherish, and take interest in the child.'   55

Without more words I pressed him
   Through the door
Within which she stood, powerless
   To say more,
And closed it on them, and downstairward bore.   60

31 doorway,] ~ *Hol.*   32 hued,] ~ *Hol.*   41 she,] ~ *Hol.*   45 won]
knew *TL*   47 snapped,] ~ *Hol.*   49 -capped,] ~ ⟨,⟩ *Hol.*

'He joins his wife—my sister,'
     I, below,
Remarked in going—lightly—
     Even as though
All had come right, and we had arranged it so   65

As I, my road retracing,
     Left them free,
The night alone embracing
     Childless me,
I held I had not stirred God wrothfully.   70

THE ROMAN ROAD

The Roman Road runs straight and bare
As the pale parting-line in hair
Across the heath. And thoughtful men
Contrast its days of Now and Then,
And delve, and measure, and compare;   5

Visioning on the vacant air
Helmed legionaries, who proudly rear
The Eagle, as they pace again
                    The Roman Road.

But no tall brass-helmed legionnaire   10
Haunts it for me. Uprises there
A mother's form upon my ken,
Guiding my infant steps, as when
We walked that ancient thoroughfare,
                    The Roman Road.   15

---

66 As] ⟨And⟩ *Hol.*   70 held] ⟨thought⟩ *Hol.*   stirred] ⟨moved⟩ stirred *Hol.*;
moved *TL*

THE ROMAN ROAD. 4 Now and Then,] ⟨*l.c.*⟩ *Hol.*   14 thoroughfare,] ∼ *Hol.*

THE VAMPIRINE FAIR

Gilbert had sailed to India's shore,
        And I was all alone:
My lord came in at my open door
        And said, 'O fairest one!'

He leant upon the slant bureau,   5
        And sighed, 'I am sick for thee!'
'My lord,' said I, 'pray speak not so,
        Since wedded wife I be.'

Leaning upon the slant bureau,
        Bitter his next words came: 10
'So much I know; and likewise know
        My love burns on the same!

'But since you thrust my love away,
        And since it knows no cure,
I must live out as best I may   15
        The ache that I endure.'

When Michaelmas browned the nether Coomb,
        And Wingreen Hill above,
And made the hollyhocks rags of bloom,
        My lord grew ill of love.   20

My lord grew ill with love for me;
        Gilbert was far from port;
And—so it was—that time did see
        Me housed at Manor Court.

About the bowers of Manor Court   25
        The primrose pushed its head
When, on a day at last, report
        Arrived of him I had wed.

THE VAMPIRINE FAIR. *Title* The Fair Vampire *Hol.*
   2 alone:] ~; *Hol.*   9 bureau,] ~ *Hol.*   19 bloom,] ~ *Hol.*   26 The
leaves were reaching red *Hol.*

'Gilbert, my lord, is homeward bound,
  His sloop is drawing near,   30
What shall I do when I am found
  Not in his house but here?'

'O I will heal the injuries
  I've done to him and thee.
I'll give him means to live at ease   35
  Afar from Shastonb'ry.'

When Gilbert came we both took thought:
  'Since comfort and good cheer',
Said he, 'so readily are bought,
  He's welcome to thee, Dear.'   40

So when my lord flung liberally
  His gold in Gilbert's hands,
I coaxed and got my brothers three
  Made stewards of his lands.

And then I coaxed him to install   45
  My other kith and kin,
With aim to benefit them all
  Before his love ran thin.

And next I craved to be possessed
  Of plate and jewels rare.   50
He groaned: 'You give me, Love, no rest,
  Take all the law will spare!'

And so in course of years my wealth
  Became a goodly hoard,
My steward brethren, too, by stealth   55
  Had each a fortune stored.

Thereafter in the gloom he'd walk,
  And by and by began
To say aloud in absent talk,
  'I am a ruined man!—   60

37 thought:] ~; *Hol.*   41 So] ~, *Hol.*   51 me, Love,] *no commas Hol.*

'I hardly could have thought,' he said,
    'When first I looked on thee,
That one so soft, so rosy red,
    Could thus have beggared me!'

Seeing his fair estates in pawn,   65
    And him in such decline,
I knew that his domain had gone
    To lift up me and mine.

Next month upon a Sunday morn
    A gunshot sounded nigh: 70
By his own hand my lordly born
    Had doomed himself to die.

'Live, my dear lord, and much of thine
    Shall be restored to thee!'
He smiled, and said 'twixt word and sign,   75
    'Alas—that cannot be!'

And while I searched his cabinet
    For letters, keys, or will,
'Twas touching that his gaze was set
    With love upon me still.   80

And when I burnt each document
    Before his dying eyes,
'Twas sweet that he did not resent
    My fear of compromise.

The steeple-cock gleamed golden when   85
    I watched his spirit go:
And I became repentant then
    That I had wrecked him so.

Three weeks at least had come and gone,
    With many a saddened word,   90
Before I wrote to Gilbert on
    The stroke that so had stirred.

92 Events that had occurred. *TL*; The crash that had occurred. *WE13*

And having worn a mournful gown,
    I joined, in decent while,
My husband at a dashing town   95
    To live in dashing style.

Yet though I now enjoy my fling,
    And dine and dance and drive,
I'd give my prettiest emerald ring
    To see my lord alive.   100

And when the meet on hunting-days
    Is near his churchyard home,
I leave my bantering beaux to place
    A flower upon his tomb;

And sometimes say: 'Perhaps too late   105
    The saints in Heaven deplore
That tender time when, moved by Fate,
    He darked my cottage door.'

THE REMINDER

While I watch the Christmas blaze
Paint the room with ruddy rays,
Something makes my vision glide
To the frosty scene outside.

There, to reach a rotting berry,   5
Toils a thrush,—constrained to very
Dregs of food by sharp distress,
Taking such with thankfulness.

Why, O starving bird, when I
One day's joy would justify,   10
And put misery out of view,
Do you make me notice you!

97 fling,] ∼ *Hol.*   98 drive,] ∼ *Hol.*   104 tomb;] ∼. *Hol.*
107 time] day *Hol.*

THE REMINDER. 5 berry,] ∼ *Hol.*   10 Fain to-day would ⟨breathe no⟩ shun a sigh,
Hol.; Fain to-day would shun a sigh, *TL*

THE RAMBLER

I do not see the hills around,
Nor mark the tints the copses wear;
I do not note the grassy ground
And constellated daisies there.

I hear not the contralto note   5
Of cuckoos hid on either hand,
The whirr that shakes the nighthawk's throat
When eve's brown awning hoods the land.

Some say each songster, tree, and mead—
All eloquent of love divine—   10
Receives their constant careful heed:
Such keen appraisement is not mine.

The tones around me that I hear,
The aspects, meanings, shapes I see,
Are those removed ones missed when near,   15
And now perceived too late by me.

NIGHT IN THE OLD HOME

When the wasting embers redden the chimney-breast,
And Life's bare pathway looms like a desert track to me,
And from hall and parlour the living have gone to their rest,
My perished people who housed them here come back to me.

They come and seat them around in their mouldy places,   5
Now and then bending towards me a glance of wistfulness,
A strange upbraiding smile upon all their faces,
And in the bearing of each a passive tristfulness.

THE RAMBLER. 11 careful] ⟨joyful⟩ *Hol.*   15 ⟨Are those not seen or heard when near,⟩ Are ⟨bygone⟩ far back ones I missed when near, *Hol.*; Are those far back ones missed when near, *TL, CP*   16 me. *Hol., WE*] ~! *TL, CP*

NIGHT IN THE OLD HOME. *Title* Home] ⟨house⟩ *Hol.*
  4 My perished] The bygone *Hol.*; The perished *TL*   7 upbraiding] pale tearful *Hol.*

'Do you uphold me, lingering and languishing here,
A pale late plant of your once strong stock?' I say to them;   10
'A thinker of crooked thoughts upon Life in the sere,
And on That which consigns men to night after showing the day
    to them?'

'—O let be the Wherefore! We fevered our years not thus:
Take of Life what it grants, without question!' they answer me
    seemingly.
'Enjoy, suffer, wait: spread the table here freely like us,   15
And, satisfied, placid, unfretting, watch Time away beamingly!'

AFTER THE LAST BREATH*

(J. H. 1813-1904)

There's no more to be done, or feared, or hoped;
None now need watch, speak low, and list, and tire;
No irksome crease outsmoothed, no pillow sloped
        Does she require.

Blankly we gaze. We are free to go or stay;   5
Our morrow's anxious plans have missed their aim;
Whether we leave to-night or wait till day
        Counts as the same.

The lettered vessels of medicaments
Seem asking wherefore we have set them here;   10
Each palliative its silly face presents
        As useless gear.

And yet we feel that something savours well;
We note a numb relief withheld before;
Our well-beloved is prisoner in the cell   15
        Of Time no more.

10 pale] poor *Hol.*   12 which] *cap. Hol.*   13 '—O] "O *Hol.*
16 beamingly!'] ~. *Hol.*

AFTER THE LAST BREATH. *Headnote om. TL*
   2 None now need wait, speak low, ⟨or⟩ and watch, and tire; *Hol.*   5 stay;] ~,
Hol.   6 aim;] ~, *Hol.*

We see by littles now the deft achievement
Whereby she has escaped the Wrongers all,
In view of which our momentary bereavement
    Outshapes but small.   20

1904.

IN CHILDBED

    In the middle of the night
Mother's spirit came and spoke to me,
    Looking weariful and white—
As 'twere untimely news she broke to me.

    'O my daughter, joyed are you   5
To own the weetless child you mother there;
    "Men may search the wide world through,"
You think, "nor find so fair another there!"

    'Dear, this midnight time unwombs
Thousands just as rare and beautiful;   10
    Thousands whom High Heaven foredooms
To be as bright, as good, as dutiful.

    'Source of ecstatic hopes and fears
And innocent maternal vanity,
    Your fond exploit but shapes for tears   15
New thoroughfares in sad humanity.

    'Yet as you dream, so dreamt I
When Life stretched forth its morning ray to me;
    Other views for by and by!' . . . .
Such strange things did mother say to me.   20

Date 190-. *Hol.*

IN CHILDBED. 8 fair] ⟨sweet⟩ *Hol.*   11 High] *l.c. Hol.*   14 vanity,]
~ *Hol.*

THE PINE PLANTERS*

(Marty South's Reverie)

I

We work here together
In blast and breeze;
He fills the earth in,
I hold the trees.

He does not notice   5
That what I do
Keeps me from moving
And chills me through.

He has seen one fairer
I feel by his eye,   10
Which skims me as though
I were not by.

And since she passed here
He scarce has known
But that the woodland   15
Holds him alone.

I have worked here with him
Since morning shine,
He busy with his thoughts
And I with mine.   20

I have helped him so many,
So many days,
But never win any
Small word of praise!

THE PINE PLANTERS. *Cornhill*, June 1903 [*Part II only*]
    Subtitle om. C, SP   Headnote (*The man fills in the earth; the sad-faced woman holds the tree upright, and meditates*). C; ⟨(*A young man and woman*)⟩ *Hol.*; (In *The Woodlanders*) SP [*Part II only*]
    2 In Winter's breeze; *TL*   21 many,] ∼ *Hol.*

Shall I not sigh to him   25
    That I work on
Glad to be nigh to him
    Though hope is gone?

Nay, though he never
    Knew love like mine,   30
I'll bear it ever
    And make no sign!

                        II

From the bundle at hand here
    I take each tree,
And set it to stand, here   35
    Always to be;
When, in a second,
    As if from fear
Of Life unreckoned
    Beginning here,   40
It starts a sighing
    Through day and night,
Though while there lying
    'Twas voiceless quite.

It will sigh in the morning,   45
    Will sigh at noon,
At the winter's warning,
    In wafts of June;
Grieving that never
    Kind Fate decreed   50
It should for ever
    Remain a seed,

---

29 Nay. Though he never *Hol.*   30 mine,] ~ *Hol.*   32 sign!] ~. *Hol.*
33 bundle at hand here] unwound bundle *C*; ⟨unwound bundle⟩ *Hol.*   34 I] We *C*;
⟨We⟩ *Hol.*   35 And set it up *C*; And set it ⟨up⟩ to stand here *Hol.*   36 Always]
Where it has *C*; ⟨Where it has⟩ *Hol.*   37 second,] moment, *C*; ⟨moment,⟩ *Hol.*
39 unreckoned] in earnest *C*: ⟨in earnest⟩ *Hol.*   43 there lying *SP, CP, WE20*]
downlying *C*; ⟨there lying⟩ *Hol.*; down lying *TL, WE13*   51 It could not ever
C, TL09   52 seed,] ~ *Hol.*

And shun the welter
    Of things without,
Unneeding shelter
    From storm and drought.   55

Thus, all unknowing
    For whom or what
We set it growing
    In this bleak spot,   60
It still will grieve here
    Throughout its time,
Unable to leave here,
    Or change its clime;
Or tell the story   65
    Of us to-day
When, halt and hoary,
    We pass away.

THE DEAR*

I plodded to Fairmile Hill-top, where
    A maiden one fain would guard
From every hazard and every care
    Advanced on the roadside sward.

I wondered how succeeding suns   5
    Would shape her wayfarings,
And wished some Power might take such ones
    Under Its warding wings.

The busy breeze came up the hill
    And smartened her cheek to red,   10
And frizzled her hair to a haze. With a will
    'Good-morning, my Dear!' I said.

68 We've passed away. *C*

THE DEAR. *Monthly Review*, June 1902
   5–8 *om. MR*   8 warding] shielding *Hol.*   11 And hazed her
hair. Commiserate still, *SP*

She glanced from me to the far-off gray,
      And, with proud severity,
'Good-morning to you—though I may say   15
      I am not *your* Dear,' quoth she:

'For I am the Dear of one not here—
      One far from his native land!'—
And she passed me by; and I did not try
      To make her understand.   20

1901.

ONE WE KNEW*

(M. H. 1772-1857)

She told how they used to form for the country dances—
      'The Triumph', 'The New-rigged Ship'—
To the light of the guttering wax in the panelled manses,
      And in cots to the blink of a dip.

She spoke of the wild 'poussetting' and 'allemanding'   5
      On carpet, on oak, and on sod;
And the two long rows of ladies and gentlemen standing,
      And the figures the couples trod.

She showed us the spot where the maypole was yearly planted,
      And where the bandsmen stood   10
While breeched and kerchiefed partners whirled, and panted
      To choose each other for good.

She told of that far-back day when they learnt astounded
      Of the death of the King of France:
Of the Terror; and then of Bonaparte's unbounded   15
      Ambition and arrogance.

ONE WE KNEW. *Tatler*, 2 Dec. 1903; *Harper's Weekly*, 12 Dec. 1903
   Title Remembrance *HW*   *Headnote om. HW*
   6 sod;] green; *HW*   8 And the couples that tripped between. *HW*
11 whirled,] ~ *Hol.*   13 far-back] distant *T, HW*

Of how his threats woke warlike preparations
  Along the southern strand,
And how each night brought tremors and trepidations
  Lest morning should see him land.   20

She said she had often heard the gibbet creaking
  As it swayed in the lightning flash,
Had caught from the neighbouring town a small child's
    shrieking
  At the cart-tail under the lash. . . .

With cap-framed face and long gaze into the embers—   25
  We seated around her knees—
She would dwell on such dead themes, not as one who
    remembers,
  But rather as one who sees.

She seemed one left behind of a band gone distant
  So far that no tongue could hail: 30
Past things retold were to her as things existent,
  Things present but as a tale.

                                        May 20, 1902.

A WET NIGHT

I pace along, the rain-shafts riddling me,
  Mile after mile out by the moorland way,
  And up the hill, and through the ewe-leaze gray
Into the lane, and round the corner tree;

---

19 tremors] terrors *T, HW, Hol.*   20 morning] morn *HW*   23 neigh-
bouring town] neighbour borough *T*; distant borough *HW*
    Date *om. T, HW*

A WET NIGHT. 4 tree;] ∼ , *Hol.*

Where, as my clothing clams me, mire-bestarred,   5
And the enfeebled light dies out of day,
Leaving the liquid shades to reign, I say,
'This is a hardship to be calendared!'

Yet sires of mine now perished and forgot,
When worse beset, ere roads were shapen here,   10
And night and storm were foes indeed to fear,
Times numberless have trudged across this spot
In sturdy muteness on their strenuous lot,
And taking all such toils as trifles mere.

BEFORE LIFE AND AFTER

A time there was—as one may guess
And as, indeed, earth's testimonies tell—
Before the birth of consciousness,
        When all went well.

None suffered sickness, love, or loss,   5
None knew regret, starved hope, or heartburnings;
None cared whatever crash or cross
        Brought wrack to things.

If something ceased, no tongue bewailed,
If something winced and waned, no heart was wrung;   10
If brightness dimmed, and dark prevailed,
        No sense was stung.

But the disease of feeling germed,
And primal rightness took the tinct of wrong;
Ere nescience shall be reaffirmed   15
        How long, how long?

13 ⟨Making no plaint of their less kindly lot,⟩ *Hol.*

BEFORE LIFE AND AFTER. 1 guess] ∼ , *Hol.*   2 earth's] *cap. Hol.*   13 feeling
germed,] ⟨thought engermed,⟩ *Hol.*   14 took the tinct of] ⟨was transformed to⟩
Hol.   wrong;] ∼ .— *Hol.*

NEW YEAR'S EVE*

'I have finished another year', said God,
    'In grey, green, white, and brown;
I have strewn the leaf upon the sod,
Sealed up the worm within the clod,
    And let the last sun down.'   5

'And what's the good of it?' I said.
    'What reasons made you call
From formless void this earth we tread,
When nine-and-ninety can be read
    Why nought should be at all?   10

'Yea, Sire; why shaped you us, who "in
    This tabernacle groan"—
If ever a joy be found herein,
Such joy no man had wished to win
    If he had never known!'   15

Then he: 'My labours—logicless—
    You may explain; not I:
Sense-sealed I have wrought, without a guess
That I evolved a Consciousness
    To ask for reasons why.   20

'Strange that ephemeral creatures who
    By my own ordering are,
Should see the shortness of my view,
Use ethic tests I never knew,
    Or made provision for!'   25

NEW YEAR'S EVE. *Fortnightly Review*, 1 Jan. 1907. *MS1* (*FR*) HRC
  4 clod,] ~ *MS1*   6 said.] ~, *MS1, FR, Hol.*   7 you] *cap. MS1, FR*
8 we] I *MS1, FR*; ⟨I⟩ *Hol.*   11 you] *cap. FR*   who "in] 'who in *TL, CP*
12 groan"—] ~ '?— *MS1, FR*; ~?'— *Hol.*   13 herein,] ~ *MS1*   16 he:]
cap. MS1, FR   *no dashes MS1, FR*   20 why.] ~! *MS1, FR*   21 'Strange]
"~, *MS1, FR*

He sank to raptness as of yore,
  And opening New Year's Day
Wove it by rote as theretofore,
And went on working evermore
  In his unweeting way.   30

1906.

GOD'S EDUCATION*

I saw him steal the light away
  That haunted in her eye:
It went so gently none could say
More than that it was there one day
  And missing by-and-by.   5

I watched her longer, and he stole
  Her lily tincts and rose;
All her young sprightliness of soul
Next fell beneath his cold control,
  And disappeared like those.   10

I asked: 'Why do you serve her so?
  Do you, for some glad day,
Hoard these her sweets—?' He said, 'O no,
They charm not me; I bid Time throw
  Them carelessly away.'   15

Said I: 'We call that cruelty—
  We, your poor mortal kind.'
He mused. 'The thought is new to me.
Forsooth, though I men's master be
  Theirs is the teaching mind!'   20

26 yore,] ~; *MS1*   30 his] *cap. MS1, FR*
     Date om. *MS1, FR, Hol.*

GOD'S EDUCATION. *Title* His Education *TL*
    13 ⟨Hoard these dismantled sweets?"— "O no,⟩ *Hol.*   sweets—?'] ~?"— *Hol.*
14 me;] ~. *Hol.*   15 Each promptly to decay." *TL*

TO SINCERITY

O sweet sincerity!—
Where modern methods be
What scope for thine and thee?

Life may be sad past saying,
Its greens for ever graying,   5
Its faiths to dust decaying;

And youth may have foreknown it,
And riper seasons shown it,
But custom cries: 'Disown it:

'Say ye rejoice, though grieving,   10
Believe, while unbelieving,
Behold, without perceiving!'

—Yet, would men look at true things,
And unilluded view things,
And count to bear undue things,   15

The real might mend the seeming,
Facts better their foredeeming,
And Life its disesteeming.

February, 1899.

TO SINCERITY. *Review of the Week*, 14 July 1900
   1 A shunned Sincerity! . . . . *RW*   sincerity!—] *cap. Hol.*   5 greens] green *RW*
6 Its faiths by stealth decaying: *RW*   decaying;] ~, *Hol.*   7 it,] such, *RW*
8 it,] such; *RW*; it; *Hol.*   9 The watchword is: "Disown such: *RW*   cries:] ~,
Hol.   10 rejoice,] ~ *Hol.*   11 Believe, without believing, *RW*   Believe,]
~ *Hol.*   12 Behold, while unperceiving." . . . . *RW*   Behold,] ~ *Hol.*
13 at] for *RW*   14 And unilluded] And questioningly *RW*; ⟨Without ⟨⟨delu⟩⟩
illusion⟩ *Hol.*   17 The fact the dread foredeeming, *RW*; ⟨Fact better its foredeeming,⟩
Hol.
    Date om. RW

PANTHERA*

(For other forms of this legend—first met with in the second century—see Origen contra Celsum; the Talmud; Sepher Toldoth Jeschu; quoted fragments of lost Apocryphal gospels; Strauss; Haeckel; etc.)

Yea, as I sit here, crutched, and cricked, and bent,
I think of Panthera, who underwent
Much from insidious aches in his decline;
But his aches were not radical like mine;
They were the twinges of old wounds—the feel   5
Of the hand he had lost, shorn by barbarian steel,
Which came back, so he said, at a change in the air,
Fingers and all, as if it still were there.
My pains are otherwise: upclosing cramps
And stiffened tendons from this country's damps,   10
Where Panthera was never commandant.—
The Fates sent him by way of the Levant.

He had been blithe in his young manhood's time,
And as centurion carried well his prime.
In Ethiop, Araby, climes fair and fell,   15
He had seen service and had borne him well.
Nought shook him then: he was serene as brave;
Yet later knew some shocks, and would grow grave
When pondering them; shocks less of corporal kind
Than phantom-like, that disarranged his mind;   20
And it was in the way of warning me
(By much his junior) against levity
That he recounted them; and one in chief
Panthera loved to set in bold relief.

    This was a tragedy of his Eastern days,   25
Personal in touch—though I have sometimes thought
That touch a possible delusion—wrought
Of half-conviction carried to a craze—
His mind at last being stressed by ails and age:—
Yet his good faith thereon I well could wage.   30

PANTHERA. *Headnote* (For other forms of ⟨the⟩ this legend—first met with in the second century—*vide* Origen *contra* Celsum; the Talmud; Tol⟨e⟩doth Jes⟨c⟩hu; quoted fragments of ⟨lost writings⟩ lost Apocryphal writings; ⟨Schöttgen;⟩ Strauss; Haeckel; etc., etc.) *Hol.* gospels;] writings; *TL09*
  1 crutched,] ~ *Hol.*   cricked,] ~ *Hol.*   15 Araby,] ~ — *Hol.*   fell,] ~ — *Hol.*   25 This] It *Hol.*

I had said it long had been a wish with me
That I might leave a scion—some small tree
As channel for my sap, if not my name—
Ay, offspring even of no legitimate claim,
In whose advance I secretly could joy.   35
Thereat he warmed.
                            'Cancel such wishes, boy!
A son may be a comfort or a curse,
A seer, a doer, a coward, a fool; yea, worse—
A criminal. . . . *That* I could testify!' . . .
'Panthera has no guilty son!' cried I   40
All unbelieving. 'Friend, you do not know,'
He darkly dropt: 'True, I've none now to show,
For *the law took him*. Ay, in sooth, Jove shaped it so!'

———————

'This noon is not unlike', he again began,
'The noon these pricking memories print on me—   45
Yea, that day when the sun grew copper-red,
And I served in Judæa . . . 'Twas a date
Of rest for arms. The *Pax Romana* ruled,
To the chagrin of frontier legionaries!
Palestine was annexed—though sullen yet,—   50
I, being in age some two-score years and ten,
And having the garrison in Jerusalem
Part in my hands as acting officer
Under the governor. A tedious time
I found it, of routine, amid a folk   55
Restless, contentless, and irascible.—
Quelling some riot, sentrying court and hall,
Sending men forth on public meeting-days
To maintain order, were my duties there.

'Then came a morn in spring, and the cheerful sun   60
Whitened the city and the hills around,
And every mountain-road that clambered them,
Tincturing the greyness of the olives warm,

39 *That*] *rom. TL, CP*   43 Ay; in sooth Jove ordered so!" *Hol.*   44 again]
then *Hol.*   46 Yea, that day] A past day, *TL*   48 *no ital. Hol.*   52 And
having] Having *Hol.*   53-4 Part under my command. A tedious time *TL*

And the rank cacti round the valley's sides.
The day was one whereon death-penalties 65
Were put in force, and here and there were set
The soldiery for order, as I said,
Since one of the condemned had raised some heat,
And crowds surged passionately to see him slain.
I, mounted on a Cappadocian horse, 70
With some half-company of auxiliaries,
Had captained the procession through the streets
When it came streaming from the judgment-hall
After the verdicts of the Governor.
It drew to the great gate of the northern way 75
That bears towards Damascus; and to a knoll
Upon the common, just beyond the walls—
Whence could be swept a wide horizon round
Over the housetops to the remotest heights.
Here was the public execution-ground 80
For city crimes, called then and doubtless now
Golgotha, Kranion, or Calvaria.

'The usual dooms were duly meted out;
Some three or four were stript, transfixed, and nailed,
And no great stir occurred. A day of wont 85
It was to me, so far, and would have slid
Clean from my memory at its squalid close
But for an incident that followed these.
Among the tag-rag rabble of either sex
That hung around the wretches as they writhed, 90
Till thrust back by our spears, one held my eye—
A weeping woman, whose strained countenance,
Sharpened against a looming livid cloud,
Was mocked by the crude rays of afternoon—
The mother of one of those who suffered there 95
I had heard her called when spoken roughly to
By my ranged men for pressing forward so.
It stole upon me hers was a face I knew;
Yet when, or how, I had known it, for a while
Eluded me. And then at once it came. 100

64 sides.] ⟨bank⟩ *Hol.*   74 verdicts] sentence *Hol.*   78 swept] seen *TL*
82 Kranion,] Cranion, *TL*, *WE13*, *CP19*   83 "The usual sentences were acted out;
Hol.   84 stript,] roped, *TL*   93 looming livid] rising cliff of *Hol.*

'Some thirty years or more before that noon
I was sub-captain of a company
Drawn from the legion of Calabria,
That marched up from Judæa north to Tyre.
We had pierced the old flat country of Jezreel,   105
The great Esdraelon Plain and fighting-floor
Of Jew with Canaanite, and with the host
Of Pharaoh-Necho, king of Egypt, met
While crossing there to strike the Assyrian pride.
We left behind Gilboa; passed by Nain;   110
Till bulging Tabor rose, embossed to the top
With arbute, terabinth, and locust growths.

   'Encumbering me were sundry sick, so fallen
Through drinking from a swamp beside the way;
But we pressed on, till, bearing over a ridge,   115
We dipt into a world of pleasantness—
A vale, the fairest I had gazed upon—
Which lapped a village on its furthest slopes
Called Nazareth, brimmed round by uplands nigh.
In the midst thereof a fountain bubbled, where,   120
Lime-dry from marching, our glad halt we made
To rest our sick ones, and refresh us all.

   'Here a day onward, towards the eventide,
Our men were piping to a Pyrrhic dance
Trod by their comrades, when the young women came   125
To fill their pitchers, as their custom was.
I proffered help to one—a slim girl, coy
Even as a fawn, meek, and as innocent.
Her long blue gown, the string of silver coins
That hung down by her banded beautiful hair,   130
Symboled in full immaculate modesty.

   'Well, I was young, and hot, and readily stirred
To quick desire. 'Twas tedious timing out
The convalescence of the soldiery;
And I beguiled the long and empty days   135
By blissful yieldance to her sweet allure,
Who had no arts, but what out-arted all,
The tremulous tender charm of trustfulness.

103 *om. Hol.*   105 pierced] crossed *TL09*   108 king] *cap. Hol.*
136 allure,] ~ *Hol.*

We met, and met, and under the winking stars
That passed which peoples earth—true union, yea,   140
To the pure eye of her simplicity.
    'Meanwhile the sick found health; and we pricked on.
I made her no rash promise of return,
As some do use; I was sincere in that;
I said we sundered never to meet again—   145
And yet I spoke untruth unknowingly!—
For meet again we did. Now, guess you aught?
The weeping mother on Calvaria
Was she I had known—albeit that time and tears
Had wasted rudely her once flowerlike form,   150
And her soft eyes, now swollen with sorrowing.

    'Though I betrayed some qualms, she marked me not;
And I was scarce of mood to comrade her
And close the silence of so wide a time
To claim a malefactor as my son—   155
(For so I guessed him). And inquiry made
Brought rumour how at Nazareth long before
An old man wedded her for pity's sake
On finding she had grown pregnant, none knew how,
Cared for her child, and loved her till he died.   160

    'Well; there it ended; save that then I learnt
That he—the man whose ardent blood was mine—
Had waked sedition long among the Jews,
And hurled insulting parlance at their god,
Whose temple bulked upon the adjoining hill,   165
Vowing that he would raze it, that himself
Was god as great as he whom they adored,
And by descent, moreover, was their king;
With sundry other incitements to misrule.
    'The impalements done, and done the soldiers' game   170

---

140 true union,] a marriage, *TL*   142 pricked] marched *TL*   149 time]
grief *TL09*   158 wedded] ⟨married⟩ *Hol.*   165 bulked] ⟨rose⟩ *Hol.*
170–6   "The impalements duly done, a legionary,
        Longinus, pierced the young man with his lance
        To silence him. And when he had breathed his last
        The woman went. I saw her never again.... *Hol.*   [*cont. on p. 342*]

Of raffling for the clothes, a legionary,
Longinus, pierced the young man with his lance
At signs from me, moved by his agonies
Through naysaying the drug they had offered him.
It brought the end. And when he had breathed his last   175
The woman went. I saw her never again . . . .
Now glares my moody meaning on you, friend?—
That when you talk of offspring as sheer joy
So trustingly, you blink contingencies.
Fors Fortuna! He who goes fathering   180
Gives frightful hostages to hazardry!'

Thus Panthera's tale. 'Twas one he seldom told,
But yet it got abroad. He would unfold,
At other times, a story of less gloom,
Though his was not a heart where jests had room.   185
He would regret discovery of the truth
Was made too late to influence to ruth
The Procurator who had condemned his son—
Or rather him so deemed. For there was none
To prove that Panthera erred not: and indeed,   190
When vagueness of identity I would plead,
Panther himself would sometimes own as much—
Yet lothly. But, assuming fact was such,
That the said woman did not recognize
Her lover's face, is matter for surprise.   195
However, there's his tale, fantasy or otherwise.

Thereafter shone not men of Panthera's kind:
The indolent heads at home were ill-inclined
To press campaigning that would hoist the star
Of their lieutenants valorous afar.   200

"The impalements duly done, a legionary,
Longinus, pierced the young man with his lance
At signs from me, moved by his agonies.
It brought the end. And when he had breathed his last
The woman went. I saw her never again. . . . *TL*

177 friend?—] ~? *Hol.*   188 condemned] ⟨doomed⟩ deathed *Hol.*   190 Panthera]
Panther *Hol.*   193 Yet seldom. But assuming it was such; *Hol.*   fact] it *TL*

Jealousies kept him irked abroad, controlled
And stinted by an Empire no more bold.
Yet in some actions southward he had share—
In Mauretania and Numidia; there
With eagle eye, and sword and steed and spur,   205
Quelling uprisings promptly. Some small stir
In Parthia next engaged him, until maimed,
As I have said; and cynic Time proclaimed
His noble spirit broken. What a waste
Of such a Roman!—one in youth-time graced   210
With indescribable charm, so I have heard,
Yea, magnetism impossible to word
When faltering as I saw him. What a fame,
O Son of Saturn, had adorned his name,
Might the Three so have urged Thee!— Hour by hour   215
His own disorders hampered Panthera's power
To brood upon the fate of those he had known,
Even of the one he always called his own—
Either in morbid dream or memory . . . .
He died at no great age, untroublously,   220
An exit rare for ardent soldiers such as he.

THE UNBORN*

I rose at night, and visited
        The Cave of the Unborn:
And crowding shapes surrounded me
For tidings of the life to be,
Who long had prayed the silent Head   5
        To haste its advent morn.

212 Yea,] And *TL09*   214 Son] ⟨*l.c.*⟩ *Hol.*   218 the *DCM3*] that *all other texts*

THE UNBORN. *Wayfarer's Love*, ed. Duchess of Sutherland (London: 1904). *MS1* (*WL*) Berg
   Title Life's Opportunity *WL*
   4 life] *cap. MS1*   be,] ~ — *MS1, WL*   5 Long having prayed the Eternal
Head *MS1*; Long having prayed the silent Head *WL*   6 haste] speed *WL*

Their eyes were lit with artless trust,
      Hope thrilled their every tone;
'A scene the loveliest, is it not?
A pure delight, a beauty-spot   10
Where all is gentle, true and just,
      And darkness is unknown?'

My heart was anguished for their sake,
      I could not frame a word;
And they descried my sunken face,   15
And seemed to read therein, and trace
The news that pity would not break,
      Nor truth leave unaverred.

And as I silently retired
      I turned and watched them still,   20
And they came helter-skelter out,
Driven forward like a rabble rout
Into the world they had so desired
      By the all-immanent Will.

                                        1905

THE MAN HE KILLED

          'Had he and I but met
            By some old ancient inn,
      We should have sat us down to wet
            Right many a nipperkin!

11 true] ~, *MS1*, *WL*   14 word;] ~, *MS1*   16 therein,] ~ *MS1*, *WL*
17 pity] *cap. MS1*   18 truth] *cap. MS1*
19–24   A voice like Ocean's caught afar
                  Rolled forth on them and me:—
            "For Lovingkindness life supplies
            A scope superber than the skies.
            So ask no more. Life's gladdening-star
                  In Lovingkindness see." *WL*
      (*MS1* = *WL*, *except* 19 voice] *cap.*   caught] heard; 20 Rolled] Broke; 21 life] *cap.*)
23 world] life *Hol.*   24 all-immanent] great nescient *Hol.*
      Date *CP23*

THE MAN HE KILLED. *Harper's Weekly*, 8 Nov. 1902; *Sphere*, 22 Nov. 1902. *MS1* (*S*) Berg
   Headnote SCENE: *The settle of the Fox Inn, Stagfoot Lane*. CHARACTERS: *The speaker (a
returned soldier), and his friends, natives of the hamlet.* HW, S
   stanzas numbered, rom. *HW, S*   4 nipperkin!] ~. *MS1, HW, S, Hol.*

'But ranged as infantry,   5
And staring face to face,
I shot at him as he at me,
And killed him in his place.

'I shot him dead because—
Because he was my foe,   10
Just so: my foe of course he was;
That's clear enough; although

'He thought he'd 'list, perhaps,
Off-hand like—just as I—
Was out of work—had sold his traps—   15
No other reason why.

'Yes; quaint and curious war is!
You shoot a fellow down
You'd treat if met where any bar is,
Or help to half-a-crown.'   20

1902.

GEOGRAPHICAL KNOWLEDGE*

(A Memory of Christiana C——)

Where Blackmoor was, the road that led
To Bath, she could not show,
Nor point the sky that overspread
Towns ten miles off or so.

7 him] ~, *MS1, HW, S*   9 dead] ~, *MS1, HW, S*   11 Just so;] You see;
HW, S   13 perhaps,] ~ *Hol.*   17 "Yes; ⟨?⟩ quaint ⟨real⟩ and curious
war is! *MS1*   18 You] —You *MS1*   19 That you would treat where any
bar is, *MS1*
    Date om. *MS1, HW, S, Hol.*

GEOGRAPHICAL KNOWLEDGE. *Outlook,* 1 Apr. 1905
    Headnote om. *O*; [In memory of Christiana C——] *Hol.*
    1 was,] lay, *O*   2 show,] ⟨tell⟩ *Hol.*   3 point] tell *O*   4 ten]
twelve *O*

But that Calcutta stood this way,   5
    Cape Horn there figured fell,
That here was Boston, here Bombay,
    She could declare full well.

Less known to her the track athwart
    Froom Mead or Yell'ham Wood   10
Than how to make some Austral port
    In seas of surly mood.

She saw the glint of Guinea's shore
    Behind the plum-tree nigh,
Heard old unruly Biscay's roar   15
    In the weir's purl hard by. . . .

'My son's a sailor, and he knows
    All seas and many lands,
And when he's home he points and shows
    Each country where it stands.   20

'He's now just there—by Gib's high rock—
    And when he gets, you see,
To Portsmouth here, behind the clock,
    Then he'll come back to me!'

THE REJECTED MEMBER'S WIFE*

We shall see her no more
    On the balcony,
Smiling, while hurt, at the roar
    As of surging sea

---

6 Cape Horn] That Horn *O*   10 Mead] ⟨*l.c.*⟩ *Hol.*   16 Amid the weirs'
hard by. . . . *O*; ⟨Amid the weir's hard by. . . .⟩ *Hol.*
16a–d   At last came explanation why
                           Her mind should be so clear
                        On distant scenes, and blank wellnigh
                      On places that were near. *O only*

THE REJECTED MEMBER'S WIFE. *Spectator*, 27 Jan. 1906. *MS1* (*S*) HRC
    Title The Rejected One's Wife *MS1*; The Ejected Member's Wife *S*
    2 the] that *S*   3 *no commas MS1, S*   at] ⟨by⟩ *MS1*

From the stormy sturdy band   5
    Who have doomed her lord's cause,
Though she waves her little hand
    As it were applause.

Here will be candidates yet,
    And candidates' wives,   10
Fervid with zeal to set
    Their ideals on our lives:
Here will come market-men
    On the market-days,
Here will clash now and then   15
    More such party assays.

And the balcony will fill
    When such times are renewed,
And the throng in the street will thrill
    With to-day's mettled mood;   20
But she will no more stand
    In the sunshine there,
With that wave of her white-gloved hand,
    And that chestnut hair.

                January 1906.

ONE RALPH BLOSSOM SOLILOQUIZES

('It being deposed that vij women who were mayds before he knew them have been brought upon the towne [rates?] by the fornicacions of one Ralph Blossom, Mr. Maior inquired why he should not contribute xiv pence weekly toward their mayntenance. But it being shewn that the sayd R. B. was dying of a purple feaver, no order was made.'—*Budmouth Borough Minutes:* 16—.)

When I am in hell or some such place,
A-groaning over my sorry case,
What will those seven women say to me
Who, when I coaxed them, answered 'Aye' to me?

5 the] our *S*   10 wives,] ~ *MS1, S*   11 zeal] zest *S*   12 lives:]
~; *MS1, S*   16 More party-assays. *S*   20 mood;] ~;— *MS1, S*
23 hand,] ~ *MS1, S, Hol.*
    Date *om. S*

'I did not understand your sign!'   5
Will be the words of Caroline;
While Jane will cry, 'If I'd had proof of you,
I should have learnt to hold aloof of you!'

'I won't reproach: it was to be!'
Will drily murmur Cicely;   10
And Rosa: 'I feel no hostility,
For I must own I lent facility.'

Lizzy says: 'Sharp was my regret,
And sometimes it is now! But yet
I joy that, though it brought notoriousness,   15
I knew Love once and all its gloriousness!'

Says Patience: 'Why are we apart?
Small harm did you, my poor Sweet Heart!
A manchild born, now tall and beautiful,
Was worth the ache of days undutiful.'   20

And Anne cries: 'O the time was fair,
So wherefore should you burn down there?
There is a deed under the sun, my Love,
And that was ours. What's done is done, my Love.
These trumpets here in Heaven are dumb to me   25
With you away. Dear, come, O come to me!'

THE NOBLE LADY'S TALE*

(*circa* 1790)

I

'We moved with pensive paces,
    I and he,
And bent our faded faces
    Wistfully,
For something troubled him, and troubled me.   5

ONE RALPH BLOSSOM. 7 cry,] say, *Hol.*   18 Sweet Heart!] ⟨*l.c.*⟩ *Hol.*

THE NOBLE LADY'S TALE. *Harper's Weekly*, 18 Feb. 1905; *Cornhill*, Mar. 1905
    Title The Noble Lady's Story *HW*

'The lanthorn feebly lightened
  Our grey hall,
Where ancient brands had brightened
  Hearth and wall,
And shapes long vanished whither vanish all.   10

'"O why, Love, nightly, daily,"
  I had said,
"Dost sigh, and smile so palely,
  As if shed
Were all Life's blossoms, all its dear things dead?"   15

'"Since silence sets thee grieving,"
  He replied,
"And I abhor deceiving
  One so tried,
Why, Love, I'll speak, ere time us twain divide."   20

'He held me, I remember,
  Just as when
Our life was June—(September
  It was then);
And we walked on, until he spoke again: 25

'"Susie, an Irish mummer,
  Loud-acclaimed
Through the gay London summer,
  Was I; named
A master in my art, who would be famed.   30

'"But lo, there beamed before me
  Lady Su;
God's altar-vow she swore me
  When none knew,
And for her sake I bade the sock adieu.   35

8 ⟨Where ancient brands had brightened⟩ ⟨Where flaming brands once brightened⟩
Hol.   24 Though 'twas then; *HW, C*; ⟨Though 'twas⟩ *Hol.*   26 ⟨"'Susie,⟩
⟨"'I was⟩ *Hol.*   27 ⟨Much-acclaimed⟩ ⟨Su, acclaimed⟩ *Hol.*   28 the]
⟨each⟩ *Hol.*   29 ⟨Was I, framed⟩ ⟨As one—named⟩ Was I;—named *Hol.*
30 ⟨As one to head his art, and to be famed.⟩ ⟨As like to head his art, among the famed.⟩
Hol. my] ⟨my⟩ ⟨his⟩ *Hol.*   32 Su;] ∼: *Hol.*

'"My Lord your father's pardon
    Thus I won;
He let his heart unharden
    Towards his son,
And honourably condoned what we had done;   40

'"But said—recall you, dearest?—
    As for Su,
I'd see her—ay, though nearest
    Me unto—
Sooner entombed than in a stage purlieu!   45

'"Just so.—And here he housed us,
    In this nook,
Where Love like balm has drowsed us:
    Robin, rook,
Our chief familiars, next to string and book.   50

'"Our days here, peace-enshrouded,
    Followed strange
The old stage-joyance, crowded,
    Rich in range;
But never did my soul desire a change,   55

'"Till now, when far uncertain
    Lips of yore
Call, call me to the curtain,
    There once more,
But *once*, to tread the boards I trod before.   60

'"A night—the last and single
    Ere I die—
To face the lights, to mingle
    As did I
Once in the game, and rivet every eye!"   65

38 He] ⟨Who⟩ *Hol.*   40 honourably] ⟨nobly he⟩ *Hol.*   41 But] ⟨He⟩
Hol.   42 *Su,*] ⟨*Sue,*⟩ *Hol.*   44 *Now to you*— HW, C; *Now* ⟨*un*⟩*to you*—
Hol.   55 change,] ~ ⟨;⟩, *Hol.*   56 when far] the far HW, C; ⟨a voice⟩ *Hol.*
57 Lips of] Voice of HW, C; ⟨As from⟩ *Hol.*   58 Call, call] Calls—calls HW, C;
⟨Calls, calls⟩ *Hol.*   curtain,] ~ ⟨;⟩, *Hol.*   65 Once] ⟨Ere⟩ ⟨Erst⟩ *Hol.*

'Such was his wish. He feared it,
    Feared it though
  Rare memories so endeared it.
    I, also,
Feared it still more; its outcome who could know?   70

'"Alas, my Love," said I then,
    "Since it be
  A wish so mastering, why, then,
    E'en go ye!—
Despite your pledge to father and to me . . ."   75

' 'Twas fixed; no more was spoken
    Thereupon;
  Our silences were broken
    Only on
The petty items of his needs while gone.   80

'Farewell he bade me, pleading
    That it meant
  So little, thus conceding
    To his bent;
And then, as one constrained to go, he went.   85

'Thwart thoughts I let deride me,
    As, 'twere vain
  To hope him back beside me
    Ever again:
Could one plunge make a waxing passion wane?   90

'I thought, "Some wild stage-woman,
    Honour-wrecked . . ."
  But no: it was inhuman
    To suspect;
Though little cheer could my lone heart affect!   95

---

70 more;] ~ : *Hol.*   know?] ~ ! *Hol.*   75 me . . .'] ~ ' . . . *Hol.*   86 "Thwart]
⟨"Sick⟩ *Hol.*   90 plunge] ⟨fling⟩ *Hol.*   waxing] ⟨ruling⟩ *Hol.*
95 affect!] ~ . *Hol.*

II

'Yet came it, to my gladness,
    That, as vowed,
He did return.—But sadness
    Swiftly cowed
The joy with which my greeting was endowed.   100

'Some woe was there. Estrangement
    Marked his mind.
Each welcome-warm arrangement
    I had designed
Touched him no more than deeds of careless kind.   105

'"I—*failed!*" escaped him glumly.
    "—I went on
In my old part. But dumbly—
    Memory gone—
Advancing, I sank sick; my vision drawn   110

'"To something drear, distressing
    As the knell
Of all hopes worth possessing!" . . .
    —What befell
Seemed linked with me, but how I could not tell.   115

'Hours passed; till I implored him,
    As he knew
How faith and frankness toward him
    Ruled me through,
To say what ill I had done, and could undo.   120

'"*Faith—frankness.* Ah! Heaven save such!"
    Murmured he,
"They are wedded wealth! *I* gave such
    Liberally,
But you, Dear, not. For you suspected me."   125

---

110 sank sick;] ⟨collapsed;⟩ *Hol.*   120 and] ⟨or⟩ *Hol.*   121 Ah!] ⟨Ha!⟩
Hol.

'I was about beseeching
   In hurt haste
More meaning, when he, reaching
   To my waist,
Led me to pace the hall as once we paced.   130

   '"I never meant to draw you
      To own all,"
Declared he. "But—I *saw* you—
      By the wall,
Half-hid. And that was why I failed withal!"   135

   '"Where? when?" said I—"Why, nigh me,
      At the play
That night. That you should spy me,
      Doubt my fay,
And follow, furtive, took my heart away!"   140

   'That I had never been there,
      But had gone
To my locked room—unseen there,
      Curtains drawn,
Long days abiding—told I, wonder-wan.   145

   '"Nay, 'twas your form and vesture,
      Cloak and gown,
Your hooded features—gesture
      Half in frown,
That faced me, pale," he urged, "that night in town.   150

   '"And when, outside, I handed
      To her chair
(As courtesy demanded
      Of me there)
The leading lady, you peeped from the stair."   155

128 he,] ~ *HW, C, Hol.*   129 waist,] ~ *HW, C, Hol.*   146 '"Nay, 'twas]
⟨'"It was⟩ *Hol.*   147 ⟨Cloak-wrapt gown,⟩ ⟨Cloak-sheathed gown,⟩ *Hol.*
151-5 *om. HW, C; inserted in margin Hol.*

'Straight pleaded I: "Forsooth, Love,
  Had I gone,
I must have been in truth, Love,
  Mad to don
Such well-known raiment." But he still went on   160

'That he was not mistaken
  Nor misled.—
I felt like one forsaken,
  Wished me dead,
That he could think thus of the wife he had wed!   165

'His going seemed to waste him
  Like a curse,
To wreck what once had graced him;
  And, averse
To my approach, he mused, and moped, and worse.   170

'Till, what no words effected
  Thought achieved:
It was my wraith—projected,
  He conceived,
Thither, by my tense brain at home aggrieved.   175

'Thereon his credence centred
  Till he died;
And, no more tempted, entered—
  Sanctified—
The little vault with room for one beside.'   180

III

Thus far the lady's story.—
  Now she, too,
Reclines within that hoary
  Last dark mew
In Mellstock Quire with him she loved so true.   185

158 been] ~, *HW, C, Hol.*   165 wed!] ~. *HW, C, Hol.*   166–70 *om. HW, C; inserted in margin Hol.*   166 'His] "That *TL*   168 Spoil all that once had graced him; *TL*   171 'Till,] "Well: *HW, C;* ⟨"Well:⟩ *Hol.*   174 He] ⟨We⟩ *Hol.* 176 his] ⟨our⟩ *Hol.*   178 entered—] ~ *HW, C, TL, CP*   179 Sanctified—] ~, *HW, C, TL, CP*   183 ⟨Within that scant and hoary⟩ *Hol.*   184 ⟨Lovers' mew⟩ *Hol.*   185 In] ⟨At⟩ *Hol.* Quire] ⟨rests⟩ ⟨Church,⟩ Quire, *Hol.*

A yellowing marble, placed there
      Tablet-wise,
And two joined hearts enchased there
      Meet the eyes;
And reading their twin names we moralize: 190

Did she, we wonder, follow
      Jealously?
And were those protests hollow?—
      Or saw he
Some semblant dame? Or can wraiths really be?   195

Were it she went, her honour,
      All may hold,
Pressed truth at last upon her
      Till she told—
(Him only—others as these lines unfold.)   200

Riddle death-sealed for ever,
      Let it rest! . . .
One's heart could blame her never
      If one guessed
That go she did. She knew her actor best.   205

UNREALIZED

Down comes the winter rain—
      Spoils my hat and bow—
Runs into the poll of me;
      But mother won't know.

193 Was her denial hollow?— *TL*   195 ⟨Some semblant dame, or her wraith
verily?⟩ *Hol.*

UNREALIZED. *Queen's Carol* (London: 1905)
    Title Orphaned/A Point of View *QC*
    3 of] o' *QC*   4 know.] ~! *QC*; ~ ⟨!⟩. *Hol.*

We've been out and caught a cold,   5
    Knee-deep in snow;
Such a lucky thing it is
    That mother won't know!

Rosy lost herself last night—
    Couldn't tell where to go.   10
Yes—it rather frightened her,
    But mother didn't know.

Somebody made Willy drunk
    At the Christmas show:
O 'twas fun! It's well for him   15
    That mother won't know!

Howsoever wild we are,
    Late at school or slow,
Mother won't be cross with us,
    Mother won't know.   20

How we cried the day she died,
    Neighbours whispering low . . .
But we now do what we will—
    Mother won't know!

---

5 We played and caught a cold *QC*   cold,] ~ *Hol.*   9 Rosy, she got lost one
night— *QC*   14 show:] ~; *Hol.*   15 O] Oh, *QC*   16 won't]
didn't *QC*   19 Mother's never cross with us— *QC*
21–4   How we cried the day she died;
                           How we miss her. . . . Though
                       We may now do what we will,
                           Mother won't know! *QC*

                       'Cause she's dead. The neighbours say
                           'Tis our ruin. No!
                       We may now do what we will—
                           Mother won't know. *Hol.*

                       How we cried the day she died!
                           All the folk said, "Oh,
                       It's those children's ruin!"—Still,
                       We may now do what we will—
                           Mother won't know. *TL*

21 died,] ~! *CP*   22 low . . .] ~! . . . *WE13*   24 know! *ME*] ~ . *WE, CP*

WAGTAIL AND BABY

A baby watched a ford, whereto
  A wagtail came for drinking;
A blaring bull went wading through,
  The wagtail showed no shrinking.

A stallion splashed his way across,   5
  The birdie nearly sinking;
He gave his plumes a twitch and toss,
  And held his own unblinking.

Next saw the baby round the spot
  A mongrel slowly slinking;   10
The wagtail gazed, but faltered not
  In dip and sip and prinking.

A perfect gentleman then neared;
  The wagtail, in a winking,
With terror rose and disappeared;   15
  The baby fell a-thinking.

ABERDEEN*

(April: 1905)

'And wisdom and knowledge shall be the stability of thy times.'—Isaiah xxxiii. 6.

I looked and thought, 'All is too gray and cold
To wake my place-enthusiasms of old!'
Till a voice passed: 'Behind that granite mien
Lurks the imposing beauty of a Queen.'

                       [no stanza break]

WAGTAIL AND BABY. *Albany Review*, Apr. 1907
  Subtitle An Incident of Civilization *AR*
    1 whereto] ⟨wheretoward⟩ *Hol.*   2 came] ⟨down⟩ *Hol.*   3 through,]
~ *Hol.*   15 Rose terrified and disappeared . . . *AR*   disappeared;] ~. *Hol.*

ABERDEEN. *Alma Mater* [Aberdeen University] Sept. 1906. *MS1* (*AM*) Aberdeen University
Library
  Epigraph footnote to line 8 AM
    1 looked] ~; *MS1, AM*   'All] "She *AM, Hol.*   2 To wake the warm
enthusiasms of old!" *AM*

I looked anew; and saw the radiant form
Of Her who soothes in stress, who steers in storm,
On the grave influence of whose eyes sublime
Men count for the stability of the time.

GEORGE MEREDITH*

1828–1909

Forty years back, when much had place
That since has perished out of mind,
I heard that voice and saw that face.

He spoke as one afoot will wind
A morning horn ere men awake;   5
His note was trenchant, turning kind.

He was of those whose wit can shake
And riddle to the very core
The counterfeits that Time will break. . . .

Of late, when we two met once more,   10
The luminous countenance and rare
Shone just as forty years before.

So that, when now all tongues declare
His shape unseen by his green hill,
I scarce believe he sits not there.   15

No matter. Further and further still
Through the world's vaporous vitiate air
His words wing on—as live words will.

May, 1909.

6 Of Her who stays in stress, who guides in storm; *AM*

GEORGE MEREDITH. *Times* 22 May 1909
   Title G. M./1828–1909 *T, TL*
   6 turning] smart, but *T, Hol.*   7 wit] words *T*   9 counterfeits] falsities *T*
14 His shape] He is *T*   18 live] strong *T*
   Date om. T

YELL'HAM-WOOD'S STORY

Coomb-Firtrees say that Life is a moan,
    And Clyffe-hill Clump says 'Yea!'
But Yell'ham says a thing of its own:
        It's not 'Gray, gray
        Is Life alway!'   5
        That Yell'ham says,
Nor that Life is for ends unknown.

It says that Life would signify
    A thwarted purposing:
That we come to live, and are called to die.   10
        Yes, that's the thing
        In fall, in spring,
        That Yell'ham says:—
    'Life offers—to deny!'

                                    1902.

A YOUNG MAN'S EPIGRAM ON EXISTENCE*

A senseless school, where we must give
Our lives that we may learn to live!
A dolt is he who memorizes
Lessons that leave no time for prizes.

                    16 Westbourne Park Villas, 1866.

YELL'HAM-WOOD'S STORY. 2 Clyffe-hill] Dudd-hill *Hol.*   3 ⟨But Yell'ham says a thing of its own:⟩ But Yell'ham-Wood says things of its own: *Hol.*

A YOUNG MAN'S EPIGRAM. *Title* Epigram on Existence *Hol.*
    Place/date 16 W. P. V., 1866. *TL*

EXPLANATORY NOTES

Epigraph to the Present Edition

Hardy wrote the epigraph (from Job 15: 17) on the title-page of his copy of *Collected Poems* (1923), with a note to himself to 'verify'. This is the copy (now in DCM) in which he also entered many of his late revisions to his poems. Siegfried Sassoon, a friend of Hardy's last years, also entered the epigraph on the title-page of his own copy of *Collected Poems*, noting there that Hardy 'thought of putting these words here'. Sassoon's copy is in the Holmes collection.

Wessex Poems

History of Composition and Publication

On 24 November 1898, Hardy wrote to his friend William Archer: 'At the beginning of Dec. I am going to send and ask you to accept a copy of my volume of verses, which will come out about then. I have been going to publish it for years. But please don't expect to find much in them.' (*Letters* II, p. 206.) Hardy had had such a collection in mind for at least six years; in 1892 he wrote in his journal: 'Title:—"Songs of Five-and-Twenty Years". Arrangement of the songs: Lyric Ecstasy inspired by music to have precedence.' (*LY*, p. 3.) Five-and-twenty years would reach back to 1867, and a third of the fifty-one poems in Hardy's first book of verse are dated in the late sixties, the years when Hardy was working as an architect in London. According to Hardy's own account he wrote very few poems during the middle period of his novel-writing career (only three poems in *Wessex Poems* are dated in the 1870s, and only one in the 1880s), but in the nineties the flow of verse increased rapidly, 'though at first with some consternation he had found an awkwardness in getting back to an easy expression in numbers after abandoning it for so many years; but that soon wore off'. (*LY*, p. 66.)

Only four of the poems had previously been published: 'The Bride-Night Fire' (under its earlier title, 'The Fire at Tranter Sweatley's') in periodicals in England and America in 1875; 'The Sergeant's Song' in *The Trumpet Major* (1880); 'The Stranger's Song' in Hardy's story, 'The Three Strangers' (1883); and 'Lines' in the *Dorset County Chronicle* (1890).

Wessex Poems must have been substantially prepared by 4 February 1897, when Hardy recorded in his journal not only his final title, but also his plan to include 'Sketches of their Scenes by the Author'. An agreement to publish was signed with Harper & Brothers in September 1898, and the book was published that winter—in December 1898 in England, and in January 1899 in America. In 1902 Macmillan & Co. became Hardy's publishers, and a 'new Edition' of *Wessex Poems*, printed from the corrected Harper plates, was issued under the Macmillan imprint in August 1903 as volume XVIII of *Thomas Hardy's Works*, the so-called Uniform Edition. This 'edition' was reprinted in 1911, 1916, and 1923.

Other significant editions of *Wessex Poems* are:

The Pocket Edition (with *Poems of the Past and the Present*), volume XVIII of 'Macmillan's Pocket Hardy' (1907). This 'edition' was printed from the Harper plates, as corrected for Macmillan's Uniform Edition, but contains a few further corrections.

The Wessex Edition (with *Poems of the Past and the Present*), Verse Volume I (1912, reprinted with some corrections, 1920): a new setting of type and one of the major revisions of the text.

The Mellstock Edition (also with *Poems of the Past and the Present*), volume XXXIV (1920): a resetting of the Wessex Edition text, but with some further revisions.

Collected Poems (1919): a substantial revision.
Collected Poems (1920): a few further revisions.
Collected Poems (1923): minor revisions to another fourteen poems.

The holograph of *Wessex Poems*, a fair copy used as printer's copy, is in the Birmingham City Museum and Art Gallery. It contains numerous corrections, and some divergences from the printed text. It also includes the thirty-two original drawings that Hardy made as illustrations (see Appendix A below). In the holograph the last six poems appear under the collective heading 'Addenda'. This was changed in *Wessex Poems* to 'Additions', and then dropped.

Explanatory Notes

PREFACE TO WESSEX POEMS. ll. 3-4 Four poems in *Wessex Poems* parallel passages in the novels: 'She, to Him I' (*Desperate Remedies*), 'Valenciennes' and 'The Alarm' (*The Trumpet-Major*), and 'In a Wood' (*The Woodlanders*). For particulars of these connections, see notes to the individual poems below.

l. 13 The early editions were illustrated by the writer. (H) The illustrations are reproduced in Appendix A of this volume.

Postponement. Collins (pp. 22-3) reports the following exchange with Hardy concerning this poem:

C.: I am not clear what is the human application of the last stanza—'Ah, had I been . . . born to an evergreen nesting tree.'

H.: You see, earlier in the poem the young man is described as not being able to marry for want of money; and the woman as not waiting, but marrying someone else.

C.: I understand that. The 'being born to an evergreen tree' means, then, simply and solely having money?

H.: Yes.

A Confession to a Friend in Trouble. In *Hol.*, the poem is written without stanza breaks, which are indicated by pencil marks. Purdy identifies the friend as Horace Moule.

She at his Funeral. Dated 1873 in 'A Chronological List of Thomas Hardy's Works', MS in Hardy's hand, DCM.

She, to Him I-IV. In a letter to Macmillan (24 March 1925), Hardy wrote that 'the four "She to him" sonnets [are] to be reckoned as one poem, which they are

. . .'. (BL Add. MS 54925.) The sonnets are described in *EL* (p. 71) as 'part of a much larger number which perished'. Professor Michael Millgate (*Thomas Hardy, A Biography* (Oxford: 1982)), identifies the speaker with Eliza Nicholls.

She, to Him II. Hardy wrote on the holograph of this poem 'prosed in "Desperate Remedies"', and made the point more generally in his preface to *WP* (see above, p. 5) and in his preface to the *WE* of the novel. Purdy cites a passage in Ch. VI. 1 of the novel (*WE*, pp. 95-6) as a possible parallel, but a closer one is the following:

And perhaps, far in time to come, when I am dead and gone, some other's accent, or some other's song, or thought, like an old one of mine, will carry them back to what I used to say, and hurt their hearts a little that they blamed me so soon. And they will pause just for an instant, and give a sigh to me, and think, 'Poor girl!' believing they do great justice to my memory by this. But they will never, never realize that it was my single opportunity of existence, as well as of doing my duty, which they are regarding; they will not feel that what to them is but a thought, easily held in those two words of pity, 'Poor girl!' was a whole life to me; as full of hours, minutes, and peculiar minutes, of hopes and dreads, smiles, whisperings, tears, as theirs: that it was my world, what is to them their world, and they in that life of mine, however much I cared for them, only as the thought I seem to them to be. (*Desperate Remedies*, Ch. XIII. 4 (*WE*, pp. 278-9).)

Ditty. E. L. G. is Emma Lavinia Gifford (1840-1912), Hardy's first wife. They met in 1870, in the remote village on the west coast of Cornwall where Emma was living with her sister and brother-in-law, the vicar of the village church. They were married in 1874.

The Sergeant's Song. Published in "The Trumpet-Major", 1880. (H)
    The first and fourth stanzas were first published in the serial version of *The Trumpet-Major* (in *Good Words*, February 1880), and in the first edition of the novel, published in the same year. Stanzas two and three were added in the Sampson, Low edition of 1881. In the novel-text, the poem is syllabized and stress-marked to indicate the rendition of the song by Sergeant Stanner and Festus Derriman. (*WE*, pp. 34-6.)

Valenciennes. Corporal Tullidge tells the story, briefly, in *The Trumpet-Major*, Ch. IV. (*WE*, pp. 30-1.) In *Hol.* the first five stanzas and the ninth stanza have opening quotation marks.

San Sebastian. Hardy's principal source appears to have been W. F. P. Napier's *History of the War in the Peninsula* (1828-40), Book XXII, Ch. 2, which provided not only details of the assault and military terminology, but also mentions a rape. Napier writes of the conclusion of the attack:

This storm seemed to be the signal of hell for the perpetration of villainy which would have shamed the most ferocious barbarians of antiquity. At Ciudad Rodrigo intoxication and plunder had been the principal object; at Badajos lust and murder were joined to rapine and drunkenness; but at San Sebastian, the direst, the most revolting cruelty was added to the catalogue of crimes. One atrocity of which a girl of seventeen was the victim, staggers the mind by its enormous, incredible, indescribable barbarity.

Hardy owned a set of Napier's *History*, in the 1892 edition.

The Stranger's Song. Printed in "The Three Strangers", 1883. (H)

Hardy dramatized the story as *The Three Wayfarers* in 1893. A revised version of the play was produced by the Dorchester Debating and Dramatic Society in November 1911. For this performance Hardy provided a musical setting for the song; the music was printed, in a facsimile of Hardy's manuscript, in the play programme, and also in the *Dorset Year-Book* for 1912-13, where the tune is described as 'a traditional one in the County of Dorset, and very old'. This manuscript is reproduced in Appendix B. The typescript of the Dramatic Society production is in the library of the University of California, Riverside.

The Burghers. The cancelled *WE* subtitle, the illustration, and the place-names all locate the poem in Dorchester.

l. 45 Hardy revised this line in *DCM1* to the *SP* version; he restored the original line in *DCM4*.

Leipzig. Hardy used passages from the poem (ll. 23-4, 42-4, 101-8, 117-32) in the Leipzig scenes of *The Dynasts*: Part Third, III. ii-v.

l. 79 Isaiah 2: 4.

The Peasant's Confession. The poem was conceived in the spring of 1898, when 'Hardy did some reading at the British Museum with a view to *The Dynasts*, and incidentally stumbled upon some details that suggested to him the Waterloo episode embodied in a poem called "The Peasant's Confession"'. (*LY*, p. 74.) The epigraph is from Adolphe Thiers's *Histoire du Consulat et de l'Empire* (Paris: 1862), vol. 20, p. 258. Hardy owned a French edition of this work, as well as an English translation by D. Forbes Campbell (London: 1862). He marked the quoted passage in his English edition.

In Hol. two tentative pencilled revisions, later erased, can be made out.

l. 8 Below the line Hardy tried out the alternative lines:

> Thronged Salon, Parc and Bois.
> Dallied with gay sangfroid.

l. 12 Above the word *enwrapt* (the Hol. version) he wrote and erased *involved*.

Hardy defended the diction of the poem in a letter to William Archer (21 December 1898): 'Your happy phrase, "seeing all the words of the dictionary on one plane" (anent the Peasant's Confession) touches, curiously enough, what I had thought over. Concluding that the tale must be regarded as a translation of the original utterance of the peasant I thought an impersonal wording admissible.' (*Letters* II, p. 207.)

The Alarm. The reference to *The Trumpet-Major* is to Ch. XXVI, 'The Alarm'. The 'one of the writer's family' who was a Volunteer was Hardy's grandfather, also named Thomas.

Her Death and After. Of this poem and the next Hardy wrote to his friend Sir George Douglas (3 April 1901): 'As you have been re-reading my books I shall ask you when I see you what you think of my opinion that "Her Death and After," and "The Dance at the Phoenix" . . . are two as good stories as I have ever told?' (*Letters* II, p. 283.)

The Dance at the Phoenix. l. 49 *moved me of yore*: in *DCM3* Hardy underlined these words and pencilled in the margin, also underlined: *?did heretofore*.

The Casterbridge Captains. Lea and Purdy identify the captains as John Bascombe Lock, Thomas Henry Gatehouse Besant, and J. Logan, all of Dorchester. The church, All Saints, stands in High East Street, Dorchester, but is no longer in use.

A Sign-Seeker. Hardy copied the seventh and ninth verses of this poem into the autograph book of his friend Dora Sigerson Shorter (wife of the editor Clement Shorter). The book is in the collection of the Philip H. and A. S. W. Rosenbach Foundation, Philadelphia.

My Cicely. In a letter to Mr Pouncy (29 December 1908), regarding a recitation of Hardy's poems, Hardy wrote: 'if you wanted more views, or rather new things to say, the poem "My Cicely" in the "Wessex Poems" would afford a capital panoramic treatment of the Great Western Road from London to Exeter—accompanied by your recitation of the journey with the galloping movement of the verses.' (Berg.) On his journey the traveller passes Basing House, near Basingstoke, scene of a Civil War siege (l. 25); Salisbury Cathedral (l. 27); Blandford Forum (l. 37); Weatherby Castle, an Iron Age earthwork near Puddletown (l. 41); Maiden Castle (l. 49); Eggardon Hill (l. 51); and Poundbury Camp (l. 52); earthworks near Dorchester; and Nine Stones, a Bronze Age stone circle near Winterborne Abbas (l. 53); he also crosses four rivers—the Stour, the Bride, the Axe, and the Otter. As Bailey observes (p. 86), the movement is backward through history as well as westward (though neither Hardy's geography nor his history is in exact order).

For a possible connection with Hardy's cousin Tryphena Sparks see the note to 'Thoughts of Phena' below.

The Ivy-Wife. Hardy's first wife, Emma, apparently took the poem personally. In a letter to Rebekah Owen (27 December 1899) she wrote: 'Of recent poetry perhaps you admire "The Ivy Wife." Of course my wonder is great at any admiration for it . . .'. (Colby.)

Friends Beyond. Some of the friends appear in other Hardy works: William Dewy in *Under the Greenwood Tree*, *Tess of the d'Urbervilles* (Ch. XVII), and 'The Dead Quire' (*TL*), Reuben Dewy in *Under the Greenwood Tree*, 'The Dead Quire', and 'The Fiddler of the Reels' (*Life's Little Ironies*), Farmer Ledlow in *Under the Greenwood Tree*, Lady Susan in 'The Noble Lady's Tale' (*TL*). Lady Susan's story is also related in *EL*, pp. 11–12 and 213–14, and *LY*, pp. 12–13.

l. 30. In *Hol.* below the line Hardy wrote and erased:

London	*coach*
City	stage

Thoughts of Phena. *EL* (p. 293) quotes the following from Hardy's diary for 5 March 1890: 'In the train on the way to London. Wrote the first four or six lines of "Not a line of her writing have I". It was a curious instance of sympathetic telepathy. The woman whom I was thinking of—a cousin—was dying at the time, and I quite in ignorance of it. She died six days later. The remainder of the piece was not written till after her death.' 'Phena' was Hardy's cousin, Tryphena Sparks (1851-90), who lived at Puddletown, near Hardy's boyhood home at Higher Bockhampton. Her education and experience as a teacher may have provided Hardy with material for the career of Sue Bridehead in *Jude the Obscure*, and her marriage to a hotel-keeper near Exeter may have suggested the situation of 'My Cicely'.

Middle-Age Enthusiasms. M. H. is Hardy's sister, Mary (1841-1915).

In a Wood. The poem is 'from *The Woodlanders*' in the sense that novel and poem share an informing idea. The passage in the novel closest to the poem is the following:

> They went noiselessly over mats of starry moss, rustled through interspersed tracts of leaves, skirted trunks with spreading roots whose mossed rinds made them like hands wearing green gloves; elbowed old elms and ashes with great forks, in which stood pools of water that overflowed on rainy days and ran down their stems in green cascades. On older trees still than these huge lobes of fungi grew like lungs. Here, as everywhere, the Unfulfilled Intention, which makes life what it is, was as obvious as it could be among the depraved crowds of a city slum. The leaf was deformed, the curve was crippled, the taper was interrupted; the lichen ate the vigour of the stalk, and the ivy slowly strangled to death the promising sapling. (Ch. VII (*WE*, pp. 58-9).)

The first of the two dates attached to the poem, 1887, is the date of publication of *The Woodlanders*.

Nature's Questioning. In a letter to Alfred Noyes (19 December 1920), Hardy wrote in defence of this poem: 'A poem often quoted against me, and apparently in your mind in the lecture, is the one called "Nature's Questioning", containing the words, "some Vast Imbecility", etc.—as if these definitions were my creed. But they are merely enumerated in the poem as fanciful alternatives to several others, and have nothing to do with my own opinion.' The letter, slightly misquoted, is in *LY*, pp. 216-18; the original is in the Taylor Collection, Princeton University Library.

At an Inn. Lea says, presumably on Hardy's authority, that the poem was written at the George Inn, Winchester. Purdy suggests that it may be associated with Mrs Henniker. (See 'A Note on the Hon. Mrs. Arthur Henniker', Purdy, pp. 342-8.)

The Bride-Night Fire. The poem was written in 1866 or 1867—Hardy gives both dates (see *EL*, p. 141)—and was published in the *Gentleman's Magazine* (November 1875) in England and in *Appleton's Journal* (6 November 1875) in America. When John Lane wrote to Hardy in 1894 asking permission to include the poem in Lionel Johnson's *The Art of Thomas Hardy*, Hardy offered to provide 'a copy of the original ballad, which was Bowdlerized for the magazine'. (*Letters* II, p. 61.) He also offered to correct a proof of the poem, and he must have done so, for the text printed in Johnson's book differs in many particulars from the manuscript (both the manuscript and Hardy's letter to Lane are in Bancroft). Hardy changed the title and added glossarial footnotes for the *WE* (1912).

For the text of the bowdlerized version see below, Appendix C.

Heiress and Architect. Sir Arthur William Blomfield (1829-99) was the architect, best known for his church designs and restorations, for whom Hardy worked during his London years, 1862-7. Hardy identified a number of his early poems as having been written at 8 Adelphi Terrace, the address of Blomfield's drawing-office. (See *EL*, p. 48 and *LY*, p. 11.)

Lines. Headnote: on *MS2* Hardy added in the margin, in pencil: *this* (*Wednesday*) *afternoon July 23, 1890*. The poem was quoted in part in the *Pall Mall Gazette* on the day of the performance (23 July 1890), and on the following day in the *Pall Mall Budget*, and was commented on in notices of the performance in the *Globe* and the *Daily News* (both on 24 July). The *Globe* reviewer thought the lines 'poor stuff, poetically', and Hardy wrote on the same day to the critic of the *World*, asking him to publish a defence of the verses, 'considering that they were written for a charitable purpose, and . . . in great haste, while the accomplished lady who recited them was waiting for the manuscript.' (*Letters* I, p. 215.) A statement, using Hardy's own words, appeared in the *World* on 30 July.

Hardy's haste may not have been quite as great as he suggested; Mrs Jeune's manuscript copy of the poem, now in the collection of Professor Richard Purdy, is dated 20 July, and in a letter dated 21 July, addressed to Augustin Daly, manager of the company of which Miss Rehan was the star, Hardy wrote that he had already sent the poem to Miss Rehan, and enclosed three corrections:

line 3—for 'grave objects' read 'grave projects.'
line 11 [line 15 in present text]—for 'cadaverous pallor' read 'lymphatic pallor.'
line 25—for 'Launched into *cabins*,' etc. read 'Launched into *domiciles surcharged* before.'

(The letter is in the library of the University of California, Los Angeles.)

'*I look into my glass*.' As Pinion notes (pp. 27-8), the same theme occurs in *The Well-Beloved*. In Part II, Ch. XII (*WE*, p. 136), Pierston thinks: 'When was it to end—this curse of his heart not ageing while his frame moved naturally onward?'; and in Part III, Ch. IV (*WE*, pp. 175-6), Pierston, seeing himself in a looking-glass, thinks that 'the person he appeared was too grievously far, chronologically, in advance of the person he felt himself to be . . . While his soul was what it was, why should he have been encumbered with that withering carcase . . .?' *The Well-Beloved* was published in the *Illustrated London News*, October-December 1892; while it was appearing, Hardy wrote in his journal: 'I look in the glass. Am conscious of the humiliating sorriness of my earthly tabernacle, and of the sad fact that the best of parents could do no better for me . . . Why should a man's mind have been thrown into such close, sad, sensational, inexplicable relations with such a precarious object as his own body!' (*LY*, pp. 13-14.)

Poems of the Past and the Present

History of Composition and Publication

Hardy's second volume of poems differs from his first in being made up almost entirely of recently written poems. Of the ninety-nine poems in the collection, only two are dated in the 1860s. Most of the other twenty-seven dated poems are occasional: nine from Hardy's European tour in 1887 and two from a trip to Switzerland in 1897; eight related to the Boer War, written in 1899; and one on the death of Queen Victoria in 1901. Fourteen of the poems had previously been published in periodicals, including seven of the war poems and the elegy to Victoria.

The agreement between Hardy and his publisher, Harper & Brothers, was signed on 28 May 1901, for a book at that time entitled *Poems of Feeling, Dream, and Deed* (Purdy, p. 118). Hardy spent the summer weeks preparing copy, and the holograph printer's copy was sent off at the end of August (the preface is dated 'August, 1901'). The book was published in England in November 1901 (though post-dated 1902), and in America the following month. A corrected second impression, inaccurately described on the title-page as the 'second edition', was printed in January 1902.

Macmillan, Hardy's publisher from 1902, first published *Poems of the Past and the Present* in August 1903, as volume XIX of Hardy's *Works* in the Uniform Edition. This printing is identified on the verso of the title-page as 'Second Edition'; it was printed from the corrected Harper plates, but has some ten further corrections. It was reprinted in 1911 and 1919.

Other significant editions of *Poems of the Past and the Present* are:

The Pocket Edition (with *Wessex Poems*), as volume XVIII of 'Macmillan's Pocket Hardy' (1907): printed from the plates of the 1903 Macmillan 'Second Edition', with which it is textually identical.

The Wessex Edition (with *Wessex Poems*), Verse Volume I (1912, reprinted 1920); a new setting of type and a substantially revised text.

The Mellstock Edition (with *Wessex Poems*), Volume XXXIV (1920), a resetting of the Wessex Edition text, with some corrections.

Collected Poems (1919): a substantial revision.
Collected Poems (1920): minor revisions.
Collected Poems (1923): minor revisions.

The holograph of *Poems of the Past and the Present*, a fair copy with some corrections, is in the Bodleian Library, Oxford (MS. Eng. poet. d. 18). Hardy prepared it as printer's copy, and his instructions to the printer, written in pencil at the head of the first poem and later erased, can be made out. They read:

To the printer:
— Words in IZE to be spelt as in MS.
— Punctuation to be as in MS.
— Poems copied here in double columns to be in single columns only.

In the holograph table of contents, 'The Bedridden Peasant to an Unknowing God'

has been moved from a position above 'God-forgotten' to a place immediately
below it. One title, 'The Complaint of the Common Man', has been cancelled. The
final group of poems, subtitled 'Retrospect' in the published text, is labelled
'Conclusion' in the holograph.

   Manuscripts of seven individual poems also exist: two of the War Poems ('At the
War Office, London' and 'The Souls of the Slain'), two of the Poems of Pilgrimage
('Shelley's Skylark' and 'Rome: At the Pyramid of Cestius'), and three others:
'Wives in the Sere', 'The Darkling Thrush' (under its earlier title, 'By the
Century's Deathbed'), and 'The Lost Pyx'.

Explanatory Notes

Preface. 'The Literary Week', a column of literary news in the *Academy*, 12 October
1901, quotes the last sentence of Hardy's preface as follows: 'The road to a true
philosophy of life seems to lie in humbly regarding divergent impressions of its
meaning as they occur.' Purdy (p. 110n.) infers that the *Academy* had an early
proof of the volume: see also, below, notes to the following poems: 'In the Old
Theatre, Fiesole', 'The Bedridden Peasant', 'Mute Opinion', 'To an Unborn
Pauper Child', and 'His Immortality'.

Embarcation. Hardy wrote to Mrs Henniker (9 November 1899): 'I fancy you
thought my sonnet on the departure too tragic? But I was not at Southampton
on the Saturday when you were there—I went Friday, and saw off 5000 alto-
gether . . .'. (*Letters* II, p. 236.) To the *Daily Chronicle* text Hardy added a note that
no copyright was claimed for the poem.

The Going of the Battery. Hardy wrote to Mrs Henniker (9 November 1899): 'The
fact is, the incidents of departure have rather come in my way by accident. The
latest was the going of our Battery of Artillery (stationed in this town) and as they
left at 10 at night, and some at 4 in the morning, amid rain and wind, the scene was
a pathetic one.' (*Letters* II, p. 236.) In a letter two weeks later he added: 'It was
almost an exact report of the scene and expressions I overheard.' (*Letters* II,
p. 238.)

At the War Office, London. Hardy wrote to Mrs Henniker (19 December 1899): 'I
have not run up to London after all, this month; but I have written a little poem, of
2 stanzas only, on the scene at the War Office after a battle, which, though I have
not witnessed it, I can imagine with painful realism.' (*Letters* II, p. 241.)

A Christmas Ghost-Story. The first appearance of Hardy's poem, in the *West-
minster Gazette*, 23 December 1899, prompted a Christmas Day leader in the *Daily
Chronicle*: 'Mr. Thomas Hardy has pictured the soul of a dead soldier in Natal
contemplating the battlefield, and wondering where is that peace on earth which
is the Christian ideal of Christmastide. A fine conception, but we fear that
soldier is Mr. Hardy's soldier, and not one of the Dublin Fusiliers who cried
amidst the storm of bullets at Tugela, "Let us make a name for ourselves!"
Here is another ideal which conflicts, alas! with the sublime message we celebrate
to-day . . .'.

Hardy replied in a letter dated 25 December:

Sir:

In your interesting leading article of this morning, on Christmas Day, you appear to demur to the character of the soldier's phantom in my few lines entitled 'A Christmas Ghost Story' (printed in the *Westminster Gazette* for Dec. 23), as scarcely exhibiting the primary quality of, say, a Dublin Fusilier, which is assumed to be physical courage; the said phantom being plaintive, embittered, and sad at the prevalence of war during a nominal Æra of peace. But surely there is artistic propriety—and, if I may say so, moral and religious propriety—in making him, or it, feel thus, especially in a poem intended for Christmas Day. One's modern fancy of a disembodied spirit—unless intentionally humorous—is that of an entity which has passed into a tenuous, impartial, sexless, fitful form of existence, to which bodily courage is a contradiction in terms. Having no physical frame to defend or sacrifice, how can he show either courage or fear? His views are no longer local; nations are all one to him; his country is not bounded by seas, but is co-extensive with the globe itself, if it does not even include all the inhabited planets of the sky. He has put off the substance, and has put on, in part at any rate, the essence of the Universal.

If we go back to the ancient fancy on this subject, and look into the works of great imaginative writers, they seem to construct their soldier-shades much on the same principle—often with a stronger infusion of emotion, and less of sturdiness. The Homeric ghost of Patroclus was plaintively anxious about his funeral rites, and Virgil's military ghosts—though some of them certainly were cheerful, and eager for war news—were as a body tremulous and pensive. The prophet Samuel, a man of great will and energy when on earth, was 'disquieted' and obviously apprehensive when he was raised by the Witch of Endor at the request of Saul. Moreover, the authors of these Latin, Greek, and Hebrew fantasies were ignorant of the teaching of Christmas Day, that which alone moved the humble Natal shade to speak at all.

In Christian times Dante makes the chief Farinata exhibit a fine scornfulness, but even his Caesar, Hector, Æneas, Saladin, and heroes of that stamp, have, if I am not mistaken, an aspect neither sad nor joyful, and only reach the level of serenity. Hamlet's father, impliedly martial in life, was not particularly brave as a spectre. In short, and speaking generally, these creatures of the imagination are uncertain, fleeting, and quivering, like winds, mists, gossamer-webs, and fallen autumn leaves; they are sad, pensive, and frequently feel more or less sorrow for the acts of their corporeal years.

Thus I venture to think that the phantom of a slain soldier, neither British nor Boer, but a composite, typical phantom, may consistently be made to regret on or about Christmas Eve (when even the beasts of the field kneel, according to a tradition of my childhood) the battles of his life and war in general, although he may have shouted in the admirable ardour and pride of his fleshtime, as he is said to have done: 'Let us make a name for ourselves!'

Your obedient servant,
Thomas Hardy.

Hardy's letter was published in the *Daily Chronicle* on 28 December 1899, and on the following day in W. G. Stead's anti-Boer-War paper, *War Against War in South Africa*. The letter is reprinted in Orel, pp. 201-2. The manuscript is in the Taylor Collection, Princeton University Library.

The *Westminster Gazette* text of the poem bears the footnote: *Not copyright*.

Drummer Hodge. Hardy wrote to Macmillan (7 January 1914) that he had changed the title of the poem from 'The Dead Drummer' to 'Drummer Hodge', 'the former title being that of a poem by another writer'. (BL Add. MS 54924.) For Hardy's views on Hodge, the traditional name for a rustic character, see *Tess of the d'Urbervilles*, Ch. XVIII (*WE*, p. 152), and his essay, 'The Dorsetshire Labourer' (Orel, pp. 168-89).

A Wife in London. Line 1: Above this line in *Hol.* Hardy wrote, and then erased, (*Best*) *She.* This no doubt indicates that he had chosen the third-person form rather than the original first-person for the poem.

The Souls of the Slain. Hardy wrote to Mrs Henniker (3 April 1900): 'I was gratified to hear that my visionary verses pleased you. I sent them off all on a sudden, having put them away when I wrote them, early in the winter, thinking that the fancy might be too peculiar to myself to interest other people.' (*Letters* II, p. 253.)

The *Cornhill* version of the poem includes the following headnote:

[NOTE.—The spot indicated in the following poem is the Bill of Portland, which stands, roughly, on a line drawn from South Africa to the middle of the United Kingdom; in other words, the flight of a bird along a 'great circle' of the earth, cutting through South Africa and the British Isles, might land him at Portland Bill. The 'Race' is the turbulent sea-area off the Bill, where contrary tides meet. 'Spawls' are the chips of freestone left by the quarriers.]

First sentence. *MS1* reads *Isle of* for *Bill of* and *would be nearly over* for *might land him at*. In subsequent publications only the second sentence was retained, as a footnote to l. 3.

Last sentence. This is omitted from *P1*; it was evidently added after the printer set *sprawls* for *spawls* in this proof.

l. 16 *Hol.* reads *night-birds*, with *moths* written in above the line; neither word is cancelled.

Song of the Soldiers' Wives and Sweethearts. Hardy wrote to Mrs Henniker (24 December 1900): 'My Soldiers' Wives' Song finishes up my war effusions, of which I am happy to say that not a single one is Jingo or Imperial—a fatal defect according to the judgment of the British majority at present, I dare say.' (*Letters* II, p. 277.)

To Mr Dunn [of the *Morning Post*] Hardy wrote (28 November 1900): 'On an impulse I send up the accompanying effusion.... If too late for the homecoming of the Household Cavalry, it might do later on.' (*Letters* II, p. 275.)

In *DCM1* the title has been altered in pencil to 'Hope Song', and the alteration then erased.

The Sick Battle-God. 'A long study of the European wars of a century earlier had made it appear to him that common sense had taken the place of bluster in men's minds; and he felt this so strongly that in the very year before war burst on Europe he wrote some verses called "His Country", bearing on the decline of antagonism between peoples; and as long before as 1901 he composed a poem called "The Sick Battle-God", which assumed that zest for slaughter was dying out. It was seldom he had felt so heavy at heart as in seeing his old view of the gradual bettering of human nature, as expressed in these verses of 1901, completely shattered by the events of 1914 and onwards. War, he had supposed, had grown too coldly scientific to kindle again for long all the ardent romance which had characterized it down to Napoleonic times, when the most intense battles were over in a day, and the most exciting tactics and strategy led to the death of comparatively few combatants.

Hence nobody was more amazed than he at the German incursion into Belgium, and the contemplation of it led him to despair of the world's history thenceforward.' (*LY*, p. 162.)

l. 29 *thought outbrings*: in *DCM1* Hardy tried *vision brings* in pencil, and then erased it.

l. 31 *With foes as friends*: in *DCM1* Hardy tried *To foes and friends* in pencil, and then erased it.

Poems of Pilgrimage. Hardy and his first wife made two continental journeys: to Italy in March and April 1887 (see *EL*, pp. 244-58), and to Switzerland in June and July 1897 (see *LY*, pp. 66-70).

Genoa and the Mediterranean. 'Leaving for Turin they stayed there awhile, then duly reached Genoa, concerning the first aspect of which from the train Hardy wrote a long time after the lines entitled "Genoa and the Mediterranean", though that city—so pre-eminently the city of marble—"everything marble", he writes, "even little doorways in slums"—nobly redeemed its character when they visited its palaces during their stay.' (*EL*, p. 246.)

In the Old Theatre, Fiesole. 'In a sonnet on Fiesole called "In the Old Theatre" Hardy makes use of an incident that occurred while he was sitting in the stone Amphitheatre on the summit of the hill.' (*EL*, p. 251.) The *Academy* version appears to be based on an earlier text—perhaps a proof copy of *PP*. See the note to 'Preface', p. 368 above, and Purdy, p. 110n.

Rome: on the Palatine. '. . . the musical incident which, as he once said, took him by surprise when investigating the remains of Caligula's palace [was the source] of another [poem].' (*EL*, p. 248.)

Rome: Building a New Street in the Ancient Quarter. Hardy wrote to Gosse (31 March 1887): 'I am so overpowered by the presence of *decay* in Ancient Rome that I feel it like a nightmare in my sleep. Modern Rome is full of building energy—but how any community can go on building in the face of the "Vanitas vanitatum" reiterated by the ruins is quite marvellous. For my part if I were going to erect a mere shed I shd say Is it worth while?' (*Letters* I, p. 163.)

Rome: The Vatican: Sala delle Muse. '. . . his nearly falling asleep in the Sala delle Muse of the Vatican was the source of another poem, the weariness being the effect of the deadly fatiguing size of St. Peter's . . .' (*EL*, p. 248.)

Rome: At the Pyramid of Cestius. 'A visit to the graves of Shelley and Keats was also the inspiration of more verses—probably not written till later . . .' (*EL*, p. 248.)

l. 14 Acts 9: 1, 'And Saul, yet breathing out threatenings and slaughter against the disciples of the Lord, went unto the high priest.'

Lausanne. In *Hol.* Hardy wrote and then cancelled the following footnote to l. 16: *Prose Works: "Doctrine and Discipline of Divorce."* In *DCM1* he expanded the note as follows:

"Truth is as impossible to be soiled by any outward touch as is the sunbeam; though this ill-hap wait on her nativity, that she never comes into the world, but like a bastard, to the ignominy of him that brought her forth."—the Doctrine and Discipline of Divorce.

Hardy's note on the flyleaf of the volume shows that this footnote was not sent to Macmillan with other corrections for the 1920 reprint of the Wessex Edition. The quotation is from Milton's introductory address 'To the Parliament of England', *The Doctrine and Discipline of Divorce.*

Zermatt. Hardy and his wife visited Zermatt and the Matterhorn in late June or early July 1897, and the poem was begun then, though finished later (see *LY*, p. 69). Hardy had met Edward Whymper, the only English survivor of the first party to climb the Matterhorn, at the home of his friend Edward Clodd in 1894 (see *LY*, p. 30).

The Bridge of Lodi. Note to title: Pronounce "Loddy." (H)
   Hardy's account of his visit to Lodi is given in *EL*, pp. 256-7.

On an Invitation to the United States. The *New York Times Saturday Review of Books and Art* gives the date of the poem as 1899.

The Mother Mourns. EL quotes two relevant journal entries (the words in brackets are in the *EL* text, and indicate Florence Hardy's interpolations):

November 17 [1883]. Poem. We [human beings] have reached a degree of intelligence which Nature never contemplated when framing her laws, and for which she consequently has provided no adequate satisfactions. [This, which he had adumbrated before, was clearly the germ of the poem entitled 'The Mother Mourns' and others.] (*EL*, p. 213.)

April 7 [1889]. A woeful fact—that the human race is too extremely developed for its corporeal conditions, the nerves being evolved to an activity abnormal in such an environment. Even the higher animals are in excess in this respect. It may be questioned if Nature, or what we call Nature, so far back as when she crossed the line from invertebrates to vertebrates, did not exceed her mission. (*EL*, pp. 285-6.)

A Commonplace Day. 1. 20 In *Hol.* below the line Hardy wrote and then erased:
   There stirs in me.
   1. 21 In *Hol.* above and below the line respectively, erased: *nothing keenly please* and *keenly please in him*

The Problem. 1. 8 *that*: in *DCM3* Hardy underlined this, pencilling in the margin *it?*

The Bedridden Peasant, Mute Opinion, To an Unborn Pauper Child. The *Academy* versions of these poems appear to be based on an earlier text—perhaps a proof copy of *PP*. See the note to the 'Preface', p. 368 above, and Purdy, p. 110n.

To Lizbie Browne. Lizbie Browne was a red-haired gamekeeper's daughter, a year or two older than Hardy. (See *EL*, pp. 33 and 270.)
   1. 10 *archly*: in *DCM3* Hardy underlined this and wrote in the margin *?weave a.*

The Well-Beloved. 'Its setting (in the Wessex Edition) is at Jordan Hill, near Weymouth—the ancient Roman station Clavinium—where there are the remains of a Roman temple, tessellated pavements, and other relics of the Roman occupation.' (Lea, p. 270.) See also James Dyer, *Southern England: An Archaeological Guide* (London: 1973).

Her Reproach. Pasted on to the rear flyleaf of Hardy's copy of *CP23* is a cutting from the *Saturday Westminster Gazette*, dated 20 February 1904, reporting the results of a competition to turn the last six lines of Hardy's poem into Latin Elegiacs. There were ninety-five entries.

A Broken Appointment. Purdy (p. 113) associates the poem with Hardy's friendship with Mrs Henniker, and identifies the setting as the British Museum.

'*I need not go*'. '. . . the prime fact [is] that Stinsford Churchyard holds the tomb in which *She* lies.' (Lea, p. 270.)

The Coquette, and After. The idea and much of the language of the poem appear in *Jude the Obscure*, Part 6, Ch. III (*WE*, pp. 426–7).

The Widow Betrothed. Hardy wrote to Gosse (18 February 1918): 'I am puzzled about the date of "The Widow", (or as it is called in the Wessex Edn "The Widow Betrothed"). Anyhow, though I thought of it about 1867 when looking at the house described, which is near here, it must have been written after I had read Wordsworth's famous preface to Lyrical Ballads, which influenced me much, and influences the style of the poem, as you can see for yourself.' (BL Ashley MS A858.)
ll. 1–2 In *DCM1* Hardy wrote in, and then erased, the *PP* version of these lines.
l. 45 *know*: In *Hol.* above this word Hardy wrote and erased *ken*. Below the line he wrote and erased: *words are truth* [?] *they evince*.

His Immortality. The *Academy* version appears to be based on an earlier text. See the note to Hardy's 'Preface', p. 368 above, and Purdy, p. 110n.

The To-be-Forgotten. Below the cancelled headnote of *Hol.* Hardy wrote in pencil and then erased:

(In All Saints Churchyard Casterbridge)

The cancelled epigraph is Ecclesiastes 9: 5. Hardy also tried it, and then cancelled it, as the epigraph to 'Sapphic Fragment' (see below).

Birds at Winter Nightfall. Dated December 1899, in 'Chronological List of Thomas Hardy's Works', *DCM.*

The Puzzled Game-birds. In *DCM1*, where the poem is titled 'The Battue', Hardy wrote and then cancelled the following footnote: *At a* Battue *near Sturminster Newton, numbers of the birds ran into the keeper's house for shelter.* [*footnote in future edition*].
In a letter to Mrs Henniker dated 11 October 1899 Hardy wrote: 'I was about to send a few rhymed lines to some paper, on Game Birds, but shall probably keep them by me now, for other slaughter will fill people's minds for some time to come.' (*Letters* II, p. 232.) The 'other slaughter' was the Boer War.

Winter in Durnover Field. l. 4 In *DCM1* Hardy cancelled the marks of elision, ending the line with a full stop.

l. 6 *be*: in *DCM1* Hardy changed this to *you*, then erased the change.

The Darkling Thrush. Weber (in *Hardy of Wessex*) and, following him, Bailey and Pinion, cite the following passage from W. H. Hudson's *Nature in Downland* (London: 1900, pp. 249-52) as a possible source of Hardy's thrush:

Mid-winter is the season of the missel-thrush . . . when there is no gleam of light anywhere and no change in that darkness of immense ever-moving cloud above; and the south-west raves all day and all night, and day after day, then the storm-cock sings his loudest from a tree-top and has no rival. A glorious bird! . . . you must believe that this dark aspect of things delights him; that his pleasure in life, expressed with such sounds and in such circumstances, must greatly exceed in degree the contentment and bliss that is ours, even when we are most free from pain and care, and our whole beings most perfectly in tune with nature. . . . The sound is beautiful in quality, but the singer has no art, and flings out his notes anyhow; the song is an outburst, a cry of happiness.

The Comet at Yell'ham. In a letter to Dr T. Herbert Warren, Vice-Chancellor of Oxford (24 October 1909), Hardy wrote: 'I have read the proof of your interesting and able address at the celebration of the Jubilee of the Oxford Museum, and I am much honoured by your quoting my little poem about the comet. It appeared, I think, in 1858 or 1859—a very large one—and I remember standing and looking at it as described.' (Colby.)

The Dame of Athelhall. Lea (p. 271) identifies Athelhall as Athelhampton, 'a magnificent example of Tudor building with some evidences of earlier work, and one of the oldest and most beautiful in the county'. It is located east of Puddletown, not far from Dorchester. Hardy wrote in December 1901 to the then owner of the house: 'I send on with much pleasure the copy of the poems I had reserved for you. You will find the story of the irresolute lady who lived in your house at p. 182 [the page number in *PP*]. I don't want to alarm you, but I fancy that the brief remainder of her life was unhappy, and that she "walks" in the Hall, occasionally.' (*Letters* II, p. 305.)

l. 29 In the 'Errata' list in his copy of PP01 (Adams) Hardy wrote:

Home, home to Athel I must take

The Milkmaid. l. 13 In the 'Errata' list in his copy of *PP01* (Adams) Hardy wrote:

189, l. 5—for She bends read She throws.

This revision was also made in his copy of *CP23* (*DCM3*), where he added a note: ["*bends*" *just above*]—i.e. in l. 4.

The Levelled Churchyard. Lea identifies the churchyard as that of Wimborne, where Hardy lived from 1881 to 1883. Hardy had also had direct experience of churchyard-levelling during his architectural career in London: see *EL*, pp. 58-9.

l. 15 Reviewing *PP*, the *Spectator*'s reviewer wrote (5 April 1902): 'In one piece in this collection [Hardy] permits himself a Swiftian turn such as was pardonable, or at least not surprising, in Swift two centuries ago, but which we do not expect, and which ought not to be sprung upon us in a book by an English writer of repute in the twentieth century.' Hardy changed *p——ing place* to *porch or place* in *WE*, though it remained *p——ing place* in *CP19*.

The King's Experiment. l. 34 Hardy's 'Errata' list in his own copy of *PP01* (Adams) reads:

for   Ere her too   read   Before her

The Self-Unseeing. 'He was of ecstatic temperament, extraordinarily sensitive to music, and among the endless jigs, hornpipes, reels, waltzes, and country-dances that his father played of an evening in his early married years, and to which the boy danced a *pas seul* in the middle of the room, there were three or four that always moved the child to tears, though he strenuously tried to hide them.' (*EL*, p. 18.)

In *Hol.*, the title is pasted over an earlier title, 'Unregarding'.

In Tenebris I. Epigraph: Psalm 101: 5 in the Vulgate. The Authorized Version (Psalm 102: 4) reads: 'My heart is smitten, and withered like grass.'

In Tenebris II. Epigraph: Psalm 141: 5 in the Vulgate. The Authorized Version (Psalm 142: 4) reads: 'I looked on my right hand, and beheld, but there was no man that would know me: . . . no man cared for my soul.'

The cancelled epigraph is Psalm 2: 1 in the Vulgate. The Authorized Version reads: 'Why do the heathen rage, and the people imagine a vain thing?'

l. 8 1 Corinthians 15: 8, 'And last of all he was seen of me also, as of one born out of due time.'

In Tenebris III. Epigraph: Psalm 119: 5-6 in the Vulgate. The Authorized Version (Psalm 120: 5-6) reads: 'Woe is me, that I sojourn in Mesech, that I dwell in the tents of Kedar! My soul hath long dwelt with him that hateth peace.'

l. 18 Revelation 10: 10, 'And I took the little book out of the angel's hand, and ate it up; and it was in my mouth sweet as honey: and as soon as I had eaten it, my belly was bitter.'

The Church-Builder. The cancelled title is from Psalm 126: 3 in the Vulgate: 'Nisi Dominus custodierit divitatem; frustra vigilat, qui custodit eam.' The Authorized Version (Psalm 127: 1) reads: 'Except the Lord build the house, they labour in vain that build it: except the Lord keep the city, the watchman waketh but in vain.'

The Lost Pyx. On a lonely table-land above the Vale of Blackmore, between High-Stoy and Bubb-Down hills, and commanding in clear weather views that extend from the English to the Bristol Channel, stands a pillar, apparently medieval, called Cross-and-Hand or Christ-in-Hand. One tradition of its origin is mentioned in *Tess of the d'Urbervilles*; another, more detailed, preserves the story here given. (H): *WE*.

First sentence. In *Hol.* Hardy first wrote *Cross-in-Hand*, then cancelled *in* and replaced it with *and*.

Last sentence. In *Sphere* and *PP* this reads: *Among other stories of its origin a local tradition preserves the one here given.*

H. J. Moule, then Curator of the Dorset County Museum, and a friend of Hardy, recounted the legend in a note in the *Folk-lore Journal*, VII (1889), 25-6.

Hardy wrote to Clement Shorter, editor of the *Sphere* (10 December 1900): 'The only thing I have which bears at all on Christianity—and I suppose Christmas verse should do this?—is the legend sent herewith, which I might have revised and condensed if you had not been in such a hurry.... The tradition, I may say, is a real one.' (*Letters* II, p. 275.)

The abbeys are Sherborne, *north of Blackmore Vale* (l. 27), and Cerne Abbas, *south thereof* (l. 28); of the latter, only ruins remain. The Cross-in-Hand pillar still stands on Batcombe Hill, north-west of Cerne Abbas. For Hardy's other version of the legend, see *Tess of the d'Urbervilles*, Ch. XLV (*WE*, pp. 396-8).

The Supplanter. In *Hol.*, Hardy wrote *iii* below l. 10, as though the second stanza ended there; he then cancelled the number and added ll. 11 and 12.

Sapphic Fragment. The epigraphs are from Edward FitzGerald, *The Rubáiyát of Omar Khayyám*, stanza XLVII, and *Henry V*, I. ii. 229. The Greek text is Fragment 55 in *Poetarum Lesbiorum Fragmenta*, ed. Edgar Lobel and Denys Page (Oxford: 1955):

> κατθάνοιϲα δὲ κείϲηι οὐδέ ποτα μναμοϲύνα ϲέθεν
> ἔϲϲετ' οὐδὲ †ποκ'†ὔϲτερον· οὐ γὰρ πεδέχηιϲ βρόδων
> τὼν ἐκ Πιερίαϲ· ἀλλ' ἀφάνηϲ κἀν Ἀίδα δόμωι
> φοιτάϲηιϲ πεδ' ἀμαύρων νεκύων ἐκπεποταμένα.

In *Hol.* Hardy first wrote, and then cancelled, the epigraph from Ecclesiastes 9: 5 ('Neither have they any more a reward; for the memory of them is forgotten') that he also tried, and then cancelled, as the epigraph to 'The To-Be-Forgotten' (see above, p. 373).

LY (pp. 60-1) quotes a letter from Hardy to Swinburne, written about 1897, in which Hardy wrote: 'one day, when examining several English imitations of a well-known fragment of Sappho, I interested myself in trying to strike out a better equivalent for it than the commonplace "Thou, too, shalt die", etc., which all the translators had used during the last hundred years. I then stumbled upon your "Thee, too, the years shall cover", and all my spirit for poetic pains died out of me. Those few words present, I think, the finest *drama* of Death and Oblivion, so to speak, in our tongue.' The reference is to Swinburne's 'Anactoria', ll. 189 ff.

Catullus: XXXI. The Latin text reads:

31

> Paene insularum, Sirmio, insularumque
> ocelle, quascumque in liquentibus stagnis
> marique uasto fert uterque Neptunus,
> quam te libenter quamque laetus inuiso,
> uix mi ipse credens Thuniam atque Bithunos
> liquisse campos et uidere te in tuto.
> o quid solutis est beatius curis,
> cum mens onus reponit, ac peregrino
> labore fessi uenimus larem ad nostrum,
> desideratoque acquiescimus lecto?
> hoc est quod unum est pro laboribus tantis.
> salue, o uenusta Sirmio, atque ero gaude
> gaudente, uosque, o Lydiae lacus undae,
> ridete quidquid est domi cachinnorum.

After Schiller. A translation of the first stanza of Schiller's 'Ritter Toggenburg'. The German text reads:

> Ritter, treue Schwesterliebe
> Widmet Euch dies Herz,
> Fordert keine andre Liebe,
> Denn es macht mir Schmerz.
> Ruhig mag ich Euch erscheinen,
> Ruhig gehen sehn.
> Eurer Augen stilles Weinen
> Kann ich nicht verstehn.

In his notebook headed 'Literary Notes II', and dated '188–, onwards', Hardy copied out the first eight lines of Schiller's poem, and wrote beside them this translation:

> ⟨Sir Knight, a sister's love for thee⟩ Knight! a true sister-love
>   This breast ⟨shall retain⟩ retains;
> Ask me no other love:
>   That way lie pains!
>
> Calm can I view thee come
>   Calm see thee go,
> ⟨Thine eyes silent weeping⟩ Thy silent tearfulness
> ⟨My eyes cannot⟩ I must not know!

Song From Heine. From the *Buch der Lieder* ('Die Heimkehr', 23). The German text reads:

> Ich stand in dunkeln Träumen
> Und starrte ihr Bildniß an,
> Und das geliebte Antlitz
> Heimlich zu leben begann.
>
> Um ihre Lippen zog sich
> Ein Lächeln wunderbar,
> Und wie von Wehmuthstränen
> Erglänzte ihr Augenpaar.
>
> Auch meine Tränen flossen
> Mir von den Wangen herab –
> Und ach, ich kann es nicht glauben,
> Daß ich dich verloren hab'!

From Victor Hugo. A translation of 'A une femme', from *Les Feuilles d'Automne.* The French text reads:

> Enfant! si j'étais roi, je donnerais l'empire,
> Et mon char, et mon sceptre, et mon peuple à genoux,
> Et ma couronne d'or, et mes bains de porphyre,
> Et mes flottes, à qui la mer ne peut suffire,
>   Pour un regard de vous!
>
> Si j'étais Dieu, la terre et l'air avec les ondes,
> Les anges, les démons courbés devant ma loi,
> Et le profond chaos aux entrailles fécondes,
> L'éternité, l'espace, et les cieux, et les mondes,
>   Pour un baiser de toi!

Cardinal Bembo's Epitaph on Raphael. The Latin text reads:

> Hic ille est Raphael, metuit quo sospite vinci
> Rerum magna parens, et moriendo mori.

ἈΓΝΩΣΤΩι ΘΕΩι. The title is from Acts 17: 23, 'For as I passed by, and beheld your devotions, I found an altar with this inscription, TO THE UNKNOWN GOD. Whom, therefore, ye ignorantly worship, him declare I unto you.'

In 1906, when A. L. Gowans, a popular anthologist, wrote to Hardy for permission to include 'Hap' in a collection to be called 'The Ways of God', Hardy agreed, but added: 'If you use more than the one aforesaid, I should like the last in "Poems of the Past and the Present"—To the Unknown God (ἈΓΝΩΣΤΩι ΘΕΩι), to be chosen.' (Bancroft.) The anthology was never published.

Time's Laughingstocks

History of Composition and Publication

The poems of *Time's Laughingstocks* were written over nearly half a century. Of those given a date either in a manuscript or in some published edition, ten are the work of Hardy's twenties, the decade of the 1860s: all but one of these are in the group here entitled 'More Love Lyrics'. Only two date from the seventies, and only one from the eighties—'He Abjures Love', which closes the 'Love Lyrics' section. Five poems are dated in the nineties, and another nineteen are from the years 1901-9—the years, that is, since the publication of *Poems of the Past and the Present*. There are fewer occasional poems among the dated ones, and more narratives: 'tragic narrative poems, like the Trampwoman's Tragedy, seem to be liked most,' Hardy wrote to Macmillan (22 September 1910), 'and I can do them with ease'. (BL Add. MS 54923.) After the publication of his first two books of verse Hardy began to find his poems in demand from editors of periodicals both in England and in the United States. Of the ninety-four poems in *Time's Laughingstocks*, twenty-nine had been published previously, including seven in American journals.

Hardy offered the new volume to Macmillan in January 1909. In May he proposed that the title be *Time's Laughingstocks, and other verses*, or if that seemed unsatisfactory, *A Trampwoman's Tragedy, and other verses*. He preferred the first title, and kept it for the volume even after he had renamed the title poem (see textual notes to 'The Revisitation', above, p. 237).

The holograph printer's copy of the volume, now in the Fitzwilliam Museum, Cambridge, shows that Hardy had considerable trouble in selecting and ordering the poems to his satisfaction. He rearranged the order of the poems, added some, and deleted at least one. That poem, 'Looking Back', remains in the holograph, but is not in the printed text, where it was replaced by 'In the Crypted Way' ['In the Vaulted Way' in the present text]. Other late additions were 'He Abjures Love' and 'By the Barrows'. Hardy also changed the titles of two groups of poems. In the holograph the group here called 'More Love Lyrics' was first entitled 'Love Poems of Past Years' and then 'Love Poems of Past Days'; in *Time's Laughingstocks* it appears simply as 'Love Lyrics'. For the poems grouped as 'Pieces Occasional and Various' Hardy first tried the collective title 'Miscellaneous Verses' and then 'Miscellaneous Pieces' in the holograph. For two poems, 'The Revisitation' and 'The Noble Lady's Tale', he inserted into his printer's copy the manuscript that he had first prepared for periodical publication.

Copy was sent to the publisher early in September 1909, but Hardy recalled the final pages almost at once in order to revise 'Panthera', writing to Macmillan (18 September 1909) that he feared it would 'provoke acrimony amongst well-meaning but narrower minded people'. (Quoted in Simon Nowell-Smith, ed., *Letters to Macmillan* (London: 1967), p. 133.) The book was published on 3 December 1909. Reviews were on the whole favourable, but a remark in the *Daily News* (13 December 1909) that 'throughout . . . the outlook [is] that of disillusion and despair' moved Hardy to protest. 'If this were true,' he wrote to the paper, 'it might be no bad antidote to the grinning optimism nowadays affected in some quarters; but I beg leave to observe that of the ninety odd poems the volume contains, more than half do not answer to the description at all—as can be seen by a mere glance through it—while of the remainder many cannot be so characterized without exaggeration.' (*Daily News*, 15 December 1909.)

Two weeks after publication Hardy sent Macmillan an errata list, and followed it a few days later (2 January 1910) with a 'little correction' for the preface. A second impression was published early in 1910, with a small change of phrasing in the preface, and minor revisions to seven of the poems. A third impression, described on the verso of the title-page as the 'Second Edition', and containing a few variants in punctuation, was printed in 1915. The volume in the Uniform Edition, published in 1919, incorporates most but not all of the *Collected Poems* revisions, and is of no textual significance.

Other significant editions of *Time's Laughingstocks* are:

The Wessex Edition (with *The Dynasts*, Part Third), Verse Volume III (1913, reprinted 1920), a new setting of type containing small changes in nearly half the poems, and with the poems arranged in a slightly different order.

The Mellstock Edition, volume XXXV (1920). A resetting of the Wessex Edition, with a few minor corrections.

Collected Poems (1919), the poems also substantially revised, but not identical with the Wessex Edition, and probably an earlier revision.

Collected Poems (1923): a very few, minor revisions.

The order of the poems in the present edition follows that of the Wessex and Mellstock Editions.

Explanatory Notes

The Revisitation. For the original title of the poem, 'Time's Laughingstocks', Pinion (p. 64) suggests a source in Tennyson's *The Princess*, iv. 496. Tennyson's line reads:

> The drunkard's football, laughing-stocks of Time.

A Trampwoman's Tragedy. Of this poem, Hardy wrote to Gosse on 15 November 1903: 'It was written between one and two years ago, after a bicycle journey I took across the Poldon Hill described, and on to Glastonbury. I wish you could see the view from the top. "Marshal's Elm" you will find on any map of Somerset. The circumstances have been known to me for many years. You may like to be told that the woman's name was Mary Ann Taylor—though she has been dust for half a century.' (BL MS Ashley A3335.)

Hardy first submitted the poem to the *Cornhill Magazine*, but it was rejected by the editor 'on the ground of not being a poem he could possibly print in a family periodical'. (*LY*, p. 101.) It was never published separately in England, though it appeared in America, and gained some notice there: when Hardy wrote to Macmillan proposing a new volume of poems (13 January 1909) he noted that 'one of these, by the way, caused quite a run on the North American Review when it appeared there'. (BL Add. MS 54923.) In later years Hardy cited the history of the poem as an example of the way in which English editors imposed censorship on writers; a letter on this subject written to Edward Garnett in 1907 is in the Adams collection, and another, to Austin Harrison, editor of the *English Review*, dated 13 March 1910, is in HRC.

l. 27 "King's Stag" (Stanza IV) was an inn down to 1829, and I know not how much later. (H): *DCM3 only*.

"Windwhistle" (Stanza IV). The highness and dryness of Windwhistle Inn was impressed upon the writer two or three years ago, when, after climbing on a hot afternoon to the beautiful spot near which it stands and entering the inn for tea, he was informed by the landlady that none could be had, unless he would fetch water from a valley half a mile off, the house containing not a drop, owing to its situation. However, a tantalizing row of full barrels behind her back testified to a wetness of a certain sort, which was not at that time desired. (H)

Last sentence. *MS1* reads *the abundance of a liquor* for *a wetness*.

l. 30 *renowned*: in lists of corrections that he sent to Macmillan in 1919 and 1920 for use in *ME* and *WE20* Hardy proposed two different revisions, *for quaffs* and *for rest*. The latter was adopted in *WE20*, but *ME* retained *renowned*. Hardy also entered both revisions in *DCM1*, but later cancelled them and restored the original reading.

l. 44 "Marshal's Elm" (Stanza VI) so picturesquely situated, is no longer an inn, though the house, or part of it, still remains. It used to exhibit a fine old swinging sign. (H)

l. 79. "Blue Jimmy" (Stanza X) was a notorious horse-stealer of Wessex in those days, who appropriated more than a hundred horses before he was caught, among others one belonging to a neighbour of the writer's grandfather. He was hanged at the now demolished Ivel-chester or Ilchester jail above mentioned—that building formerly of so many sinister associations in the minds of the local peasantry, and the continual haunt of fever, which at last led to its condemnation. Its site is now an innocent-looking green meadow. (H)

First sentence. *TL* omits *among . . . grandfather*.

See F. E. Dugdale [later Mrs Hardy], 'Blue Jimmy: the Horse-Stealer', *Cornhill*, February 1911.

l. 81 The editor of the *North American Review*, writing to Hardy on 10 December 1903, regretted that 'in revising the proof, you altered the pathetic line, "Thereaft I traipsed the world alone," by substituting "walked" for the more picturesque word. The latter seemed so natural on this trampwoman's lips, and her use of it in her hopeless sorrow surely emptied it of the slightest trace of the idea of jauntiness or light-heartedness and left only that aimless wandering through a friendless world.' (Adams.)

The Two Rosalinds. When the poem first appeared in the *English Review* (April 1909), it was grouped with 'Reminiscences of a Dancing Man' under the general title 'London Nights'. According to *EL* (p. 298), it might have been suggested by a performance of *As You Like It* that he saw in June 1890. For an earlier experience of the play, and two poems associated with it, see 'To an Impersonator of Rosalind' and 'To an Actress' below.

A Sunday Morning Tragedy. Hardy sent this poem to the *Fortnightly Review* in the autumn of 1907. It was rejected by the editor, W. L. Courtney, who wrote the following explanatory letter:

Dear Mr. Hardy,

    I have read with deep interest the poem you were good enough to send me, entitled 'A Sunday Morning Tragedy'. You know how proud I am that you send your poems to me, and how glad I have been on several occasions to publish them. But I fear that I cannot possibly publish your latest poem, because of its subject. Personally I sometimes have a doubt whether even the greatest art can illustrate certain themes, or rather a certain class of horrors. I remember hearing a great lawyer say once that the worst cruelties were hidden away in law reports, and rightly so hidden, because if they were published to the world the world could not endure them.

    Pray forgive my inability, which you must put down to the fact that the 'Fortnightly Review' circulates among families! (DCM.)

Hardy then sent the poem to Ford Madox Hueffer, editor of the newly founded *English Review*, with a covering letter in which he explained:

The Editor of the review, who returned it, merely said that he would have personally liked to print it, but that his review circulated amongst young people. Of course, with a larger morality, the guardians of young people would see that it is the very thing they ought to read, for nobody can say that the treatment is other than moral, and the crime is one of growing prevalence, as you probably know, and the false shame which leads to it is produced by the hypocrisy of the age. (Adams.)

    In 1909 Hardy submitted written testimony, in the form of a letter to John Galsworthy, to the Joint Committee of Lords and Commons which had been appointed to inquire into the censorship of plays. 'All I can say', he wrote,

is that something or other—which probably is consciousness of the Censor—appears to deter men of letters, who have other channels for communicating with the public, from writing for the stage.

    As an ounce of experience is worth a ton of theory, I may add that the ballad which I published in the *English Review* for last December, entitled 'A Sunday Morning Tragedy', I wished to produce as a tragic play before I printed the ballad form of it; and I went so far as to shape the scenes, action, etc. But it then occurred to me that the subject—one in which the fear of transgressing convention overrules natural feeling to the extent of bringing dire disaster—an eminently proper and moral subject—would prevent my ever getting it on the boards, so I abandoned it.

The letter was published with other written testimony in *The Times* for 13 August 1909. Two drafts of Hardy's abandoned play, one entitled 'Birthwort' and the other 'A Sunday Morning Tragedy', are in DCM.

    Lea (p. 303) locates the calling of the banns in the parish church of Piddlehinton, 'in circumstances reputed to be veracious'.

Autumn in King's Hintock Park. In *DCM3* Hardy inserted the word *Melbury* in brackets after *Hintock*.

    In a letter to Gosse (11 November 1906) Hardy wrote: 'though the scene as I witnessed it was a poem, it is quite another question if I have conveyed it to paper. (It happened at Lady Ly's daughter's park at Melbury, by the way).' (Adams.) Lady Ly is Lady Londonderry, a friend of Hardy's for many years; her daughter was Lady Ilchester. Hardy described the occasion of the poem in a letter to Mrs Henniker, 21 December 1906:

I happened to be walking, or cycling, through [the Ilchesters' park] years ago, when the incident occurred on which the verses are based, and I wrote them out, though I had no intention of publishing them in a newspaper. I think I may have told you that my interest in that park arises from the fact that a portion of it belonged to my mother's people centuries ago, before the Strangways absorbed it. (*ORFW*, p. 131.)

For Hardy's claim to a connection with King's Hintock Park, see *EL*, p. 7.

Shut out that Moon. l. 8 *Lady's Chair*: the constellation Cassiopeia.

Reminiscences of a Dancing Man. Hardy first danced at Almack's Rooms in 1862 (see *EL*, p. 56 and *LY*, p. 44).
   l. 30 Jullien, Louis Antoine (1812–60), composer of popular music, and conductor (mainly in London) of concerts at which very large orchestras played both popular and classical music.

The Division. Purdy (p. 141) associates the poem with Mrs Henniker. She quoted the second and third stanzas, without acknowledgement, in her novel, *Second Fiddle* (London: 1912). Her text is that of *TL*, without significant variants.

Her Father. In *Hol.*, the last three lines have been pasted on.

In the Mind's Eye. In his own copy of *TL*, Hardy underlined the title ['The Phantom' in that version], and wrote in the margin *Ghost-face*. (DCM).
   In *DCM3* Hardy wrote in the margin opposite this poem: [*In the Selection this is called 'In the Mind's Eye' there being already 'The Phantom Horsewoman.'*]

The Sigh. The final stanza echoes Job 14: 14. See also 'Waiting Both' in *Human Shows*.

The Conformers. In *Hol.*, on the verso of the text, the following lines have been written and cancelled:

> Yes; we'll wed, my little fay
>   And you shall write you mine,
> And in a cot of brown or gray
>   We'll house, and sleep, and dine.
> But those night-screened divine

The Dawn after the Dance. *EL* (p. 85) suggests that the poem 'is supposed, though without proof, to have some bearing' on the dancing-classes that Hardy attended at Weymouth in 1869. Collins (p. 23) reports the following exchange:

C.: What is 'that which makes man's love the lighter and the woman's burn no brighter'?
H.: I suppose when they got intimate . . . I think perhaps I originally wrote '*the* brighter.'

   l. 11 In *DCM3* Hardy transposed the seventh and eighth words, and then erased the mark of transposition.

To an Impersonator of Rosalind. On 21 April 1867 Mrs Scott-Siddons was playing Rosalind in *As You Like It* at the Theatre Royal, Haymarket, London. She is also presumably the actress addressed in 'To an Actress', below. See also 'The Two Rosalinds'.

To an Actress. See note above.

He Abjures Love. In 1920, in a letter to Alfred Noyes defending himself against the charge of pessimism, Hardy wrote of this poem: 'The poem called "He Abjures Love", ending with "And then the curtain", is a love-poem, and lovers are chartered irresponsibles.' (*LY*, p. 218.) In *Hol.*, the following note, written at the top of the page and then erased, can be made out: [*Insert at the end of 'Love Poems' after 'The Minute before Meeting'*].

Let Me Enjoy. In *DCM4* a note at the top of the page, in Hardy's hand, reads:

?Minor Key *p. 222 Coll Edn. Possibly these words are not required here when the poem is detached from "A Set of Country Songs".*

An arrow has been drawn to the space below the title, where the words *Minor Key* appear in all texts except *SP*, which Hardy was here revising for *Chosen Poems*. The words were not added in *Chosen Poems*.

l. 10 In *DCM4* Hardy added a comma at the end of the line, and then cancelled it with the note: *Omit in Collected Edn etc.*

At Casterbridge Fair. Hol. shows that 'A Set of Country Songs' originally began here.

A Wife Waits. "The Bow" (line 3). The old name for the curved corner by the cross-streets in the middle of Casterbridge. It is not now so inscribed, and the spot has to be designated by a circumlocution, to the inconvenience of market-men in their appointments. (H)
    This note is pasted on to the bottom of the page in *Hol.*
    Second sentence. This was omitted from *CP* and *WE*, no doubt because in the interim since the publication of *TL* a sign had been placed at the corner, at Hardy's expense. See Denys Kay-Robinson, *Hardy's Wessex Re-appraised* (London: 1971), p. 24.

After the Fair. "The Chimes" (line 6) will be listened for in vain here at midnight now, having been abolished some years ago. (H)
    The note is omitted from *Hol.*

Julie-Jane. It is, or was, a common custom in Wessex, and probably other country places, to prepare the mourning beside the death-bed, the dying person sometimes assisting, who also selects his or her bearers on such occasions. (H)

News for Her Mother. l. 7 In an obituary notice of Hardy published in the *Dorset Year-Book* in 1928, the editor, Stanley I. Galpin, wrote: 'I have before me as I write his proof [of "News for her Mother"] in which he has altered one word, but what a masterpiece that alteration is—Cyder *made* to-year altered to Cyder *wrung* to-year.' Galpin adds that this revision was noted in the *Daily Mail* review of the *Year-Book*, as 'an illuminating example of the constant care which great poets give to their work.' (*Dorset Year-Book* (1928), p. 4.)

The Homecoming. Hardy wrote to Clement Shorter, editor of the *Graphic*: 'Had I known that the poem would appear in the Xmas number I wd have sub-titled it "a Xmas reverie." ' (Berg.)

A Church Romance. The poem is quoted in *EL* (p. 17) as an account of his mother's first view of his father. The date is there given as '*circa* 1836'.

The Rash Bride. l. 29 *Michael* (*Michael Mail* in the *Graphic* version): a member of the Mellstock Quire in *Under the Greenwood Tree.*
    l. 60 On the printed programme for the funeral of Hardy's father, 31 July 1892, Psalm 90 is identified as 'The Grave-side Hymn of this Parish down to about 1840'. Hardy Senior would have been one of the choir that played it in those years: he was a member of the Stinsford parish church choir until about 1842 (*EL*, pp. 11–15). A copy of the funeral programme is in DCM.

The Dead Quire. In *Hol.* Hardy first wrote stanza XXIII above stanza XXII, and then marked it with an arrow to move it to its present position.
    ll. 9-12, 89-92 *Dewy, Reuben, Michael, Bowman*: members of the Mellstock Quire in *Under the Greenwood Tree.* See *EL*, p. 122.

A Dream Question. Hol., TL, and *WE* omit closing quotation marks around the second stanza. *CP* inserts closing quotation marks at the end of l. 12, but omits the opening marks at the beginning of l. 7. I have inserted both opening and closing marks, which the sense clearly requires.

By the Barrows. ll. 2-3 Bailey (p. 239) notes two uses of this image in Hardy's novels: in *The Mayor of Casterbridge*, Ch. XLV (*WE*, p. 381), and in *Tess of the d'Urbervilles*, Ch. XLII (*WE*, p. 358).

A Wife and Another. In *Hol.* the last line is pasted on, replacing a line or lines that have been cut off.

After the Last Breath. Hardy's mother, Jemima Hardy, died 3 April 1904.

The Pine Planters. l. 51 In *Hol.* the line *It could not ever* is emended in pencil to read: *It could for ever*. This emendation was not made in *TL*. For the parallel scene in *The Woodlanders* see Ch. VIII (*WE*, pp. 73–4).

The Dear. Hardy wrote to Henry Newbolt, editor of the *Monthly Review* (in which the poem was first published) that it was 'made on a real incident that seemed worth recording for its own sake'. (Sotheby & Co., *Catalogue of Valuable Printed Books etc.*, for sale on 22 and 23 June 1959, p. 53.)

One We Knew. M. H. is Mary Head Hardy, the poet's grandmother. See *LY*, p. 231.

New Year's Eve. In a letter to his friend Edward Clodd (2 January 1907), Hardy wrote:

Many thanks for your letter about my New Years' fantasy or dream in the F. R. [*Fortnightly Review*]. It was written some years ago. As you say, people will no doubt mistake it for a belief.
    It is Feuerbach who says that God is the product of man, which is only another way of stating that he has the 'best excuse' you allude to. On the other hand I quite enter into

[Herbert] Spencer's feeling—that it is paralyzing to think what if, of all that is so incomprehensible to us (the Universe) there exists no comprehension anywhere. (BL MS Ashley B 1920.)

See also *L Y*, pp. 121 and 217. *Hol.* is cut off below the last line, and the zigzag mark indicating the end of the poem is on a pasted-on piece below; so there may have been further lines.

ll. 11-12 2 Corinthians 5: 4, 'For we that are in this tabernacle do groan, being burdened: not for that we would be unclothed, but clothed upon, that mortality might be swallowed up of life.'

God's Education. See *L Y*, p. 217.

Panthera. Hardy did considerable research on the Panthera legend. A notebook in DCM, labelled 'Facts', contains notes from Bellamy's 1660 translation of Origen's *Contra Celsum*, Thomas Taylor's translation of Jacques Basnage's *Histoire des Juifs* (1706-7), and Ernest Crawley's *The Tree of Life* (1905). He had also read *The Riddle of the Universe at the Close of the Nineteenth Century*, a translation of Ernst Haeckel's *Die Welträtsel* (1899), and David Friedrich Strauss's *Das Leben Jesu* (1837), in George Eliot's translation. A copy of the latter, in the 1898 edition, was in Hardy's personal library.

Hardy was concerned that the poem might 'provoke acrimony amongst well-meaning but narrower minded people'. He submitted it for reading in manuscript to a number of people, including John Bagnell Bury, Regius professor of modern history at Cambridge, and his friend Edward Clodd, and was encouraged to publish it; but he also met with some objections. In September 1909 he sent the holograph of *TL* to be published, but almost immediately recalled the final pages, beginning with 'Panthera', because, he said, a revision had occurred to him. He described what this revision was in a letter to Macmillan dated 18 September: 'I have rewritten the poem, and made the events a possibly erroneous fantasy of the narrator—which I think removes all objection.' He added, however, that Macmillan must decide whether to include the poem in the volume. (Quoted in Simon Nowell-Smith, ed., *Letters to Macmillan* (London: 1967), pp. 133-4.)

Headnote. The immediate source appears to be a footnote in Strauss concerning the name Panthera; Strauss's note cites Origen, Schöttgen (a name that appears in Hardy's holograph), and Toledoth Jeschu (the spelling that Hardy used, and then altered, in the holograph).

ll. 44-5 and 181-2 The short rules that separate Panthera's own story from the narrative frame appear in *Hol.* only. In *TL* the first rule is replaced by a wide space, but the second is an ordinary paragraphing-space. *WE* and *CP* do not distinguish either interval from others in the text.

l. 89 In all printed texts this line is indented, with opening quotation marks. But *Hol.* is not indented, and the opening quotation marks appear not to be Hardy's. I have omitted both the indention and the quotation marks.

l. 218 *the*: an erased note at the back of *DCM3* shows that Hardy had also considered *o' the* as a revision.

The Unborn. In his letter to Noyes, defending himself against the charge of pessimism, Hardy wrote of this poem: 'though the form of it is imaginary, the sentiment is one which I should think, especially since the war, is not uncommon or unreasonable.' (*LY*, p. 218.)

Hardy's dating of the poem is either a slip of the pen or, as Purdy suggests (p. 147), a reference to the date of the revision.

Geographical Knowledge. Purdy (p. 147) identifies 'Christiana C——' as Mrs Christiana Coward, the postmistress at Bockhampton.

The Rejected Member's Wife. For the *Dorset County Chronicle*'s account of the election scene in Dorchester, see Bailey, p. 206. The rejected member in the election of January 1906 was Colonel William Ernest Brymer, a Conservative.

The Noble Lady's Tale. Lady Susan Fox-Strangways (1743-1827), daughter of the first Earl of Ilchester, eloped with an Irish actor, William O'Brien (1738-1815) in 1764. They lived at Stinsford House, next to the parish church attended by the Hardy family; Hardy's grandfather built their burial vault. *EL* refers to Lady Susan's story twice (pp. 11-12 and 213-14), citing Horace Walpole's letters as a source. In the notebook labelled 'Facts' (in DCM) he quotes another source, *A Series of Letters of the first Earl of Malmesbury, his family and friends from 1745 to 1820*, edited by his grandson, the Earl of Malmesbury, 2 vols. (London: 1870). Lady Susan's elopement is described in vol. 1, p. 108. There are also letters from Lady Susan in *The Journal of Mary Frampton, from the year 1779, until the year 1846* (London: 1885), which Hardy knew.

Aberdeen: 1905. Hardy received an honorary LL.D. from Aberdeen University in April 1905; for an account of the occasion see *LY*, pp. 108-10. He sent the poem to the university magazine on 30 July 1906.

Collins (p. 23) quotes the following exchange:

C.: Who is the 'Queen'?

H.: Knowledge. That might apply to any University town—though, of course, not the granite.

George Meredith. Meredith died on 18 May 1909. According to Hardy's account (*LY*, p. 137) he saw the death announced on a poster while he was walking along a London street. He went on to the Athenaeum and wrote the poem, and sent it to *The Times*, where it was published on 22 May, the day of Meredith's funeral.

A Young Man's Epigram on Existence. Hardy wrote to Alfred Noyes that he had found the lines in a drawer, and had published them 'merely as an amusing instance of early cynicism'. (*LY*, p. 217.) In *Hol.* this poem is written at the bottom of the page containing 'Aberdeen', and preceding 'G. M.' ['George Meredith'].

APPENDIX A

A Note on the *Wessex Poems* Drawings

Hardy made thirty-two drawings for *Wessex Poems*, of which thirty-one were included in the volume (though the title-page reads 'with thirty illustrations by the author'). The thirty-second, the tailpiece to 'The Casterbridge Captains', is here reproduced in its proper place for the first time. The original drawings are with the holograph of the poems in the Birmingham City Museum and Art Gallery.

Hardy mentioned the drawings in letters to two of his close friends. In February 1899 he wrote to Edmund Gosse: 'The truth is I have been out of conceit with the Poems ever since they were printed—owing to a sense of my inexcusable carelessness in revising them so perfunctorily. My interest lay so entirely in the novel occupation of making the drawings that I did not remove defects of form in the verses which lay quite on the surface, and might have been cured in a couple of hours.' (*Letters* II, p. 214.) And in March of the same year he told his friend Edward Clodd that 'the illustrations to the Wessex Poems, that take your fancy, had for me in preparing them a sort of illegitimate interest—that which arose from their being a novel amusement, and a wholly gratuitous performance which could not profit me anything, and probably would do me harm'. (*Letters* II, p. 217.)

The following list identifies scenes and subjects where that is possible:

p. 1 (Frontispiece) 'Friends Beyond'. Stinsford Church from the north.

p. 7 'The Temporary the All'. A tower on Max Gate, Hardy's house in Dorchester. The sundial, which Hardy designed, was not actually put in place until after his death.

p. 14 'She at his Funeral'. Stinsford Church from the south-east.

p. 16 'Her Dilemma'. The south-west aisle of St. George's Church, Fordington, Dorchester. Hardy has taken some liberties in the drawing—for example in the capitals of the pillars—but the resemblance is clear. Of the churches in the Dorchester area, St. George's is the only one in which the floor level was altered, revealing Saxon and Norman graves below the floor.

p. 18 'She to Him I'. Clavel Tower, on the cliff to the east of Kimmeridge Bay, south Dorset. I am indebted to Professor Michael Millgate for this information.[1]

---

[1] Michael Millgate, *Thomas Hardy, A Biography* (Oxford: 1982).

p. 23 'Sergeant's Song'. Head of Napoleon.

p. 24 'Valenciennes'. Ramparts, with a distant view of Valenciennes.

p. 27 'San Sebastian'. San Sebastian at night, from the south-east.

p. 31 'The Burghers'. High West Street, Dorchester, facing west.

p. 34 'Leipzig'. The Markt-Platz, Leipzig.

p. 39 'Leipzig'. The Old Ship Inn, High West Street, Dorchester.

p. 46 'The Alarm'. Signal fire on Rainbarrow, near Hardy's birthplace at Higher Bockhampton.

p. 48 'The Alarm'. The Dorchester-Weymouth Road, with Weymouth and Portland Bill in the distance.

p. 53 'Her Death and After'. Dorchester Cemetery and Maumbury Rings, with Dorchester in the background.

p. 56 'Her Death and After'. West Walks, Dorchester.

p. 57 'The Dance at the Phœnix'. The music of 'Soldier's Joy'.

p. 62 'The Dance at the Phœnix'. Stinsford Hill, east of Dorchester.

p. 65 'A Sign-Seeker'. The Dorchester sky line from Yellowham Hill, east of Dorchester.

p. 67 'My Cicely'. The Great Western Road, west of Dorchester, with the earthworks of Maiden Castle on the left.

p. 72 'My Cicely'. The towers of Exeter Cathedral.

p. 74 'Her Immortality'. Landscape near Dorchester (?).

p. 86 'Nature's Questioning'. For the superstition of the broken key see *Far From the Madding Crowd*, Ch. XXXIII (*WE*, p. 249).

p. 87 'The Impercipient'. Salisbury Cathedral.

p. 92 'In a Eweleaze near Weatherbury'. Landscape near Puddletown (?).

APPENDIX B

Hardy's setting for 'The Stranger's Song'. From the original in the Dorset County Museum.
Reproduced courtesy of the Museum, and its Curator, R. N. R. Peers.

APPENDIX C

THE FIRE AT TRANTER SWEATLEY'S.

A Wessex Ballad.

By Thomas Hardy,

AUTHOR OF *Far From the Madding Crowd*, *A Pair of Blue Eyes*, *The Hand of Ethelberta*, Etc.

They had long met o' Sundays—her true-love and she—
　　And at junketings, maypoles, and flings;
But she dwelt wi' a crabbed old uncle, and he
Swore by noon and by night that her husband should be
Naibour Sweatley (a man often weak at the knee
From taking o' sommat more cheerful than tea),
　　Who tranted, and moved people's things.

She cried, "O pray pity me!"—Nought would he hear;
　　Then with wild rainy eyes she obeyed.
She chid when her Love was for clinking off wi' her:
The passon was told, as the season drew near,
To throw over pulpit the names of the pair
　　As fitting one flesh to be made.

The wedding-day dawned and the morning drew on:
　　The couple stood bridegroom and bride:
The evening was passed, and when midnight had gone
The folks horned out "God save the King," and anon
　　To their home the pair gloomily hied.

The lover, Sim Tankens, mourned heart-sick and drear
　　To be thus of his darling deprived:
He roamed in the dark around field, mound, and mere,
And, a'most without knowing it, found himself near
The house of the tranter, and now of his dear,
　　Where the moving lights showed they'd arrived.

The Gentleman's Magazine (Nov. 1875).

The bride sought her chimmer so calm and so pale
    That a Northern had thought her resigned;
But, to eyes that had seen her in seasons of weal,
Like the white cloud of smoke, the red battle-field's veil,
    That look told of havoc behind.

The bridegroom yet loitered a beaker to drain,
    Then reeled to the linhay for more;
When the candle-snoff kindled the chaff from his grain—
Flames sprout and rush upwards wi' might and wi' main,
    And round beams, thatch, and chimley-tun roar.

Young Sim in the distance, aroused by the light,
    Through brimbles and underwood tears,
Till he comes to the orchet, where slap in his sight,
Beneath a bowed codlin-tree, trimbling wi' fright,
In an old coat she'd found on a scarecrow bedight,
    His gentle young Barbara appears.

Her form in these cold mildewed tatters he views,
    Played about by the frolicsome breeze;
Her light-tripping totties, her ten little tooes,
All bare and besprinkled wi' Fall's chilly dews,
While her great frightened eyes through her ringlets so loose
    Shone like stars through a tangle of trees.

She eyed him; and, as when a weir-hatch is drawn,
    Her tears, penned by terror before,
Wi' a rushing of sobs in a torrent were strawn,
Till her power to pour 'em seemed wasted and gone
    From the heft of misfortune she bore.

"O Sim, my *own* Sim I must call 'ee—I will!
    All the world hev turned round on me so!
Can you help her who loved 'ee, though acting so ill?
Can you pity her misery—feel for her still?
When, worse than her body so quivering and chill,
    Is her heart in its winter of woe!

"I think I could almost hev borne it," she said,
    "Had my griefs one by one come to hand;
But O, to be slave to an uncle for bread,

And then, upon top o' that, driven to wed,
And then, upon top o' that, burnt out o' bed,
   Is more than my nater can stand!"

Sim's soul like a lion within him out-sprung—
(Sim had a great soul when his feelings were wrung)
   "Feel for 'ee, dear Barbie?" he cried:
Then his warm working jacket about her he flung,
Made a back, horsed her up, till behind him she clung:
Like a chiel on a gipsy her round figure hung
   As the two sleeves before him he tied.

Over piggeries, and mixens, and apples, and hay,
   They stumbled, straight into the night,
And finding at length where a bridle-path lay
By dawn reached Sim's mother's—who, up with the day,
In round kindly spectacles glared every way,
   To gather some clue to the sight.

Then old Mis'ess Tankens she searched here and there
   For some closet—though fearing 'twas sin—
Where Barbie could hide, and for clothes she could wear,
A task hard enough with a creature so fair,
Who half scrammed to death, sat and cried in a chair
   To think what a stoor she was in.

The loft, up the ladder, seemed safe; and all day
   In that hiding she laid her sweet limbs;
But most of the time in a terrible way,
Well knowing that there'd be the piper to pay
When 'twas found that, instead of the element's prey,
   She was living in lodgings at Sim's.

"Where's the tranter?" said men and boys, "Where can he be?"
   "Where's the tranter?" said Barbie alone.
"Where on earth is the tranter!" said everybody:
They sifted the dust of his perished roof-tree,
   And all they could find was a bone!

Then the uncle cried, "Lord, pray have mercy on me!"
   And in sorrow began to repent:
But before 'twas complete, and till sure she was free,

Barbie drew up her loft-ladder, tight turned her key—
Sim handing in breakfast, and dinner, and tea—
    Till the crabbed man gied his consent.

There was skimmity-riding with rout, shout, and flare,
In Weatherbury, Stokeham, and Windleton, ere
    They had proof of old Sweatley's decay:
The Mellstock and Yalbury folk stood in a stare
(The tranter owned houses and garden-ground there),
But little did Sim or his Barbara care,
    For he took her to church the next day.

INDEX OF TITLES

INDEX OF FIRST LINES